A Nation of Empire

A Nation of Empire

The Ottoman Legacy of Turkish Modernity

MICHAEL E. MEEKER

University of California Press

BERKELEY LOS ANGELES LONDON

University of California Press
Berkeley and Los Angeles, California

University of California Press, Ltd.
London, England

Library of Congress Cataloging-in-Publication Data

Meeker, Michael E.
A nation of empire : the Ottoman legacy of Turkish modernity / Michael E. Meeker.
p. cm.
Includes bibliographical references and index.
ISBN 0-520-22526-0 (alk. paper)—ISBN 0-520-23482-0 (pbk. : alk. paper)
1. Elite (Social sciences)—Turkey—Black Sea Coast—History. 2. Black Sea Coast (Turkey)—Social conditions. 3. Black Sea Coast (Turkey)—Politics and government. 4. Islam and politics—Turkey—Black Sea Coast—History. I. Title: Ottoman legacy of Turkish modernity. II. Title.

HN656.5.B57 M44 2002
306'.09565—dc21 2001004242

Manufactured in the United States of America
9 8 7 6 5 4 3 2 1 0

10 9 8 7 6 5 4 3 2 1

The paper used in this publication meets the minimum requirements of ANSI/NISO Z39 0.48-1992(R 1997) (Permanence of Paper).⊗

In memory of Ahmet Hızal

In friendship with Mehmet Bilgin

In recognition of Hasan Umur

Contents

Maps, Tables, and Figures

Maps

Tables

Figures

Preface

As its title suggests, my book examines the imperial legacy of the Turkish Republic. By this phrase, I refer not to those fragments of the old regime that somehow survived the radical reforms carried out by the nationalist movement but to key pieces of the imperial system that became active, even formative, principles in the new regime. As I explain in the first two chapters, the discovery of such principles as a force within the public life of the nation came to me as a surprise some years after my first period of fieldwork. My training in anthropology and history had not prepared me for it, and my interlocutors in the province of Trabzon, otherwise so helpful, had been unable to lead me to it. So the legacy in question was—and still is—beneath the surface, one altogether different from those features of the Ottoman past that have recently become a subject of nostalgic reminiscence. But while beneath the surface, and therefore not easily identifiable, the legacy has contributed to both the dynamism of modern society in Turkey and by implication some of the country's most intractable political problems. My work has thus unfolded as an effort to make recognizable what might well be called counterrevolutionary practices and beliefs that nonetheless served as the hidden devices of the nationalist revolution itself.

My study has its origins in a program of anthropological research on the role of local elites in the public life of a Turkish town in the province of Trabzon. Those local elites whom I encountered during my fieldwork in the 1960s were almost always descendants of individuals who had been prominent during the last years of the Ottoman Empire. I therefore understood that my account would necessarily combine ethnography with history, but I initially had no intention of theorizing the character of Ottoman official thinking and practice. On the contrary, I had at first assumed, out of sheer ignorance, that the region where I was working could be considered a remote backwater, only superficially touched by the imperial system. More than ten years after my residence in Trabzon, I had an inkling of my mistake in the course of reading the reports of British and French consular officials who came to reside in Trabzon during the first decade of the nineteenth century. Gradually, as my archival and historical research deepened, I came to realize that the lands of the old province of Trabzon featured striking transgressions of what had been, not so many years ago, conventional Ottoman and Republican historiography. The imperial system—sometimes portrayed as an extreme example of state exclusivity and centralism—had never been entirely closed. An official governmental hierarchy had always been only the visible part of a much larger complex of nonofficial elites leading nonofficial coalitions at the local level.

Because the imperial system had been open to outsiders, it had refashioned multiethnic, multilinguistic, and multireligious populations into ottomanist provincial societies during the later centuries of the Ottoman Empire. This being the case, the nationalists who founded the Turkish Republic enjoyed an important resource for an otherwise daunting project. As they set about to create a new population of Turks for the country that would be called Turkey, they were able to rely on an already existing state society that could be moved from Empire to Republic. Taking advantage of this, the nationalists resorted to an imperial practice, supplementing an official governmental hierarchy with nonofficial social oligarchies. As they did so, the new national regime came to exhibit a combination of institutional flexibility and rigidity, not wholly unlike what had previously characterized the old imperial regime.

In the remainder of this preface, I shall place my study in the context of scholarly understandings of the transition from Empire to Republic. To do so, I shall use the opening remarks of a classic work as a reference point.

In the introduction to *The Emergence of Modern Turkey* (1961), Bernard Lewis begins with a characterization of the object of his study: "We may then distinguish three main streams of influence that have gone to make modern Turkey: the Islamic, the Turkish, and a third, composite one that for want of a better name we may call local."[1] By this assessment, the Ottoman Empire did not figure as a main influence in the making of modern Turkey.

1. Lewis 1961, 3.

An imperial system that had survived seven hundred years would appear to have vanished without a trace by the close of the third decade of the Turkish Republic. Having been a significant piece of the world system for almost a millennium, the old regime had more or less vaporized, its ruling devices having at long last exhausted their political potential. In contrast to western European imperialism, deemed virtually ineradicable by postcolonial scholarship, this peculiar version of an "other" European imperialism was without aftermath.

To draw such a conclusion from the citation is unfair, although not as unfair as it might first seem. Lewis was most certainly aware of the continuing existence of all kinds of "ottomanisms" in the Turkish Republic. Even though Lewis was at an early stage of his academic career, few other scholars would have been better equipped to address this subject. So he did not mean to imply that the Ottoman Empire had left nothing behind when he omitted it as an influence in the making of modern Turkey. Instead, he regarded the Empire as an earlier accomplishment of the "Turkish" and "Islamic" people of Asia Minor, just as he saw the Republic as their later accomplishment. According to such an analysis, it did not make sense to consider the influence of the Empire on the Republic, since the people in question had abandoned the first as they set about to realize the second. Accordingly, Lewis focused instead on the meaning of such a move, and he concluded that it signified a shift from latent to manifest nationalism. The Empire had been a nonmodern state system designed to govern a vast multiethnic, multilinguistic, and multireligious population. The "Turkish" and "Islamic" people of Asia Minor had therefore remained unconscious of themselves as a people in the course of making and sustaining it. In contrast, the Republic was a modern state system that represented only one people, not many. The "Turkish" and "Islamic" people of Asia Minor had consequently become conscious of themselves as they moved from the imperial to the national phase of their history.

When Lewis published his study, its introduction would not have been welcomed by many Turkish citizens, especially those who might be described as the Kemalist establishment: state administrators, military officers, and schoolteachers.[2] Many such individuals would have taken exception to the view that the Turkish people were either closely associated with Islam or responsible for the Empire. To understand why, we must have

2. The terms "Kemalist" and "Atatürkist" are commonly applied to supporters of Mustafa Kemal (Atatürk), founder of the Turkish Republic. The same terms are also applied to political ideologies and programs associated with the founder.

some understanding of the mission of the Kemalist establishment. The nationalist movement began as an effort to resist the occupation of Asia Minor by Greece, Britain, France, and Italy (1918–22). After achieving success, it evolved into a revolutionary movement aimed at replacing the Ottoman Empire with the Turkish Republic. Once this course was taken, the problem of defining both the nation-state and the nation-people arose. Under the leadership of Mustafa Kemal (Atatürk), the members of the National Assembly took steps to invent a new public life based on secularism, as well as to destroy the old public life based on religion. As they did so, the Kemalists adopted policies that favored the identities and traditions of some citizens and disfavored those of others. For example, the Kemalists came to see the Alevis of Turkey as representative of the original Turkish nation that had settled Asia Minor *before* it had been spoiled by the Ottomans. They took this view because many of the Alevis had retained ancient beliefs and practices of Central Asian origin; however, they had done so precisely because they had been remote forest or mountain peoples relatively untouched by imperial institutions. So they had been perceived as representative of the original Turkish nation precisely because they were free of the stigma of Empire, and also of the stigma of Sunni Islam.

Although Lewis had written an introduction that contradicted the views of the existing Kemalist establishment, he had accurately predicted a watershed in public life. At the time, more and more citizens were moving toward the idea that a Turkish and Islamic people had first built the old regime, and then built the new. And some twenty years later, even state administrators, military officers, and schoolteachers would embrace such a doctrine. Astonishingly, Lewis had anticipated nothing less in his introduction. He had flatly stated that the Kemalist program of secular reforms could never have succeeded in displacing Islam. After only a temporary eclipse, he observed, Islamic belief and practice were once again becoming an important part of public life. Noting this trend, he affirmed that it would continue, if not accelerate, precisely because the state could not help but orient itself to its people in a modern Turkey.

While Lewis was moving with a trend in the thinking of Turkish citizens, he was moving against a trend in the thinking of historians, sociologists, and anthropologists. With the de-colonization of many parts of Asia and Africa, academics had begun to take an interest in the gap between nationalist ideals and realities. In principle, the destiny of every nation-people was defined by the task of achieving independence through the founding of a nation-state. In practice, every nation-state came into being as a result of language policies and educational programs that encouraged a diverse population to think and behave as a homogeneous nation-people. In other words, a people did not create their own state so often as a state created its own people.

By the 1980s, two theorists of nationalism had articulated the shift in perspective in distinct but equally provocative analyses. Anderson and Gellner explained that the modern nation was the result of a political process, one in which the state system was used as an instrument for generating national identity and commitment.[3] In doing so, they separated the problem of the origin of the modern nation from the problem of its propagation. And in discussing the latter, they gave special notice to "modular nationalism."[4] This last concept refers to the following sequence of events.

The first nation-states representing nation-peoples emerged during the later eighteenth century in different parts of the Euro-American sphere. But once in place, they provided a recipe by which other governments, whatever their character, could concoct a nation-state representing a nation-people. The mechanisms for doing so involved all the machinery of the modern state, such as promoting a standardized vernacular in print, institutionalizing public education, building monuments of commemoration, mobilizing an army of citizens, and so on. So it was that nation-states representing nation-peoples came into being in the rest of the world. And of all the many instances of modular nationalism, the Turkish Republic stood as one of the most impressive examples of a top-down project of nation-building, one that explicitly embraced the example of the nations of western Europe.

The theorists of nationalism would seem to require a radical revision in *The Emergence of Modern Turkey.* However, a number of cosmetic changes—replacing the word "emergence" in the title with "making," for example—suffice. For as Lewis had cogently pointed out, the Muslim peoples of Asia Minor did not think of themselves as Turks or their country as Turkey at the beginning of the twentieth century. They would only adopt these self-descriptions some years later, after Ottoman defeat and collapse,

3. Anderson 1991 [1983] and Gellner 1983. Also see Hobsbawm (1990), who gives a fuller account of what can be called "imperial nationalism" in late-nineteenth-century Europe (but neglecting the instance of the Ottoman Empire). See Deringil (1998), who demonstrates that the Ottomans pursued policies of imperial nationalism in the same manner and at the same time as other late European empires.

4. The specific designation "modular nationalism" presumably belongs to Anderson (1991), but other theorists of nationalism describe a similar process without so naming it.

borrowing them from long-standing usages in western Europe.[5] And although he did consider that both the country and the people had existed latently before they existed manifestly, his account is otherwise largely consistent with the concept of modular nationalism.[6] He describes how the Turkish Republic was more or less modeled on "Euro-American" states representing peoples, placing some special emphasis on the French Revolution.[7] He describes how this modeling enabled the Islamic and Turkish peoples of Asia Minor to understand themselves as a nation. The historian of modern Turkey differs from the theorists of nationalism only in regard to the question of whether the state actually created or merely stimulated national consciousness.

On the other hand, this is hardly a negligible difference. According to Lewis, the Kemalist establishment had "mis-identified" the people. As time would tell, the real Turkish nation was religious, not secular. But according to the theorists of nationalism, any such contention necessarily came in the company of a politics of the "proper" nation. And indeed, the fulfillment of Lewis's prediction featured precisely such a politics. By 1980, a large segment of the political elite in the Turkish Republic, including many members of the Kemalist establishment, had reached a new consensus, inconsistent with the program of secular reforms. The political elite in question were reacting to a decade of unstable coalition government accompanied by growing unrest among youths in the larger cities. To reaffirm the importance of order and discipline, they had begun to promote a "proper" Turkish and Islamic nation in which the two qualities were deemed essential for a strong state and stable society.[8] Eventually, as a consequence of their advocacy, state policies of cultural de-legitimization and political exclusion gained ground, the targets of these policies including all kinds of individuals and groups. Some among them could easily be deemed not Turkish (linguistic minorities) or not Islamic (religious minorities), but some could be deemed not Turkish or not Islamic politically rather than empirically.[9]

5. Lewis 1961, 1. See Kayalı's (1997) study of the extent to which Ottoman elites remained committed to the imperial system even into the years of the Great War.

6. Lewis 1961, 478–79.

7. Ibid., 53–55.

8. I have in mind various currents of authoritarianism that were current in Turkey around 1980, and in particular the "Turk-Islam" (*Türk-İslam*) movement as represented by the "Hearth of the Enlightened" (*Aydınlar Ocağı*). See Zürcher 1993, 302, 303).

9. The range of targets was very broad. It included feminists, leftists, Kurds, and Alevis. Once the Motherland Party (*Anavatan Partisi*) of Turgut Özal came to power, these policies were tempered and in some instances reversed.

Kurdish and Turkish Alevis, many of whom were subjected to official blacklisting (*şeritli*), are notable examples of each of these categories.[10]

But I do not wish to find fault with the historian of modern Turkey; for the weakness of his work as politics is also its strength as history. Lewis was pointing to something very real when he described a "Turkish" and "Islamic" people who had moved from Empire to Republic. He had located the counterrevolution within the revolution, even if he would never use such terminology, and he had sensed that the counterrevolution was gaining ground. This insight is impressive even if it was gained at the cost of his own "mis-identification," that is, mistaking a part of the Turkish nation for the whole. To see how this is so, we must reassert the dictum of the theorists of nationalism—states make people, people do not makes states—and then apply it to the Ottoman Empire.

It is certainly true that "Turkish" and "Islamic" streams of influence were important, if not dominant, among the population in parts of the Middle East, Asia Minor, and the Balkans for many hundreds of years. It is also indisputable that the classical imperial system of Sultan Mehmet II was shaped in a fundamental way by rivulets among these streams of influence. On the other hand, the Ottoman Empire was built and sustained by individuals of diverse backgrounds, some of whom were of Turkish and Islamic background, some of whom were not.[11] As we shall see in the instance of the old Ottoman province of Trabzon, participants in the imperial system included large numbers of Turks, Lazis, Greeks, Armenians, and Kurds, as well as some number of Circassians, Georgians, Bosnians, and Albanians. Representatives of these same peoples would have also been participants in the imperial system in other Ottoman provinces, along with still other peoples, most notably Arabs, Persians, and Jews, not to mention some scattering of Hungarians, Poles, Russians, Italians, Frenchmen, and Germans. The imperial project was joined by peoples of diverse backgrounds, and in so joining it, they acquired behaviors that featured its peculiar "Turkish" and "Islamic" qualities.

So the Empire generated a state people even before the Republic generated a state people. The capacity of the imperial project to mobilize the population would have a direct bearing on the capacity of the national project to mobilize the population. For to reform a state people that already existed, it would be necessary to address the very elements that composed

10. For a recent assessment of the place of the Alevis in the politics of religion, see Shankland 1999.

11. For a discussion of this aspect of early dynastic history, see Kafadar 1995.

that state people, replacing in each instance an imperial formula with the equivalent of a national formula: hats for turbans, shoes for slippers, tubs for hamams, a romanized script for an Arabic script, a secular law for a sacred law. This means that the Republic would inevitably feature a derivative and imitative character with reference to the Empire.[12]

Mustafa Kemal (Atatürk) (d. 1938) and Mehmet the Conqueror (d. 1481) had indeed charted a similar course at a distance of almost five hundred years.[13] The accomplishments of both involved a series of prescriptions that could be said to constitute a project of modernity, conceived in response to challenges from abroad. Launch a project of state that is cut free from a past of degeneracy and corruption. Clear out all that is rotten from a landscape littered with ancient ruins in order to construct the capital city of a new political utopia. Assemble a body of supporters by inculcating a discipline of interpersonal association distinct from that of any pre-existing communal grouping. With the assistance of this body of supporters, constitute a regime that draws together peoples of diverse backgrounds and traditions. Guarantee all these peoples the honor and dignity of subjects on the condition that they take their proper place in the new utopia. By such steps, convert fatal circumstances of ethnic fragmentation into an opportunity to propagate a state society that transcends the disabilities of parochial loyalties and affiliations.

The imperial project therefore prefigures the national project.[14] The former, usually judged traditionalist, appears as modernist while the latter, usually judged an unprecedented departure, appears as repetition. Insofar as this is the case, the old imperial project represents something far more formidable than the inertia of a degenerate and corrupt tradition. Until re-

12. Cf. Tapper and Tapper (1987), who argue that Turkish nationalism has a certain kinship with Islamic fundamentalism. Accordingly, they trace nationalist authoritarianism to the Semitic religious tradition. Delaney (1991) takes a similar view. I would argue instead that the authoritarianism of both Kemalists and Islamists is more directly an imperial legacy, and that religion was itself shaped by this imperial legacy.

13. The comparison of Empire and Republic is inspired by Foucault's (1975) analysis of "modern" western European institutions in terms of a microphysics of power that works through a disciplinary tactic. I have attempted to understand "modern" Ottoman institutions as based on an entirely different microphysics of power working through a different disciplinary tactic. Although this approach is perhaps not exactly that recommended by Asad (1993), I am nonetheless indebted to his critique of anthropological studies in terms of their emphasis on symbols to the neglect of disciplines.

14. Cf. Mardin 1969 on the parallels between the state officials of the Empire and the Republic.

cently, however, the posing of such a question has been blocked by two presumptions backed by scholarly consensus. *The Emergence of Modern Turkey,* a landmark in Ottoman and Turkish studies in its time, provides a useful example of these two presumptions.

Having accounted for the three main influences that went into the making of modern Turkey, Lewis devoted his first chapter to "The Decline of the Ottoman Empire." The story began with the virtual collapse of the classical imperial system during the seventeenth century: "The breakdown in the apparatus of government affected not only the supreme instruments of sovereignty but also the whole of the bureaucratic and religious institutions of the Empire. These suffered a catastrophic fall in efficiency and integrity, which was accompanied by the growing change in methods of recruitment, training, and promotion."[15] By this assessment, the Empire was twice removed from the Republic. The classical imperial regime (fifteenth and sixteenth centuries) had been based on a narrow military and administrative elite who set themselves apart from a much larger subject population. The efficiency and integrity of this military and administrative elite had vanished during the post-classical imperial period (seventeenth and eighteenth centuries). There could have been no influence of the Ottoman Empire of Sultan Mehmet II on modern Turkey. The classical imperial period he initiated with the conquest of Constantinople had come to an end three hundred years before the founding of the Turkish Republic and had left no trace of itself on the majority population that was to become its citizenry.[16]

Recent studies of local elites in the core Ottoman provinces have cast a clearer light on the dark figure in the preceding citation, the "growing change in methods of recruitment, training, and promotion."[17] Sometime during the seventeenth century, under the direct pressure of internal instability and external competition, the Ottomans took more radical steps to widen the circle of participation in imperial institutions in the core provinces

15. Lewis 1961, 23.

16. By Lewis's estimation, there was hardly anything left of the old Ottoman Empire by the end of the first great Ottoman reform, the "Reordering" (*Tanzimat*): "The destruction of the old order had been too thorough [by 1871] for any restoration to be possible; for better or for worse, only one path lay before Turkey, that of modernization and Westernization" (ibid., 125).

17. The works in question are cited in parts 2 and 3. Those that have been most important to the present study are: Akarlı 1988, Aksan 1999a, 1999b, Aktepe 1951–52, Barkey 1994, İnalcık 1977, Kafadar 1995, Kunt 1983, Nagata 1976, Özkaya 1977, Sakaoğlu 1984, and Veinstein 1975, 1991. I am also especially indebted to the distinguished local historians of Of and Sürmene, Umur (1949, 1951, 1956) and Bilgin (1990), respectively.

of the Empire. By the beginning of the eighteenth century, the countryside was here and there teeming with representatives of the lower echelons of the military and religious branches of the imperial system.[18] And during the course of the eighteenth century, some of these elements began to emerge as the principals of regional social oligarchies comprising a major proportion of the local population. The state policies of the post-classical period therefore had the potential to generate state societies, partly as a consequence of their intentional and judicious application, but also partly as a consequence of their manipulation and infringement at the local level.

In this regional study, I shall examine how peoples of different ethnic origins, speaking different languages and ascribing to different religions, came to form such a state society in the old province of Trabzon. Through participation in imperial institutions, a large population of townsmen and villagers adopted universal standards of social thinking and practice in the course of bringing themselves into alignment with the imperial system. As they did so, they lost their sentimental attachment to their existing customs that they came to consider degenerate and corrupt, even though they did not entirely abandon them. In this respect, the large majority of the inhabitants in the old province of Trabzon could be said to have been more modern than traditional. They had not incidentally participated in imperial institutions but had identified themselves with a world project that was conceived as a move toward reform and renewal.

My argument can be summarized as follows. Local elites backed by local coalitions had the ability to tax commerce, raise armies, requisition supplies, impose labor, apprehend fugitives, and exact punishment, that is, to do everything that higher state officials of the centralized government might be able to do. They could do so, even though the latter might sometimes attempt to prevent them, because they were able to do what the proper imperial system could do: to deploy the sovereign power of a family line through a following based on a discipline of interpersonal association.[19] The rise of regional social oligarchies can therefore be understood as coincident with the dissemination of an imperial tactic: the exercise of sovereign power by means of a discipline of interpersonal association. Such an imperial tactic, together with contradictions inherent within in it, had been transmitted outward and downward into the core Ottoman provinces, and

18. The widening of the circle of participation is considered in chaps. 3, 4, and 5, where I rely on Barkey's (1994) study of state policies relating to this issue during the sixteenth and seventeenth centuries.

19. Cf. Mardin 1969 on the local elites imitating the palace.

especially into the old province of Trabzon.[20] The result was the decentralization of the state system, and, during periods of crisis, the vertical and horizontal fracturing of the structure of political authority.[21]

Once in place, the regional social oligarchy in the province of Trabzon was both a resource and a problem for the state system. Higher state officials could enter into agreements with local elites, granting them local sovereign powers in return for administrating or policing the local population. On the other hand, local elites frequently opposed official policies that reinforced centralized government. When such policies were nonetheless adopted, local elites proved adept at repenetrating and recolonizing the new state system. In such a manner, they were able to reinhabit the state system after periods of "revolutionary" change. From the 1830s to the 1840s, they moved from the post-classical imperial system into the westernized imperial system of the "Reordering" (*Tanzimat*). From the 1920s to the 1930s, they moved from the late Empire into the early Republic. The dissemination of a basic piece of the classical imperial system had led to the rise of a state society that was able to accommodate itself, first to the reformed state system of the later Empire, and then to the reformed state system of the early Republic.[22]

My study is divided into four different parts. Parts 1 and 4 are primarily based on fieldwork. Parts 2 and 3 are primarily based on historical research.

In part 1, I begin by telling the story of my encounters with local elites in the district of Of during my first period of fieldwork in the 1960s (chap. 1 and 2). Initially, I could not understand how these local elites represented a regional social oligarchy of imperial origin that had gradually come to dominate public life during the later decades of the Turkish Republic. As for my

20. State protocol and ceremony is considered in chap. 4, where I rely on Necipoğlu's (1991) study of the imperial palace.

21. The period of decentralization in Trabzon is considered in chaps. 3, 4, and 5, where I rely on İnalcık 1977.

22. Here I shall mention how my regional study departs from Keyder's (1987) analysis of state and class in the Turkish Republic. For Keyder, the statist orientation of contemporary Turkish society is an imperial legacy, but only insofar as it represents a continuation of an official, Ottoman "statolatry." The question is then why this statolatry was never successfully challenged and defeated by bourgeois ideology, even with the rise of a commercial class during the later Republic. To find an answer, Keyder relies on dependency theory, analyzing the place of the Turkish polity and economy in the world system. In my analysis, I have considered how the official state system was supplemented by a nonofficial state society.

interlocutors among the residents in the district Of, they too were unable to explain how this had come about, as it contradicted their commitment to official nationalist ideology and history. It was only years later, in the course of reading consular reports from the nineteenth century, that I became aware of the extent to which public life in the 1960s featured an imperial legacy.

Part 2 examines how diverse peoples speaking various languages in the old province of Trabzon became an ottomanist provincial society during the seventeenth and eighteenth centuries. I begin by analyzing the ways in which topography and environment consistently encouraged its inhabitants to participate in the wider market and state systems (chap. 3). I then consider the channels by which the local elites of these rural societies could have identified with and participated in the imperial system (chap. 4). To do so, I analyze the relationship of sovereign power and disciplinary association as displayed in the architecture and ceremony of the Ottoman palace. I then consider evidence for the provincial dissemination of this relationship during the late seventeenth and early eighteenth century (chap. 5). This came about as an important segment of the population in the old province of Trabzon became affiliated with imperial military and religious institutions.

Part 3 addresses the character of local elites in the old province of Trabzon from the later eighteenth to the early nineteenth century. I first show how local elites composed a tiered state society, the uppermost tier being inside the state system and the lowermost tier being outside the state system (chap. 6). I then examine how western European consuls misunderstood the character of this imperial state society. As a result, they mistakenly declared its local elites to have been suppressed by the central government during the 1830s, even though they continued to be part and parcel of the imperial system (chap. 7). I then show how the consular assessment of the local elites was later adopted by higher Ottoman officials as they adopted a westernist theory of centralized bureaucratic government (chap. 8). As a result, both consuls and officials of the later nineteenth century were repeatedly surprised to find that local elites were able to manipulate, if not subvert, the central government at the local level.

In part 4, I analyze the process by which the old regional social oligarchy of the eastern coastal region came to inhabit the Turkish Republic, citing the district of Of as a case study. The first two chapters account for the return of the old regional social oligarchy. I begin by describing how the nationalist revolution succeeded in undermining the legitimacy of local elites, even as state officials continued to rely on them for governmental assistance (chap. 9). I then describe the resurgence of a regional social oligarchy following the first free and direct elections in 1950 (chap. 10). The last two chapters illustrate the ability of local elites to accommodate changing economic and political circumstances. I examine cooperatives and coffeehouses during the 1960s as a case study of the flexible relationship between official institutions and social relations (chap. 11). The last chapter examines the effects of urbanization on social formations among the natives of Of, both at home and in Istanbul, during the 1970s and 1980s (chap. 12).

Acknowledgments

Since the research on which this study is based spans three decades, I cannot hope to recognize all the individuals who have given me assistance over these many years. I am especially grateful to the residents of the town and district of Of, who welcomed me during my stay there in the 1960s. I would like to mention in particular the kindness of Ahmet Hızal, Ziya Ramoğlu, Kaymakam Nihat Zeki Özerin, Ali Yakupoğlu, Elias Kaptanoğlu, Hasan Tahsin Saral, Miktat Saral, Necati Çakır, Dursun Ali Karnapoğlu, Mustafa Karnapoğlu, Niyazi Abdik, Şahmeran Taka, and Kazim Tellioğlu. In later years, I also greatly benefited from the hospitality and expertise of Mehmet Bilgin in Sürmene, Haşim Albayrak in Istanbul, Mehmet Necef and İsmail Zengingönül in Antalya, Paul Stirling in Kent, Anthony Bryer in Birmingham, Nancy Lindisfarne and Richard Tapper in London, Heath and Demet Lowry in Istanbul, Reşat Kasaba in Seattle, Maria Pia Di Bella and Baber Johansen in Paris, and Ildiko Beller and Chris Hann in Berlin.

I am especially appreciative of Gesine Meeker, Hasan Kayalı, Luce Giard, and Nazanin Wahid, who read drafts of the manuscripts with special care and offered valuable comments and criticisms. I also want to thank Dale F. Eickelman, Frederick G. Bailey, and Michael Rogin for reading and commenting on substantial sections of the manuscript; Frank La Rosa for kindly providing me with a sketch of the palace to illustrate the argument in chapter 4, and Hasan Kayalı and Engin Akarlı for patiently helping me with a number of Ottoman documents. I also owe a very special debt for the wisdom and friendship of Lloyd Fallers, Margaret Fallers, Nur Yalman, Şerif Mardin, Frederick G. Bailey, Clifford Geertz, Alan Duben, Mübeccel Kıray, Ned Levine, Yurdanur Salman, and Ali Gheissari. My discussions with colleagues at the University of California at San Diego, James Holston,

Suzanne Brenner, and Vincent Rafael, have shaped my understanding of modernity and cities. My discussions with James Siegel have also influenced my thinking over the years, so thoroughly as to defy comment. I would also like to thank my graduate students, especially William Reese, Jeffrey Snodgrass, Joseph Masco, Leila Madge, Marcia Rego, and Jon Bialecki, for their enthusiasm about the kinds of anthropological questions that have been my concern.

I would never have been able to complete this project without the love and support of Gesine Meeker. Her assistance has been essential from its beginning to its conclusion. Both my daughters have become young women during the years that I was writing this book. Their keen interest in their own Turkish experiences was always an encouragement.

My research in Anatolia from 1966 to 1968 was supported by the National Institutes for Mental Health. My research in Istanbul from 1986 to 1988 was supported by the Fulbright Commission in Turkey, with special thanks to Hüsnü Ersoy and Ersin Onulduran. My research in the archives of the Public Record Office and the Ministère des Affaires Étrangères was supported by the Social Science Research Council, with funding from the Mellon Foundation. My writing and research from 1991 to 1992 were supported by a President's Fellowship from the University of California and by the Institute for Advanced Study in Princeton, with funding from the Mellon Foundation.

Explanations

Pronunciation

The sound values for the Turkish alphabet are as follows:

a	like *o* in *possible*
e	like *a* in *payday*
i or İ	like *ee* in *feet*
ı or I	like *u* in *puddle*
o	like *ow* in *low*
ö or Ö	like the German *ö*
u	like *oo* in *tool*
ü or Ü	like the French *u* or German *ü*
ç or Ç	like *ch* in *church*
ğ	like *w* in *newer*
ş or Ş	like *sh* in *shake*

Dates

When a single date is cited without a slash, as in "Hasan Umur (b. 1880)," the date refers to the common era. When two dates are cited separated by a slash, as in "the Trabzon yearbook (*salname*) for 1869/1286," the first date refers to the common era and the second date refers to the Islamic era.

Old and New Place Names

The names of many villages, towns, and districts were changed during the Republican period. For example, most of the villages in the district of Of had Greek names until 1965, when a new set of Turkish names was adopted. When the name of a village, town, or district is followed by another name in brackets, as in Paçan [Maraşlı], the first name is the old and the second is the new. Otherwise, I have always used "Istanbul" for the name of the imperial capital, except for a few references to Mehmet II's conquest of "Constantinople."

Personal Names in the District of Of

I have adopted fictitious names for the two large patronymic groups that dominated the two coastal towns in the district of Of, but I have otherwise used the actual names of all other patronymic groups. I have also adopted fictitious personal names for the members of the two large patronymic groups who were active in public life during the twentieth century, but I have retained the personal names of their members who appear earlier in the historical record. When citing names that appear in official documents from the Ottoman period, I have cited the personal name before the family name, thereby reversing the order in which the names usually appeared in the documents.

References to Locales and Their Inhabitants

The name of the town that serves as an administrative center for a district or province usually has the same name as the district or province. Hence, the town of Of is the center of the district of Of, whereas Sürmene is the center of the district of Sürmene. Correspondingly, the towns of Rize and Trabzon are also the centers of the districts Rize and Trabzon, as well as the capitals of the provinces Rize and Trabzon, respectively.

The names of the inhabitants of a place, be it a village, town, district, or province, are formed by adding the particle "li/lı/lü/lu." Thus, the Oflus are the inhabitants of Of, the Çaykaralıs are inhabitants of Çaykara, and the Sürmenelis are the inhabitants of Sürmene. Similarly, the Trabzonlus and the Rizelis are the inhabitants of the corresponding towns, districts, or provinces (as indicated by context).

English Versions of Turkish and Ottoman Terms

English equivalents have been used in place of some Turkish and Ottoman terms and titles, for example, agha instead of *ağa,* pasha instead of *paşa,* and hodja instead of *hoca.*

Photographs

All the photographs were taken sometime between 1965 and 1978 by the author.

PART I

AGHAS AND HODJAS

The Republican District of Of

1 Amnesia

Clan-Society and Nation-State

A FIRST ACCOUNT OF ARRIVAL AND DISCOVERY

In August of 1965, during my first trip to Turkey, I was traveling by minibus eastward along the coastal road from Trabzon, hopping from town to town, taking first one van and then another, intending to reach Rize by the evening. Sometime after noon, taking advantage of a stop at the small town of Eskipazar in the district of Of, I decided to have lunch in a restaurant that catered to the travelers making bus connections in the market center. Just as I had begun to relish a dish of chicken pilaf, the room fell silent as several men, some of them dressed in suits and ties, abruptly rose from their chairs, standing at attention as though soldiers presenting themselves to a commanding officer. An elderly bearded man who had just then entered the room with a perfunctory greeting motioned to the men to sit and then ordered two of the waiters to carry a suitcase and a millstone from the nearby market to a minibus that he was about to board on his way to Trabzon. The waiters followed him from the restaurant to do his bidding while the patrons, having taken their seats again, resumed eating and talking as before.

Impressed that someone without any apparent official standing would be accorded this kind of deference in a public place, I decided to return to the district of Of as soon as I had finished my tour of the eastern Black Sea coast from Rize to Hopa. When I did so a week or so later, I was able to question a university student whom I had met in one of the coffeehouses in the town of Of. After describing the scene in the restaurant, my acquaintance was able to explain to me exactly what I had seen. He told me that the elderly bearded man and all the other men who had risen to salute him would have been members of the same large family grouping, as was most of the population in the vicinity of Eskipazar. The older man, whose identity he was able to guess, was one of the more prominent elders (*büyüklerinden*) of this family. The younger men had stopped eating and talking and stood at attention as a sign of their respect (*hürmet ediyorlardı*) for a senior relative.[1] Some of them might have been his own sons or grandsons, but others would have been more distant junior agnates (*amcaoğlu*).

I expressed surprise that the majority of the residents near a major district market consisted of a single kin-group composed of many households. My host, who was not displeased by my reaction, explained that this situation was not at all remarkable. The majority of the population in the vicinity of the town of Of, where we sat, also belonged to a second large family grouping. Each of the two families consisted of hundreds of households, and each was concentrated around one of the two small coastal towns of the district. Moreover, the members of these two families dominated the public life of the two little towns. As my acquaintance explained it, leading individuals from the two families had, by virtue of the support of their numerous kinsmen, monopolized all the higher official positions that were open to locals in each town. Except for a certain number of district state officials, the heads of municipal government, agricultural cooperatives, nationalist associations, and political parties were drawn from one of two large family groupings, the Muradoğlu in the town of Eskipazar and the Selimoğlu in the town of Of.[2]

As our conversation continued, my host told me that the two families had been in a dominant position in the district as far back as anyone could remember, that is to say, for well over a hundred years. Throughout the final decades of the Ottoman Empire, they usually monopolized the higher official positions open to locals. More often than not, they were able to intimidate, if not coerce, local representatives of the provincial government. After the declaration of the Turkish Republic, the two families were set back politically for only a few years. Toward the end of the one-party system, from 1945 on, leading individuals from the Muradoğlu and Selimoğlu rose in prominence through participation in political parties. Now, the two families were fierce rivals with one another, each aligned with a different national political party and competing against the other to bring govern-

1. According to the conventions of showing respect, younger men do not eat or talk before senior male relatives unless bidden by them to do so, standing ready to perform any task that might be asked of them.

2. Muradoğlu and Selimoğlu are not the actual names of the families in question. In an earlier publication (Meeker 1972) I used other fictitious names, Karahasanoğlu and Hadjimehmedoğlu, for the same two families. I have adopted the new names because they are easier to print and read.

ment projects to Eskipazar and Of, respectively. The "Oflus" (native residents of the district), as well as the district state officials who served among them, were more or less resigned to the fact that members of the two families would dominate public life in the district. Some considered this situation a kind of scandal, running counter to the democratic principles of the multiparty period, but no one expressed such an opinion openly.

I wrote down a summary of the remarks of my coffeehouse acquaintance with a sense of excitement. I had stumbled upon a situation that posed exactly the kind of questions on which I had intended to focus my research. When I came to the Turkish Republic as a graduate student in anthropology, I had been interested in understanding how local tradition had played a role in shaping the course of economic and political modernization. I was searching for a site, preferably a district center, where I could study these two sides of everyday provincial life. I had the idea that interpersonal relationships in villages and towns had not been transformed by the nationalist movement to the same degree as in the major cities of the Turkish Republic. Presuming that the Ottoman Empire had left most localities to fend for themselves, I expected to discover a rich variety of local social and cultural systems.

I was therefore anticipating that townsmen and villagers had responded to the nationalist project of state modernization in different ways, and I was hoping to demonstrate that local traditions were sometimes the basis for both positive and negative engagements with modernity. I had been specifically attracted to the eastern Black Sea coast by the reputation of its inhabitants. They were said to be unusually conservative in their social relations but nonetheless successful as officials, professionals, and entrepreneurs.

In the district of Of, I had now encountered just the profound contrast between a local tradition and state modernity for which I had been looking. An "order" of a social system, consisting of leading individuals from large family groupings, could be clearly differentiated from an "order" of the nation-state, consisting of representative government, state administration, and public associations. By this distinction, the elites of a local social order had succeeded in infiltrating the new national order. These elites, whose conduct of social relations was apparently conservative, familial, and religious in orientation, dominated a public sphere that was in principle reformist, nationalist, and secularist in orientation. The district of Of therefore seemed an excellent place for a study of the way in which local social formations had adapted themselves to state projects of political and economic modernization. Using the methods of anthropology—the ethnographic study of interpersonal relationships—I could hope to uncover the limits of "top-down" reforms that a study of government policies and institutions could not easily detect. From the outset, I had assumed the existence of two separate but interacting orders at the local level: a traditional social system and a modern state system.

A SOCIAL SYSTEM DIVIDED FROM THE STATE SYSTEM

What I had observed as the result of an incidental stop for lunch would not have ordinarily come to the attention of a passing traveler. Normally, there was nothing to be seen or heard in either the market of Eskipazar or the town of Of to indicate the dominant position of the Muradoğlu and Selimoğlu. It was not openly announced by any kind of sign, building, or plaza. The town of Of, where I was eventually to conduct my fieldwork, actually offered a strong first impression of the new state rather than the old society. By the design of its streets and squares, and by the appearance of its offices, shops, and residences, this was a town of the Turkish Republic, even more so than its counterparts elsewhere in the country.[3] Forty years earlier, when the Ottoman Empire came to an end, it was hardly a town at all.[4] Its public spaces and structures, most of which had come into being since that time, were therefore almost entirely the creations of the new nation-state. Some body of state officials and experts, probably in Ankara, had devised a definition of what a Turkish town should be. The town of Of, such as it was during the summer of 1965, conformed to this nationalist canon far more perfectly than other Turkish towns, some of which were cluttered with Ottoman, Seljuk, Byzantine, or even Roman leftovers.

What first struck the eye of a casual visitor was therefore very much a "republican" town (see fig. 1).[5] There was a new government building (*hükümet*), designed in a spare modernist style and larger than any other building. Here, a district officer (*kaymakam*), two district judges (*hakim*), and a district prosecutor (*savcı*), none of them natives of the district, conducted their affairs and received visits from citizens. A large central square

3. The population of the town of Of was in the range of one to two thousand during the first two-thirds of the twentieth century, after which it began to soar.

4. See the Trabzon yearbooks (*salname*) from the late Ottoman period, in particular, the re-publications supervised by Emiroğlu (1993–95).

5. I use the words "republican" and "ottomanist" to refer to attributes of the new and old regimes, respectively.

Figure 1. View of the town of Of.

(*meydan*) had been laid out before the government building for the purpose of national commemorations and ceremonies. A bust of Mustafa Kemal (Atatürk) was located at the center of one side of this square, always to be seen looking to the west—and so, specifically, not to the east. On national holidays, state officials, local worthies, military bands, schoolchildren, and villagers assembled in the square before the bust in order to pay homage to the founder of the Turkish Republic.

With the government building and central square as its center, the town spread out along the coastline. To the west, where the small nucleus of a late Ottoman town had been laid out around the turn of the century, the grid of streets was more compact, but the roads were still rectilinear rather than winding and irregular. Most of the shops, workshops, and warehouses of the town were located here, as well as most of its coffeehouses, hotels and dormitories, and restaurants. To the east, two wide avenues ran parallel to one another, interspersed with vegetable gardens and citrus groves. The residences of officials, the gendarmerie and military posts, the primary and secondary schools, and the public health and social services agencies were all located here.

The town was centered around the government building and central square, the administrative and ceremonial spaces of the Turkish Republic. By the arrangement of the two, which had been determined sometime around the early 1930s, one could detect the principle that had inspired the Kemalist one-party regime.[6] Although barely a stone's throw from the coastline, the government building and central square had been oriented landward rather seaward, so that they were facing away from a spectacularly beautiful vista. Given the sensitivity to architectural siting and views in Turkey, the pair of them seemed to insist, "We do not represent the people of this district to the world so much as we represent the central government to the people of this district."

Such a reading of the town plan is more simplification than exaggeration. From the later 1920s, the Kemalist leadership of the nationalist movement had faced the difficult task of transforming a citizenry of Ottoman Muslims into a citizenry of Republican Turks. To do so, they encouraged a certain degree of popular participation in various kinds of governmental and nongovernmental organizations. In this way, a new kind of public life would be propagated, one based on republican rather than ottomanist principles. All these governmental and nongovernmental organizations had always been subject to official regulation, even closure and banning. Nonetheless, resident state officials did not have direct control over a certain number of genuinely public organizations whose numbers and functions had gradually multiplied over the first four decades of the Turkish Republic.

The most important of these public organizations, in terms of their services and their financing, were the municipal government and four agricultural cooperatives.[7] Just to the west of the central square, toward the older section of town, the municipal government was located in a new concrete building, along with the water, electric, and telephone utilities. The town mayor and council, who had their offices there, were residents of Of and natives of the district. They had assumed their posts after facing other candidates in free and open elections. Elsewhere in the older section of the town, the four agricultural cooperatives maintained separate offices and warehouses. They consisted of a loan cooperative for purchasing agricultural tools and supplies, founded in the 1930s; a cooperative for hazelnut producers, founded in 1942; and two cooperatives for tea growers, founded in 1955 and 1965. Each of the four agricultural cooperatives had a director,

6. Lewis 1961, chap. 8, and Zürcher 1993, chap. 11.

7. The district center had been a municipality as early as the 1870s, but its financing was limited. See Emiroğlu 1993–95.

councilmen, membership rolls, annual meetings, and a written constitution. The director and councilmen were elected by the membership from a list of nominees during the annual meeting. The elections, which were by secret ballot, were observed by government inspectors, who ratified the results. The membership of each cooperative varied from somewhat fewer than a thousand to more than two thousand, and the annual budget of each varied from about a half million to more than two million Turkish lira, a very considerable sum of money at the time.[8]

In addition to the municipal government and agricultural cooperatives, there were also a number of local branches of national public associations. Most of the latter had first been organized in the larger cities during the early years of the Turkish Republic with the express intention of facilitating, but also guiding, popular participation in political, cultural, and charitable activities. Each branch office had appeared in the district of Of not long after the association's founding at the national level. The Republican People's Party (*Cumhuriyet Halk Partisi*) had been founded by Mustafa Kemal (Atatürk) in 1922, shortly before the declaration of the Turkish Republic. The RPP had a chairman in the town of Of no later than 1927, and probably several years earlier than that.[9] The People's Houses (*Halkevleri*), which were directly linked with the RPP, were culture clubs for the promotion of local history, folklore, music, and literature.[10] First founded in Istanbul in 1924, the People's Houses had established a local branch in Of no later than the 1940s, and probably by the 1930s. It had become defunct when the national organization was closed down by the government in 1951.[11] The Turkish Air Association (*Türk Hava Kurumu*), founded on the national level sometime after 1922, was in existence in the town of Of by 1925. This association collected contributions—principally the hides of sheep sacrificed during the annual religious festival (*Kurban Bayramı*)—for the building of a national air force. The Red Crescent Society (*Kızılay*

8. The exchange rate was 9 Turkish lira to $1 U.S. during the mid-1960s. Robinson (1963, 207) cites estimates of the average annual *per capita* income for 1953 and 1956 as just over 500 TL. By this estimate, the average annual *per capita* income during the mid-1960s would have been somewhere between 500 and 1,000 TL.

9. Local branches of other political parties had been opened in the town of Of starting in 1945, but they were still of little importance to the town during the 1960s.

10. The People's Houses were based on the Turkish Hearths (*Türk Ocağı*), an early nationalist club first founded in 1912 (Lewis 1961, 376).

11. After the Democrat Party defeated the Republican People's Party in the national elections of 1950, the government abolished the People's Houses and seized their assets (Zürcher 1993, 233).

Cemiyeti) raised relief funds for victims of disasters. There was a local branch during the 1940s, and probably by the 1930s. The Primary and Middle School Parent-Teacher Associations (*İlk Okul/Orta Okul Aile Birliği*) were in existence by the 1940s. They had a chairman who called an annual meeting at least once a year to discuss issues regarding the schools. A local branch of the Small Businessmen's Association (*Küçük Esnaf Derneği*) was organized in the town of Of in 1966, soon after it was first founded at the national level. Its officers managed a loan fund for the promotion of small businesses.

Like the municipal government and the producer cooperatives, most of these local branches of national organizations were supposed to manage their affairs according to a written constitution that had been legally approved and registered. Their membership was to elect a chairman and councilmen during an annual assembly in accordance with prescribed procedures. Their officers were to maintain a membership roll, keep a record of dues paid, announce meetings, conduct open discussion, and so on.

The municipal government, the producer cooperatives, and the local branches of national associations were therefore in principle the means by which private individuals in the town of Of were able to participate in the public life of the Turkish Republic. During the period of their existence in Of, their directors, councilmen, and membership were almost always composed of natives of Of who were not themselves state officials. And yet, popular participation in the public life of the town was certainly not in any way free and open.

At the time of my arrival, the top officer of every public association in the town was a member of the Selimoğlu family. This included the mayor of the municipality, the headman of the central municipal quarter, the directors of the four producer cooperatives, the chairman of the Republican People's Party, the chairman of the district Turkish Air Association, the chairman of the district Red Crescent Association, the chairman of the Parent-Teachers' Associations, and the chairman of the Small Businessmen's Association. As for the councilmen and committeemen in these same public associations, they included a few more individuals from the Selimoğlu, but for the most part consisted of their friends and allies, many of whom were the members of other large family groupings. As I was eventually to learn, this situation was not at all transitory. The monopoly of the directorships and chairmanships by the Selimoğlu, together with their support by other associated large family groupings, spanned many years, going back to the first two decades of the Turkish Republic.

At first it seemed that this situation was not altogether surprising or unusual. Since a majority of the residents of the town may have had the same surname, one could expect most officeholders would be selected from the Selimoğlu. Similarly, one could also explain the large proportion of the members of other large family groupings who appeared as councilmen and committeemen. Nothing more than the common tendency for voters to support their relatives, whether close or distant, would have probably produced such a result. But once I was able to determine the exact identity of the directors, chairmen, councilmen, and committeemen, it was clear that the pattern was no simple artifact of a normal electoral process.

With only one exception, all the individuals who served as directors or chairmen in the town of Of were the sons or grandsons of one man, so they were not at all randomly selected from among all the qualified members of the Selimoğlu family (see fig. 2).[12] Ferhat Agha Selimoğlu (c. 1860 – c. 1931) is remembered as the last preeminent public figure of the old regime in the town of Of. In the 1960s, during the fourth decade of the Turkish Republic, the sons of the eldest son of this one man held the top office in as many as seven different public associations at the same time. The officeholders in the town of Of appeared to be the "dynastic successors" of the last "reigning" member of the family during the late Ottoman Empire.

Members of other large family groupings were similarly predominant among the councilmen and committeemen. These individuals came from large family groupings that were not necessarily settled in or even near the town of Of. They appeared as councilmen and committeemen by virtue of some kind of friendship or partnership among large family groupings, not as a consequence of the voting preference of an organized membership. So it appeared that the public life of the town, although not directly subject to state officials, was nonetheless under the strictest supervision by some other kind of authority.

A variation on the same pattern prevailed in the vicinity of Eskipazar, which was dominated by leading individuals from the Muradoğlu. This area was little more than a marketplace with some shops, warehouses, coffeehouses, and dormitories. Although it was not a subdistrict and had not yet been incorporated as a municipality, producer cooperatives and nationalist associations were appearing in Eskipazar just as they had earlier in Of.

12. The one exception, a father's brother's great grandson of Ferhat Agha, was a significant departure from usual practice. See the analysis of the tea cooperatives in chap. 11.

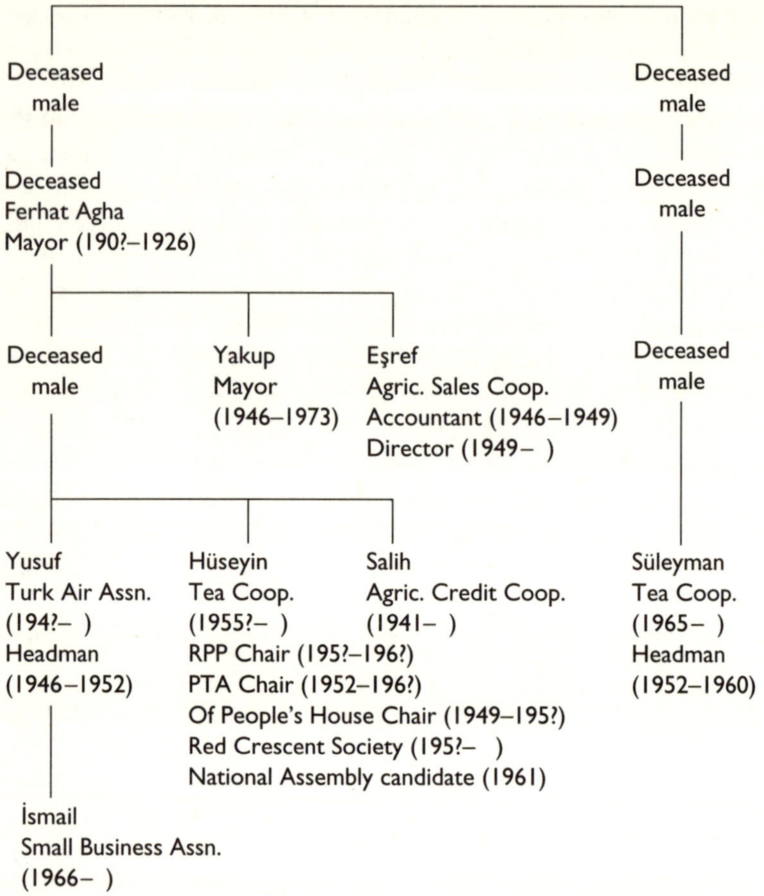

Figure 2. Prominent sons and grandsons of Ferhat Agha (c. 1960s).

Moreover, the Muradoğlu had recently been far more successful than the Selimoğlu in bringing government installations and factories to their area. So the vicinity of Eskipazar was on its way toward becoming an *ostensible* "republican" town, rivaling the *ostensible* "republican" town of Of.[13] In effect, the formation of public institutions and organizations in these "republican" towns was working through the rivalries of leading individuals

13. In 1986, one of the villages of the Muradoğlu just to the west of Eskipazar was incorporated as a municipality, rather than Eskipazar itself, by then a town center. See chap. 12 for the significance of this move.

from the Muradoğlu and Selimoğlu. These were towns where popular participation in public life was not so much under the regulation of the state system as under the regulation of a social system internal to the district of Of. Or so it seemed to me during the first period of my fieldwork.

THE ETHNOGRAPHIC ANALYSIS OF A CLAN-SOCIETY

Soon after my return to the district in 1966, I began to consider how best to understand the Selimoğlu and Muradoğlu as local social formations. I was more or less familiar with the state system, because the ideology and institutions of the Turkish Republic had been studied so thoroughly, but I did not know anything about the social system that had come to my attention in the district of Of, since I had read of nothing like it in the anthropology of Turkey. So I eagerly set about to define and analyze what I considered to be my anthropological discovery.

Although the Selimoğlu and Muradoğlu were the most prominent family groupings in Of, they were but two of many other similar family groupings in the district. The names of these family groupings were always constructed in the same way. The names of large family groupings are composed of the putative personal name, attribute, or title of an ancestral father (never a mother) plus a suffix, "*oğlu*," which means "son of" (never "daughter of"). So, for example, Selimoğlu and Muradoğlu can be translated as "the son(s) of Selim" and "the son(s) of Murad," respectively.[14] These names can therefore be described as *patronyms*. They refer literally and narrowly to groups of agnatically related men (not their mothers, daughters, or wives) who are conceived to be the descendants of a single individual. These groups of agnatically related men can be described as *patronymic groups*.[15]

Before the adoption of official "Turkish" surnames some years after the declaration of the Turkish Republic, patronyms of the type described were very common in the coastal districts that had comprised the old province of Trabzon, all the way from Batum to Ordu.[16] Probably most men (but not

14. The patronymic suffix is usually expressed in the singular, but sometimes in the plural, "sons of" (*oğulları*), as in Selimoğulları or Muradoğulları.

15. This is a paraphrase of the analysis of large family groupings in the district of Of that appears in my dissertation (Meeker 1970).

16. The new province of Trabzon is bounded by the provinces of Rize in the east and Giresun in the west.

any women) identified themselves with a patronym that signified their membership in a patronymic group.[17]

The prevalence of patronyms as well as the salience of patronymic groups was a regional peculiarity. In other parts of rural Turkey, groups of agnatically related males often designated themselves by a nickname, but they did not consistently take the form of a patronym. Correspondingly, the nicknames for descent groups, so common elsewhere in rural Turkey, did not have their counterparts in most of the eastern coastal districts of the old province of Trabzon.[18] This was an odd contrast that had never received any attention but that seemed significant, given my interest in local variation and diversity. I began to consider the patronymic group as a local social formation more or less distinctive of the eastern Black Sea coast without any exact equivalent in other parts of the country. There was other evidence that this might be the case.

The patronymic group was called an "*akraba*" in the district of Of as well as in neighboring districts to the east and west. So, for example, my interlocutors sometimes spoke of the Selimoğlu or the Muradoğlu as an *akraba*. Sometimes, however, the word was used in a different way, so that it had a more inclusive meaning. Instead of referring only to the males who comprised a patronymic group, the term "*akraba*" referred to all the patriarchal households (*hane*) of a patronymic group. In this case an *akraba* took the form of a "great patriarchal family," which included men, women, and children. All these usages, like the patronyms themselves, were peculiar to the eastern coastal districts and not at all typical of Anatolia.[19] I concluded that the patronymic groups could be appropriately described as "clans." This term, which correctly pointed to their qualities as bounded

17. One can say that women come from the group of males designated by a patronym, for example, "His wife is from the Muradoğlu" (*Ailesi Muradoğlundan*) or "She is from the Mehmet Muradoğlu group [of the Muradoğlu]" (*Mehmet Muradoğlunun takımından*). For other examples of local patronyms, see Umur (1951, 1956).

18. The contrast is described in my dissertation (Meeker 1970), but my attempt to explain it there is flawed.

19. Ibid. Elsewhere in rural Turkey, the word "*akraba*" normally referred to kinsmen, relatives or family in the broadest sense, that is, both males and females, including relatives by both blood and marriage. This means that the word "*akraba*" did not refer to any kind of bounded collectivity. Elsewhere in rural Turkey, the word "*sülale*" was commonly used to refer to "descent line" but without the meaning of a "descent group" as in the expression, "He is from my family line" (*sülalemdendir*). I rarely heard this word in the district of Of, probably because they were more preoccupied with descent groups than with descent lines.

patriarchal collectivities, was a move toward a certain theory of the division of society and state, as we shall see.

On the basis of more or less random inquiries, I estimated that the large majority of clans ranged from ten to fifty households.[20] The residences of such ordinary clans were usually territorially grouped within a village, so that they extended across a hillside or along a ridge. Otherwise, the prominence and population of clans varied enormously. About a score of the dominant clans were very much larger than the average, so that they comprised more than a hundred, and sometimes several hundred, households.[21] These larger clans sometimes made up virtually the entire population of the quarter (*mahalle*) of a village or even an entire village (*köy*). In a few instances, the very large clans comprised the population of two or three villages. During the 1960s, I estimated that the score of very large clans represented a minimum of 15% to 20% of the total district population.[22] So a major proportion of the entire population belonged to a very large clan (*akraba*). Taken together, these large clans were significant social and political factors in the district, if for no other reason than their sheer numbers.

I concluded that I was confronted with a "clan-society." The local social order took the form of a political system altogether independent of the national order. Almost every male in the district of Of recognized his attachment and loyalty to a clan. This suggested that membership in a clan was the basis of personal and familial security.[23] The size of a clan was correlated with its social and political prominence. This suggested that large clans had dominated small clans on the basis of force and numbers.[24] Two of the very

20. Ibid., 159–60. The households are assumed to be headed by a descendant of the putative ancestor of the patronymic group. The households are otherwise of variable composition. They might include a couple and their unmarried children or a couple, their married children, and their unmarried children, or they might include other relatives of the household head, or even relatives of his spouse in some instances.

21. In rural areas of central and western Turkey in the 1960s, by contrast, patrilineages consisting of more than 100 households would have been considered extraordinary.

22. Meeker 1970, 158–59. The estimate, which is a conservative one, applies to the villages of the district of Of as newly constituted in 1948. It is based on interviews, a partial census of the Selimoğlu, official census results by village, and official vote counts by village.

23. The local usage of the word "*akraba*" seemed to confirm that this was so since it indicated that the clan was a basic unit of the social system.

24. This was sometimes asserted to be a fact of life in the district of Of: "Here among us large families crush small families" (*bizde büyük akrabalar küçük akrabaları ezilir*).

largest clans appeared to have subverted the public life of the nation-state in the marketplace of Eskipazar and the town of Of. This suggested that these two large clans were able to face down provincial state officials responsible for regulating local public institutions and organizations.

If all this was correct, I could apply, or at least adapt, existing anthropological theories to the clans in the district of Of. These theories proposed that concepts of unilineal descent could provide the basis of a political system among peoples who otherwise lacked centralized government.[25] By simply historicizing these theories, which were synchronic rather than diachronic, I could argue that a principle of agnatic solidarity would be reinforced if a state system weakened or failed. Given concepts of kinship that favored patrilineal descent, near agnates would have become the first line of political identity and support during times of insecurity. This would explain why almost all the males in the district of Of had become members of patrilineal descent groups (clans) at some time during the post-classical imperial period.[26] Furthermore, these theories would also explain why groups of agnates, that is, the members of different patrilineal descent groups (clans), would unite with and divide from one another. The members of each clan would look for allies in order to protect themselves from enemies, and they would generally find these allies among more distant clans, rather than among neighboring clans, who would be their nearest competitors. By this logic, a checkerboard pattern of clan alliances and oppositions could be expected to emerge during conditions of insecurity. Such a pattern would constitute a political system based on the principles of balanced opposition and lineage mediation. When a dispute or conflict occurred, two broad coalitions of clans would oppose one another. The resulting stalemate would force a resort to political settlement that would be worked out by mediators who were outsiders to the clan-society. The return of centralized government would be understood by all the clans as an assault on the broad range of their mutual agreements and arrangements. The two coalitions of clans could therefore be expected to have come together to resist interference in their local affairs by state officials.

Such an analysis seemed plausible in consideration both of the facts I was assembling and of the explanation of those facts by my interlocutors. I de-

25. The classical statements of these anthropological theories are to be found in Evans-Pritchard (1940, 1949) and in Evans-Pritchard and Fortes (1940).

26. I use the phrase "post-classical period" to refer roughly to the seventeenth and eighteenth centuries. Later, in chap. 4, I will also use the phrase "period of decentralization," following Hourani (1974, 71) and İnalcık (1977).

cided to focus my research on the two clans that seemed to be the key to the local political system. The results of my initial findings were encouraging.

The Selimoğlu and Muradoğlu were among the largest of all the clans in the district of Of. I was eventually able to arrive at a good estimation of their population and location in each of the two valley-systems that comprise the district (see map 1):

> The Muradoğlu are reported to consist of about 700 households or about 4,000 individuals. Most of these people are settled in three villages at the foot of the eastern valley-system. These villages are set in the midst of the more prosperous agricultural region in the district, especially so after the introduction of tea cultivation. The leading individuals of this group dominate the nearby market town of Eskipazar, where they are estimated to constitute 80% of the population.
>
> The Selimoğlu are reported to consist of about 350 households and 2,000 individuals in two different areas. One group is settled in their "home" village about 20 kilometers up the western valley-system. A second group is settled in and around the town of Of, which is the district center, an incorporated municipality, and the most extensive market. The leading individuals of this group dominate the municipality where they are said to constitute a majority, but no more than 60%, of the population.[27]

These two clans were preeminent among all the larger clans because of their strategic coastal locations. Many of their households were concentrated near the shoreline at the foot of each of the two valley-systems that comprised the district. Here, leading individuals from each of the two clans were in a good position to serve as intermediaries between the district population and outsiders. Officials, merchants, and travelers inevitably came under their surveillance, whether they landed on the shore, traversed the coastal tracks, or descended the valley-systems. About a score of other very large clans, scattered throughout the lower reaches of the eastern and western valley systems, had also dominated their vicinities at some time in the past, just as they continued to do in the present. They, too, were located near a point of commercial significance, such as a marketplace, a trade route, an anchorage, or a pass. All claimed a kind of social, if not political, ascendancy over the smaller clans who were their neighbors.

The members of all these large clans were said to be mutually associated by partnership, friendship, and marriage. For example, my interlocutors would say that the Muradoğlu or the Selimoğlu were allied to (*çok yakınız*),

27. Meeker 1970, 158.

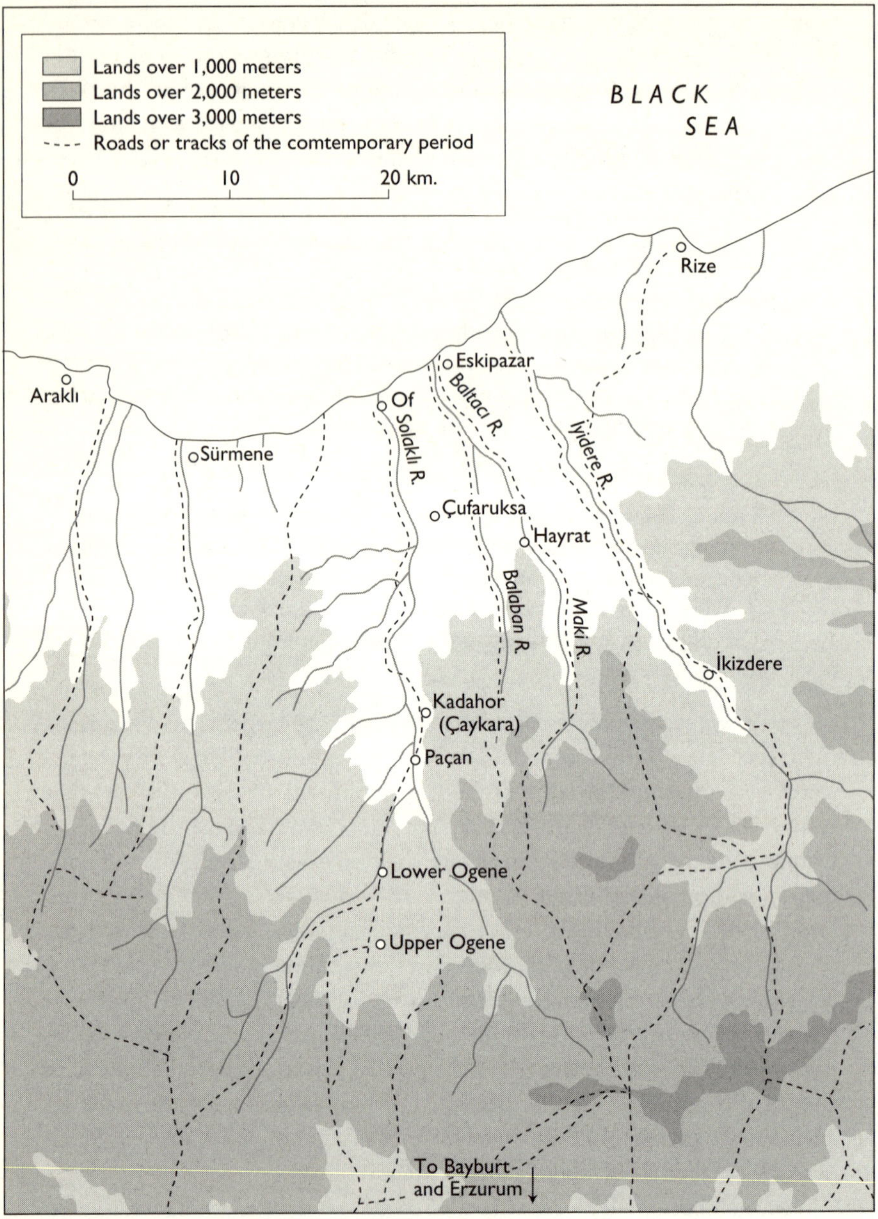

Map 1. Lands of Rize, Of, and Süreme (c. 1923)

related to (*hısımlığımız var*), or friendly with (*dostuz*) this or that other group. Some claimed that the large families were grouped into two district-wide coalitions, separately led by the Selimoğlu and Muradoğlu, that competed for social honors, government influence, and control of public affairs. The leading individuals from the large clans in the district of Of also had close relationships—by marriage, friendship, or partnership—with leading individuals from large clans in the districts to the west and east of Of. These relationships were mutually exclusive, so that the families in other districts allied to the Selimoğlu would be rivals of those allied to the Muradoğlu. Some of my respondents claimed that there had long been a patchwork of competitive coalitions that ranged up and down the coast. There were also indications that this might have still been the case in the eastern Black Sea districts during the 1960s.

Eventually I began to encounter evidence that the clan-society was associated with competitive displays of force and numbers. During my first visit to the district of Of, when I was still a bachelor, my acquaintances in the market of the town sometimes invited me to their residences in the mountain villages just beyond the town. On one of these occasions, late in the morning on a warm summer day, a series of distant explosions began to reverberate through the mountain valleys. When I asked my host what this could be, he said matter-of-factly that it was a marriage (*düğün*), as though this were a sufficient explanation. Seeing that I still did not understand, he promised me a demonstration. After leaving for a moment, he returned with what appeared to be a small mass of dough and invited me to come outside, into the garden. There he placed a fuse into the dough, lit it with a cigarette lighter, and flung it into the brush. A few seconds later there was a deafening explosion.

After my return to Of the following year, I was able to witness the fetching of the bride that takes place at one point in the celebration of a marriage. If the groom and the bride come from different villages and different families, the bride-takers would organize a caravan of supporters equipped with firepower.[28] Cars, trucks, and buses were assembled to transport the scores, and sometimes hundreds, of individuals who might participate in such an event. There were always at least a few women in one of

28. I have argued elsewhere (1976a; 1976b) that marriage at a distance was more common in the eastern Black Sea region than in other parts of Turkey. The logic of my analysis depended on the inability or reluctance of women to press their legal right to property inheritance, both under the Ottoman and Republican legal code. Since the probability that women may press their claims to property is increasing, endogamous marriages may be increasing accordingly, as a device for main-

the cars to assist the bride on the return trip, but the remainder of the celebrants was men. As such a caravan proceeded on its way to fetch the bride, other villagers, who were not part of the festivities, would venture to test the resolve of the bride-takers by barricading the roadway with fallen trees or piles of stones. If the caravan traveled along a major highway, oncoming trucks and buses might suddenly swerve across the tarmac in order to bar the passage of the bride-takers.[29] Even the gendarmerie would sometimes attempt to stop the caravan if it passed near one of their guard posts.[30] In each instance, the groups who blocked the road would demand money before they agreed to allow passage. Only the bravest of souls had the courage to challenge a caravan of bride-takers, since these groups were usually heavily armed with pistols, rifles, and explosives. As a caravan left the main road and climbed into the mountain areas, gunfire and explosions would break out. When the caravan arrived at the village of the bride, the men descended from their vehicles and advanced upon the house of the bride with more gunfire and more explosions, like a skirmish line advancing against the enemy. After taking the bride from her house, the caravan then made its return, again with a noisy manifestation of numbers and force.

The fetching of the bride seemed to confirm that a clan-society, based on masculine solidarity and military power, existed alongside the nation-state. Moreover, these two principles appeared to be deeply ingrained in masculine personal identity, hence, something more than a quaint way of celebrating a wedding. The preoccupation with firearms along the eastern Black Sea coast had come to my attention during the first days of my second residence in the district of Of in 1966. I had been obliged to go to the provincial capital, the town of Trabzon, in order to apply for a residence permit. When I arrived there late in the day, I found a harried clerk who was anxious to leave the office and did not want to hear my business. He brusquely waved me away saying, "No more gun permits today, come back tomorrow." The clerk was unaccustomed to foreigners applying for residence permits, but all too familiar with citizens who somehow felt it necessary to carry guns. I soon became aware that more than a few of my acquaintances in the

---

taining male control over property. Cf. Hann and Beller-Hann (2001), who conclude that marriage to close kin is common in the Lazi districts from Pazar to Hopa.

29. In the 1960s, one encountered these large caravans along the coastal road from Rize to Trabzon during the warmer months. I do not know if they were also typical of the coastal districts further east or further west.

30. The use of firearms during wedding celebrations was illegal, but the gendarmerie looked the other way during the 1960s.

town of Of carried handguns underneath their suit jackets, such that they could be glimpsed when they leaned forward to tie a shoe or pick up a dropped key. Miraculously, these concealed firearms always vanished during the periodic sweeps of the coffeehouses by the gendarmerie, and they were rarely discovered and confiscated. When I asked my acquaintances who carried concealed weapons why they did so, they said they were obliged to do so because they had enemies (*düşman*), as they also had friends (*dost*). The carrying of firearms was then an artifact of a local social order in which individuals were politically allied to some and politically opposed to others.

The local social order of a clan-society, nowhere written into law, was incompatible with the national order of state officials and public associations. The two orders referred to two incompatible kinds of sovereign power, one nonofficial, based on force and numbers, the other official, based on legal procedures and judicial enforcement. By state law, one was not allowed to parade along streets and roads in large numbers firing off weapons and tossing dynamite. One was not allowed to carry a gun in the district of Of or anywhere else in Turkey without a permit. The local social order was thereby divided from the state order. Or so I presumed during the first period of my fieldwork.

THE CLAN-SOCIETY BELONGS TO THE PAST, NOT THE PRESENT

I have described a path of investigation inspired by my notion of a clan-society divided from the state system. But all along, this direction of my fieldwork had been faced with an unresolvable difficulty. I could not really locate a system of rights and duties that was uniquely linked with the clans, the *sine qua non* for the anthropological theories to which I was appealing. The patronymic groups were not associated with either a rule of marriage, an obligation to give or receive bride-price, the taking of vengeance, or the payment of blood money. Even the fetching of the bride was not really an occasion when a bride-taking clan was opposed to a bride-giving clan. The armed participants were largely composed of individuals from many patronymic groups, some related and some not related to the groom's patronymic group. So the fetching of the bride only demonstrated a connection of military power with broad social formations, but not with bounded patriarchal collectivities.

Ultimately, I had to qualify my concept of a clan-society in the district of Of with a series of negative conclusions. The patronymic groups in the district of Of lacked the minimum attributes by which anthropologists had defined a political system based on unilineal descent groups. I duly drew up a list of the essential "missing" features:

1. Assembly and Ceremony. The members of a patronymic group did not assemble on any occasion or unite for any collective purpose. They did not observe any distinctive ceremony associated with their common descent, either separately or collectively.

2. Property or Territory. The members of a patronymic group did not have a mutual share or claim to any property or endowment. Some large family groupings were associated with specific vicinities, but neither patronymic groups nor any of their constituent patrilines claimed collective ownership over a demarcated territory.[31]

3. Vengeance Obligations and Blood Money. The members of a patronymic group did not collectively recognize any obligation to take vengeance for an injury or insult that was inflicted by an outsider on one of their agnatic relations. They did not collectively pay or accept blood money on the occasion of a homicide involving one of their agnatic relations.

4. Marriage Rule and Bride-price Payments. The members of a patronymic group were not obliged to consult with agnates about marriages or to follow any kind of endogamous or exogamous marriage rule. They did not collectively contribute to the bride-price paid by a member of their patronymic group. They did not collectively receive a portion of the bride-price received on the occasion of the marriage of a daughter of a member of their patronymic group.

5. Mediators. There were local specialists in the sacred law of Islam who could be considered outsiders to the clan-society. They were often consulted on matters of religion by individuals and families, but there were no reports that they served as mediators on the occasion of conflicts among clans.[32]

These generalizations applied to both large and small patronymic groups. The "clans" of Of were little more than amorphous groupings of men who claimed descent from the same patronymic ancestor and referred to themselves as a patronymic group. Otherwise, they did not constitute a "corporate group" in the technical sense of the anthropological theory of unilineal descent groups. Similarly, the patrilines of a patronymic group could be

31. The patronymic groups in Of were sometimes associated with one or more village quarters, or one or more entire villages. This was a stronger relationship of patronymic group and a specific territory than usually existed in the villages of western Turkey at the time (Meeker 1970, 147, 149).

32. The tradition of religious study in the district of Of is the subject of chap. 2.

separately designated, but such a patriline also did not constitute what anthropologists have described as an "effective lineage."[33]

In the absence of collective institutions or organizations, the patronymic groups could not be represented by specific individuals, could not support or challenge one another, and could not enter into collective contracts and agreements. This being the case, the clans did not comprise a political system in their own right. This meant that I had failed to discover how the Selimoğlu and Muradoğlu had dominated the public life of the district. Given this difficulty, I turned to a strategy of anthropological reconstruction. The patronymic groups in the present must be but a pale reflection of a more structured and institutionalized clan-society in the past. Once upon a time, when the authority of the central government was either weak or absent, there must have been a clan-society in the eastern coastal districts. Now its shadowy legacy continued to distort and subvert the institutions of the nation-state. As my theory of a social order divided from the state order was seriously mistaken, one might have expected that such a study of history would immediately reveal the flaws in my thinking. On the contrary, my errors were reinforced and compounded by the sources available to me.

Aghas and Clans

Questioning my acquaintances in the town of Of, I began to piece together a picture of leading individuals from large family groupings during the late Ottoman Empire. Since it appeared they had been even more socially prominent and politically powerful at that time, I assumed the local social order had been more assertive during the old imperial regime than during the new nationalist regime. The leading individuals from large clans, I was told, had then been locally accorded the title "agha" (*ağa*) and had played a significant role in governing the district of Of.[34] Some of my interlocutors believed that the backing of a large clan was necessary for someone to qualify as an agha, and, consistent with this presumption, they designated those large families that had once been the base of their support as "agha-families" (*ağa akrabası*). Some of my interlocutors in Of also spoke of "the time of

33. See Fortes (1953) for a discussion of unilineal descent groups as "corporate groups" and "effective lineages" and Stirling (1965) for a limited application of these concepts to villages in central Anatolia.

34. The word "*ağa*" is translated in English-Turkish dictionaries as "chief," "master," or "lord." Cf. Meeker 1972. At the time of my fieldwork, I assumed that the aghas of the nineteenth century were local elders and leaders. I failed to understand they had been appointed and titled by state officials, who assigned them certain governmental tasks in designated groups of villages. See chaps. 6, 7, and 8.

the aghas" (*ağa devresi*), when aghas from agha-families had been able to defy state officials and rule segments of the district as their personal possessions. During this period, they levied and collected taxes, assembled soldiers, arrested lawbreakers, and imposed forced labor.

Accordingly, my interlocutors also said that the aghas in the district were at loggerheads with officials from Trabzon, but they inconsistently described the confrontation of the two. Sometimes it would be said the aghas had protected the people from rapacious state officials always eager to raise more troops and more funds. At other times it was said that state officials had protected the people from the aghas who imposed illegal taxes, seized fertile lands, kidnapped women, and suppressed opponents. I was easily able to reconcile these inconsistencies in terms of a division between two separate political systems, one a social order based on patrilineal descent groups and the other a state order based on administrators, police, courts, and laws. Each of these two political systems could lapse into its own peculiar version of exploitative subjection. The tyranny of the agha was warm and familiar while the tyranny of the official was cold and formal.

The "Five" and "Twenty-five" Parties

When speaking of the old days, some respondents recalled a definite structure of rivalries and alliances in the district of Of as well as elsewhere in the old province of Trabzon. My interlocutors also recalled two opposed hierarchies of aghas in the district. A greater agha of the Selimoğlu and a greater agha of the Muradoğlu were said to have been preeminent along the western and eastern coastlines, respectively. Other lesser aghas, distributed in checkerboard fashion through the western and eastern valley-systems, aligned themselves with either the agha of the Selimoğlu or the agha of the Muradoğlu. Just as the latter were personal rivals, so the two networks of aghas saw themselves as rivals with one another. These personal rivalries and alignments extended to their supporters to include all the members of their respective clans. Moreover, all the aghas also had allies and partners among the prominent members of ordinary clans, who were also supported by all the members of their clans. So the two networks of aghas and clans, opposed as factions, included many, perhaps most, of the individuals and families in the district of Of.

My interlocutors also said that these hierarchies had once formed two "parties" (*fırka*) in the district during the time of the aghas, one designated "Five" and the other "Twenty-five." Each party had a kind of coat of arms (*arma*) that was carved on a wooden slate marked by the number five or twenty-five and placed near the fireplace in the house. The two parties are thought to have been led by the aghas of the Selimoğlu and Muradoğlu but included many of the individuals and families throughout the two valley-systems. The presence of coat of arms markings on the fireplaces of old houses, even those belonging to ordinary households, confirmed extensive participation in the Five and Twenty-five parties.[35] According to one interlocutor, a man's personal relationships were directly determined by membership in one or the other party. If a man visited a house and saw the coat of arms of the other party, he politely said goodbye and went on his way. To illustrate this legacy, an acquaintance of mine, born in the early twentieth century, was able to draw up a list of the names of the clans that had been associated with the Five and Twenty-five parties at some time during the nineteenth century.[36] He recorded fifteen family names under the Selimoğlu, the Five Party, and six family names under the Muradoğlu, the Twenty-five Party.[37] He was of the opinion that a pattern of marriages, friendship, and partnerships among the members of all these clans still followed the lines of their membership in the Five and Twenty-five parties.[38]

I was pleased to discover that a local historian of Of had described the old social system in terms that almost exactly fit my suppositions. Hasan Umur (1880–1977) had been born early enough to hear first-hand reports of the period when the authority of the central government was either weak or absent. In one of his books he argued that the aghas, clans, and parties constituted an alternative political system. According to Umur, this system first arose with the breakdown of central government in the 1200s (1785–95). This was the "time of the aghas" (*ağa devresi*), which continued until the end of the 1240s (1834), when it was brought to an end by a provincial governor of Trabzon, Osman Pasha Hazinedaroğlu. It seemed possible to accept what he had written as only one step removed from an eyewitness account:

35. Umur 1949, 18.

36. I have chosen not to publish this list of twenty family names, all of them of the "oğlu" form, but I shall be using the list to evaluate historical documents in later chapters. I have preserved the families' anonymity in order to avoid associating family members, who are many in number, with the activities of leading individuals, who are few in number.

37. He wrote down the name of one patronymic group under both parties, saying that its members had recently split between the groups.

38. I carried out a census of a large number of households from the Selimoğlu. This census confirmed that leading families from the Selimoğlu had repeatedly intermarried with leading families from other large family groupings of the Five Party in the district of Of (Meeker 1970).

> So it was that the people [of Of], who joined parties because of the weakness of the government, gradually became enmeshed in a state of perpetual conflict by depending on their membership in parties. In the absence of a government that would have protected them and preserved the law, and with the natural thought that they might try to secure their lives by means of the parties which they blindly took for granted, the people participated in the spirit of the affair by searching for the means to either kill their enemy or save themselves from their enemy. Every leading agha, in as much as he could do so, tried to protect those who belonged to his party, as though they were his subjects.[39]

Umur went on to explain that membership in a party was based on membership in a clan. In doing so, he arrived at his own formulation of the anthropological theories of unilineal descent groups. He even included the principles of balanced opposition and lineage mediation:

> Sometimes the clans (*kabîle*) who were adversaries made peace among themselves. As I heard it from an elderly man in my village: "Peace was made between the Boduroğulları (the clan of which I am a member) and the Ceburoğulları and a celebration was held." The elderly man related that he had witnessed this celebration when he was a child. . . . And let me add this further point. While the clans (*kabîle*) who were adversaries were continually agitated and in a state of tumult, there were also neutral clans. These did not recognize any side but went along getting by on their own. The sides who were adversaries did not intervene on their behalf.[40]

Looking into the past seemed to be a way of understanding what could be glimpsed only obscurely in the present. In the course of my interviews, the outlines of a social order, apart from the state order, seemed to come more clearly into focus. Furthermore, I had also learned that the district of Of was in no way unique or peculiar. A social order that had come into being with a breakdown in the state order had been duplicated, not only in the near neighboring districts to the east and west, but throughout the old province of Trabzon. A patchwork of aghas and clans had once existed in all the coastal districts from Batum to Ordu during the last centuries of the old regime.

39. Umur 1949, 18–19. Umur later conducted an extensive program of archival research on the district of Of. He may well have revised his views after completing this research.

40. Ibid. Umur uses the Turkish word "tribe" (*kabîle*) instead of "family" (*akraba*) to refer to the clans, thereby choosing to emphasize their extra-state character.

Mansions

Indeed, I had both heard of and seen clear physical evidence of such an old order of aghas and clans in the form of the remains or ruins of mansions (*konak*) that once existed throughout the eastern Black Sea coast. All the greater aghas from the larger clans were said to have been "valley lords" (*derebey*), independent rulers of their separate domains. As such, they had constructed large, semi-fortified mansions to serve as their personal residences, seats of government, and reception halls. According to my interlocutors, there had once been at least a score of these mansions in the district of Of alone. During my travels along the eastern Black Sea coast, I was told of the remains of foundation stones or ruined walls of such structures that had once existed on this promontory or that hilltop. All these mansions of the old social order were said to have been razed in the 1830s by the aforementioned Osman Pasha. He was credited with having restored centralized government in the coastal region, but only by resorting to drastic measures. Large numbers of troops invaded and occupied the outlying districts, where they burned the mansions of the aghas and destroyed the villages of their followers.

Inexplicably, a number of the old mansions had somehow escaped these depredations and remained standing. Here and there I had observed these old, dilapidated structures, many times larger than ordinary houses and always situated in a prominent location. They had stone foundations, massive doorways and hearths, spacious storerooms, and pleasingly decorated salons fitted with wood panels and conical fireplaces.[41] Oddly, and contrary to the report of their destruction, these existing mansions were those of the most powerful aghas, that is, just the mansions one would have expected Osman Pasha to have put to the torch.

I concluded, with some prompting from my hosts, that the mansions had been essential architectural instruments of the old social order. In light of their ownership and location in the district of Of, they could be reliably correlated with the aghas, clans, and parties. The mansions had been built by individuals of prominence who were now remembered as the ascendants of large clans. The mansions had all been located near markets, crossroads, routes, or anchorages. So wherever there had been leading individuals from large family groupings, there had also been a mansion. And wherever

41. I saw five such mansions in the old district of Of and heard reports of a few others that had fallen into ruins. For a description of one of the old mansions east of the town of Trabzon, see Winfield et al. (1960).

there had been a mansion, one could be assured that its location was of strategic significance. For its chief residents, a mansion was a necessary physical infrastructure for bringing together relatives, friends, and allies. In this manner, a mansion became a center of political authority that first replaced and then later challenged state officials. The handful of dilapidated mansions appeared to stand as testaments to the existence of a local political system that had once been distinct from the central government during the first decades of the nineteenth century.

AGHAS CREATE CLANS, CLANS DO NOT CREATE AGHAS

But again, this second path of investigation, like the first, became less and less credible as I learned more. Public life, social memory, local history, and architectural leftovers all pointed toward the same conclusion. But the conclusion was dependent on a logic of analysis that was inconsistent with what is known about the social history of the eastern Black Sea coast.

A mass of other details, all conveniently suppressed in the preceding arguments, could not be reconciled with the idea that the aghas, mansions, clans, and parties were a local social system divided from the state system. One of these "details" stands out in all the discussion that has preceded as a blatant contradiction. According to all authorities, Osman Pasha had brought the "time of the aghas" to an end in 1834. And yet leading members of the Muradoğlu and the Selimoğlu had dominated the public affairs of the district of Of during the remaining eighty years of the Empire, and then appeared soon again to repeat this performance during eighty years of the Turkish Republic. How could a local social order that was outside the state system continue to exist inside the state system for well over a hundred years?

The simplest kind of anthropological facts finally pointed toward a resolution of this contradiction. As I have indicated in the preceding discussion of the leftover mansions, the pattern of aghas and clans that I had discovered in Of was also more or less characteristic of the eastern coastal region from Batum to Ordu during the nineteenth, if not the twentieth, century. Everywhere one found the same kind of local elites, backed by the same kind of large family groupings, designated by the same type of patronyms, and aligned in the same type of rivalrous alliances. That is to say, the same kind of clan-society was found throughout the coastal region. If concepts of patrilineal descent had originally provided the elements for this pervasive pattern, then a specific idiom of kinship must have been common to, or at least dominant among, all the peoples of the coastal region. And if this was the case, there must have been a common ethnic tradition that was the same everywhere throughout the eastern coastal region. In other words, the thesis of a clan-society separate from the state system demanded the presence of a "primary folk" in the coastal region, which raised the question of "which folk?"

Since the patronyms, which were everywhere current in the coastal districts, were Turkic in form, I first considered that the clan-society might be traceable to a "Turkic folk." This solution was not acceptable on the basis of the comparative ethnography of rural Anatolia. There was a plethora of lineage and tribal names of Turkic origin in other parts of Asia Minor, but they only sometimes and exceptionally took the "*oğlu*" form. They tended to vary in their character and composition, even from village to village, so that one did not normally find the same type of names across a broad region. This inconsistency was compounded by other considerations. In many parts of the eastern Black Sea region (and especially where leading individuals and large family groupings were most prevalent), Turkic settlement had occurred much later and in lesser numbers than elsewhere in Asia Minor.[42] So it was difficult to explain why a clan-society of Turkic origin would be more important and developed in a region where Turkic peoples had settled at a later date and in fewer numbers than in other parts of Anatolia.[43]

This raised the possibility that the clan-societies might be traceable to some underlying non-Turkic ethnicity that had been subsequently Turkicized in its overt forms if not in its substance. Perhaps the patronyms were simply a Turkicized version of the family names of another ethnicity (the "son of" construction being a common practice among many non-Turkic peoples in northeast Asia Minor).[44] The role of non-Turkic peoples in the social history of the Muslim population in the eastern Black Sea region was

42. See the analysis in chap. 3.

43. Nonetheless, Sümer (1992) has argued that prominent individuals and families along the eastern coastal region were traceable to the late arrival of Çepni Turkic peoples.

44. Some years ago I argued the possibility that the aghas and clans could be an artifact of the settlement of the eastern coastal region by Kartvelian peoples (Meeker 1971). Recently, Toumarkine (1995) has pointed out a weakness in my argument. If the dominant pattern of social organization all along the coast is derived from a Kartvelian kinship system, one must explain why almost all the peoples who feature such a dominant pattern failed to retain any consciousness of their Kartvelian origins. To address this problem, he devised an ingenious hypothesis. However, I have since concluded that the aghas and clans are artifacts of local participation in the imperial system and so not associated with any one of the many ethnic groups who settled in the eastern coastal region.

undisputed. The problem was that none of these non-Turkic groups could be considered to have been a preponderant influence throughout the coastal districts. The Muslim population in this part of Turkey was formed relatively recently out of many different ethnic groups, including peoples of Turkic, Lazi, Kurdish, Greek, and Armenian background. The influence of each of these ethnic groups varied in different parts of the region, from valley to valley as well as from the lower to the upper parts of a single valley.[45] The pattern of aghas, mansions, clans, and parties, which was more or less the same throughout the eastern coastal region, could therefore not be explained in terms of an underlying ethnic tradition, since the latter was variable throughout the coastal region. As there had been so many folk in the eastern coastal region, it was impossible to argue that any of them could claim the status of a primary folk.

An obvious and simple solution had always been at hand but seemed unthinkable given the prevailing climate at the time of my early fieldwork. The aghas, mansions, clans, and parties could only be derived from some kind of uniform sociopolitical process that had been common to all the coastal districts of the eastern Black Sea region. And the only general condition that could have determined such a process would have been the state system of the late Ottoman Empire, given the variable ethnic, linguistic, and religious backgrounds of its inhabitants. The aghas, mansions, clans, and parties in the eastern coastal region were not essentially outside of, or consistently opposed to, the central government. They had arisen as district social formations in the course of local participation in the imperial system. What was recalled as a breakdown in the central government was more precisely a spread of certain kinds of imperial thinking and practice that moved outward and downward into the coastal districts.

With this conclusion, local memories and traditions that had once seemed to me so unanimous and convincing now appeared both contradictory and questionable. Setting aside everything that I had been told and shown in the district of Of, I drastically revised my assessment of the aghas, mansions, clans, and parties:

1. Aghas. During the post-classical imperial period, the aghas were local elites who always claimed and usually held some kind of position in the state system. They were invariably the descendants of individuals who themselves had claimed or held some kind of position or appointment in the state system.

45. See the analysis in chap. 3.

2. Patronyms. The patronym ("*oğlu*" or "*zade*") had its origin in official references to local elites who received government positions and appointments. To claim a patronym was therefore to claim descent from an individual who had some kind of standing in the imperial system.

3. Agha Clans. The aghas were able to set down family lines (*ağa akrabası*) because their positions in the state system were perpetuated from generation to generation.[46] It was always aghas who made large clans and never large clans who made aghas. Upon a review of my field notes, I discovered that the ascendant of every large family grouping with which I was familiar was said to have held some kind of state position or appointment.

4. Mansions. The mansions of the aghas were not local in origin but were constructed to emulate the residences of state officials. They symbolized their occupants' claim to the right to participate in the state system by collecting taxes, conscripting recruits, imposing forced labor, and enforcing judicial decisions. When my interlocutors had said the mansions were like a "government," they were citing a memory of aghas having usurped the sovereign power of the state system.

5. Patronymic Groups. The ubiquity of family groupings taking the form of patronymic groups was not the simple and direct result of a reaction to the threat of anarchy (*pace* Hasan Umur). By membership in a patronymic group, one also claimed descent from an individual who once had a role in the imperial system, that is, someone who was more than a mere farmer or villager. The ubiquity of patronymic groups along the eastern Black Sea coast points to a greater degree of participation in the imperial system than was typical of most parts of rural Anatolia.

6. Parties. The Five and Twenty-five parties had been linked with irregular or regular military regiments. The members of the two parties had been rivals, but specifically for precedence and privilege in the imperial system. Membership in a patronymic group was usually correlated with membership in one or the other party. The aghas were then social leaders of social formations, but also military leaders of military formations.

7. Force and Numbers. There was always a certain amount of rivalry among different aghas and hence also among their followers. Through displays of force and numbers the aghas and their followers claimed sovereign power on the inside, not the outside, of the state system. This rivalry sometimes degenerated into military skirmishes and sieges.

46. I use the English phrase "family line" as a translation of the Turkish word "*akraba*" but with its special meaning in the district of Of, that is, a descent line which is also a descent group. See note 19, above.

8. Vengeance and Vendetta. The militarization of the population of the coastal districts did compromise legal statutes and judicial procedures (but the latter were never completely overturned). The solidarity of patronymic groups did become a refuge against insecurity, and this did lead to the law of talion. But these tendencies were directly related to local participation in the imperial system rather than a breakdown in the central government.

By such revisions, the aghas, mansions, clans, and parties were not based on the elaboration of a local system of kinship. They were country extensions of the imperial military and administrative establishment. I therefore dropped the term "clan" since it evoked the idea of a local social system complete in itself.[47] Thus, by this new approach, the outlying coastal districts of the old province of Trabzon were anything but marginalized and isolated with respect to governmental institutions and activities. Local elites at the head of large followings had always had a close relationship with state officials of the central government, even if not always according to the terms that the latter would have wished to impose upon the former.[48] This was then the "solution" to the problem of the existence of aghas, mansion, family lines, and parties throughout the coastal region.

Of course, the "solution" brought with it other kinds of problems. The anthropological theories by which I was trying to describe and analyze the social order of aghas, mansions, family lines, and parties only made sense if the central government was weak or absent. All the structural features of local social order—leading individuals, large family groupings, a checkerboard pattern of alliances and oppositions, and binary coalitions—were understood to be responses to insecurity that arose with a power vacuum. If the aghas, mansions, family lines, and parties were instead the consequence of participation in the imperial system, a wholly new kind of analysis was necessary. Why did state officials permit local elites to become part of the imperial system? What did local elites have to gain from becoming part of the imperial system? Why did participation in the imperial system result in such extensive social formations? Why were the latter associated with the principle of force and numbers, and, as a consequence, divided into rivalrous factions?

47. I retained the terms "family grouping" and "patronymic group" as two translations of the broader and narrower meanings of the local term "*akraba.*"

48. This problem will be examined in chap. 6. See Van Bruinessen (1978) for an assessment of the relationship of local elites and the state system among the Kurdish-speakers of eastern Anatolia.

All these questions pointed to the necessity of a theory of a society within, rather than against, the state. This suggested that a full understanding of the local societies in the coast districts would be dependent on an understanding of the imperial regime of which they were a part. Even before any such analysis had been undertaken, however, the abandonment of the concept of a clan-society had led to an important conclusion. The aghas, mansions, family lines, and parties were examples of state phenomena because they had come into being through local participation in the imperial system. But at the same time, the aghas, mansions, family lines, and parties were also social phenomena because they took the form of an oligarchy woven together by agnation, affinity, partnership, and friendship. With this provisional conclusion, we can return to the question of local memories and traditions.

A REGIONAL SOCIAL OLIGARCHY OF THE POST-CLASSICAL EMPIRE

Why was it that my interlocutors could not understand that participation in the imperial system had produced a regional social oligarchy? One might object. Perhaps I was asking for too much. After all, local memories and traditions are never fully reliable, and the time of Osman Pasha was long, long ago. But the issue was a matter of remembering as well as forgetting. If the Oflus had simply "forgotten," they would have no understanding of the aghas, mansions, family lines, and parties at all. This was most certainly not the case. They "remembered" them, saying they had appeared with the breakdown and vanished with the restoration of the central government. I was therefore obliged to consider memories and traditions as desire rather than fact.

My interlocutors did not want to believe that a regional social oligarchy had anything to do with the state system. They therefore insisted it had arisen only under the conditions of the absence or weakness of centralized government. By this thesis, they were driven to the conclusion that the aghas, mansions, family lines, and parties must have vanished with the restoration of centralized government. So it was that they analyzed the old social order as impeccably as any social anthropologist, demonstrating how its characteristics were perfectly consistent with the absence or weakness of the state system. So it was that they focused on Osman Pasha, deeming him to be a transitional figure between governmental breakdown and restoration.

If my supposition was correct, the motivating desire that had generated so many deductions seemed to have a kind of origin or center: the figure of

Osman Pasha during the 1830s. How was it that this particular man in this particular period could be imagined as an epochal divide, thereby clouding all that was the same before and after him? Was it possible that Osman Pasha had accomplished something during the 1830s to make the relationship of the present to the past incomprehensible? These questions led me toward a third path of investigation: the writings of western Europeans who had visited the old province of Trabzon. These "outsiders" had described what they had seen and heard, entirely unencumbered by the burden of local history. Perhaps these "outsiders" might reveal what Osman Pasha had actually accomplished in the 1830s and why this accomplishment left behind so much confusion.

During the first decades of the nineteenth century, foreign diplomats, soldiers, and explorers—most of them French and British—had begun to visit the province of Trabzon in increasing numbers. What they reported was indeed revealing, but not by way of an explanation of what had really happened during the 1830s. In their accounts, they wholly agreed with local memories and traditions in the district of Of. The French and the British consuls affirmed that the aghas, mansions, family lines, and parties were a distinct form of government outside of and opposed to the central government. They also affirmed that Osman Pasha had suppressed and abolished this alternative political system and so restored the authority of the central government. But it was not their agreement with Oflu memories and traditions that cast a new light on the aghas, mansions, family lines, and parties. Instead, their affirmations were inconsistent with other archival sources, as well as inconsistent with their own accounts of what they had seen and heard during their travels. In other words, I had rediscovered in the accounts of western Europeans the same desire that I encountered among my interlocutors in the district of Of.[49] They did not want to believe that a regional social oligarchy had anything to do with the state system.

As a provisional demonstration of this, I shall cite one of the most knowledgeable of all the western European visitors to Trabzon during the period in question. From 1821 until 1833, Victor Fontanier intermittently served as a naturalist, political observer, commercial advisor, and consular official attached to the French embassy in Istanbul. During this time, he resided in Trabzon on at least two occasions, first as a visitor in 1827, a time of deepening political crisis. Just months previously, Sultan Mahmut II had succeeded in abolishing the old central army of the janissaries (*yeni çeri*),

49. See chaps. 6, 7, and 8 for a fuller discussion of French and British consular reports.

opening the way to reforms in the military establishment. Osman Pasha Hazinedaroğlu had assumed the provincial governorship in the midst of these destabilizing events, and the local elites of the coastal districts were testing his mettle. Fontanier described the situation as a confrontation of two kinds of government, that of a weak state system, as represented by Osman Pasha, and that of a strong feudal system, as represented by aghas, mansions, family lines, and parties in the coastal district:[50]

> The pasha of Trabzon is appointed by the Porte [Ottoman government] and placed under the command of the chief of staff in Erzurum; his authority is not great owing to the division of his territory among several chiefs who for the most part are hereditary, and in open revolt against him. These chiefs *have the title of aghas,* and were formerly called *derebey;* but the Porte, desiring to seize their fiefs, has suppressed this last denomination. This institution is *precisely the feudal system of thirteenth-century Europe;* the *aghas reside in fortified mansions,* sometimes equipped with cannons, where they preserve their families and treasures; they go about *surrounded by servants and armed partisans,* impose laws, raise taxes, and take refuge in their retreats, from where they defy the authority of the pasha, even the fermans [decrees] of the sultan. [Italics mine][51]

A few years later, Fontanier returned to Trabzon once again, this time to take up residence as French consul. In the intervening years, Osman Pasha had consolidated his hold on provincial government and taken advantage of the military reforms. Impressed with all that had been accomplished since his previous visit, Fontanier submitted a report in which he once again described the feudal system, now to declare that the aghas, mansions, family lines, and parties had been decisively and permanently suppressed. Writing as a consular official on January 31, 1831, he took care to be precise, citing the names of individuals and their places of residence:

> The pashalik (province) of Trabzon has for a long time been divided into small feudal domains [*petites féodalités*] whose chiefs [*chefs*] resided in fortified strongholds, some of which were located in the city itself. The most important of these chiefs were situated at Trabzon, Şatıroğlu and [illegible] oğlu; at Tonya, a town twelve hours from Trabzon, Hacı Salihoğlu; at Rize, Tuzcuoğlu; at Of, Selimoğlu and Cansızoğlu; and finally at Gönye [between Hopa and Batum], Fatzanoğlu. Other less important chiefs were affiliated with these and provided their clients. But as often

50. Fontanier may have received this idea from P. Fourcade, who preceded him as French consul in Sinope. See chap. 7.

51. Fontanier 1829, 17–18.

> happens in governments of this sort, they made war on one another and sought the good graces of the pashas [at Trabzon] and the Sublime Porte [at Istanbul].[52]

Fontanier leaves his reader the impression he is listing the names of the "chiefs" in the different districts, but in every instance he does not give the personal name of an individual but rather the patronymic of a family line. The two patronymics that he associates with Of are those of two large family groupings that I encountered when I was carrying out my fieldwork during the 1960s.[53] Otherwise, all the other patronymics in the consular report save one refer to the ascendants of family groupings that are still prominent in the eastern coastal region today.[54]

As the report continued, Fontanier described how the feudal system had threatened the very existence of the provincial government: "these chiefs combined to form formidable coalitions [*coalitions redoutables*] . . . sometimes managed to drive the officers of the Ottoman sultan from the sandjak [sub-province]." On several occasions, he observed, "the Imperial Divan attempted to destroy them by setting them against one another but was never strong enough or capable enough to achieve this end."[55] But now, Fontanier declared, the aghas, mansions, family lines, and parties were a thing of the past; thanks to the vigor and energy of Osman Pasha's provincial government, they "no longer existed."[56] And yet, within months, the populations of outlying coastal districts were once again refusing to forward taxes or conscripts to the provincial government, and within two years, another formidable coalition had besieged the town of Trabzon, forcing Osman Pasha to take refuge in his citadel, then to vacate his capital.[57]

Osman Pasha did eventually settle the "revolts" of the 1830s, but neither he nor any of his successors ever fulfilled Fontanier's declaration. For decades, aghas would continue to be appointed, mansions would still be built,

52. MAE CCCT L. 3, No. 11, Jan. 1831. British consul Brant reported a similar assessment, PRO FO 524/1, Jan. 26, 1831.

53. The first, Selimoğlu, already known to us, is remembered as the preeminent family line of the old Five Party. The second, Cansızoğlu, is remembered by some as the preeminent family line of the old Twenty-five Party during the time of Osman Pasha.

54. The exception is the Fatzanoğlu. I do not know if this family line is today a large family grouping in the vicinity of Hopa.

55. MAE CCCT L. 3, No. 11, Jan. 1831.

56. Ibid. British consul Brant had reached the same conclusion (PRO FO 524/1, Jan. 26, 1831).

57. PRO FO 524/2 p. 29, Feb. 1833. Brant acknowledges the reports of a force of twelve thousand but believes that it is a force of only six thousand.

family groupings would grow ever larger, and district networks would remain in place. Nonetheless, Fontanier's erroneous report of the end of the aghas, mansions, family lines, and parties was but the first statement of what eventually became a fixed consular opinion during the later nineteenth century.[58] The "valley lords" had been a separate form of government, but Osman Pasha had abolished them once and for all. And yet this consular opinion, announced and re-announced, was repeatedly contradicted by incidents that confirmed that leading individuals, large family groupings, district networks, and coastal coalitions still existed and still participated in the provincial government, bottom to top. As the Ottomans eventually moved to reform the imperial system by borrowing "western" technology and methods, a regional social oligarchy in the province of Trabzon adapted itself to the new bureaucratic centralism and continued to play a role in the state system. Nonetheless, the consular opinion, despite all the evidence to the contrary, never retreated but instead spread. By the later nineteenth century, Ottoman officials and citizens in Trabzon also believed what Osman Pasha had most likely never believed, that he had put down the "valley lords" once and for all. Ottoman officials and citizens, and later Turkish officials and citizens, would therefore find themselves "surprised" by incidents revealing that leading individuals from large family groupings still permeated district and provincial government.

Why, then, did Osman Pasha come to be remembered for something he did not accomplish, even in the coastal region itself? A provisional, and thus imperfect, answer to this question is as follows. The officials and citizens of the Ottoman Empire had come to believe what the consuls believed for similar reasons but by a different path. A new thinking and practice about the proper relationship of state and society had migrated from western Europe into the Ottoman Empire during the later nineteenth century, eventually to be carried over into the Turkish Republic. By this new thinking and practice, the centralized government should have taken the form of an official association of professional bureaucrats. Accordingly, the state system should not have included aghas, mansions, family lines, and parties. And yet, the state system did include the latter, necessarily so, since it would have been impossible for the association of professional bureaucrats to perform the most elementary governmental acts without relying on them. As the new thinking and practice gained ground among the ordinary citizenry of the coastal districts, a fracture appeared in local memory and

58. See chaps. 6, 7, and 8.

tradition. It was no longer possible to reconcile the existence of leading individuals, large family groupings, district networks, and coastal coalitions with principles of government. So it was no longer possible to understand how the aghas, mansions, family lines, and parties had come from inside the state system and so continued to serve the state system as a mechanism of local control in the years and decades after Osman Pasha. The citizenry of the eastern coastal districts therefore came to believe that the aghas, mansions, patronymic groups, and parties had arisen from outside the state system during a period of governmental breakdown. Accordingly, by this belief, they could not explain either the perpetuation of leading individuals from large family groupings or, more importantly, the ability of the latter to monopolize public institutions and organizations.

Osman Pasha had thereby come to be credited with suppressing an alternative political system in the 1830s that still endured in the 1960s. He marks the onset of a period of incomprehension when first western European consuls, then the public of Trabzon, could not understand the place of a regional social oligarchy in the state system. This is the significance of Osman Pasha and the 1830s. Why then did the unacceptable, a regional social oligarchy, remain in place, even after the Empire was replaced by the Republic? This is a harder question that will be tackled in the later chapters of this study.

A SECOND CHANNEL OF IMPERIAL PARTICIPATION

As I have noted, the aghas, mansions, family lines, and parties point to a society within, rather than against, the state. In later chapters, I will undertake a step-by-step demonstration of this theory of the imperial system. First, however, I must address an issue that has loomed ever larger as I have moved toward my conclusion. I have argued that Osman Pasha faced the necessity, which was also an opportunity, of retaining the aghas as his assistants and intermediaries. They were at the same time more dangerous than any kind of anti-state clan-society but also more useful, precisely because they represented social formations oriented toward the state system. But if this was the case, what exactly was the foundation of these social formations in terms of everyday interpersonal interactions and association? By the previous arguments, it would appear to have arisen from participation in the imperial system, and given the nature of the imperial system in question, it would have some kind of connection with Islamic belief and practice. So representatives of peoples of different backgrounds, Turkic, Kurdish, Lazi, Armenian, and Greek, would have come to constitute a regional social oligarchy by a process of Islamization. That is to say, they would have turned away from parochial customs and habits and turned toward the universal norms of the imperial system.

I must now confess that I had become aware of a second avenue of local participation in the imperial system at an early stage of my fieldwork. Scores of religious academies, hundreds of religious professors, and thousands of religious students had once been scattered through the villages of the district of Of. All these academies, professors, and students had been officially recognized by the imperial religious establishment before going underground some years after the declaration of the Turkish Republic. There were then two separate channels by which the inhabitants of the district of Of had once participated in the state society of the imperial system. That of the aghas, mansions, family lines, and parties was linked with the military and administrative establishment, while that of the teachers, schools, and students was linked with the religious establishment.

2 Prohibition
Social Relations and Official Islam

A SECOND ACCOUNT OF ARRIVAL AND DISCOVERY

In August of 1965, traveling by minibus eastward along the coastal road from Trabzon, I reached the town of Rize in the late afternoon. Wanting to shower and rest, I took a room in a comfortable hotel, patronized for the most part by businessmen, professionals, and officials. That evening, some of the guests invited me to join them in the lobby of the hotel and asked me questions about my university studies. When I found the opportunity, I told them about the elderly bearded man in Eskipazar for whom the restaurant patrons had stood at attention. My hosts were impressed with the story but unable give me any further information about what I had seen. They explained that they had never visited the district of Of and were poorly informed about its peoples and villages. They had the impression that many of the Oflus were exceptionally hardworking and successful in business, but socially conservative. One of them described the Oflus as backward (*gerici*) and fanatical (*mutaassıb*) in their religious outlook. Another said there had once been numerous religious academies (*medrese*) in the mountain villages of the district of Of, but these had all been closed down soon after the declaration of the Turkish Republic in 1923. With this comment, someone spoke of country religious teachers who came from the district of Of, the very mention of which provoked laughter.[1]

As I was to learn later, the "hodja from Of" (*Oflu hoca*) represented a stereotype for educated urbanites everywhere in the Turkish Republic. He

1. The term "hodja" (*hoca*) would have commonly designated a religious teacher during the Ottoman period. The term is now used to refer to any kind of teacher, whether religious or secular. On the other hand, the phrase "hodja from Of" would always be understood to refer to a country religious teacher.

brought to mind a man with a trimmed beard, an education limited to a few religious texts, little or no knowledge of the world beyond the small towns and villages of Anatolia, and a literal, if not erroneous, interpretation of the sacred law of Islam (*şeriat*). A district that was little known by outsiders had somehow become notorious for its religious teachers. The obvious questions this posed eventually became an important part of my fieldwork. Why had there once been religious academies in a district that was entirely rural and remotely situated? Why was the hodja from Of still notorious all over the Turkish Republic four decades after the National Assembly had imposed strict penalties on all forms of unauthorized religious teaching and learning?

SOCIETY CONFORMS TO ISLAMIC BELIEF AND PRACTICE

When I returned to the town of Of some days later, I took a room at the Crystal Palace Hotel and Teahouse. The name, which has metropolitan associations, was probably inspired by a downstairs room enclosed by large glass windows where men from the villages took refreshments during their visits to the town. In my first conversations with those whom I met there, I raised questions about Islamic belief and practice, since I had always intended to make religion part of my study. My queries, together with my ability to speak a little Turkish, were immediately taken as a sign of my readiness to convert, hence to become a "Turk." During my first few days in the town, I was repeatedly "called to Islam," usually before crowds of people in coffeehouses or in the market. Even when I declined to accept, my acquaintances were not discouraged. As far as they were concerned, I was on my way to the truth, and my acceptance of Islam was a virtual certainty. Soon I found that I had been "adopted," breathtakingly transformed from foreigner to companion.

In the Crystal Palace, I had made contact with a group of friends and partners from different villages involved in a variety of business enterprises (see fig. 3). They managed the hotel and teahouse, bought and sold farm products, rented a warehouse in the town, managed a stall during the weekly town market, leased and operated a truck, and so on. Their houses were in the villages of the foothills not far from the town, but they resided in the town for most of the week rather than return each night to their wives and children. Some of them frequented the markets along the coast, buying and selling hazelnuts. Some traveled to nearby cities such as Erzurum, Rize, and Trabzon, buying and selling cheese. Some took the truck on long-distance hauls to other parts of Turkey, such as Adana, Ankara, or Istanbul.

Figure 3. Friends at the Crystal Palace Hotel.

Overnight, they had set about to make me part of their little business association, and for a while I no longer had time for anything else. During the remainder of that summer in Of, I was always in the company of others.

My new companions plied me with refreshments during hours of conversation in the coffeehouses. They insisted I join them in their lunches and dinners. They assigned me tasks to perform, including even collecting and holding the cash from sales. They gave me a new name, changing my Christian name, Michael, into a Muslim name, Mahmut. They expressed concern if I was not feeling well or low in spirits. They offered to prepare hot water and to pour it for my baths, an occasion that was as much social and moral as hygienic. They invited me to their homes in their villages and introduced me to their aging fathers and mothers (but not their wives or daughters). They took me with them on excursions to Erzurum and Trabzon, where I accompanied them to markets, mosques, restaurants, and nightclubs. During our trips, we might walk together as couples, hand-in-hand. In the cities, during our entertainment, we might sing to each other, groom one another, two-by-two. When I sometimes left the town to travel alone to other towns—partly in search of respite from their attention—

they urged me to look up their relatives and friends and to stay with them during my visit.

Some of my friends from the Crystal Palace were lax in their religious observance until the approach of the month of Ramadan. In the course of their trips outside Of, some drank alcohol, smoked cigarettes, gambled at cards, and visited prostitutes, all of which met with strong disapproval in the district of Of during the 1960s. But others were strictly observant, regularly performing their prayers throughout the year and keeping the fast during Ramadan. Despite these differences in religiosity, they formed a circle of intimacy based on notions of obligation, cooperation, and sociability that referenced Islamic belief and practice. Both the bad and the good Muslims had accepted me because of my interest in Islam, and they were all excited at the prospect of my conversion. When I asked about Islamic belief and practice, they were usually able to provide explanations, and, if not, they summoned a friend whom they thought might address my question more authoritatively. They assured me of their wholehearted support. They welcomed me into their community. I could settle in their district forever. They offered me land for gardens and a house to live in. They would find me a wife. Why should I ever return to Chicago, a city of racists and gangsters? Accept! Join us! Stay with us!

The news of my coming to Islam, outrunning the event itself, spread to other parts of the district. I would hear stories about myself during my travels to this or that market or village. After introducing myself as a visiting American, my interlocutor would exclaim, "You are an American. Have you met one of your countrymen who has recently come to Of to accept Islam? You should do the same. Study our religion. You will find it is true and right." At the same time, I found myself trapped by the topic of religion whenever I visited the coffeehouses in the town of Of. My interlocutors would describe for me correct religious practice, the performance of the daily prayers or the pilgrimage, the keeping of the fast at Ramadan, the obligation to pay alms, and so on. Sometimes they would raise questions of a philosophical nature. How could one recognize the truth? How did this recognition affect one's actions? Why did some individuals refuse the truth? What were the consequences of this refusal? Even a visit to the barber, a store, or a workshop would result in a religious debate with a gathering of three to six individuals. And when I sat on the terrace of a coffeehouse, a conversation about religion would soon attract a larger crowd of listeners. At moments when my response to a challenge appeared weak or defensive, the audience might urge me to accept Islam, seeing my hesitation as a fleeting recognition of the truth.

On one occasion in the tiny square of the old town center, I was surrounded by younger men urging me to accept Islam. Then, to my surprise, one of them with whom I had gone swimming in the sea that day revealed that I was circumcised. The crowd was ecstatic. They knew I was interested in Islam and surprisingly well informed about it. Now they had learned that this painful but necessary operation had already been performed. They suspected I had hesitated to accept Islam for fear of the knife, but no such obstacle stood in the way. Come with us to the mosque! Do it now! Accept! Join us! Stay with us! There was a place for me, stranger and foreigner, in the district of Of. I had no family or relatives there, but that would come in the course of time. Someone like myself—that is, anyone at all no matter who he was—could become an Oflu through interpersonal association, underwritten by Islamic belief and practice.

Only very reluctantly, I came to realize that social thinking and practice in the district of Of was not so much "parochial," that is, based on a local system of kinship, as "universal" in orientation. My companions' business association included men who were related and unrelated to one another. They came from different patronymic groups. They even came from different villages. They had gradually become both friends and partners in the course of working together, but it was their mutual acceptance of a discipline of Islamic sociability that had made it possible for them to do so. An ethic of face-to-face exchanges—sitting, conversing, and sharing—was the basis of their business association. Seeing others and showing oneself, speaking and listening in turn, gestures of respect and tokens of affection, all fostered sentiments of intimacy and contracts of reciprocity. Their circle was certainly not independent of kinship relations, but the latter had been channeled through Islamic regulations and courtesies.[2]

In this respect, my acceptance and inclusion were in no way extraordinary but were consistent with the mixed composition of their little group. In the course of time, as my Turkish improved, they marveled at my gradual acquisition of their language and were pleased when I adopted their social thinking and practice. In time, someone noticed that I bore an uncanny resemblance to the Oflus.[3] This provoked a discussion about what might possibly account for this. One of my companions asked me directly about

2. Elsewhere (Meeker 1994a), I have given another account of Islamic sociability in Of.

3. The peoples of the eastern Black Sea coast are thought to conform to a certain physical type, with tall stature, light complexion, narrow head, and large nose. While I fit this type, many Oflus do not.

my family origins, and I replied that I was an American, as he well knew. "No, no," he said. "All Americans come from somewhere else. What about your forefathers?" Relenting, I told him that the Meekers were said to be Flemish or Dutch people from Belgium or Holland. "That's it," he replied. "You are descended from a Turk! The Ottomans conquered the Low Countries (*Belçika*) in the seventeenth century!" The experience of intimacy and familiarity, gained through a discipline of sociability, had led gradually to a sensation of resemblance, then finally to a revelation of common identity.

I did not arrive at the preceding understandings either quickly or easily. From the moment of my arrival, my interest had been in leading individuals and large family groupings. On any occasion that was possible, I steered my companions away from Islam toward the topics of descent lines, marriage rules, vengeance obligations, and dispute mediation. These efforts were not especially rewarding, since my companions seemed to have no concept at all of balanced opposition or lineage mediation.[4] This was extremely annoying and frustrating to me. I was an aspiring anthropologist engaged in a study of a uniquely "local" society and culture. If I could not discover such a phenomenon, if my informants were going to refer their conventional thinking and practice to the sacred law of Islam, my fieldwork made no sense at all. I began to think that my first queries about religion had been a serious mistake. When I came to be perceived as a potential convert, everything "local" had been pushed to the background and the issue of Islam had come to the foreground. I therefore made a renewed effort to uncover a substratum of local society and culture "untainted" by Islam. I began to ask my companions about stories and legends, rituals and shrines, witchcraft and sorcery—anything of an exotic or marginal character that could be opposed to Islamic belief and practice. And, of course, I was able to find such material, although extremely little during my initial, shorter visit. What impressed me, however, was the hostility with which some of my acquaintances greeted my interest in these "lies" (*yalan*) and "nonsense" (*saçmalama*).

Attempting to outwit my interlocutors, whom I suspected of exaggerating their piety for the benefit of the potential convert, I devised another tactic to uncover a layer of Oflu society and culture that was "outside" conventional Islam. I was able to discover certain local customs that were either forbidden or disapproved in the learned Islamic tradition. These included

4. These are classical anthropological concepts. See, for example, Evans-Pritchard (1940, 1949) and Evans-Pritchard and Fortes (1940).

such matters as the payment of bride-price, the marriage of daughters without their consent, the exclusion of women from land inheritance, and the belief in possession by spirits (*cin, peri*). When I pointed out these disparities, I was astonished that my remarks were enthusiastically received with expressions of guilt and apology. My companions were not at all surprised by my examples, but told me they had long been subjects of controversy in the district. As it happened, local customs (*örf ve âdet*) were commonly evaluated by reference to Islam; moreover, such evaluations were not recent but seemed themselves an aspect of district "tradition." Even insignificant gestures might be subject to an Islamic critique. For example, one man told me that the Oflus incorrectly greeted one another in the coffeehouses by touching their fingers to their forehead. "Our hodjas have told us that we should instead greet one another by touching the flat of our right hand to our heart." I began to glimpse a history of Islamization whereby local habits had been subjected to revision according to the sacred law of Islam.

Ordinary Oflus, lacking common family or village origins, were able to form a business association by virtue of a discipline of Islamic sociability. Similarly, they could accept a stranger who did not know the local dialect and came from a distant country on the basis of his anticipated acceptance of that same discipline of Islamic sociability. The inhabitants of what I took to be remote and isolated mountain valleys were somehow able to see themselves as participants in a greater Islamic society. By my experiences in the Crystal Palace, I was fitfully coming to understand that religious teaching and learning, through a process of criticism and argument, had left its mark on the district of Of. In the 1960s, however, the hodjas from Of were a more or less forbidden topic.

LOCAL ELITES CONFORM TO ISLAMIC BELIEF AND PRACTICE

During intermittent visits to Rize and Trabzon I heard further reports about religious teaching and learning in the district of Of, at some time in the past, or perhaps still in the present. Meanwhile, in the district of Of, I had difficulty finding anyone who would speak to me openly about such matters. For example, no one ever explained to me the simple fact that scores of religious academies (*medrese*), hundreds of professors (*müderris*), and thousands of students (*talebe*) were officially listed in the district during the final years of the Ottoman Empire. My interlocutors were understandably reticent. The tradition of religious study had gone underground sometime after its prohibition during the first years of the Turkish Republic. At the time of my visit, unauthorized religious instruction could still result in a prison term, even though many public prosecutors chose to look the other way. No one was eager to delve into the sensitive subject of proscribed religious activities with a foreigner who had appeared out of nowhere, even if he was a potential convert.

At last one of my regular interlocutors commented on the local tradition of religious study when I pressed him about the issue. "Oh yes, there were once religious academies in Çaykara [a sub-district of Of that had become a separate district after 1948], but they are no longer in existence and they were not located here [in the new district of Of]." By this response, the hodjas from Of were set at a double remove, both in time and in space. The man who made this comment was the director (*müdür*) of the middle school (*orta okul*), or so I erroneously considered him to be. He was about forty years old and resided in a nearby village. He usually wore the standard dress of local officials, a necktie, hat, dress shirt, and suit. He sometimes spoke of the backwardness of the villagers and made condescending remarks about their accents, expressions, food, and dress. By his conversation and appearance, I took him to be a radical nationalist (*Kemalist, Atatürkçü*), and by that fact an enthusiastic secularist.[5] He seemed exceptionally well informed about contemporary affairs and was something of a polemicist on the subject of the place of Islam in the Republic. This was not especially surprising to me, given his (supposed) position as a school administrator. He had no doubt developed arguments to counter local religious conservatives. Based on such presumptions, I came to depend on him as an authority when I had questions about religion in Of, failing to recognize numerous clear indications that he was not at all what I had taken him to be.

On one occasion, the "school director" had delivered an eloquent lecture, or should I say a "sermon" (*hutbe*), ostensibly for my benefit, but in fact for a crowd that surrounded us before one of the coffeehouses. He explained to me, now and then turning to his audience, how the Turkish Republic was not an "innovation" (*bid'at*) but was compatible with the sacred law of Islam.[6] He went on to argue that the National Assembly and Constitution of the Turkish Republic had their direct counterparts in the first

5. During the early years of the Turkish Republic, the National Assembly, under the leadership of Mustafa Kemal (Atatürk), had adopted various laws that encouraged or required new forms of "secular" (*lâik*) dress and behavior, usually of western European origin.

6. The word "*bid'at*" is usually translated as "innovation" or "heresy." It is a technical term in the Islamic sciences that some believers use to condemn behavior they consider un-Islamic.

community of Muslims at Medina and the Charter of Medina drawn up by the Prophet Muhammad. I was impressed with his cleverness in defending secular national institutions by references to Islamic history. He knew his listeners were resentful of the restrictions that the early nationalist movement had placed on religious observance. He had therefore chosen to undercut their objections by defending the Turkish Republic as conforming to Islamic tradition. I surmised that the "school director" had composed his little lecture by way of familiarity with the writings of nineteenth-century Islamic modernists, such as Afghani and Abduh. The thought even crossed my mind that he might have read these authors as part of the curriculum of a government training institute for school administrators. Perhaps the works of Islamic modernists had been included in the curriculum, precisely as a way of countering religious reactionaries.[7] And so I kept missing the significance of our private conversations that took on the color of public harangues.

During another conversation, or at least what had begun as such, the "school director" told me a parable about the Sufi mystic and poet Celalettin el-Rumî, founder of the Mevlevi religious brotherhood (*tarikat*). The two of us were seated facing one another in the old town square, surrounded by a crowd of adolescent boys. He spoke directly to my face but in a louder voice than necessary since his intended audience was really not I but all the boys around us:

> One day a man saw Celalettin put something under his robe as he came out of a shop. Curious, this man began to follow the great mystic and poet. As he did so, he met others who asked him where he was going. He explained that he was following Celalettin in hopes of learning what he was hiding. These others then joined him until at last a large, noisy crowd was trailing along behind the sage. Upon noticing that he was followed by a throng of people, Celalettin turned to ask what it was they wanted from him. Their leader replied that he wished to learn what he had concealed beneath his robe. "Bread," Celalettin replied, exposing the loaf for all to see.

The "school director" concluded with the moral: "A man will wish to see the face and body of a woman that much more when she is covered up. The practice of veiling does not keep the peace but sows discord among the believers."

7. This would have been very unlikely. During the first decades of the Turkish Republic, there was very little dialogue between Kemalist and Islamist partisans. See Esposito (1991) for an account of the Islamic modernists.

I correctly understood the narrow meaning of the story at the time, even if its wider implications had escaped me. The "school director" was obviously criticizing local veiling practices that were regarded as Islamic by most villagers during the 1960s. When women of the villages in the surrounding countryside came to the weekly market, they covered their hair with white scarves and their heads with large shawls of various sizes and colors in accordance with the convention of their particular village. If they happened to encounter a man on the way to the market, or if they asked a shopkeeper a question about price or quality, these women would often draw the shawl across their nose and lips as they did so. The "school director" had told his story in response to my questions about this kind of behavior, and he had concluded it by mocking village women, drawing his hand across his face as though concealing his nose and lips.

I had my first hint of the gravity of what the "school director" had said only a few days later. Hitching a ride with an Oflu trucker near the town of Giresun on my way back to Of, I told the driver about Celalettin's loaf of bread, simply by way of making conversation. By the time I had finished, the trucker was almost bouncing out of his seat, so angry that he considered stopping his rig and asking me to get out. I regained his good graces only by telling him that it was not *my* story but a story told to me by one of his own countrymen. "And who was the man who told you this lie?" he asked. This was only the first of many occasions that proved to me how seriously women's dress was taken. In the 1960s, all the women who were natives of Of, whether they lived in towns or villages, covered their head and hair as I have described, while wearing blouses, skirts, and aprons that concealed their lower arms and legs. When my wife accompanied me to Of the following year, she decided the best course would be to respect local custom because we were guests. She therefore adopted the use of a headscarf and wore a long coat when she left our house to go to the marketplace. This behavior was rewarded with gifts of anchovy pilaf and fresh yogurt brought to our door in thanks for our respect for Islam. On the other hand, the wife of the pharmacist, also an outsider, was less compromising. Having moved to Of from Istanbul only after her marriage, she was an avowed secularist who detested all forms of veiling. She purposely went to the marketplace with her head uncovered, provoking some of the village women to curse and spit at her.

In retrospect, I realized that the "school director" had been expressing an inflammatory opinion in a loud voice in the middle of the town square, and that it was as though some invisible barrier protected him from any kind of challenge. The trucker had been on the right track when he had asked for his identity. He was indeed a man of a certain social position and background, but not at all the one I had supposed. I am embarrassed to recall that I did not immediately understand that the "school director" himself was a hodja who had studied in a religious academy of the district. Knowing only that he worked at the middle school, I had assumed that he was the highest functionary of that institution by virtue of his reception among the town worthies. The directors and chairmen of public associations invited him to their tables in restaurants to share their meals, listened respectfully to his opinions, and addressed him as "my hodja" (*hocam*) rather than by his personal name. Without really thinking about it, I had assumed that the title accorded him referred to an earlier career in the classrooms of state schools. After all, it was common practice for Turkish citizens to address their former teachers by the title "my hodja" all their lives. Only toward the end of my initial visit did I realize he was merely the school secretary (as I shall henceforth refer to him). The town worthies deferred to him not because of his employment, which was a post of no particular distinction whatsoever, but rather by virtue of his religious studies, which were entirely unofficial, even illegal, in character.

I was later to learn of various partnerships between leading individuals and religious teachers, especially in the past but continuing during my residence. These took the form of friendships of convenience between an uneducated but socially prominent individual and an educated but socially humble individual. The town worthies did not extend their hospitality to everyone engaged in religious study, far from it. Instead, they welcomed and hosted the school secretary because he was a hodja from Of who spoke with and for them. As I came to understand some years later, his arguments were not intended to persuade religious conservatives that the Republic and Kemalism conformed with Islam. They were instead intended to justify the dominant position of his kinsmen, friends, and associates in public institutions and organizations. To see how this is so, the lessons I learned from my companions in the Crystal Palace must first be applied to leading individuals from large family groupings.

As I have explained, it was my initial presumption that the town worthies had come to dominate the public life of the district by means of clan solidarity and alliances. However, my experiences at the Crystal Palace had indicated that social relations in the district of Of were based on a discipline of Islamic sociability rather than any parochial system of descent and marriage. Like my companions at the Crystal Palace, the town worthies also engaged in day-to-day interactions of sitting, conversing, and sharing. By these activities, they, too, were bound together by sentiments of intimacy and contracts of reciprocity. So the town worthies had come together to dominate public life in much the same way that my companions at the Crystal Palace were able to come together to engage in multiple entrepreneurial adventures.

Leading individuals of the Selimoğlu and Muradoğlu were the principals of two circles of interpersonal association in the district of Of. But the latter were but unusual examples of many other circles of interpersonal association among townsmen and villagers, such as the one that had adopted me at the Crystal Palace. Leading individuals of the Selimoğlu and Muradoğlu were different only in their ability to extend and reinforce their circles of interpersonal association by dominating public institutions and organizations. The least seepage of power or resources out of the hands of state officials had always resulted in the consolidation of their social networks. Moreover, their interpersonal associations had been purposely perpetuated from generation to generation by the collusion of state officials who had relied on them for local social control, now in the Republic as formerly in the Empire. Anyone who might oppose the Selimoğlu or Muradoğlu would therefore take on more than a single individual with a few friends and partners. They would confront entrenched district social oligarchies that had been and still were supported by the state system.[8]

So leading individuals from large family groupings controlled public institutions and organizations by using them to consolidate their position in interpersonal associations based on a discipline of Islamic sociability. And yet at the same time, they dominated these same public institutions and organizations, not for the most narrow and selfish reasons, but to assert their claims to take part in the sovereign power of the state system. They therefore presented themselves as members of a national political elite. In the instance of the Selimoğlu in the town of Of, this fusion took the form of a curious strategy that I shall characterize as "Kemalo-Islamism." To explain

8. By comparison, the circles of interpersonal association among ordinary Oflus were both more flexible and more evanescent. Economic opportunities that required group cooperation and organization stimulated a *potential* for sociability derived from Islamic belief and practice and so spawned a little circle of interpersonal association that did not exist before the fact. Correspondingly, as economic conditions changed during the early 1970s, their little circle began to change in its membership and activities. Two brothers who were key members of the group became more and more involved in long-distance trucking. This was a demanding occupation that entailed extended absences from the town. Eventually the two brothers no longer worked together with their old associates, but made new friendships and partnerships among Oflus residing outside the district.

this phenomenon, I must first mention how the old rivalries had more recently come to work through national political parties.

The Selimoğlu and their friends and partners, once associated with the old Five Party (*fırka*), were aligned with the Republican People's Party (RPP), the political party founded by Mustafa Kemal (*Atatürk*). The RPP had been the only legal political party from 1925 to 1945. During this period, the RPP had implemented the Kemalist program of secular reforms that placed certain restrictions on religious observance and was much resented by some believers. The Muradoğlu and their friends and partners, once associated with the old Twenty-five Party (*fırka*), were aligned with the Justice Party (JP), successor to the Democrat Party (DP). The DP (now the JP) had turned the RPP out of the government in the first openly contested, national elections held in 1950. Since that time, the DP (now the JP) had been able to appeal to those believers who resented the restrictions placed on religious observance.

So, then, the rivalry between the Selimoğlu and the Muradoğlu was a rivalry between the defenders and the critics of the Kemalist principle of secularism. Accordingly, the town worthies who were most active in public affairs declared themselves to be Kemalists and defended the principle of secularism. And yet they were also scrupulous in their observance of Islamic beliefs and practices, more so than their friends and partners (see fig. 4). They performed their daily prayers punctiliously, and not only during the month of Ramadan. Then, during Ramadan, they demonstrated exceptional piety. They kept the fast in full view of the public, sitting in their coffeehouse. They joined the supererogatory prayers (*teravih*) in the old town mosque each evening. They received visitors in their public offices during the holiday *Şeker Bayram*, which followed the month of Ramadan. Very few if any of them ever touched a drop of alcohol or smoked a cigarette so far as I could determine, and the coffeehouse they attended had banned card playing, not to mention gambling. The town worthies of Of therefore led a kind of double life that drew together contradictory principles. They would extol the radical secularist policies of the RPP in the midst of a coffeehouse discussion, then suddenly excuse themselves to perform their ablutions and prayers. They wore hats, neckties, dress shirts, and suits in accordance with the strictest Kemalist codes, but would not fail to be present at the Friday prayers.[9] Echoing official RPP policy of the day, they condemned the JP

9. The fusion of Republican and Islamic principles was a common feature of public life in the district of Of in the 1960s. The holders of the most important public offices, including the district officer (*kaymakam*) and the executive director (*müdür*)

Figure 4. A descendant of Ferhat Agha (in fedora), relatives, friends, and others.

and its predecessor, the DP, for injecting religion into politics, even as they took care to display their religious piety.

If we recall the aghas of the 1830s during the time of Osman Pasha, this contradictory behavior becomes familiar rather than strange. The ascendants of the Selimoğlu and the Muradoğlu were a local elite exercising sovereign power in the state system. They had built immense mansions and maintained large households, more or less in the manner of higher state officials, but they had also been recognized by the central government on the basis of their position in district networks and coastal coalitions. Now during the Turkish Republic, their descendants were still a local elite exercising sovereign power in the state system. While they no longer had mansions and households, they held directorships and chairmanships in national associations, supported national party ideologies and programs, and were recognized by RPP and DP party officials. So the Selimoğlu had become Kemalists who donned hats and neckties and defended the principle

of the tea factory, neither of whom were Oflu, "officially" recognized major religious holidays in various ways. For example, during the holidays concluding the month of Ramadan, the district officer personally greeted the crowds who issued from early morning prayers in the mosque, and the executive director received visitors in his office in the tea factory.

of secularism, and the Muradoğlu had become populists who dressed like country squires and criticized official curbs on religious observance.[10] But neither of the two had achieved public prominence on the basis of their commitment to (and certainly not their understanding of) their respective party ideology and programs.[11] They were the leaders of circles of interpersonal association that spread from their coastal settlements into all the villages of the district. And because these district social oligarchies were based on a discipline of Islamic sociability, they performed the prayers and kept the fast more visibly if not more scrupulously than most other Oflus.

The Kemalo-Islamism of the town worthies largely fits into what we have already learned in the preceding chapter regarding the aghas, mansions, family lines, and parties. Party officials (and, by that fact, state officials as well) recognized the town worthies because they could not possibly ignore them, just as Osman Pasha could not ignore their forebears in the 1830s. And yet, the preceding analysis, based on drawing an analogy between my companions at the Crystal Palace and the town worthies in public offices, has most definitely led us to a discovery: In order for an individual to position himself in the state system (whether as leader, follower, or subject of the district social oligarchies), he was obliged to accommodate himself to a certain kind of Islamic belief and practice. That is to say, he had to be a certain kind of Muslim, not just any kind of Muslim. The school secretary had already announced such a principle in his two "sermons", but I had been unable to recognize it during the period of my fieldwork.

On the occasion of his first "sermon," the school secretary cited the first Muslim community at Medina as an Islamic precedent for the National Assembly and Constitution. As I saw it, he was cleverly responding to criticisms of religious reactionaries who saw the Turkish Republic as an unacceptable "innovation." However, he never really addressed the basic principle of republican government at all. Neither the parliamentary representation of a body of citizens nor the constitutional balancing of state powers appeared in his analysis. Rather, by his analogy, the National Assembly was a kind of community (like the Muslims at Medina), while the National Constitution was its charter (like the Charter of Medina). In other words, an exclusive political elite (Kemalists) who formed an interpersonal association (Muslims) came into his mind when he contemplated the Turkish Republic.

10. The "Kemalo-Islamism" of the Selimoğlu in Of was matched by the "Libero-Islamism" of the Muradoğlu in Eskipazar.

11. Cf. Lewis 1961, 280.

On the occasion of his second "sermon," the school secretary cited the story of Celalettin's loaf of bread as an Islamic precedent for the disapproval of women's seclusion and veiling. I had assumed he was defending Kemalist standards of dress and behavior by meeting religious conservatives on their own ground. However, he never made a case for the active role of women in public life, which was the point of the Kemalist attack on seclusion and veiling. Rather, the school secretary concluded with the moral that ordinary villagers who practiced seclusion and veiling (they were not good Kemalists) were beset by social discord (they were not good Muslims) and thus unfit to manage their affairs. By way of contrast, the town worthies were fit to share in the sovereign power of the state system (that is, they were good Kemalists) because they formed a proper interpersonal association (that is, they were good Muslims).

The school secretary, a hodja from Of, was able to please the town worthies. He could articulate their embarrassing Kemalo-Islamist predicament as a coherent political philosophy. For our purposes, his exotic views are significant because they indicate that the domination of the state system by circles of interpersonal association had placed a kind of pressure on Islamic belief and practice. As we shall see, an oligarchy of leading individuals from large patronymic groups had evolved in tandem with the tradition of religious study in the district of Of.

THE HODJAS FROM OF

Toward the end of my initial visit, my interlocutors had more difficulty evading my questions about religious teachers and students. I had repeatedly encountered individuals in the streets of the town who had been introduced to me as a "hodja."[12] Almost none dressed in a manner that was consistent with the conventions of the Turkish Republic (see fig. 5). Many compromised these conventions by wearing berets and overcoats, western apparel that was tolerated by authorities but consistent with an Islamic sensibility.[13] Some wore scarves wrapped around their heads to form a turban, a gesture for which one could be prosecuted, if the authorities wanted to

12. During the 1960s, the government was opening religious schools at the middle and high school levels. These were designated "prayer-leader and sermon-giver school" (*imam hatip okulu*). Since there was no such school in the district of Of at the time, the hodjas were clearly the result of illegal religious teaching and learning.

13. Many believers were reluctant to accept brimmed headgear, since the forehead must touch the ground during prayer, or tight-fitting outer clothing, since it is identified with secular life.

Figure 5. Village hodjas (in berets, turbans) bid pilgrims farewell.

make a case of the matter. Most of them also had well-trimmed beards, signifying they had performed the pilgrimage to Mecca.[14]

When I asked the school secretary about all these berets, turbans, overcoats, and beards, he attempted to belittle the question with a joke. "But of course, after our local squash (*kabak*), we Oflus are most famous for our hodjas!" In other words, religious teachers, like the humble squash for which the Oflus were indeed famous, were also a matter of little importance. Each time I questioned the school secretary about hodjas, he refused to attribute any significance to them. They had existed in the past but not in the present. And if they somehow did exist in the present, they were not here in Of but only in Çaykara. And if they were somehow here in Of, they were of no more importance than squash. As a dis-informant, the school

14. In this respect, the hodjas were not alone. By the time of my first visit to Of in 1965, the government had eased currency and passport controls that severely restricted the ability of Turkish citizens to perform the pilgrimage. After the easing, the pilgrimage had become highly organized as a commercial business. A convoy of buses departed from the district each year on the same day.

secretary was a revealing informant, but only after I could understand how and why he was misleading me.

During the later Ottoman Empire, the largest numbers of professors, academies, and students were to be found in the upper western valley-system, which had later become the district of Çaykara.[15] This part of the old district of Of had not been settled until the sixteenth century, at which time it became a place of refuge for Pontic Greek-speaking Orthodox Christians who subsequently converted to Islam. More isolated and mountainous than the rest of the district, the upper western valley-system lacked fertile soil and level land, and the growing season was shorter. Grain deficits were therefore persistent, and the absence of fodder precluded large flocks or herds. Under such circumstances, its villagers had been pressed to use whatever skills they had to make up for the lack of material resources. These skills appear to have included reading and writing and, quite possibly, even before conversion, religious teaching and learning.[16] After a shift from Greek literacy and Byzantine Orthodoxy to Arabic literacy and Ottoman Islam, a tradition of religious study had not only continued but even flourished in the upper western valley-system.[17] According to one of my interlocutors, the conventional manner of addressing an elder in this part of Of had recently been "O teacher" (*Ey hocam*), in contrast to "O father's uncle" (*Ey amcam*) or "O mother's uncle" (*Ey dayım*) elsewhere in the district.

Perhaps the tradition of religious study had first begun in the upper western valley-system, but if this was the case, it had also spread to other villages.[18] Ultimately, the professors, academies, and students had become a local industry of impressive proportions all over the old district of Of. And although most of the fee-paying students were residents of the district of Of, some came from other parts of the coastal region as well as from the interior highlands. As a pathway toward some level of learning in the Islamic sciences, the religious academies in Of were affordable, beyond the

15. The religious academy in the village of Paçan [Maraşlı], not far from Kadahor [Çaykara], may have been one of the first. See chap. 5.

16. See chap. 5 for a fuller discussion of the historical documentation of the tradition of religious study in the old district of Of.

17. It is probable that the first religious academies in Of were founded in the upper western valley-system, but it is not altogether certain that the first professors and students in these early religious academies were Greek-speakers. See chap. 5.

18. Umur (1949, 22–40) lists the religious academies in the eastern valley-system, citing them by name and by village.

immediate oversight of government inspectors, and most importantly, perhaps, open to almost anyone, regardless of their social background. The religious academies therefore exported large numbers of graduates, both Oflus and non-Oflus, in the manner of any contemporary university system. A few would continue their studies in the more prestigious religious academies in the major cities. A few would become religious officials in the middle to upper ranks of the imperial religious establishment. But most would seek appointments as prayer-leaders and sermon-givers in the towns and villages of Anatolia.[19] It was the latter, the very large majority, who had come to be known as "hodjas from Of," famous and infamous throughout Asia Minor during the Empire and then again during the Republic.

The professors, academies, and students in the district of Of therefore represented the outer, marginal reaches of the imperial religious establishment. In this regard, the local tradition of religious study was both inside and outside the state system, legal and proper in some respects, but illegal and improper in others. Many hodjas from Of were officially recognized as sermon-givers and prayer-leaders in the mosques of towns and villages all over Anatolia. But many others made a living from what was called "imaming" (imamlık) without official assignments or licenses.[20] Most of these illegal hodjas from Of provided religious advice and services for a fee in the course of pursuing other itinerant occupations. When the occasion arose in the course of plying a trade—peddling, tinning, cooper-working, or carpentry—they were always ready to give a sermon, lead the prayers, conduct a burial, conclude a marriage contract, or perform a circumcision for a modest gratuity. All the hodjas from Of, the legal and the illegal, were of variable character and judgment. By my own experiences during the 1960s, some of them would have been relatively thoughtful and educated. Others would have been "*şeriatçi,*" subscribing to an interpretation of the sacred law of Islam so literal as to bar any kind of music or dancing, not to mention the use of alcohol and tobacco. And still others would have been "*cinci,*" engaging in shady practices such as casting spells for the lovelorn (*büyüme*), performing cures (*okuma*) for the possessed, and selling charms (*nuska*) to fend off the evil eye.[21]

19. So the hodja from Of is not necessarily from Of at all but is rather an individual who pursued his studies there for some period of time.

20. The staff of an official mosque—for example, the prayer-leader (*imam*) and the caller-to-prayer (*müezzin*)—required official approval in both the Ottoman and Republican periods.

21. Strasser 1995. See also Hann and Beller-Hann (2001) for an account of such a hodja from Of in the eastern district of Pazar. Even though some of the hodjas in-

When I had mentioned berets, turbans, overcoats, and beards, the school secretary had thought of the practitioners of imaming. These were the hodjas who came from the poorest villages, like those of Çaykara, villages that had no leading individuals and no large family groupings.[22] With this low end of the tradition of religious study in mind, the school secretary had compared the local hodjas with the local squash. The most impoverished of the Oflus had been able to supplement the income of their families either by peddling religion or by peddling squash. Both were produced in the district of Of, and both could be put up for sale in the towns and villages of Anatolia. The comparison appropriately directs our attention to a "religious market."

The professors, academies, and students in the district of Of represented only one kind of Islam, the official Sunni Islam of the imperial religious establishment. Elsewhere in Anatolia, other kinds of Islam were to be found among the townsmen and villagers of the later Ottoman Empire. There were leaders and followers of religious brotherhoods (*tarikat*), some closer to and some distant from the official Sunni Islam. There were also what might be called non-Sunni Islams, such as the Alevis and Bektaşis, who varied in their beliefs and practices from group to group. And finally, there were folk Islams that featured Islamic, Christian, and Judaic influences as well as Hellenic, Central Asian, and Anatolian influences.

If the tradition of religious study in the district of Of flourished during a certain period of imperial history, this increase in the "supply" of hodjas versed in official Islam must have been the result of an increase in the "demand" for this kind of Islam. The likely correlate of such a change in the religious market has been mentioned in the conclusion to the last chapter. An important segment of the population along the eastern Black Sea had begun to participate in imperial military institutions during the post-classical period. Those who did so would have most likely been motivated to bring themselves into conformity with the behavioral standards of the imperial system, that is to say, official Islam. If this is correct, the aghas, family lines, and parties were linked with the professors, academies, and students.

---

dulged in shady practices at least some of the time, this should not obscure their other, more prosaic function as modest religious experts in the sacred law of Islam.

22. Although there were some hodjas from large family groupings (as was the school secretary), the individuals who worked as itinerant prayer-leaders and sermon-givers were rarely the descendants of aghas or the members of their family lines. I was sometimes told that individuals had pursued the profession of imaming for lack of economic opportunities in the district of Of and as a means to escape domination by or collaboration with the aghas.

Before this last issue is considered, we have to know more about the tradition of religious study, its "upward" relationship to the state system, and its "downward" relationship to ordinary townsmen and villagers. In the next two sections, I shall examine each of these matters in turn as they appear in recollections of the professors, academies, and students during the transition from Empire to Republic.

PROFESSORS, ACADEMIES, AND STUDENTS

The professors, academies, and students in Of had been officially recognized by the imperial religious establishment during the eighteenth and nineteenth centuries.[23] But does recognition alone demonstrate that the tradition was really representative of the imperial system of religious education? The writings of Hasan Umur (1880–1977), our local historian, provide an answer to these questions.[24] Umur received his early schooling in one of the local religious academies before pursuing further study in Istanbul. Some years before the Great War, he left Istanbul and returned to Of, where he carried out an "investigation" of the conditions of religious education, a project that brought him into contact with teachers and students all over the district.[25]

According to Umur, the teaching duties of the professors, the course loads of the students, the methods of instruction, the kinds of courses offered, and the granting of diplomas in the district of Of all more or less conformed with official standards. Indeed, he tells us, this was exactly what was wrong with the local tradition of religious study, since it consequently suffered from all the many problems of the imperial system of religious education. The professors had to teach too many subjects for too many hours each week so that they never dealt with any topic as they should have. Their methods of instruction retarded the progress of the students so that they never properly learned Arabic after many years of study. The official

23. For the later nineteenth century, see the citations of the Trabzon yearbooks (*salname*) for 1869/1286 and 1888/1305 in chap. 8 (notes).

24. Umur, a native of Yığa [Yarlı] village, received his first diploma in the district Of and completed his studies at the Beyazit Mosque in Istanbul before returning to the district of Of. When the Russian army occupied the district in 1916, he left the district again to become an activist in the nationalist movement, serving as the mayor of Samsun from 1935 to 1936. Sometime later, he turned from politics to commerce before retiring in Istanbul. In his retirement, he carried out an extensive program of archival research on the history of Of. The published results of this work are cited in later chapters.

25. Umur 1949, 25–28.

curriculum was excessively narrow, being entirely limited to courses in the Islamic sciences.[26] Since students were never given instruction in basic subjects, such as writing, arithmetic, history, and geography, they could not progress satisfactorily in their studies of the higher Islamic sciences.[27] The absence of any kind of examinations meant that many graduates received their diplomas without learning anything at all.[28]

Umur paints a bleak picture of religious education in the district of Of.[29] In addition to its pedagogical deficiencies, he also refers in passing to widespread corruption, which he preferred not to discuss.[30] Still, Umur admired the old tradition of religious study, to which he felt personally indebted. As an example of the best of what it had to offer, he gives a brief account of the accomplishments of his own teacher in the district of Of, Zühtü Efendi Veli Efendi Oğlu. This man, still famous for his erudition during the 1960s, appears to have offered his students a rigorous and demanding program of study. He had himself received his diploma, or "authorizing certificate" (*icazet*), sometime during the middle of the nineteenth century, at the age

26. He lists the subjects taught as grammar (*sarf*), syntax (*nahiv*), logic (*mantık*), semantics (*maânî*), rhetoric (*beyan*), jurisprudence (*fıkıh*), applied jurisprudence (*usulü fıkıh*), study of the Koran (*kelâm*), commentary on the Koran (*tefsir*), and study of the Tradition (*hadîs*). This list appears to include the full range of subjects that would have been offered in a religious academy of the Ottoman Empire.

27. After his first return to the district of Of, sometime around 1910, Umur is reported to have offered such supplementary courses. According to Albayrak (1986, 68–70), this was the first time such basic subjects had been taught in the district of Of during the late Ottoman period. Umur is also said to have given instruction in Persian and Arabic.

28. Examinations, once a part of the system of religious education, had been abolished by official decree sometime during the later Ottoman period.

29. Umur (1949, 25–28) formulated a program of reform for religious education in Of and submitted it as a proposal to the müftü. He recommended that a new kind of academy be set up in Çufaruksa (Uğurlu) village. This new kind of academy would be financed by public contributions (an idea that suggests Umur's views were shared by other Oflus). Its professors would use different teaching methods and offer a different course of study. There would still be religious courses and instruction as before, but they would be supplemented by secular courses and instruction. The müftü was never able to implement his proposal because of the crises that were to accompany more than a decade of warfare.

30. He writes that he will leave unmentioned irregularities that were characteristic of the religious academies in Of (ibid., 27). I would guess he is referring to the offering of authorizing certificates for a flat fee. The status of certified religious teacher would have sometimes been useful for escaping conscription during the later nineteenth century. Umur also writes that a good system of religious education is necessary in order to protect the people from charlatans (ibid., 30–31). I would guess he has in mind the hodjas who worked spells and cures. See chap. 8 for further discussion of the significance of this practice.

of twenty-eight. So it would appear he had studied for many years before qualifying for his diploma.[31] By time of his death at an advanced age, he had granted thirty-one authorizing certificates. Since this number is considered exceptionally large, it would appear that many of the teachers offered courses of study that were not easily or quickly completed. The character of the thirty-one certificates provides a hint of the intentions of his students. Thirteen had been "general" authorizing certificates (*büyük icazet*), confirming that the graduate had mastered the complete course of study in the religious academy. These individuals may have been hoping to qualify themselves for appointment as minor officials in the imperial religious establishment.[32] The remaining eighteen had been "inheritance" authorizing certificates (*feraiz icazet*), confirming that the graduate had mastered the law of inheritance, but nothing more than this. These individuals may have been content to provide advice and counsel to clients among townsmen and villagers.[33] Knowledge of the law of inheritance would have enabled them to give plausible assistance in regard to the writing of wills, the distribution of property, bills of sale, and the arrangement of marriages.

From Umur's account, we can conclude that the professors, academies, and students were most certainly a local branch of the imperial system of religious education. Their "upward" relationship to the state system confirmed, I shall now examine the tradition of religious study as it continued after the imperial religious establishment was no more. Once the superstructure of the state system had been swept away, the "downward" relationship of the tradition to townsmen and villagers was all the more clearly exposed.

THE UNDERGROUND TRADITION OF RELIGIOUS STUDY

Under the leadership of Mustafa Kemal (Atatürk), the National Assembly abolished the Ottoman Sultanate (1922) and declared the Turkish Republic (1923). Soon afterwards, steps were taken to remove Islam from the public life of the new nation-state. The Caliphate followed the Sultanate into oblivion (1924), and along with it the upper hierarchy of the imperial

31. Ibid., 36–37.

32. See chap. 8 for a review of the number of Oflus in the imperial religious establishment in the later Empire.

33. The Ottoman Civil Code (*mecelle*), compiled between 1869 and 1876, was based on the sacred law of Islam but took the form of a modernized legal code (Lewis 1961, 120–21).

religious establishment, the Şeyh-ül-İslâm, the Ministry of the Şeriat, the Şeriat courts, and the religious academies and schools.[34] This accomplished, the National Assembly adopted the Swiss civil code and Italian penal code (1926), thereby removing the last traces of the sacred law of Islam from the state legal system.[35] For a short while, the nationalists contemplated a reform of the system of religious education and so permitted a number of new religious academies to reopen during the later 1920s. Then, after serious incidents in which religious conservatives challenged the Kemalist program of reforms, all religious academies were closed and all religious instruction was banned (1931).[36] Religious study in Of was henceforth largely useless as an official path toward any kind of position in the state system, just as the religious expertise of its graduates had no relevance whatsoever to the official legal system. And yet, religious teaching and learning did not come to an end in the district of Of. Why was this the case?

With the collapse of the Empire and the founding of the Republic, "Muslim subjects" had become "Turkish citizens." To take part in public institutions and organizations, they would henceforth be obliged to conform to a new nationalist standard of behavior. In the district of Of during the 1960s, the changes in masculine dress were still keenly remembered. Turbans, baggy pants, and slippers were out. Hats, trousers, and shoes were in. These examples of the transformation of masculine attire are but superficial indicators of a wide range of profound changes whose significance should not be minimized. But, this admitted, it must also be said that the old standards of personal conduct and social relations were still very much in place in the context of family, relatives, friends, and partners. That is to say, everyday interpersonal association was still based on a discipline of Islamic sociability. So there was still a demand for religious expertise regarding official Islam, even after the transition from Empire to Republic,

34. Ibid., 259–60, 266–69. The nationalists did not ignore official Islam. A new Ministry of Religious Affairs and Ministry of Pious Endowments took the place of the old imperial institutions. See Zürcher (1993, 195).

35. Ibid.

36. The nationalists discussed reform of the existing religious schools (*medreses*) during the Independence War (1921–22). Later, in 1924, they abolished these schools but opened new İmam-Hatip schools "to train enlightened [*aydın*] imams," and reopened the faculty of theology, which had been closed in 1919 (Akşit 1991, 161). Then new, more restrictive policies were adopted. An İmam-Hatip school that had been opened in the town of Of in 1925 was closed down in 1928 (Tursun 1998, 45). By 1929, instruction in Arabic and Persian was abolished in secondary education, and the last two İmam-Hatip schools in the country were closed in 1931 (Lewis 1961, 409).

and the teachers and students of Of, tucked away in their mountain fastnesses, would have a near monopoly on the supply for a while.

Toward the end of my first period of fieldwork, I had known some residents of the town of Of for more than two years. Over this period of time those who had become my friends had told me what they knew about the tradition of religious study. One of these men had traveled and worked among Oflus in all parts of Turkey. He had a wide network of friends in the district, and he had always been interested in its history. Born in 1908, he was able to write Turkish in the old Arabic letters and was familiar with the official terms and offices of the late imperial period.[37] He offered me the following synopsis of religious study during the first decades of the Turkish Republic, saying that it still continued as before:

> A student might come to the village of a reputed hodja during the summer or winter for a few months in order to receive lessons from him for a certain fee. They would meet in the dwelling of the teacher or in the mosque of his village. [The speaker did not use the defunct official terminology, "professor" (*müderris*) or "academy" (*medrese*), even though he was familiar with these words.] This student might be from some other village in the district or he might come from elsewhere in Anatolia. He would continue his studies under the tutelage of his teacher for several years until he had mastered a course of study of some kind. A student required at least four years to complete a course of study, more if he were not especially gifted. The average course of study normally took six years. [However, it has already been stated that teacher and student met together during only part of the year.] The lessons would involve the memorization of the Koran, the study of the Arabic language, instruction in the sacred law, explanations of passages in the Koran, and other matters. Eventually, the student would meet certain requirements stipulated by his teacher. In recognition of this, he would be awarded an "authorizing certificate," a written document also known as a "permission" (*izin*). The written document recorded the name of the student, the course of study he had followed, the name of his teacher, and the scholarly lineage (*silsile, zincir*) of the latter. For example, the scholarly lineage might pass from the Prophet Muhammad to Hazreti Ali, or sometimes Hazreti Abubakr, or one of the other four rightly guided Caliphs, thence to Mustafa Samarkanti, or another Konyavi, Bagdadi, Hindustani, or Andalusi, and finally to an Ofi [Oflu], after

37. In 1928, the National Assembly adopted a new Latin alphabet for printed Turkish and prohibited the public use of the old Arabic alphabet. See Lewis (1961, 271–74) and Zürcher (1993, 196–97).

> which the name of the student is given.[38] The hodjas are very anxious to grant these authorizing certificates to the students who work with them and very upset should a student choose to leave them in order to work with someone else.[39]

Judging from this account, the tradition of religious study in Of had continued to resemble the old system of professors and academies even after the latter became illegal.[40] The one-on-one relationship of teacher and student, the subject matter of the courses taught, the period of study required, and the granting of authorizing certificates all remained similar. On the other hand, my friend's account, by contrast with Hasan Umur's analysis of the religious academies, underlines the *ad hoc* character of the tradition of religious study. The teacher and student met one another from time to time, in any place of convenience, for a number of years. At some moment, without examination, the teacher decided the course had been completed and granted a written slip of paper to that effect.

Given the ad hoc character of instruction, not only in Of but also in Istanbul, the religious teachers and students in the district of Of would have found themselves in a singular position soon after the disestablishment of Islam. The upper level personnel of the imperial system of religious education, situated in the major cities such as Istanbul, would have been under the nose of state officials. So the implementation of the Kemalist program of reforms would have been especially successful in curbing or suppressing their activities. In contrast, the professors, academies, and students of Of had always been at the outer reaches of the state system. They had, in effect, penetrated and colonized the imperial religious establishment from its fringes. By virtue of their more or less marginal position, the hodjas from Of had adapted and adjusted their activities to suit themselves and their clients. Already during the imperial period, they had streamlined courses

38. When I interviewed the müftü of Of in 1988, he told me that the authorizing certificate would not list a chain of authorities but only the name of the student's teacher and the name of a teacher's teacher, usually a sheikh (*şeyh*) of a Nakşibendi religious brotherhood (*tarikat*). It is possible that this comment reflects a change in the character of the authorizing certificate over the intervening period. See chap. 8 (notes) for further comment on religious brotherhoods in the district of Of.

39. The passage fuses together the results of two interviews with the same individual, one in the fall of 1966 and another in the fall of 1967.

40. When I interviewed the müftü of Of in 1988, he told me he was the last graduate of one of the last academies during the early 1940s. By his account, I have concluded that his early religious education in Of at that time was but a fragment of the old system of religious education as described by Hasan Umur.

of study, granted diplomas for a fee, and worked without licenses. It was precisely all these illegalities and subversions that Umur Hasan had chosen not to discuss when he referred darkly to the widespread corruption.

During the years immediately following the declaration of the Republic, it seems, the tradition of religious study in the district of Of remained more or less the same. The professors, academies, and students had lost their official and legal status, but the ban on unauthorized religious instruction was not enforced, at least in the mountains of Of. Then, from the early 1930s, state officials became *more* vigilant in meeting any challenge to the Kemalist program of reforms, and thus vigorously enforced the ban on religious instruction. When this happened, the numbers of teachers and students in the district of Of probably declined for a while. By the later 1940s, however, the tradition of religious study had moved underground, where it began to flourish anew. For a few years, before the re-opening of official religious academies in the later 1950s, the hodjas from Of became the principal suppliers of religious expertise responding to a rising demand.

One of my acquaintances in the district of Of had been a schoolteacher in the sub-district of Kadahor (later called Çaykara) at that time. The following passage is an edited version of my notes:

> He told me that it was certainly true that many individuals had received religious instruction in Çaykara and had gone elsewhere in Turkey to work as imams in villages and towns. This was a result of the restrictions that the government had placed on the training of prayer-leaders and sermon-givers. Because Çaykara had a tradition of religious academies, it had become an ideal place for meeting the shortage of imams that had arisen as a consequence of the government ban on religious education. In more remote villages of the district, the Çaykaralıs were able to continue religious teaching and learning in secret. On a one-by-one basis, those individuals with religious training had trained just a few young men at a time, usually in the mosques. When their course of study was completed, they moved out to other parts of Turkey in order to serve as prayer-leaders and sermon-givers.

The schoolteacher then told a story that pointed to the opening of a divide between state and society at just that point where they had previously been cobbled together:

> When [the hodjas from Of] left their homeland, they could not depend on the living they made from imaming alone. They also had to ply other trades. To illustrate this point, he mentioned an acquaintance of his, a schoolteacher in a secular state school who had been threatened with dismissal [for his criticism of the secular reforms]. This man had received lessons from one of the local hodjas and was prepared to look

> for work as an imam somewhere in Anatolia. He had said on this occasion, "If I am dismissed, I shall take my kit bag and put my hammer (*çekiç*) on the bottom, then I shall put my saw (*bıçkı*) on top of that, and I shall put my Koran on top of that and leave. Wherever I go, I shall certainly be able to find work."[41]

The profession of imaming had acquired a new significance by continuing its old function. Earlier, during the Empire, the hodjas from Of had provided "popular" access to a scarce resource, official Islamic belief and practice. That is to say, they had facilitated the wish of ordinary Muslims to align themselves with the normative standards of the imperial system. Now, during the Republic, the hodjas from Of still provided "popular" access to what had become a still scarcer resource. But now, in doing so, they were enabling ordinary Muslims to subvert the imposition of a new standard of thinking and practice in the public life of the nation-state.

Another interlocutor in the town of Of told me of a personal experience that also illustrates these points. At the end of World War II, he was demobilized from the army. Since he had some education and could use a typewriter, he began to work as "public secretary" (*kâtip, yazıcı*). He would sit in a small stall or even on the street before his typewriter, somewhere near a government building, and accept requests to fill out official forms, write letters to friends and family, and submit petitions to the court. During this time, he had not been able to return to his family in the district of Of but moved from town to town in accordance with changing prospects for work. On one such occasion, during the month of Ramadan, he had stopped for the evening in the town of Havza (near Amasya):

> When I arrived there, I went to a restaurant. After finishing the meal and asking what I owed, the proprietor told me, "We don't accept money from people like you" (*Böylenizden para almayız*). I was surprised but simply accepted this response. I then asked where I might find a room for the night. The proprietor then took me to a room with nothing but straw mats that were ordinarily let to travelers. But now he brought in a nice bed for me and again refused to accept my money. That evening I was taken to meet several people as a guest of the town. By then I realized that they thought I was an itinerant imam. They were trying to persuade me to stay with them and become their imam.

Townsmen and villagers had difficulty finding prayer-leaders and sermon-givers at the time because none had been officially trained for many years.

41. The citations, which are edited versions of my field notes, were recorded in 1967.

By my interlocutor's eastern Black Sea accent, the citizens of Havza realized he was from the district of Of and assumed he was a hodja. They were determined to keep him because they had no one else to instruct them in the performance of prayers, to perform marriages, or to bury the dead. They believed that he might have been summoned by a district religious official (müftü) but assumed they might be able to persuade him to abandon his official obligations:

> I told them that I did not know anything about being an imam. I had business in another town and was obliged to leave. They did not believe me. They suspected I was going to report to the müftü in that town. They urged me not to continue on my way. They said the müftü would send me to a very poor village where I would be uncomfortable. I told them I did not have any business at all with the müftü. They would not accept this. They thought I was only trying to escape from them and take a job as imam in some other village that would offer me more money. At long last I was able to escape them and reach my destination.

My interlocutor had not explained that the month of Ramadan had traditionally been the occasion for the so-called *cer.* During the old regime, religious teachers and students had traveled into Anatolia to preach to the people and lead them in prayer in return for alms to finance their studies. The religious teachers and students of Of had always done the very same thing, and they were once again going out on the *cer* during the later 1940s.[42] The citizens of Havza would have therefore been on the lookout for hodjas from Of who might serve as their prayer-leader and sermon-giver.

OFFICIAL ISLAM AS SOCIAL ISLAM

I have still not answered the question with which this chapter began, "Why so many hodjas from Of?" but the conclusions reached in the last two sections permit the question to be rephrased more precisely. Why had the hodjas specialized so exclusively in official Islam, to the neglect of all other versions of Islam? And having done so, why was the demand for official Islam at the outer reaches of the imperial system so great as to generate such

42. In 1988 I met a young man from Çaykara who told me that he had himself engaged in religious studies in his village and had gone out on the *cer* when he was in his early twenties (circa 1970), as had all the young people from his village. During the month of Ramadan, they had traveled to Çukurova, near the city of Adana, where they were received as guests by villagers and given food and lodging. However, his generation may have been one of the last to engage in this kind of activity, at least in any significant numbers.

a large supply of hodjas? These questions direct our attention to the ways in which the district of Of was similar to the other coastal districts of the old province of Trabzon.

The very large numbers of professors, academies, and students in Of were unusual, without any exact counterpart in the other eastern coastal districts.[43] But this having been said, a number of the other eastern coastal districts certainly did have important traditions of religious study, some of which produced graduates who were more successful than the Oflus in obtaining middle- and upper-level appointments in the imperial religious establishment.[44] Moreover, the dominant position of official Islam was not a unique feature of Of, but typical of most of the coastal districts of the old province of Trabzon.[45] Almost everywhere in the eastern coastal region, religious teachers, academies, and students represented official Islamic belief and practice while other versions—folk Islams, brotherhood Islams, and heterodox Islams—were strangely undeveloped or even altogether absent. So it is not just Of but all the eastern coastal districts that stand out as different. In this particular region of Asia Minor, unlike other regions, official Islam was unusually dominant while other Islams were unusually absent.[46]

This brings to mind another way in which the eastern coastal region stands out as different. As we have seen in the last chapter, aghas, mansions, family lines, and parties had been local branches of the imperial military and administrative establishment during the post-classical imperial period. And, as we have seen in this chapter, the aghas, mansions, family lines, and parties, which had comprised a major proportion of the masculine population, took the form of interpersonal associations based on a discipline of Islamic sociability. So it is possible that the rise of professors, academies, and students was somehow associated with the rise of aghas, mansions, family

43. There appears to have been at least one other country area where residents had accomplished such a massive penetration and colonization of the imperial religious establishment: the districts of Akseki and Ibradı, which are adjacent to one another in the province of Antalya. But see chap. 8 for an analysis of the differences between Of and these two districts in the Toros Mountains of southern Asia Minor.

44. See the counts of learned class officials for Batum, Arhavi, and Rize in chap. 8, table 3.

45. This was more the case toward the east than toward the west. See chaps. 3, 4, and 5 for a more precise accounting of the place of official Islam in the coastal districts.

46. Various peoples and groups affiliated with other kinds of Islam had from time to time arrived and settled in the eastern coastal districts. Eventually, however, these peoples and groups tended to re-orient themselves toward official Islamic belief and practice. See chaps. 3, 4, and 5.

lines, and parties. If so, the district of Of would certainly be an excellent place to examine the relationship of aghas and hodjas, for this particular coastal district had been just as famous for its soldiers as for its students. To explore this issue, on a *structural* rather than *historical* level, I shall return to the question of the "downward" relationship of the tradition of religious study to the inhabitants of the district of Of.[47]

The professors, academies, and students had been hosted and feted by the villagers of Of on specific occasions. A group of religious teachers, working together with the residents of one or more villages, would arrange to hold such celebrations whenever a large number of students had completed their course of studies.[48] The religious teachers called them an "authorizing certificate prayer" (*icazet duası*) or a "granting of permission prayer" (*izin duası*). But ordinary people called them an "authorizing certificate celebration" (*icazet merasimi*). The different terminology indicates that these occasions had two different but related sides. For the hodjas, they were primarily solemn ceremonies of learned Islam, while for the villagers they were communal festivals as well.

During the later Ottoman period, several "authorizing certificate celebrations" were held each year in the district of Of, and some of them had been attended by thousands of villagers.[49] By the size of the crowds they attracted, these occasions would have been without rival as public ceremonies during the old regime.[50] The same friend who described the tradition of religious study in Of gave me an account of the granting of authorizing certificates during the course of an extended interview.[51] He had attended more than one and had heard of many others.[52] He began by explaining how such occasions had initially declined but then later recovered in the course of the first two decades of the Turkish Republic:

47. See chaps. 4, 5, and 6 for further discussion of the historical connections between soldiers and students.

48. I have never heard of such ceremonies elsewhere in Anatolia, but it would be surprising if they did not have their counterparts. See chap. 8 for a discussion of the professors and academies of Akseki and Ibradı.

49. Umur 1949, 32.

50. The fairs (*panayır*) held each year during the late summer would have been attended by a larger number of people, but these were informal gatherings rather than ceremonial occasions.

51. I was not able to witness an authorizing certificate celebration, but I have spoken with a number of individuals who did attend some of them.

52. I have taken the citations that follow from my notes, breaking the text at certain points for the sake of analysis. Before analyzing their content, I edited them for grammar and redundancy. They have not been rewritten to support my commentary.

> The ceremony (*merasim*) is an occasion when the teachers in the academies give their students certificates that qualify them to practice as a teacher (*hoca*). During the period immediately following the declaration of the Republic [more probably, some years after 1931], these occasions were held in secret and were never very large. During the İnönü period [more probably, during the years following World War II], these occasions were held more or less openly but in a more secluded spot in a forest or away from the road. During the Menderes period [1950–1960], they were completely out in the open and held at the side of village mosques. At the present time, they are occurring very frequently. Many hodjas are now granting authorizing certificates to students.[53]

According to these remarks, the graduation celebrations never ceased altogether. Few villagers had participated during the period when the ban on religious education was vigorously enforced, but they had been eager to sponsor the celebrations when not faced with official reprisals. My friend then described an example of this:

> First several hodjas determine that they have a group of students who are ready to receive certificates. They come together and decide on a time for the award and they look for a village to sponsor the occasion. Such an occasion adds to the religious merit of its sponsors (*sevaptır*). So the villagers are anxious to sponsor the ceremony in their village, and they all contribute money for the occasion in accordance with their means. Different villages vie with one another for the honor of having the ceremony in their precincts because it is a matter that reflects on the honor of the village (*köy şerefi için*). It is said that some villages would not even be considered as a site for such a ceremony because of stains on their reputation. "What! You people want to have an authorizing certificate ceremony? You are all drunkards (*sarhoşsunuz*). You are lazy and shiftless (*çalışmazsınız*). You have no manners (*edipsizsiniz*). You are without morals (*ahlaksızsınız*)."

My friend spoke as a townsman who considered himself more educated and cultivated than an ordinary villager. When he said that the sponsors of the graduation ceremony wanted to gain merit or honor, he was more or less belittling them as typical villagers who were concerned with matters of

53. I have not been able to refer to descriptions of any official graduation ceremonies, which would have been held by the teaching staff of the imperial religious academies in Istanbul, so I cannot comment on the extent to which these local celebrations imitated them. One has to consider the possibility that the authorizing certificate ceremony had come under the influence of secular graduation exercises by the 1950s or 1960s.

reputation and standing. For example, he mimicked the villagers by speaking in dialect, making a face, and brusquely gesturing. But even as he so portrayed them, the words he put in their mouths—their denunciations of the ethics and morals of their competitors—implied that they strove to behave as good and proper Muslims. In this last respect, he admired them.

For my interlocutor, the residents of the district approached Islam more or less as simple villagers, but they nonetheless found in Islam something that could make them more than simple villagers. As he continued, he oscillated between these two contrasting themes. For example, he next told me that the graduation celebrations were organized as marriage celebrations. That is to say, an occasion of high religious study and learning appeared in the guise of a familiar rural festival:

> Once the village is chosen, people are invited from everywhere. Of course the families of the boys who are to receive certificates invite guests, but other people come as well.[54] It is like a marriage celebration (*düğün*).[55] Individuals and families come from Rize, Istanbul, Sürmene, and Trabzon, from everywhere. A proper ceremony is expected to host 5,000 people and as many as 10,000 is possible.[56] The invitations are sent out (*davet ederler*) to friends and relatives. They say, "There is an authorizing certificate prayer, come!" (*İcazet duası var, gel!*). The villagers begin to make preparations. They bake sweets (*baklava, tatlılar*) to be served on the occasion. As many as ten beds, or even more, might be laid out in each house. On the day or night before the ceremony, the guests begin to arrive and they are assigned to different houses.

He then adopted a very different tone as he began to describe the granting of the authorizing certificates. He was now specifically recalling a graduation ceremony that he had attended. As he did so, he became less condescending as he began to indicate how the occasion revealed special qualities of the students and teachers:

> The next day the people assemble in the village, and the ceremony begins after the morning prayers (*sabah namazı*). Let us say that there might be five teachers (*hoca*) who are awarding certificates and about twenty students (*molla*) who are receiving them. There might be about

54. This indicates that the graduates were usually adolescents during the later years of the Turkish Republic. This was confirmed by the reports I received from other individuals who were religious teachers and students.

55. The word "*düğün*" can be applied to any of the festivities that are part of the marriage, such as the fetching of the bride, the hosting of the bride-takers, or the reception of the bride.

56. Cf. Umur (1949, 32) for the Ottoman period.

> two hundred other hodjas at the ceremony. All the hodjas collect in rows at the head of the assembly, and the students are in lines in front them, sitting as though in the mosque and facing sideways one behind the other. Their heads are bowed. As the day wears on and the sun shines down on them, they perspire under their turbans (*sarık*) that they are wearing.

The students sit before their teachers, not facing them directly, but rather as though presenting themselves to God. In the course of their studies they have acquired religious learning, and we now see this achievement through a performance. The students remain in their assigned places, sitting silent and still, enduring the heat of the sun that bears down upon them. This passivity is also an activity.[57] To acquire religious learning is not just to acquire knowledge; it is also to acquire discipline.

With the picture of the teachers and students before his mind's eye, my friend began to contemplate the effect of the occasion on the audience. As he did so, he implied that their witnessing the teachers and students brought the villagers closer to Islamic belief and practice. This thought first appeared, however, in the guise of the negative example of the women in attendance:

> All the men assemble in this open square surrounding the hodjas and the mollas. The women assemble in another place apart from the men, but close enough to listen. The women want to hear what is said by the hodjas because it is meritorious (*sevaptır*) to do so. They listen to the speeches much as they listen at the back of the mosque during the festival prayers (*bayram namazı*) and the festival sermon (*bayram vaazı*). Among the 10,000 people who attend, there might be as many as 2,000 women. Sometimes the women become bored with being shunted aside and are anxious to participate [The speaker is now recalling a particular occasion]. They begin to complain and the hodjas are forced to send someone to speak to them expressly. When this happened on one occasion, they sent a hodja who was considered a "contrary" (*aksi*) person and was not liked by the women. The hodjas were simply trying to get rid of the problem presented by the women so they would no longer be bothered by them.

The women are bored and restless because they cannot see or hear the teachers and the students. Their marginal position is correlated with a lack of personal discipline, a quality instilled by Islamic belief and practice. To

57. See Meeker (1997), in which I describe the same kind of performance, silence and stillness, as a recognition and acceptance of state authority, versions of which appear in both the Empire and the Republic.

calm the women, the hodjas delegate one of their number to preach to the women.

At the same time, the hodjas have taken the opportunity to rid themselves of a troublesome character. The contrary hodja will eventually reappear as a negative example of what the teachers and students give to their audience just as the women are a negative example of what the audience receives from the teachers and students. First, however, my friend returned to the scene of the graduation ceremony:

> Eventually some of the hodjas begin to speak [in turn], not only those who have students receiving authorizing certificates, but others who are considered appropriate, such as the elder ones (*en lâyık olan hocalar konuşurlar, ihtiyarlar konuşurlar*). As they speak, the hodjas exhort the people of the assembly to live a good life (*ikna ederler*).[58] For example, Hacı Dursun Efendi, one of the well-known district hodjas, might preach to the crowd (*vaaz eder*). There might also be hodjas from Istanbul who would speak with an Istanbul accent. Their address would be more cultivated and dignified. The speeches of all these hodjas might last a few hours. When I heard Hacı Dursun Efendi speak, for example, he continued for about an hour. After the hodjas have finished speaking, they say a prayer, in Turkish or in Arabic.[59] They ask for blessings from God on the proceedings, on the village, on the people present, and so on. They ask for help that they might be good people (*iyi insanlar*), have sufficient land, or a good road. At the end of the prayer, all the people say, "Amen!" (*amin!*)"

The hodjas exhort and encourage the assembly to lead their lives as good and proper Muslims. Some hodjas address the assembly plainly and directly in the local dialect. But other hodjas will speak in a manner that reveals their ties with a center of religious study and learning. The ceremony brings the audience into contact with the simple truths of Islam but also with a world center of Islamic sophistication and cultivation.

My friend then described the granting of diplomas according to procedures that would have previously been in conformity with the criteria set by the imperial religious establishment:

58. Umur describes these exhortations as follows: "The best known of the learned class give advice and counsel [to those in attendance]. They condemn such immoral practices as dishonesty, rape, carousing, and gambling, and so they encourage the fostering of brotherhood among the Muslims and they give especially effective advice and counsel" (Umur 1949, 32).

59. My friend may be "forgetting" that public prayers were sometimes still spoken in Pontic Greek in some of the villages of Çaykara. See chap. 5, note 38, for further comment on Pontic Greek in the district of Of.

> Then when the hodjas have finished preaching, the certificates are awarded. Each of the hodjas who are awarding certificates has a notebook (*defter*) with the certificate written out, with its heading, a chain of attribution (*silsile*), and the name of the student (*molla*). He reads it out and awards it. Thus all the students receive their certificates. At the end, a hodja recites a short prayer. He announces the names of the students. He asks blessings on the people of the assembly, and he asks that the angels (*melek*) give the news of their having attended. He concludes by saying, "Let there be another one like it."

The accomplishment of the teachers and the students has enabled the villagers to gain merit and honor before God, but precisely as a proof that they are not just simple villagers. They have attended the assembly in hopes of seeing and listening such that they will be able to live as good and proper Muslims.

As he brought such an image before his mind's eye once again, my friend also recalled the contrary hodja who had been dispatched to address the women:

> The "contrary" hodja who had been sent to the women had been listening to the proceedings from afar.[60] Now, at the end, he returned and insisted on speaking. He came running up, saying to the people of the gathering, "O Assembly!" (*Ey cemaat!*). At first the hodjas tried to silence him, but they reluctantly agreed that he might speak. An elderly man, he launched into criticisms of some of the younger hodjas present. He accused one of them, who was assigned to one of the district mosques to which pilgrimages were made, of improperly accepting gifts from the people. As he made these remarks, the hodja who was being attacked began to bow his head in shame, but the contrary hodja hotly continued with his criticisms.

The contrary hodja has crossed a line. The criticism of others by appeal to religious learning results in belittling and shaming of others. The gift of expert knowledge and performance to the assembly should enable them to experience the pleasure of sociability, not mutual conflict and discord. All those present begin to remark on this difference:

> The people in the assembly began to murmur. He is not preaching to us; he is insulting individuals (*vaaz etmiyor, hakaret ediyor*). One of the hodjas then shouted out, "Don't tell us stories, preach to the people!"

60. My friend was well known for his ability to provide entertaining accounts of individual characters, reflecting their speech and behavior. The translation suffers from the absence of his mimicking of accents, facial expressions, and gestures.

> (*Halka vaaz et, bize atma!*). Finally the contrary hodja desisted. The people of the assembly scattered to the different houses, where they were then served baklava and visited with one another.[61]

The contrary hodja is silenced by a call for him to serve the assembly by exhorting and encouraging them, not by criticizing. The graduation ceremony is an occasion for both recognizing the achievement and enjoying the rewards of a discipline of Islamic belief and practice. If these rewards will only be experienced in full measure in the next world, they are partially available in this world through the pleasure of sociability. The granting of authorizing certificates having concluded, the villagers go to their separate groups of families and friends, where they enjoy one another's company.

CONCLUSION

The granting of authorizing certificates came at the end of years of effort on the part of teachers and students. In principle, if not always in fact, these efforts consisted of memorizing the Koran, learning to read and speak classical Arabic, and the mastery of some secondary canonical texts. At the same time, the graduation celebration was also a very special occasion for the villagers who attended them. By taking part in them, the inhabitants of a remote rural landscape, both men and women, could lay claim to being something much more than impoverished and ignorant villagers. During these occasions they could demonstrate to themselves that they were good and proper Muslims, and also participants in an imperial civilization whose foundations lay in the Islamic religion. This is why their engagement in and celebration of religious learning was so closely aligned with the imperial religious establishment.

My friend's description attributed to the graduation ceremony the quality of theater, with a multiplicity of performances and audiences. First of all, of course, the teachers and students, as well as the attendees assembled, performed for a divine audience who was beseeched to respond with blessing and favor. But the teachers and students also performed for one another, just as they also performed for the assembly, and the assembly performed for them. In the wings of this theater, somewhere offstage, there were yet other audiences that have gone unmentioned in my interlocutor's account.

During the later imperial period (nineteenth century), one of these other audiences would have been provincial governors, district administra-

61. The text is based on an interview that took place during the fall of 1967.

tors, judicial authorities, and military officers of the imperial system. All these state officials, who were in a position to tax, conscript, arrest, punish, and coerce, might have been impressed by a district population who so diligently took its proper place in the imperial system. So the Oflus would have been claiming a moral standing in the eyes of state officials who represented a regime that sponsored Islamic belief and practice.

But now, with this official audience in mind, let us consider the moment when the professors, academies, and students first appeared and proliferated during the post-classical imperial period (late seventeenth to early nineteenth century). During these years, all the higher state officials just mentioned would have been far away and out of sight since they had been locally replaced by aghas, mansions, family lines, and parties. These local representatives of the state system exercised the same sovereign powers as higher state officials, but they had a very different relationship with the district populations.

The rise of the aghas, mansions, family lines, and parties, let us recall, was coincident with the militarization of the population, hence the principle of force of numbers and the compromise of legal statues and judicial procedures. By local memory and tradition, the rivalry among the aghas grouped in different factions had led to anarchy and disorder, the resort to talion and the spread of vendetta. But, all this admitted, the legitimacy of aghas, mansions, family lines, and parties was also directly linked with official Islam. The aghas, mansions, family lines, and parties were local branches of the imperial military and religious establishment, but took the form of broad and deep interpersonal associations that comprised a substantial proportion of the masculine population.

So the aghas, mansions, family lines, and parties were doubly linked to the official Islam of the imperial religious establishment. First, like state officials, they claimed to exercise sovereign power in an imperial system whose legitimacy was underpinned by official Islam. And second, unlike state officials, their claim to exercise sovereign power was entirely dependent on their position in interpersonal associations based on a discipline of official Islam. This being the case, they were more significant than state officials as an audience whom ordinary villagers might hope to impress by the performance of a discipline of official Islamic belief and practice. Moreover, in so impressing them, the ordinary villagers might also advance a claim to being true and better Muslims than those who ruled them in the name of official Islam.

And so, whatever the precise origins of professors, academies, and students in the district of Of, the aghas, mansions, family lines, and parties would have provided a strong incentive for the broadening and deepening of the influence of official Islam at the expense of other versions of Islam. Ordinary townsmen and villagers, whether affiliated or not with the aghas, mansions, family lines, and parties, would have been inclined to claim moral standing and social prestige by the performance of the discipline of official Islam. And as for those who were not affiliated, they would have been inclined to align themselves with the local representatives of the imperial religious establishment.

So the rise of aghas, mansions, family lines, and parties was coordinated with the rise of professors, academies, and students. As some Oflus became soldiers of the aghas, so, too, other Oflus became students of the hodjas. The result was the "imperialization" of personhood and community, most notably in the district of Of, but also generally in all the old provinces of Trabzon. As a consequence, then, of an especially far-reaching process of ottomanization, the inhabitants of Trabzon became adherents of an official Islam to the relative exclusion of all the other kinds of Islam that were otherwise available in Asia Minor during the later centuries of the Ottoman Empire.

Osman Pasha brought the post-classical phase of the imperial period to an end in the coastal region in the 1830s, but he did not suppress leading individuals, large family groupings, district networks, and coastal coalitions. This being the case, ordinary townsmen and villagers would have continued to align themselves with the official Islam of the imperial system. As a consequence, aghas and hodjas continued to be a part of the later imperial period, right up to the declaration of the Turkish Republic. As we have seen, however, the two representatives of the post-classical period met different fates after the declaration of the Turkish Republic. By the 1960s, leading individuals and large family groupings occupied a central place in public associations, but religious teachers and students were more or less reviled by state officials as subversives and outlaws. I shall conclude with a few remarks on the Kemalist attempt to disestablish Islam.

I have already cited the comments of a retired schoolteacher who had described how the practitioners of *imaming* had defeated the ban on unauthorized religious instruction, if not during the 1930s then certainly during the 1940s. On another occasion, however, I had met a second retired schoolteacher who had also been assigned to Kadahor [Çaykara] during these same two decades. Unlike the first, this second schoolteacher had always been a firm supporter of the Kemalist program of reforms, and, not surprisingly, he had a very different recollection of the local reception of the new regime.[62] He recalled that a large speakers' platform had been constructed in the sub-district center of Kadahor on the occasion of the tenth anniversary (1933) of the declaration of the Turkish Republic. Some of the best known of the hodjas (*âlimler*) had been invited to address the crowd, and each of them had spoken eloquently in praise of the Turkish Republic. He went on to conclude that the residents of the upper western valley-system had accepted the Kemalist program of reforms, never rebelling against them as had some of the residents of Rize.

Although the second retired schoolteacher was overstating his case, he nonetheless made an important point. There were many representatives of the old tradition of religious study who became nationalist supporters, and even nationalist activists.[63] On the other hand, some other representatives of the old tradition, whose numbers were no doubt very considerable, would more reluctantly and hesitantly transform themselves from Muslim subjects into secular citizens. The schoolteacher himself continued with the following recollection seemingly designed to minimize this fact:

> I was teaching in the middle school of [Kadahor] during the year 1935. This was the peak of the program of secular reforms that had been put in place by Atatürk. A report came to the sub-district [Kadahor] that a certain individual was giving lessons from a book in the old [Arabic] script. Members of the police, the gendarmerie, and myself set out to arrest this man.[64] This was not long after the events at Menemem [a local uprising in western Turkey calling for the restoration of the sacred law of Islam].[65] As our party approached the village, a line of women [moving along a narrow trail] were returning with baskets on their backs [having been gathering crops or fodder from the fields]. When they saw us coming, one dropped her basket and ran to warn the man. The police came by one path and the gendarmerie came by another [to

62. I met this man in Sürmene in 1988. He was nearly ninety years old and had been retired for many years.

63. We have already encountered two, Hasan Umur and the school secretary. Another interesting example is Mustafa Cansız, reported to have been well read in both the Islamic sciences and Western philosophy. He is also said to have joined the Turkish Workers Party (*Türk İşci Partisi*) during the 1970s.

64. Most secular schoolteachers would have been ardent Kemalists during the 1930s.

65. The uprising occurred at a town near Izmir on December 23, 1930. More than a score of men were hanged in the aftermath. The schoolteacher may have incorrectly remembered the date of the incident in Kadahor, or, more probably, the events at Menemem may have still been fresh in his mind five years later when he accompanied the gendarmerie to the village.

> prevent the man from escaping]. The man tried to run away but he was apprehended. He was shaking with fear. They had a warrant for his arrest. But he was ninety years old. They took his books, but they didn't have the heart to take him in. He was not involved in politics. He was only teaching. They decided to put the warrant away. They did not destroy it. It would be overlooked.[66]

The example, which takes the form of a traditional moral teaching (*misal*), even though the speaker is a Kemalist, makes two points. It was only the very aged who had been unable to accept the new regime, and state officials had treated these individuals with discretion and humanity.

The Kemalists were attempting to displace Islamist associational virtues from public life so that they might be replaced with civic associational virtues. To do so, they would have to break open the closed circles of interpersonal association that dominated the institutions and organization of the old regime. Otherwise there would have been no hope of broadening and deepening the circle of citizenship. And so they were obliged to mount a challenge to, if not entirely defeat, the old imperial religious establishment. But our concern here is not intentions but rather the results of Kemalist policies in the eastern coastal districts.

As we have seen in the previous chapter, leading individuals from large family groupings gradually aligned themselves with the new nationalist standards of public life so that they were Kemalist rather than ottomanist in orientation by the close of the second decade of the Turkish Republic. It was not the old aghas that did so of course, but their sons, grandsons, nephews, and grandnephews. First they donned hats, neckties, and suits at an early period. Later they learned to defend their different party ideologies and policies. Their ability to reposition themselves with changes in the state system had always been a feature of their very existence as a local elite. They therefore instinctively sought to retain connections with state officials just as state officials sought to retain them as their assistants and intermediaries.

On the other hand, leading individuals, family groupings, district networks, and coastal coalitions were circles of interpersonal associations based on a discipline of Islamic sociability. Hence the local elites in many of the eastern coastal districts, Kemalist on the surface and Islamist below the surface, still monopolized public power and resources on the basis of the old, not the new, associational virtues. The disestablishment of Islam had there-

66. The citations, which are edited versions of my field notes, were recorded in 1988.

fore not led unambiguously to the opening up of public life beyond the old circles of interpersonal association. It had led instead to Kemalo-Islamism.

As a consequence, many ordinary villagers and townsmen could not participate as citizens in the public life of the nation-state since they were prevented from doing so by closed circles of interpersonal association. These ordinary villagers and townsmen were therefore left with their older claims to moral standing and social dignity based on Islamic belief and practice. So then a large segment of the population continued to resent its exclusion and rejection by the state system when it should have rather recognized and accepted them. And with the beginning of the multiparty period, this segment of the population became a "floating" electorate for which every political party would attempt to provide dock and anchor. Their combined efforts would eventually lead to the end of the hodjas from Of.

In the 1930s, state officials had disestablished Islam, abandoning the religious market in provincial Turkey to the low end of the religious tradition where hodjas would proliferate like squash. For a few years, from the 1940s through the 1960s, the hodjas of Of enjoyed a near monopoly as suppliers for the continuing demand for religious expertise. But sometime in the 1970s, the expansion of the state system of religious education brought an end to the old tradition of religious study in the mountain villages of Of.[67] The problems of access to public power and resources had not been resolved. The political parties had only agreed that the state should reclaim the sponsorship and propagation of official Islam.

67. A new faculty of theology was opened in Ankara in 1949, and the first new İmam-Hatip schools began to be opened in 1951. By the 1980s there were nine faculties of theology and 376 middle-level and 341 *lycée* level İmam-Hatip schools enrolling about a quarter-million students. See Akşit 1991, 147. By the 1980s, a school for prayer-leaders and sermon-givers had been opened in the town of Of. By the early 1990s, hundreds of students were enrolled in two İmam-Hatip schools in the district.

PART II

THE DISSEMINATION OF AN IMPERIAL MODERNITY

The Ottoman Province of Trabzon

3 Horizons

Markets and States

TOPOGRAPHY AND ENVIRONMENT

The Pontic Mountains run from west to east across the upper tier of the peninsula of Asia Minor.[1] The northern slopes of these mountains comprise a well-watered coastal region with a temperate climate. The southern slopes belong to the more arid, less vegetated, hot-in-summer, cold-in-winter interior highlands of Anatolia. This contrast between coast and plateau intensifies as the mountains rise from west to east (see map 2).

Along all the eastern segment of the coastline, from Ordu to Hopa, there are no large deltas, flat coastal strips are more infrequent and narrower, and the landscape is almost everywhere broken and precipitous. In the foothills near the shoreline, little hamlets with half-timbered houses pepper the foothills, sometimes barely visible among the trees and brush. Around each hamlet there are maize and bean gardens prepared by hand rather than by plough.[2] Away from the shoreline in the upland valleys, the rainfall gradually decreases, the valleys are more deeply cut, and the mountains become steeper. Here the houses, almost always timbered, are sometimes clustered together on a promontory or in a valley, sometimes dispersed across the face of a mountainside (see fig. 6). The villagers are therefore forced to construct narrow terraces on the sheer mountainsides for their maize and bean gardens, sometimes securing themselves with ropes to tend them.

1. See Bryer and Winfield (1985, 1–16) for a more detailed description of the topography and ecology of the Pontic region.

2. Issawi (1980, 199–200) lists the distribution of crops in the province of Trabzon in1863 by percent of total quantity of agricultural production: wheat 6; barley 3; maize 52; oats 3; tobacco 10; vines 1; other 25 (beans 10, nuts 5, vegetables 4, potatoes 2, olives 2, mulberry 1, hemp 1).

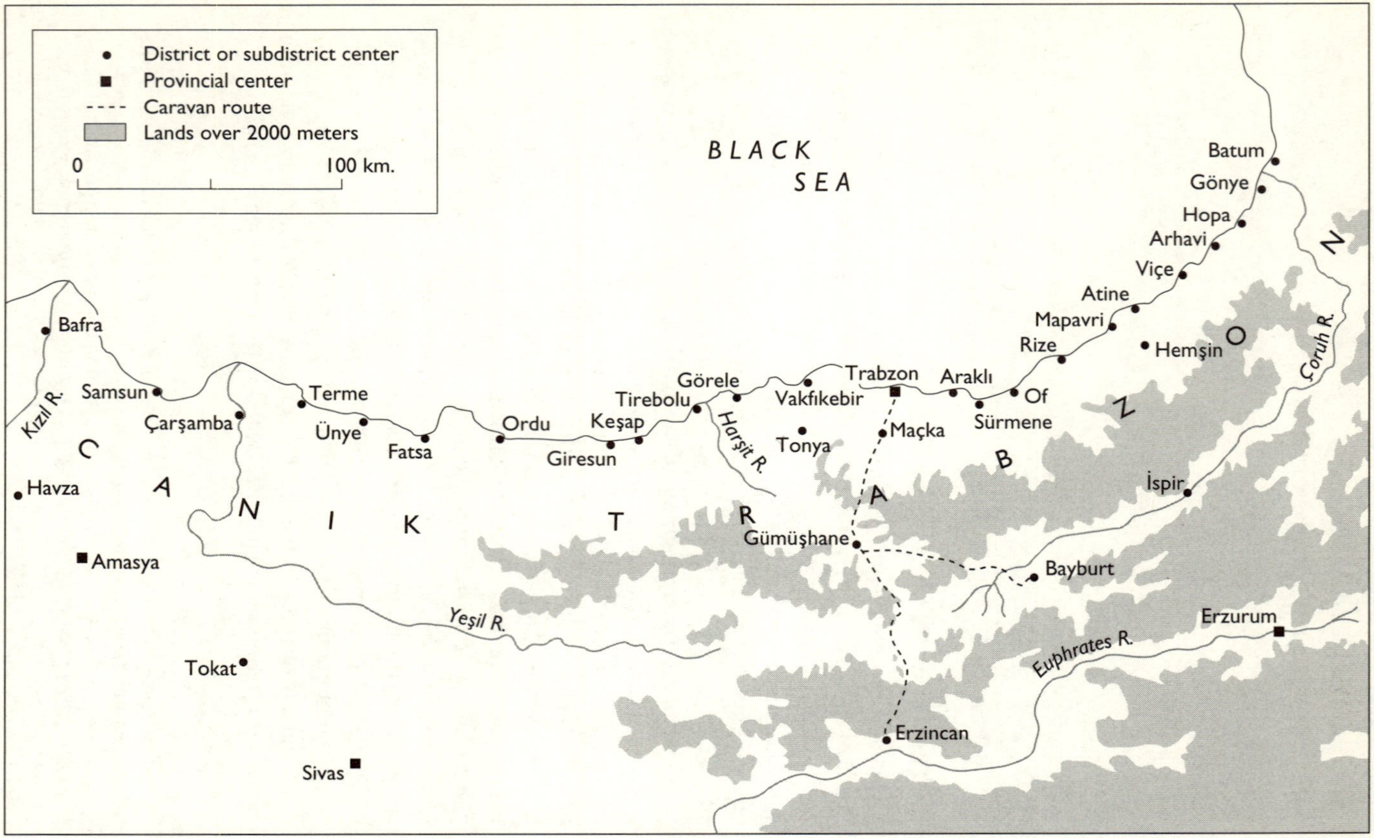

Map 2. Lands of Canık and Trabzon (early nineteenth century)

Figure 6. Wooden houses in the high mountains.

Owing to the uneven landscape, level cropland and open pasture are at a premium.[3] To this day neither animal power nor machine power has ever been widely used in agriculture in the region. Along this section of the coast, nothing more than a meager living can be extracted from farming and herding. Farming is usually limited to horticulture. Herding is usually limited to a few cows. Large estates have always been the exception rather than the rule. Nonetheless, some of the area's inhabitants are able to become something other than subsistence farmers and herders, given the relative absence of landlords and overseers. Leaving their garden farms to the care of women, the men of the eastern coastal region can look for work elsewhere in towns and cities of Anatolia.[4] As a consequence, the residents of this entirely rural area have always included impressive numbers of soldiers, teachers, merchants, craftsmen, sailors, fishermen, peddlers, and laborers.

As one moves from the west to the east, the high Pontic peaks gradually come to define an "island on the land," set apart from the remainder of Asia Minor.[5] East of the vicinity of the town of Trabzon, the littoral is not so much a greener version of Anatolia, but another kind of world altogether. Streams and rivers running north and south divide the entire eastern region into side-by-side valley-systems separated by densely vegetated foothills, falling and rising hundreds of meters to and from the water courses. Moving from one valley to another is often impractical owing to undergrowth and ravines. Instead, one must descend to the coastline, travel along the narrow shore, and then ascend into the next valley. Not so long ago, such a trek had to be made on foot or by horse. For lack of roadways, not even a cart could make its way through the foothills or across the rocky beaches. So it is that townsmen jokingly claim that the villagers did not learn of the invention of the wheel until the arrival of motor transport.

3. This paragraph is written in the present tense. It describes patterns that were still widespread when I first visited the coastal region in the 1960s. These patterns have since become less prevalent because of the growth in the cash economy and increasing migration to the larger cities.

4. An anonymous reader for the University of California Press has reminded me that women commonly tend the fields in many parts of Anatolia. My analysis is a comparative one. Because of the character of agriculture in the coastal region, the practice of labor migration by the male population is arguably older and more general than elsewhere in Anatolia.

5. I have taken the phrase from the title of the book by Carey McWilliams (1973), who applied it to southern California, another coastal enclave of a most different kind.

By contrast, the farming and herding world across the Pontic mountain chain is entirely different in character.[6] The landscape is open and treeless, sometimes rocky and barren. Winters are cold. Summers are hot. Dry-farming (wheat and barley), stream irrigation (rice and vegetables), and goats and sheep (yogurt and cheese) are the basis of subsistence agriculture. Ploughs and carts are pulled by draft animals. Houses are constructed of mud bricks. Timber, being scarce, is used only for the roof poles, doors, and sashes. Until recently, the only fuel was cattle dung, which was molded into patties (*tezek*) and dried in the sun. Highly efficient ground ovens (*tandır*) are the means for both cooking and heating.

To the north and south of the Pontic chain, rural life is governed by contrasting requirements and possibilities. Crops, flocks, tools, building materials, house designs, kitchen fuel, diet and cuisine, dress and manners, bodies and faces, accents and dialects are different. And some time ago, for a span of centuries, language, religion, and state were also not the same.

ETHNIC FRAGMENTS AND LINGUISTIC ARCHAISMS

Following the Byzantine defeat at Manzikert in 1071, Turkic pastoral peoples began to enter and occupy many sections of Asia Minor, changing the character of its villages and towns. By the thirteenth century, the interior highlands of northeastern Anatolia had been under Turco-Islamic rule for more than a century, and a majority of the population had become Turkish by language and Muslim by religion.[7] This transformation had not always come about with the displacement of the older Byzantine peoples. In many places, groups of Greek-speakers and Armenian-speakers had gradually assimilated themselves to the newcomers, first losing their languages to acquire Turkish, then losing their religion to become Muslim.[8] In contrast, the older Byzantine peoples of the eastern littoral were neither Turkicized nor Islamized until a much later date, and then by a different path.

The eastern coastal region, first as the province of Chaldia in the Byzantine Empire (until 1204), then as the Greek Empire of Trebizond (until 1461), had for a long while remained outside the orbit of the Turco-Islamic states of the interior highlands. Finally capitulating to Sultan Mehmet II,

6. This paragraph, like the preceding, is also written in the present tense, even though some of the patterns, such as the use of dung for fuel, are less prevalent than when I first visited the region in the 1960s.

7. Cahen 1968, 145–55, and Vryonis 1971, chap. 3.

8. By such a sequence, a process of social assimilation with the Turkic majority would appear to have been the precondition of conversion to Islam (Bryer 1975).

this last mainland fragment of Byzantium subsequently reemerged as the province (*paşalık*) of Trabzon. For more than a century, most of the older Byzantine peoples remained relatively unaffected by incorporation. Then, during the course of the second century of Ottoman rule, as a consequence of both conversion and immigration, the large majority of the inhabitants became Muslim. Even so, substantial numbers of the Muslims, most of them descendants of the older Byzantine peoples, continued to speak mother tongues other than Turkish. The eastern coastal region therefore stands as an "exception" twice over to what had happened in the interior highlands.[9] A Muslim majority did not emerge until the seventeenth century, almost four hundred years after the rest of northeastern Anatolia. And when this Muslim majority did emerge at last, its constituents spoke a variety of languages, such as Turkish, Lazi, Greek, and Armenian.

As both Anthony Bryer and Xavier de Planhol have pointed out, the high Pontic chain played a decisive role in determining the different course of history in the eastern coastal region.[10] The arrival of large numbers of Turkic pastoral peoples had guaranteed that the population in northeastern Anatolia would be relatively quickly Turkicized and Islamized. In contrast, the eastern littoral was far less accessible to the semi-nomadic, stock-keeping peoples of the interior highlands. The passes that cut through the mountains consisted of little more than narrow and twisting tracks, buried in deep snows during the winter. Descending into the valleys, these tracks traversed a landscape ideally suited for defensive purposes: virgin forests shrouded in mists at the upper elevations and a dense undergrowth of bushes and vines at the lower elevations.[11] By these circumstances, the rural societies of the coastal valleys were in a position to limit the numbers of pastoral newcomers who settled in their midst, just as the Greek Empire of Trebizond was in a position to resist military invasion and occupation by the Turco-Islamic states of the interior.

Viewed as a great mountain barrier, the Pontic chain explains why the rural societies of the eastern littoral were slow to change, as well as why the Greek Empire of Trebizond was to endure so long. Otherwise, topography and environment did not consistently function to isolate the coastal re-

9. Bryer 1975, 116–17.

10. Planhol (1963a, 1963b, 1966a, 1966b) was the first to point out the role of topography and environment in retarding Turkish settlement. Bryer (1975, 118 n. 11) restates and revises Planhol's conclusions.

11. Cf. Bryer 1970, 33–34.

gion from the outside world.[12] Even as the high mountains and dense vegetation defined an "island on the land," a kind of refuge area set apart from the interior highlands, its temperate climate and fertile soils were powerful magnets that lured peoples into it. The two opposed qualities of the landscape, defensibility balanced against desirability, led to a pattern of ethnic fragmentation. For whenever outsiders did succeed in penetrating the coastal region, they tended to retain elements of their distinctiveness.[13]

By the early medieval period, before the arrival of Turkic pastoral peoples in Anatolia, the northern slopes of the eastern Pontic Mountains were occupied by peoples who had colonized the region from different directions. Kartvelian-speakers from the Caucasus, eventually to be called the Lazi, had settled its eastern precincts. Greek-speakers from Sinop, eventually to be called Pontics, had settled the western precincts. Armenian-speakers from the interior highlands, eventually to be called Hemşin, had entered the eastern upper valleys above the Kartvelian-speakers and Greek-speakers.[14] Thus, the coastal region had inexorably drawn peoples from neighboring territories into its valleys, complicating the ethnic composition of the coastal region.

Almost surely, Turkic peoples appeared in most of the coastal valleys soon after their arrival in the interior highlands, perhaps as early as the eleventh century.[15] It is even likely that some of these early arrivals assimilated themselves to the existing inhabitants, losing their language and their religion, only to get them back centuries later.[16] Whatever the case,

12. Cf. Bryer 1975, 116–17, who writes of "a historic Pontic separatism." I do not mean to refute this observation entirely, but rather to expose a contrary dimension of topography and environment in the coastal region.

13. Planhol (1966b, 1972) implicitly recognizes this feature of the coastal region in his later articles on comparative geography. See his account of the Pontic, the Elburz, and the Lebanon mountains as "shelter mountains." Planhol attributes the high population of each of these coastal regions to flight from the nomadic invasions occurring in the interior. I would argue that outsiders were consistently attracted to these temperate and fertile regions over the long term.

14. See the sections on Laz and Hemşin in Andrews and Benninghaus (1989).

15. The presence of small numbers of Turkic peoples in all the coastal region during the twelfth century seems likely but is not well documented. Hasan Umur records a court case (1951, Case No. 1, dated 1575/983) involving Turcomans (*Türkmen taifesi*) who were transporting goods from the shoreline up the river valleys of the district of Of.

16. In the 1960s, it was common for Greek-speaking, Armenian-speaking, and Lazi-speaking Muslims in the eastern coastal region to claim their forefathers had been Turks. Although such claims were no doubt inspired by nationalist ideology, they cannot be discounted entirely on these grounds alone. For example, Bilgin

Turkic pastoral peoples did not initially enter and occupy the coastal region in large numbers, save where the mountains were lower and the landscape less vegetated. Çepni Turcomans, tribally organized pastoral peoples of heterodox Shi' background, first began to settle along the western littoral in the vicinity of Sinop, then reversed direction to move back toward the eastern littoral. By the thirteenth century, the emirates of these peoples governed the coastal region between Ordu and Sinop. And by the fourteenth century, Çepni Turcomans were moving still further eastward, settling the more accessible lower valleys just to the west of the town of Trabzon.[17]

At the moment of Ottoman incorporation, the overall distribution of ethnic groups in the early province of Trabzon can be roughly described as follows.[18] Greek-speakers inhabited most of the lower and upper coastal valleys near Trabzon, both to the east and to the west. This inner core of Greek-speakers was flanked by Kartvelian-speakers living in the valleys east of Rize and by Turkic-speakers living in the valleys west of Giresun. Groups of Armenian-speakers inhabited some of the upper valleys above the Kartvelian-speakers in the east.[19] Groups of Greek-speakers inhabited some of the western upper valleys above the Turkic-speakers in the west.[20]

(1990, 220–22) finds individuals with Turkish names who were paying the *ispenç*, a tax imposed on Christians, not Muslims. He argues that these were early Turcoman immigrants who had become Orthodox.

17. Bryer (1975, 127–29) places thirteenth-century Turkish emirates in the vicinity of the present-day towns of Çarşamba and Ünye. According to Bryer (1975, 132), the Çepnis had occupied the coastal region up to the Harşit River not far from the regional capital. According to Sümer (1992, 48–49), they had entered the areas of Eynesil-Kürtün, Dereli, and Giresun-Tirebolu.

18. According to Birken (1976, 151–53), who cites Evliya Çelebi, the sub-provinces (*sancak*) of the Ottoman province (*paşalık*) of Trabzon would have been Batum, Gönye, Rize, Trabzon, Maçka, and Ordu. Gümüşhane, which lies across the Pontic Mountains, was not part of the old province of Trabzon until later and not a separate sub-province thereof until 1847. Canık, the western coastal region from Ordu to Sinop, was not part of the old province of Trabzon until the later nineteenth century.

19. These Armenians are loosely termed "the Hemşin" by themselves and by outside observers. This name associates them with a specific upper valley complex where today there is a district and town of that same name in the contemporary province of Rize. See the entries for Hemşin in Andrews and Benninghaus (1989) and, especially, Benninghaus (1989a).

20. By indirect comparative evidence, it is probable that Greek-speakers had retreated to the upper valleys of the western coastal region with the arrival of the Çepni Turcomans along the shoreline. For example, Poutouridou (1997–98), citing Vakalopoulos, notes that the retreat of Greek populations to remote and mountainous regions was a common occurrence in the Balkans during the Ottoman period. Along these lines, Greek Orthodox villagers formed new settlements in the upper

This pattern of settlement then became further complicated during the period of Ottoman rule. From the later sixteenth century through the seventeenth century, large numbers of Muslim settlers, most of who were Turkish-speaking, but not necessarily Çepni Turcomans, moved into various parts of the eastern coastal region. Their arrival appears to have led to relocations and conversions among some portion of the Christian population, thereby enhancing the mixed and merged character of local communal groupings. Just as some number of Turkic pastoral peoples had probably become Orthodox during the earlier period, many of the older Byzantine peoples most certainly became Muslim during the later.[21]

Given the traces of many peoples and languages in the coastal region, travelers were consistently perplexed about the nature of its peoples, during the Roman, Byzantine, and Ottoman periods, down to the present. By what name is the population to be called? What language do they speak? With what religion are they affiliated? These questions had no simple answers given the situation of ethnic fragmentation. Groups of different peoples were unevenly distributed across the landscape, sometimes interspersed among one another, and always mixing with one another. In one valley one language would be spoken, but in the neighboring valley another language might be spoken. Furthermore, in the same valley, one language might be spoken at the lower elevations and another at the higher elevations. At the same time, several languages would be spoken in the lowland and highland markets.

But even more puzzling to outsiders than the ethnic and linguistic complexity of the population was the fact that ethnicity and language were not correlated with political identity and religious affiliation during the later Ottoman period.[22] In the coastal region, as we shall see in later chapters, the older Byzantine peoples became Muslim by participating in an imperial project rather than by assimilating to a Turco-Islamic majority.

---

valleys of the district of Of (eastern Trabzon) during the century following Ottoman incorporation. See in this regard the analysis of the Ottoman registers in the district of Of in chap. 5. The matter is disputed. Planhol (1963a, 1963b, 1966b) believes that traces of Greek Orthodox villages in the upper valleys to the west of the Trabzon were of ancient provenance. Bryer (1970, 45–47; 1975, 118 n. 11) argues that they were of more recent origin, probably no older than the seventeenth century. I suggest they may be correlated with the arrival of the Çepnis along the western coast.

21. Lowry 1977.

22. As Bryer (1969, 193) has put it, "the ethnic origins of the eastern Pontic peoples (18 are listed in an unofficial census of 1911) are probably past disentangling."

SOCIETY AND STATE IN THE PONTIC ENCLAVE

The rural societies of the eastern coastal region have been adjudicated, taxed, and conscripted by a state system from the medieval period, during which time the town of Trabzon consistently served as the region's administrative, military, religious, and commercial center. As Bryer has noted, the structure of the state system has been remarkably constant over the centuries.[23] The valley-systems that constituted districts (*bandon*) in the ninth-century Byzantine province (*thema*) of Chaldia reappeared as districts in the Greek Empire of Trebizond. Later, they became districts in the sixteenth-century province (*paşalık*) of Trabzon, and then reappeared once again as districts in the twentieth-century provinces (*vilayet*) of the Turkish Republic. This structure points to the strategic position of the regional capital and its links to other major markets and ports.

Walled and fortified from the medieval period, the town of Trabzon was situated on a rocky coastal promontory rising between two ravines. Some of the best anchorages along the eastern coast are in the vicinity, and a route from the town through the mountains is passable during both the summer and the winter. An entrepôt for maritime and overland commerce, the regional capital was inhabited by officials, mercenaries, merchants, craftsmen, travelers, and adventurers of diverse backgrounds from different homelands.[24] The rural societies flanking the regional capital were in contact with the more cosmopolitan society that appeared there, and some number of their residents lived and worked in its administrative, military, religious, and commercial centers. As we shall see, however, their links with the outside world beyond their valleys was not restricted to this single channel.

An early hint of the special relationship between rural societies and the state system appears in the works of Procopius. The sixth-century Byzantine historian refers to the inhabitants of the coastal region as the "Romans who are called Pontics." In so choosing his words, Procopius designated rural societies of the coastal valleys as a provincial population of the Byzantine

23. The coastal valleys from Rize to Giresun were the core districts of this regional state system, the farther coastal valleys, from Hopa eastward and from Ordu westward, its fringe districts (Bryer 1969, 194–95; Bryer and Winfield 1985, 10, 178).

24. There were good anchorages not far to the east and west along a coastline that otherwise featured very few natural harbors (Bryer and Winfield 1985, 7). A mountain path, suitable for animal transport, cut through the Pontic Mountains at the Zigana Pass (2025 meters) to reach the interior highlands.

Empire. He therefore conceived of a collection of different peoples speaking different languages as representatives of an imperial civilization. Much later, during the time of the Greek Empire of Trebizond, outsiders had considered the inhabitants of the coastal region to be primarily "Laz." Once again, the term in question characterized a diverse collection of peoples as the provincial population of what was then a "regional" imperial civilization.[25]

In the eighteenth century the same pattern appears again, even though the population in question was no longer either Byzantine or Christian. Outsiders commonly used the term "Laz" to describe what was now a large Muslim majority in the coastal region as a provincial population of another imperial civilization, that of the Ottoman Empire. As before, this provincial population included a diverse collection of peoples. Descendants of Turkic-speakers, Kartvelian-speakers, Greek-speakers, and Armenian-speakers had aligned themselves, however imperfectly, with official Ottoman Islam, and all of them spoke greater or lesser snatches of Ottoman Turkish. Since none of the four groups had previously featured these attributes (Turkic pastoral peoples included), they each separately indicate a strong tendency for the residents of the coastal valleys to position themselves in the larger social, economic, and political world beyond their scattered hamlets.[26]

While geography worked to preserve ethnic fragments and linguistic archaisms, it also worked to homogenize identities and relationships. The terrain of the eastern coastal region isolated the residents of the coastal valleys from local processes of social assimilation, but it also encouraged, if not necessitated, that they connect themselves with the outside world. Each valley linked oversea routes with overland trade routes. Some had good anchorages along their shorelines. Some provided easy access to the interior highlands through mountain passes. Some were located near major markets of Anatolia. Some combined all these features, so that they rivaled the regional capital at Trabzon. At the same time, each valley was also a total ecological system. Every year individuals, families, and communities moved up and down the valley. Petty traders, craftsmen, and wage laborers moved from the markets of the coastal lowlands to the markets of the interior highlands. Family members moved cattle and flocks in stages through the upper valleys, gradually ascending to the highland pastures in the spring

25. Bryer 1966, 1967, and Benninghaus 1989b.

26. The Turkic-speakers, for whom this might seem to be a natural tendency, are in fact especially revealing as an example. Many of them arrive as tribally organized Çepni Turcomans of heterodox Shi'i background, but they soon become Sunni Muslims who identify with and participate in the imperial system (Sümer 1992, 53).

and descending to their lowland hamlets in the fall. Entire villages moved between a winter settlement near the shoreline and a summer settlement in the mountains.

As homelands, the valleys were not what they first appeared to be, motley groups of people living in isolated hamlets dispersed across the landscape. The valleys were instead transit systems whose inhabitants had a large stake in the security of the people, animals, and goods moving through them. All the residents of each valley-system, whether lowlanders or highlanders, therefore had an interest in knowing one another and cooperating with one another. Accordingly, each valley-system comprised an integrated social network. That is to say, all its residents were more or less organized for the purpose of communicating information, organizing cooperative ventures, and providing mutual assistance. In this respect, the peoples of the coastal region, densely settled and agriculturally impoverished, were also oriented toward outside markets of all kinds, for labor, skills, services, and goods. And given the existence of networks of relationships and lines of communication inside their homelands, they were in a position to make their way in the world abroad beyond their coastal valleys.

As a consequence, the rural areas of the coastal valleys have been inhabited for many, many centuries by cash-croppers, soldiers, miners, carpenters, sailors, metal-workers, weavers, rope-makers, dyers, masons, cooks, laborers, and traders, as well as a small minority of extortionists, counterfeiters, smugglers, gunrunners, kidnappers, bandits, pirates, and assassins. The residents of the rural areas have plied all these legitimate and illegitimate activities in their homelands since ancient times, but they have also left their homelands to go abroad as migrants when there was an opportunity to do so. Similarly, just as these rural societies have been oriented to external market conditions, so, too, outsiders were always in a position to become insiders among them. Certain kinds of "specialists" have always infiltrated the coastal region when they had something to offer its resident peoples.[27] Among them we find animal transporters, religious teachers, military officers, stone-layers, wood-carvers, metalworkers, shipwrights, and so on. In this respect, the coastal region, which is otherwise completely rural in character, bears a resemblance to an urban center.

27. Many of the individuals whom I encountered in Rize, Of, and Sürmene told stories of their forebears migrating into the coastal region from Anatolia, Syria, or Iraq. This was true even in the district of Of, which has the reputation of being among the more insular of the coastal districts.

There were, then, two contradictory sides to the rural societies of this segment of the coastal region. Their homelands served as isolated refuges where archaic traits and dialects were preserved. And yet, their homelands, while isolated refuges, were also connected with the outside world. Topography and environment did not have a single, undivided consequence for social life in the coastal region. It worked to fragment human groups at the level of mother tongue and family life even as it also worked to unify human groups at a level of entrepreneurial, governmental, and educational engagements.

The two opposed tendencies explain why the residents of the coastal region have more or less consistently had the reputation of hicks since the medieval period. They issued from their remote valleys with outlandish accents, manners, and dress, but, unlike other rural peoples, they were nonetheless consistently present and active in provincial centers. What is significant is not that they were dismissed as rustics, but rather that they were always on the scene in the towns and cities of Asia Minor, ready and available to be designated as countrified interlopers. The peoples of the coastal region were always striving to integrate themselves into a larger state society, even as they could rarely achieve urbanity and sophistication, since most of them retained contact with their rural homelands as refuges and hideouts.[28]

Once any group of people left the interior highlands, crossed the Pontic Mountains, and settled in the coastal region, their work habits and mental outlooks were inexorably transformed. Gradually, the newcomers found it more and more difficult to conceive of the local community as an entity in itself and they came to see themselves in relation to the commercial and governmental systems beyond their valley homelands. They tended, then, both as individuals and communities, to see themselves as participants in universal projects of power and truth. Once in the coastal region, the heterodox became orthodox and the illiterate became literate. They became

28. This may explain why indigenous populations of the coastal region have vanished without a trace. The "native" populations who are associated with the coastal region in ancient times have disappeared entirely by the early medieval period. See, for example, Bryer (1966; 1967, 161, 167), especially his comments on the Tzan. So it would seem that the "native" populations were unable to preserve elements of their parochial backgrounds, despite the defensive advantages of their homelands. Since the "natives" were not part of a regional society represented by a state system, one might guess that they were therefore absorbed by more experienced, colonizing peoples (Lazis, Greeks, Armenians, and Turks).

partisans first of Romanism and Byzantinism, then of Ottomanism and Nationalism.

A further comparison of the coastal region with the interior highlands brings to light the way in which local and global factors combined to reinforce a preoccupation with, as I have chosen to phrase it, "the horizon of elsewheres."

ECONOMIC FLEXIBILITY AND ELASTICITY

Across the Pontic chain in the interior highlands, subsistence farming and herding are demanding occupations, narrowly constrained by circumstances and resources. Winters are long, requiring the maintenance of sturdy houses, stables, and barns. In the absence of trees, fuel for cooking and heating is limited but necessary for any measure of comfort. Plough farming is not possible without large draft animals, which have to be maintained year-round. The growing season is short, so farm work intensifies at specific times, when family groups must work long and hard. During the warmer months, from March through November, there is a time to sow, a time to harvest, a time to gather and store fuel, a time to pasture and corral flocks, and a time to repair roofs and walls. Moreover, each household's activities cannot be organized independently from others. The fields of the villagers are mingled together at the periphery of their nucleated settlements. Fallowing, ploughing, harvesting, pasturing, manuring, and penning are virtually impossible without collective agreements and mutual assistance.

In contrast, the subsistence activities of family groups in the coastal region are not so closely defined by climate, labor power, resources, equipment, and community. In most places the growing season is long, almost year-round near the shoreline. Water is almost never in short supply, and wood for fuel is readily available. Each hamlet is more or less isolated in the midst of its own lands, and, in many places, it stands as a kind of little kingdom on a promontory or hilltop. As a result, the villagers, especially the majority in the lower valleys, are able to organize their subsistence activities more flexibly, coordinating them with other kinds of engagements and activities. The maize and bean gardens can always be made a little larger or a little smaller.[29] The planting of potatoes and squash can be expanded or

29. Maize had replaced millet as the staple crop in the province of Trabzon from the early seventeenth century. See Humlum (1942, 90) for the beginning of maize agriculture along the Black Sea coast. The adoption of maize would have presumably led to an increase in agricultural productivity. This increase may have consol-

contracted during the warmer months, just as the planting of cabbage and leeks can be expanded or contracted during the colder months. Since there is no need for oxen, ploughs, horses, and carts, subsistence activities can also be incrementally adjusted down to a bare minimum. There can always be a few more or a few less animals in the stable beneath the house, or even no animals at all.[30]

By virtue of the flexibility and elasticity of subsistence activities, those members of the household who preoccupy themselves with subsistence activities are variable in number. Some members of the household can be absent from the hamlet for long periods of time, even during the warmer months, without seriously interrupting the cycle of farming and herding activities. When other sources of income present themselves, some members of the households can leave. It is almost always men who do so. Those remaining, some of the men and all of the women, can scale back their subsistence activities accordingly. This allows for the coordination of subsistence farming and herding with itinerant trades and crafts. Such coordination was an ancient practice in the coastal region, and especially characteristic of the later centuries of the Ottoman Empire.

If a handicraft was seasonally in demand in a town of the interior highlands, some of the men of the coastal region learned it, temporarily migrated, and practiced it. If commercial possibilities arose in some section of Asia Minor, the Caucasus, eastern Europe, or the Middle East, some went there as petty traders and wage laborers.[31] If state officials were looking for soldiers and sailors, some took this chance to gain some experience abroad. As a consequence, the men of the coastal region were never entirely bound to the peasant way of life.[32] Their thinking and practice took into account opportunities that might appear over the horizon.[33] If they had a keen

idated the elasticity and flexibility of the subsistence economy, thereby leading to a stimulation of population growth through increasing labor migration.

30. During the 1960s, when labor migration to Germany was possible, some villages were virtually deserted of men during most of the year, save for those who were very young or old. Still, these villages continued to function as subsistence farms, perhaps no less productive than before.

31. In the last century, the Oflus were accustomed to migrating to Sevastapol, Sokhum, Anapa, and Batum for work. Some men told me they had heard their grandfathers speak of trips as traders to Rumania and the Crimea.

32. Some observers describe them as miserable farmers. Describing the Oflus, whom he visited briefly in 1872, Palgrave wrote, "Their best success is in pedlary and shop-keeping; their worst in agriculture; in handicraft, iron-work especially, they are tolerable; in masonry excellent" (PRO FO 526/8 p. 39, Jan. 29, 1873).

33. Hrand Andreasyan (Bijişkyan 1969, 61, n. 12) attributes to İnciciyan the remark that the people of Of were scattered in many different areas and that an im-

sense of their local origins, they nonetheless conceived themselves in relationship to all kinds of elsewheres, even to the point that subsistence became a secondary rather than primary concern.[34] Cash-cropping, handicrafts, manufactures, and labor migration therefore tended to degrade the production of basic food stuffs.[35]

The assortment of local products continually changed and shifted with market conditions.[36] During the later Ottoman period, dried and fresh fruits, such as grapes, cherries, and citrus, were cultivated and exported in significant quantities to Istanbul. To the east, locally grown hemp and flax were used to make thread, nets, and cloths.[37] A fine linen (*Trabzon bezi, Rize bezi*) that became prized in the Middle East and Europe was also produced.[38]

---

portant segment of them were blanket-makers in Istanbul. Dupré reported that two thousand "Lazes" embarked for Constantinople "to escape the vexations of their chiefs" (MAE CCCT L. 1, No. 73, June 1808). In Of, I heard the following saying: "The cripple of the Oflu went to America, / Where did his healthy son go to?" (*Oflunun topalı Amerikaya gitti. / Bunun sağlam oğlanı nereye gitmiş?*).

34. In 1966, I asked how it was that the villagers of the agriculturally impoverished upper valleys of Çaykara often seemed to be so prosperous. My interlocutor replied that they did not hesitate to leave their villages to seek work in Izmir, Istanbul, and Adana. They were not like the villagers of the interior highlands (Bayburt), who hated to leave their villages.

35. The idea of labor migration was explicitly associated with the doctrines of capitalism. In 1967, a shopkeeper in the district of Of explained, "If a man got any capital, he left Of. There was no way that capital could be used in Of itself. Those who stayed were those with little capital."

36. For an account of the economy of Trabzon at the beginning of the nineteenth century, see the report by consul Dupré (MAE CCCT L. 1, Nivôse An XII [Dec. 1803]). Also see Peysonnel (1787), who presents a report on the economy of the southern Black Sea during the mid-eighteenth century.

37. Peysonnel (1787, 69, 91) cites hemp as an important export at Rize and the principal export at Ünye. Palgrave (1887, 18) describes the hemp and maize grown on homestead gardens in Trabzon, adding that the hemp is used to make family clothes. He also lists 90 to 100 dyers in the town of Trabzon who used indigo to dye chenille imported from Izmir (Palgrave 1887, 75–76). Fontanier (1829, 8–9) describes an encounter with an indigo cloth-dyer at Sürmene.

38. Peysonnel (1787, 67–68) refers to four manufacturers of the cloths in the town of Rize and twelve more in the surrounding villages. The cloths were made in three different qualities and called "*toile de trébizonde.*" They were the most important export of Rize and were shipped to Constantinople, Egypt, and North Africa. Dupré writes in 1803 that "All the industry in this town [Trabzon] consists of the manufacture of linen, the most of which is for making into shirts, of which use it is in great demand at Constantinople, and of a great deal of copper articles, essentially for domestic usage, of which the most part is exported" (MAE CCCT L. 1, Nivôse An XII [Dec. 1803]). The French consul reports in 1868 that the most important export from the village of Rize is a cloth called "*toile de Rize,*" which is manufactured in three qualities. The highest quality is made of pure linen, the other two being

To the west, grapes from vineyards were distilled into a powerful liqueur (*nardenk*) and exported to the Crimea for reduction into *eau-de-vie*.[39] Wooden boats (*kayık*) for transporting cargo to Black Sea ports were constructed in Hopa, Rize, and Araklı, as well as elsewhere along the coast in secluded coves invisible from the sea.[40] Copper, lead, and silver were mined, smelted, and cast in different vicinities near Trabzon.[41] Knives, swords, pistols, and rifles were manufactured no later than the nineteenth century and perhaps considerably earlier.[42] Paper money was counterfeited no later than the beginning of the nineteenth century, and one can guess that metal counterfeits had been produced from ancient times.[43] Most of the local products that flourished during later Ottoman period have declined or vanished since the beginning of the last century, only to be replaced with others. But a very few were produced for centuries, and some for much longer. Tea is a crop grown today that was first introduced between Rize and Trabzon during the mid-twentieth century, but hazelnuts have been cultivated and exported from the eastern littoral for two thousand years.[44]

By virtue of a market orientation, subsistence farming and herding placed no Malthusian limit on how many people could inhabit the eastern

---

mixed with cotton. The two inferior grades are also manufactured at Trabzon (MAE CCCT L. 8, No. 4, Aug. 1868). The French consul reports in 1901 that thread and cloth were exported from Trabzon to Bulgaria, Rumania, Turkey, and Egypt, and that textile manufactures and cotton *filé* were exported to England, Austria, and France (MAE CCCT L. 13, June 1901).

39. Dupré (MAE CCCT L. 1, Nivôse An XII [Dec. 1803]) and Peysonnel (1787, 69, 83) refer to this liqueur.

40. Large seafaring boats were still being constructed by hand at Kemer village between Sürmene and Of when I first visited the area in the 1960s. Later, in the 1970s, with help from a World Bank loan, the villagers were able to construct a sheltered anchorage and to build large motor-driven boats from steel plate. Peysonnel (1787, 71–72) appears to have had a report of shipbuilding at this site in the mid-eighteenth century, but first-hand European observers were apparently unaware of it some decades later.

41. Dupré (MAE CCCT L. 1, Nivôse An XII [Dec. 1803]). Cuinet (1890–95) counted twenty-one silver-bearing lead mines, thirty-four copper mines, three of copper and lead, two of manganese, ten of iron, and two of coal for the sub-province of Trabzon (Bryer and Winfield 1985, 3).

42. Bryer and Winfield 1985, 3. When I first visited Trabzon local foundry workers and machinists were able to turn out copies of Colt 45s and Smith & Wessons (locally pronounced as "jolt kurk besh" and "seemeeteevesson," respectively).

43. Bijişkyan (1969, 61) writes that the Oflus "are talented to the extent of being able to print counterfeit money." Smelting and casting are ancient activities. It would be surprising if they were not also applied to counterfeiting.

44. Bryer (1975, 122), correcting Planhol (1963a, 1963b, 1966b), documents the export of hazelnuts during the medieval period.

coastal region.[45] So the population of the coastal region, like that of a metropolitan area, could expand indefinitely, limited only by the ingenuity of its inhabitants to produce for a market, turn a profit in commerce, or go abroad to ply a trade or seek out work.[46] And in fact the population did expand once the coastal region became more firmly integrated into the imperial system. British consul James Brant, traveling eastward from Trabzon in 1835, made the following observation:

> I passed in succession the districts of Yemourah, Surmenah, Oph, Rizah and Lazistan. . . . The country is so wooded and mountainous, that it does not produce grain sufficient for the consumption of the population, yet not a spot capable of cultivation appears to be left untilled. Corn fields are to be seen hanging on the precipitous sides of mountains, which no plough could arrive at. The ground is prepared by manual labour, a two pronged fork of a construction peculiar to the country being used for this purpose. Indian corn is the grain usually grown and it is seldom that any other is used for bread by the people. What the country does not supply is procured from Gouriel and Mingrelia.[47]

As the population doubled, redoubled, and doubled again, grain deficits became endemic to the eastern coastal region.[48] And when such deficits were exacerbated by poor harvests and market crises, the rural societies of the coastal region suffered extreme hardship and impoverishment.[49] British

45. The population of the eastern coastal region rose sharply during most of the Ottoman period, no doubt for a variety of reasons. The reintegration of the coastal region with the interior highlands after Ottoman incorporation, and the arrival of New World crops were perhaps among the several causes.

46. Thus cash-cropping, handicrafts, and manufactures are not a local response to grain deficits so much as the cause of them. Bryer (1975, 122) notes that hazelnuts are a virtual monoculture in some districts. Palgrave observed that flax was the primary crop at Rize and that grain and maize were secondary (PRO FO 195/812 p. 487, Feb. 16, 1868).

47. Brant 1836, 192.

48. Bilgin (1990, 269) cites a document mentioning grain deficits during the early sixteenth century (before maize). Umur (1951, 67–68) cites an official document, dated 1615/1024, mentioning grain deficits in the villages of Of (also before maize). Peysonnel (1787 [1762], 66) documents grain deficits at Rize during the middle of the eighteenth century. Fontanier (1829, chap. 1) traveled by boat from Redut-Kaleh to Trabzon in 1827. The boat, captained by a Sürmeneli, had carried a cargo of citrus and dried fruit from Trabzon and was returning with a cargo of maize. For other references to grain deficits, see MAE CCCT L. 2, BPMT No. 12, Jan. 1813, in which the province is reported to be threatened with a grain deficit; and MAE CCCT L. 5, No. 25, July 1846, in which Trabzon and its surrounding villages are said to have a grain deficit.

49. In 1829, food production was disrupted by Osman Pasha Hazinedaroğlu's campaigns against the local elites in the coastal districts. In 1830 and 1831, the har-

consul William Palgrave, who resided in Trabzon from 1868 to 1873, described the miserable condition of the villagers near Trabzon in the following terms:

> The inhabitants are, with hardly an exception, wretchedly poor. The plot of ground on which each man cultivates his maize, hemp, and garden stuff, yields little more than enough for his own personal uses and those of his family; the maize-field and garden supply their staple food, and the hemp their clothing: this last coarse and ragged beyond belief. And no wonder, where a single suit has to do duty alike for summer and winter, day and night.[50]

Cash-cropping and labor migration were alternatives to the meager fare gained from gardens and stables, but they also exacerbated the precariousness of rural life. The market orientation of the villagers decreased the local production of basic foodstuffs and so increased dependency on external economic and political conditions. The villagers were ever more inclined to contemplate the possibilities and opportunities beyond their homelands as the population density climbed.

The eastern coastal region therefore represented an impressive reservoir of men who were able and eager to take up any opportunity that might be present itself. At a certain point of crisis in the imperial project, Ottoman officials took note of this fact.

OTTOMANIZATION OF TRABZONLUS, TRABZONIZATION OF THE OTTOMANS

In addition to cash-cropping, handicrafts, manufactures, and labor migration, some inhabitants of the coastal valleys had always entered governmental service. Most commonly, it seems, they served as mercenaries for all kinds of power-holders in the coastal region as well as other parts of Asia Minor. As it happened, however, the inhabitants of the eastern coastal region began to expand the extent of their participation in centralized governmental institutions during the third century of Ottoman rule. Afterward, the rural societies might have appeared to the casual observer as dispersed

---

vest was especially poor and food was very limited (Bryer 1969, 202–3; Bilgin 1990, 298). In 1880, Biliotti describes a bad harvest and severe winter that, aggravated by the aftereffects of the recent war with Russia, was responsible for usurious loans, severe inflation, banditry, and mutiny in Trabzon (PRO FO 195/1329, No. 25, July 9, 1880).

50. Palgrave 1887, 18.

and fragmented peasantries, but they had become, more than ever before, provincial extensions of the imperial system.

During the second half of the seventeenth century, official policies led to an unprecedented increase in the numbers of individuals associated with military and religious institutions in all the core provinces of the Ottoman Empire. In a context of internal instability and external competition, a significant fraction of the population joined the ranks of soldiers and preachers. Sometimes employed and sometimes unemployed, tens of thousands of individuals came to identify themselves with the imperial system. The rise in the numbers of soldiers and preachers, which would have had affected towns and villages everywhere, had a special impact on the rural societies of the coastal region, once again by reason of topography and environment.

Elsewhere among the peasant societies of Anatolia, soldiering and preaching had the potential to wreck the rural economy coming and going. By the coincidence of these activities with the growing season, they drew able-bodied men out of the subsistence economy when they were most needed, then returned them when prospects for productive activities were at a low point. In contrast, the men of the eastern coastal region could depart from and return to their homelands without seriously disrupting the subsistence economy. And given their background of participation in market and state systems, they could immediately understand how state service was an opportunity rather than a catastrophe. Soldiering and preaching were ways of insinuating themselves in the social networks of the state system. And as well, soldiering and preaching could be combined with trade and crafts.[51] As a consequence, the rural societies of the province of Trabzon did not remain Christian but became largely Muslim, as they were once again, but more than even, re-integrated within a state and market system, now global rather than regional.

Women's labor in the gardens and stables was the precondition for men's participation in the horizon of elsewheres. It was the men who soldiered and

51. When individuals from the coastal region joined military expeditions, they also continued their entrepreneurial activities. Buying and selling was always a part of a military campaign, and for some perhaps the most important part. Ferrières-Sauveboeuf (1790, 233) describes an Ottoman military campaign in eastern Europe. He writes, "The army never moves in order, and the Turks refuse to form columns, either to protect their marches against surprise or to enable their troops to move about more easily in enemy territory. Those [of the troops] who practice some kind of profession always move on ahead in order to prepare their shops, where they busy themselves as in the towns, so that the camps resemble more a fair for artisans than an army of soldiers."

preached and, in doing so, traveled to other towns, resided in dormitories, socialized in coffeehouses, set up shops and ateliers in markets, ran caravans into eastern Anatolia, and sailed transport ships along the coast. If women remained involved in the market economy, that is to say, with cash-cropping, handicrafts, and manufactures, they did so only within their mountain fastnesses. And by the logic of such circumstances, women's work in the fields and stables became the confirmation that the men of the household were something more than peasants. Women were therefore obliged to work in the fields and stables whether or not the men were absent from the homestead.

In this way, local engagement in the imperial project came to shape gender relations in the coastal valleys of the eastern littoral. Women were closely identified with subsistence tasks, which were necessary but unrewarding and undignified. Men were identified with governmental and commercial engagements beyond the hamlet, which were potentially more rewarding and certainly more prestigious and dignified. By the pressure to claim social standing, each household was organized in such a way that the men were freed from subsistence activities, regardless of their actual position or achievement. While men were absent from the homestead during the day (in principle if not in fact), women took care of the children, the house, the stable, and the fields.[52] It was just as important for a man to be seen as free from farming chores as it was for him to be involved in some other rewarding enterprise.

The issue was as much a question of propriety as economic necessity or possibility. When they were able to do so, regardless of their actual occupation, men wore the "official" attire of businessmen, professionals, and bureaucrats. Women, regardless of their circumstances, wore the peasant costumes of striped aprons (*önlük*) and shawls (*çarşaf*) or blouses and baggy pants (*şalvar*), dress suitable for heaving, carrying, digging, and clearing. Wicker baskets, a distinctive feature of the subsistence economy in the coastal region, were another indication of the differing relationship of men and women to subsistence activities. Women with baskets—some as small as a rucksack and some as large as a person—took the place of animal power and wheeled vehicles.[53] Until recently, women were seldom seen away from

52. These tasks could be performed without the assistance of men, but the result was often endless, grueling labor. During the 1960s, young women in the villages in their thirties frequently appeared to be in their fifties, and fathers attempted to marry their daughters to men whose prospects were promising so that the latter would not make their wives into drudges.

53. Meeker 1971.

their homesteads without one, gathering fodder for the stables, harvesting crops from the fields, or transporting produce and supplies.

Women were the means by which men could become something other than subsistence farmers and herders, that is to say, the means by which men could claim imperial identities and affiliations. This explains why there was competition among men for the control of women as well as why this competition was expressed during marriage festivities in terms of the assembly of large numbers of men engaging in impressive displays of firearms. One could not be a participant in the sovereign power of the state system without women's labor, hence the manifestations of numbers and firearms were necessarily linked with claims over women. Villagers who saw themselves as potential participants in the sovereign power of the state system were also villagers for whom numbers and firearms symbolized their claim to women.

In the same way, imperial engagement explains why the eastern Black Sea people are known by story and proverb as possessive and jealous. Competition for women's labor arose because men were required to be absent from the homestead, not just during the day, but also during major parts of the year. Locally, these circumstances were associated with the notion that women should be able to defend themselves with weapons in the absence of men.[54] But more tellingly, they reinforced the moralization of men's claims over women, such that a principle of manhood required respect for another man's claims over women. This moralization appears in the orientation of religious thinking and practice in the eastern coastal region. All those elements of official Islam that touch on the morality of gender relations are emphasized, if not exaggerated, in the eastern coastal region.

So it is that the eastern coastal region, by participation in imperial military and religious institutions, became famous for a "traditional" assertion of male rights over women. And since its soldiers and preachers became instrumental in the ottomanization of provincial society, so too they transmitted the moralization of gender relations to other parts of Anatolia. The male residents of the eastern Black Sea coast became soldiers and preachers only by the advantage of local circumstances. And as they did so, they carried into the state society their own special concerns that had arisen from the circumstances of their participation. As they were transformed by taking their place in the lower echelons of the imperial system, so too they

54. In the 1960s, I was told that women were given rifles to defend themselves when left alone in their homesteads and were just as skilled as men in their use.

transformed the lower echelons of the imperial system. Ottomanization of Trabzonlus led inexorably to Trabzonization of the Ottomans.

A STATE SOCIETY BEFORE CONTEMPORARY MODERNITY

Travelers and visitors have repeatedly perceived the landscape of the eastern littoral as a stabilizing foundation for social life. Xenophon in the fifth century B.C.E., Procopius in the fifth century C.E., and then French consul Fontanier in 1827 all describe the same scene of isolated hamlets scattered across the hillsides. Topography and environment, it would seem, have always regenerated the same way of life, despite the arrival and departure of various peoples. A closer look reveals, however, that this continuity of observation is misleading.

Domestic architecture is less uniform here than anywhere else in Asia Minor. Sümerkan notes that the techniques of house construction in the coastal region change every fifteen to twenty kilometers, an indication of the diverse origins and skills of its inhabitants.[55] And if some domestic implements and structures are common to all the peoples of the littoral, reappearing in every coastal valley, such devices are everywhere named by different terms from different languages. Sümerkan notes, for example, that the maize granary was designated by as many as fifteen different terms.[56] And yet all this variability at the level of everyday practical activities is strangely accompanied by uniformity at the higher level of social relations. Sümerkan notes that the terms for domestic architecture are Arabic for activity rooms, Ottoman for the sitting room, and Persian for the balcony.[57] In other words, local fragmentation and difference is accompanied as well by the disruptions and intrusions of world commerce and imperial government.

The truth of the matter is that topography and environment worked to destabilize, not stabilize, the character of social life. On the one hand, outsiders were always attracted to this fertile and temperate region, thereby disrupting the consolidation of parochial habits and custom. On the other hand, once these outsiders had become insiders, they were pressed to orient themselves to the commercial and governmental systems beyond their

55. Sümerkan 1987, 21.
56. Ibid., 28.
57. Sümerkan (1987, 30), who is specifically referring to the region of Rize, Of, and Sürmene, also notes that the terminology of the stable is primarily Greek. By his observations, those areas of the house that were social in character came under the influence of imperial civilization more than those areas that were utilitarian in character.

homelands. And as the villagers oriented themselves to the market and state systems of which they were a part, so local identities and relationships never came into balance but always remained off-center, like the world system of which they were a part. The surface appearance of an unchanging way of life, dispersed homesteads in a garden landscape, therefore concealed a history of ethnic fragmentation and imperial reorientation.

The most perceptive observers of the old province of Trabzon noticed this peculiarity of the eastern coastal region, even though they did not understand exactly why or how it had come about.[58] J. Decourdemanche, who visited the coastal region during the 1850s, described the Muslim population as a collection of diverse peoples who had coalesced to form a regional society in the imperial system. "The inhabitants of Trabzon consist of many races . . . who came closer to each other in religion and speech [in the past so that] today they are one caste which has social and political influence."[59] Alfred Biliotti, serving as the British consul in 1873, also described the Muslim population as diverse in background but nonetheless united in their imperial sentiments and participation. "However much the Muslims who live here may be from the point of view of root or structure from different races, it can be thought that they are in the same fashion close to one another in regard to the Ottoman Empire, religious belief, and political ties."[60] When these observations were made, the steamship and telegraph had only recently arrived in this part of Asia Minor. It would be almost a century more before motor transport and electronic communications would become important factors in the social life of the coastal region. Nonetheless, in the absence of technological modernity, a collection of peoples living in a rural landscape more or less without towns had become a state-oriented society.

Today, in the eastern Black Sea provinces of Turkey, from Artvin to Ordu, the traces of ethnicity, Lazi, Armenian, Greek, and Turkic, are easy to discover in language, stories, customs, and dress. And yet, in contrast to all these differences, the inhabitants of the rural societies still lack a strong interest in their parochial backgrounds and traditions.[61] With the exception

58. W. G. Palgrave, who perceived the population in terms of racial classifications, was scandalized by the "mixtures" he encountered in the population of Trabzon (PRO FO 526/8, "On the Lazistan Coast . . . ," Jan. 1873).

59. Decourdemanche 1874, 361.

60. Consular report, Sept. 1873, cited by Şimşir (1982, vol. 2, 4). Also see PRO FO 195/1141, Jan. 1877, Biliotti.

61. The Lazi would be the most likely grouping to develop some form of ethnic identity since they are a large population that is territorially concentrated. However, see Benninghaus (1989b) for a discussion of the lack of a clearly defined ethnic identity among the Lazi. Also see his citation of Marr, who observed in 1920

of a few recent authors and books, there is no developed culture of ethnicity in the eastern coastal region.[62] Instead, social manners and relations are more or less homogeneous at a certain level, a direct reflection of a local engagement in wider market and state systems, now national as once before imperial.

These conditions of social life among eastern Black Sea peoples are indirectly recognized in Anatolian folklore. The diet of cornbread and yogurt is the simple and modest fare of village life in the coastal valleys. According to villagers and townsmen in the rest of Anatolia, these food items are said to be the cause of the restless energy and quick temper for which the "Laz" are famous. Cornbread and yogurt are indeed responsible for their liveliness, but only indirectly by their correlation with cash-cropping and labor migration. To be obliged to survive on cornbread and yogurt was also to have an intense interest in the horizon of elsewheres.

---

that the Lazi did not have a strong ethnic identity or favor their language. Also see Hann and Beller-Hann (2001) for a recent evaluation of ethnic identity among the Lazi.

62. See, for example, Asan (1996) and Aksamaz (1997).

4 Empire
Gaze, Discipline, Rule

THE PROBLEM

In the last chapter, I noted that the inhabitants of the eastern coastal region eventually came to identify with and participate in the institutions of the Ottoman Empire. But if these rural peoples were inclined to align themselves with the imperial system, this does not mean that the ruling institution itself would have permitted, let alone encouraged, such an accommodation. Indeed, the very idea of a rural people becoming ottomanist in orientation contradicts the prevailing historiography of the Ottoman Empire. Most commentaries have emphasized an unbridgeable divide between its ruling (*askeri*) class of state officials and its ordinary subjects (*reaya*), both Muslim and Christian. How then could a population of gardeners residing in remote mountain hamlets find themselves a place in the imperial system?

To answer this question, I first review how the Ottomans incorporated the eastern coastal region soon after the conquest of Constantinople, at a time when they were perfecting the classical ruling institution. This done, I analyze the architecture and ceremony of the governmental complexes that they built in the new imperial capital. This analysis features a double objective: to lay bare the distinctive configuration of sovereign power in the imperial system, and to expose channels of popular identification and participation that would lead into it.

OTTOMAN CENTRALISM AND EXCLUSIVITY

From the early sixteenth century, western European observers began to perceive the Ottoman Empire as a remarkable example of the centralism and exclusivity of sovereign power. What they noticed were the features of a new imperial system that Mehmet II had developed following his conquest of Constantinople in 1453.[1] Niccolò Machiavelli's comparison of the French and Ottoman governments in *The Prince* (1515) exemplifies the contemporary assessment:

> The entire monarchy of the Turk is governed by one lord, the others are his servants; and, dividing his kingdom into sanjaks [sub-provinces], he sends there different administrators, and shifts and changes them as he chooses. But the King of France is placed in the midst of an ancient body of lords, acknowledged by their own subjects, and beloved by them; they have their own prerogatives, nor can the king take these away except at his peril. Therefore, he who considers both of these states will recognize great difficulties in seizing the state of the Turk, but, once it is conquered, great ease in holding it. The causes of the difficulties in seizing the kingdom of the Turk are that the usurper cannot be called in by the princes of the kingdom, nor can he hope to be assisted in his designs by the revolt of those whom the lord has around him. This arises from the reasons given above; for his ministers, being all slaves and bondmen, can only be corrupted with great difficulty, and one can expect little advantage from them when they have been corrupted, as they cannot carry the people with them, for the reasons assigned.[2]

The passage points to a stereotype of Ottoman government that had come to prevail in Christian Europe. The sultan ruled through a body of officials having the legal status of household slaves. Recruited from the children of Christian families and trained from adolescence within the confines of the sultan's palace, they had no independent social identities or loyalties.[3] At the same time, these slave officials (*kul*) were unchallenged by any system of estates. There was no aristocracy composed of lords who ruled their own peoples and territories, and no bourgeoisie composed of merchants or bankers who had been granted the privilege of governing their own towns and cities. The "Grand Turk," as the sultan was sometimes styled in Christian

1. İnalcık (1973, 29) regards Mehmet II as the true founder of the Ottoman Empire.

2. Machiavelli (1992), in manuscript from 1505, in print from 1515.

3. The slave official that appears in western European commentary can be considered a rhetorical figure. He is a person whose being was reduced to absolute obedience by separation from his place and family of origin. Ottoman officials of slave status (*kul*), however, might parade their ethnic origins, dressing as Circassians or Bosnians, forming factions with those of the same ethnicity in the palace and speaking among themselves in their mother languages (Kunt 1974). Despite these complications, the rhetorical figure of the slave official does accurately indicate the strategy of Ottoman recruitment and training.

Europe, seemed to enjoy a measure of sovereign power unmatched by any other monarch in early modern Europe.

Machiavelli's analysis reduced the ruling institution to a simple and static formula, thereby concealing both its complexity and instability. Still, his formula directs our attention to a distinctive feature of a new governmental system that gained ground during the early classical period. As the Ottomans launched a world imperial project during the later fifteenth century, they reinforced the centralism and exclusivity of the ruling institution. The recruitment and training of "slave" children to serve as high state officials was just one of the measures they adopted. By means of a range of policies, the Ottomans came to rely on a special class of military, administrative, and judicial officials who lacked affiliation with the governed. This raises the question of how the Ottomans incorporated a region whose peoples had such a large stake in market and state participation.

Mehmet II had annexed the Greek Empire of Trebizond (1461) just as he was beginning to devise and apply the new imperial system. Süleyman I had later reorganized the province (*paşalık*) of Trabzon as a new administrative entity (1519) at the high point of classical institutions. So the substantial Christian population of the coastal region had become subjects just as the Ottomans were perfecting the centralism and exclusivity of the ruling institution. Higher state officials were more than ever composed of slave officials, and other entry points into the ranks of officialdom were regulated more than ever. Thus the shock of conquest was compounded by the shock of subjection. The old rural societies of the coastal region and the new imperial system were exactly mismatched. The inhabitants of the province of Trabzon had become part of a governmental system based on principles that stood in direct opposition to compelling local interests.

As we saw in the last chapter, the mismatch was transitory rather than permanent. As the domains of the ruling institution reached their maximum limits, the conduct of warfare was shifting away from the use of cavalry toward the use of infantry with firearms.[4] Under these circumstances, the Ottomans came to require larger numbers of men with a wider range of skills, even before the close of the classical period. They therefore took

4. Barkey (1994) points out that the Ottomans regularly adjusted the size of their armies by either expanding or contracting military appointments and prerogatives. Even during the classical period, the high point of imperial centralism and exclusivity, they added military officials and formations when they required them, then shed them once they no longer needed them. The increasing numbers of soldiers and preachers were at least in part the intended result of state policies.

steps to widen the circle of participation in imperial military and religious institutions during the seventeenth century, in effect compromising the principles of centralism and exclusivity. As they did so, problems of imperial competition at the military frontier were joined by problems of internal instability in the core Ottoman provinces. Provincial governors had begun to defy the central government, asserting themselves by collecting illegal taxes and maintaining their own private armies. In response, the palace widened the privileges and prerogatives of provincial elites at the district level in hopes of curbing the powers of provincial governors.[5] As a result, principles of centralism and exclusivity were compromised still further. By the beginning of the eighteenth century, the distribution of sovereign power had moved outward and downward into the imperial system, weakening both central and provincial government. Higher state officials found themselves unable to rule save with the acquiescence and assistance of provincial elites.[6] The post-classical period was thereby characterized by a progressive decentralization of sovereign power.

All the core Ottoman provinces were affected by the changes I have just summarized, but the province of Trabzon is an especially revealing example of the phases of decentralization. By the close of the seventeenth century, many of the districts where the population had been almost entirely Christian at the moment of Ottoman incorporation had become almost entirely Muslim. Furthermore, large numbers of the men among these new Muslim populations had associated themselves with local branches of imperial military and religious institutions. By the close of the eighteenth century, local participation in imperial military and religious institutions had resulted in an entirely new relationship of state and society. Provincial elites at the head of armed followings asserted their prerogatives in the imperial system, sometimes defying, even threatening, higher state officials, both those in Trabzon as well as in Istanbul.

The instance of the eastern coastal region therefore poses questions of general significance for the understanding of the ottomanization of provincial society in other parts of Asia Minor and the Balkans. How did a population composed of different ethnic groups attached to different religions come to participate in imperial military and religious institutions?

5. İnalcık 1977.

6. Ibid.; Nagata 1976; Özkaya 1977; Sakaoğlu 1984; and Veinstein 1975. These authors are not in agreement on the timing of the period of decentralization, setting its beginning variously between the middle of the seventeenth and the middle of the eighteenth century.

And in doing so, how did this diverse and mixed population become state-oriented, official Muslims, given that the imperial regime was based on radical principles of centralism and exclusivity?

OTTOMAN INCORPORATION OF TRABZON

In his account of the ruling institution during the classical period, İnalcık explains how the palace, the seat of centralized government, organized and supervised the core Ottoman provinces in Asia Minor and the Balkans.[7] A hierarchy of military officers was appointed to govern a hierarchy of administrative units. There was a governor of each province (*beylerbeyi*), a few sub-governors of its several sub-provinces (*sancakbeyi*), and a large number of subordinate officers (*sipahi*) assigned to groups of villages (*tımar*) in the sub-districts of each sub-province.[8] The palace appointed the governors to their positions for a limited term, rotating them from province to province. The palace also approved the governor's appointments of subordinate officers, also for a limited term, rotating their assignments from time to time.[9] The powers of this hierarchy of military officers was further subject to certain checks and balances. The chief treasury official (*hazine kethüdası*) was responsible for seeing that the fiscal affairs of the province were in order. The chief court official (*kadı*) issued judgments in accordance with administrative and religious law. The provincial governor could dismiss both these officials, but only upon notification of the palace.

As we have seen, the military, treasury, and judicial officials were members of a special class without ties to the lands and peoples they governed. Only some members of this special class would actually have been trained in the institutions of the imperial capital, but of those who were not from Istanbul, only some would have been born and raised in the eastern coastal region. So the military, treasury, and judicial officials of the province of Trabzon had no multistranded ties with either the lands or the peoples for whom they were responsible. In this regard, they were unlike the lords and vassals of western Europe during the Middle Ages. They generally lacked castles or estates in the provinces to which they were posted, just as they lacked supporters among their inhabitants.

7. İnalcık 1973, 103–18.

8. Only a fraction of these military officers would have been raised and trained in the palace.

9. For a more detailed summary of this complex system, see Barkey (1994, chap. 3).

Furthermore, official procedures insured that the military governors would remain loyal and obedient servants of the central government rather than set down roots and build a following among the populations they governed. The *sipahi,* who were assigned to the countryside as a kind of country police force, best exemplify how this was accomplished. They came into direct contact with villagers on a routine basis in the course of collecting taxes, apprehending fugitives, imposing forced labor, and carrying out court decisions. They were therefore in a good position to build a base of local support, by favoring or disfavoring the villagers for whom they were responsible. But to counter this very possibility, the *sipahi* were subject to all kinds of controls.

The provincial governor could renew or revoke their appointment to a *tımar,* as well as allow or disallow their relatives to succeed them as a *sipahi.* So both their assignment in the countryside and their tenure as subordinate military officers were entirely dependent on higher state officials rather than local preference or election. Normally, they were rotated from district to district during the course of their service, so that they usually found themselves among peoples with whom they had no previous social contacts. They also had limited opportunity to develop social contacts since they were obliged to report for military campaigns, during which they were replaced by deputies for extended periods.[10] Treasury and judicial officials also subjected them to periodic inspections and were in a position to bring charges against them for malfeasance. Complaints could be lodged against them by townsmen and villagers and could result in dismissal if confirmed.[11]

In other words, all kinds of precautions had been adopted to prevent lower state officials from doing exactly what some would do during the period of decentralization. Policies of appointment, rotation, and inspection prevented the *sipahi* from setting down family lines and building local followings. It was as though the Ottomans had designed the institutions of the classical period in anticipation of the post-classical period that followed

10. Barkey (1994, chap. 4) describes the position of the *tımar* holder in relationship to his charges during the classical period.

11. Bilgin (1990, 240–46) has examined fifteenth- and sixteenth-century *tımar* lists for Trabzon. These lists include the name of *sipahi* to whom a *tımar* was assigned, the reason it was granted, and, more exceptionally, the reason it was revoked. Bilgin gives some examples of complaints against *sipahi* that led to revocation of their appointments, such as 1) taking a wife without proper registration of marriage, 2) killing a man, 3) getting drunk and drawing a weapon on another *sipahi,* 4) insulting the sultan, and 5) a complaint lodged by an ordinary individual (*reaya*).

it. As we shall see, this would not have been a coincidence. Those who were responsible for inventing and implementing the imperial project would have taken care to neutralize a decentralizing potential that was inherent within its logic.

Four Ottoman registers attest to the thoroughness and efficiency with which the classical system of provincial government was put into practice in the province of Trabzon. Taken once every generation during the first century of incorporation, the registers tabulate the different classes of *tımar* assignments, list the names of the *sipahi* appointed to them, and establish the tax obligations of each household head.[12] Although the same structure of government would have been operating in other parts of Asia Minor and the Balkans, the province of Trabzon was in certain respects unusual. Initially, as confirmed by the registers, the Ottomans appointed *sipahi* who had taken part in the conquest. Some of these individuals came from the western coastal region (the province of Canık), which had been Islamized and Turkicized for many years.[13] More than a few came from still further away, from other parts of Asia Minor, or even the Balkans.[14] Thus, the *sipahi* in most of the coastal valleys of Trabzon would have been even more distant from their charges than was the case in some other provinces. The villagers among whom they resided were a newly subjected Byzantine population composed mostly of Orthodox Christians. The *sipahi* and the villagers therefore observed different customs, spoke different languages, and belonged to different religions.[15]

Accordingly, the rural societies of the sixteenth-century province of Trabzon faced a bureaucratic hierarchy whose officials were part of interpersonal networks closed to ordinary townsmen and villagers.[16] The towns-

12. The dates were 1486/892, 1515/921, 1554/961, and 1583/991. Three of the registers are discussed in more detail in the next chapter.

13. Bryer (1975, 132–33) notes that Çepni *beys* were given *tımar* in Trabzon after its incorporation.

14. Of 207 *tımar* holders in Trabzon, as listed in a document dating from 1486, Bilgin (n.d. a) believes 20 were of Albanian origin. Elsewhere, citing Beldiceanu, Bilgin (1990, 136, 145) points to evidence of *tımar* holders of Albanian, Bosnian, Serbian, and Hungarian background.

15. The villagers would have largely been Lazi-, Greek-, and Armenian-speakers who were Christians.

16. The rural societies of the coastal region had taken part in the military and religious institutions of the Greek Empire of Trebizond (Bryer 1975). The defense system of the latter had extended into the upper and outlying coastal valleys, requiring the support of the local residents, Greeks and non-Greeks, Christians and Muslims. Orthodox churches, monasteries, and endowments were also dispersed

men and villagers found themselves subject to strangers who represented a foreign fiscal and legal administration. Appointments to military, administrative, and judicial positions were limited to insiders rather than open to outsiders. The entry of ordinary townsmen or villagers into the official class was unlikely. State regulations made it difficult for villagers to leave or neglect their farms. Even conversion from Christianity to Islam may have been discouraged, since every new Muslim household, no longer obliged to pay a tax (*haraç*) imposed on Christian households, would have had a negative effect on treasury receipts. The policies and institutions of the classical period were therefore incompatible with the peculiar character of the eastern coastal region as described in the preceding chapter.

And yet, as we shall see, the foundation had been laid for the "imperialization" of the rural societies in the province of Trabzon. The Ottomans had incorporated the inhabitants of the eastern littoral as a Christian population subordinated by imperial institutions. But the latter would eventually discover channels into the military and religious establishments that ruled them. In doing so, the inhabitants of the eastern littoral would evolve into a Muslim population participating in imperial institutions. To some degree, this transformation came about as local elites of the eastern coastal valleys took advantage of the breakdown of bureaucratic centralism during the period of decentralization. But this was not the most important process that led to the emergence of ottomanized rural societies in the province of Trabzon.

As we shall soon see more clearly, the official class of the ruling institution subscribed to a discipline of social thinking and practice that instilled qualities of individual behavior and disposition. Reinforced by bureaucratic policies and procedures, the exercise of sovereign power through interpersonal association bound the official class together even as it divided them from ordinary townsmen and villagers. But once individuals of the subject population were in a position to adopt this same "imperial tactic," they would be able to assert their prerogatives within the imperial system, even at the expense of higher state officials.

The dissemination of the exercise of sovereign power through interpersonal association, its spread from insiders to outsiders, was then a cause of the period of decentralization. The breakdown and corruption of bureaucratic centralism can be seen as the corollary rather than the cause of this

---

through the coastal valleys, and their staffs and tenants were drawn from a cross-section of the population.

dissemination. To understand the emergence of ottomanized provincial societies in the eastern coastal region, it is therefore necessary to clarify the social thinking and practice of the official class.

THE PALACE COMPLEX: A DEVICE OF SOVEREIGN ASSOCIATION

Soon after the conquest of Constantinople, Mehmet II initiated the construction of great monumental centers on prominent hilltop locations within the city. By the end of his reign (1451–81), a palace complex and a mosque complex, by virtue of their immensity, the numbers of their personnel, and the extravagance of their budgets, had completely transformed the city from a Byzantine into an Ottoman capital.[17] Each of the two sites had a dual purpose, both organizational and representational.[18] They were centers for implementing a new ruling institution based on radical measures of centralized government, and at the same time, they were also theaters for displaying this ruling institution in splendor and grandeur. The palace complex and the mosque complex were therefore instruments of edification as well as of government, and as such, designed to confound and enthrall, if not intimidate and terrify.

Two hundred years or so after the time of Mehmet II, as the imperial system slipped into a period of decentralization, the counterparts of these great imperial complexes began to appear in many parts of the eastern coastal region. Aghas residing in government mansions and hodjas teaching in mosque academies were in effect rural versions of the great monumental sites of Istanbul. However, these rural replicas of imperial models mimicked their originals more perfectly at the level of interpersonal association than at the level of ceremony and architecture. Neither the aghas nor the hodjas intended to emulate the courts, domes, ceremony, and protocol of the palace and mosque complex. Rather, they drew upon the ethical underpinnings of the imperial project: the exercise of sovereign power through a discipline of interpersonal association.[19]

17. The Ottoman mosque complex and the palace complex were designed to "fashion" both a Muslim state personnel and Muslim state subjects where there had been few or none before. In this respect, they were without precedent among other Islamic dynasties (İnalcık 1973; Necipoğlu 1991).

18. Necipoğlu 1991, 21.

19. I use the term "ethical" advisedly to emphasize the interpersonal character of the ceremony, a quality that linked it with Islam. This is not to say that court ritual was essentially Islamic, even if the Ottomans might wish to claim it was so.

Since the great monumental centers were designed as much for "showing" as for "ruling," their ceremony and architecture can be deciphered to expose these ethical underpinnings. I shall consider each of the two centers in turn, but devoting more attention to the palace than the mosque complex. The relationship of power and religion during the classical imperial period justifies this treatment. As we shall see, the foundation of the imperial project, sovereign power through interpersonal association, required that the palace hold Islam captive.

The Palace Machine

By its placement and appearance, the palace complex is contrived to manifest sovereignty and invincibility, but by a peculiar logic. Two striking architectural features, clearly visible from afar, suggest a coordination of seeing with ruling. The residential quarters of the sovereign are set on a promontory overlooking two continents, Europe to the west and Asia to the east. This vantage point is set behind and above a high fortress wall that surrounds the entire palace complex.[20] So the sight of the sovereign is represented by an overlook from within an interior. And the association of a personal gaze with a ruling power, already implicit in its elevated perspective, is explicitly represented by a high fortress wall adorned with watch towers and gun emplacements.

The physical structure of the palace complex announces the relationship of gaze and rule not once or twice, but over and over again. Apertures, gratings, and windows are repeatedly coordinated with balconies, overlooks, and towers. Each instance of the relationship symbolizes the sovereign situated within an interior space overlooking an external space occupied by subjects. All these instances of an elevated oversight articulate the personal presence of the unobserved sovereign as the foundation of a world ruling institution.

But exactly how is gaze translated into rule? What is the quality of vision as cause and how is it related to the quality of power as effect? Does the relationship of gaze and rule perhaps have some kinship with the panopticon, as invented by Jeremy Bentham and analyzed by Michel Foucault?[21] Or

20. The wall was not built to serve a military purpose, its watch towers and gun emplacements being of symbolic rather than practical significance (Necipoğlu 1991).

21. Bentham's panopticon (1787) consists of a central point of observation surrounded by, but invisible to, a circle of isolated cells. The individuals in each of the cells have no contact with their neighbors but are exposed to surveillance by the central point of observation. Foucault (1975) explains the panopticon as an archi-

should we not anticipate that the articulation of peculiar elements—eye, interior, oversight, rule, exterior—points to a specific language of authority and obedience? The verses of an Ottoman poet, cited in Necipoğlu's definitive study of the architecture and ceremony of the palace, seem to have been composed as an answer to this very question. Cafer Çelebi said:

> What is each window, but an eye opening to the whole world, to watch ceremonies and spectacles?
> What is each tower, but from head to foot a tongue to praise and eulogize the just shah?[22]

The verses of the poet refer to the basic elements of the overall placement and appearance of the palace complex: A personal presence, symbolized by windowed interiors set in tower overlooks, bespeaks of sovereign power. But now the poet composes these elements to articulate a somewhat strange message.

According to the conceit, the palace complex works like a machine that mediates between the eye of its resident and the imperium beyond its walls. Its overlooking windows (set in towers) are telescopes that expose the whole world to his sight. Its elevated towers (pierced by windows) are megaphones that speak to the whole world of his rule. So by this combination of mechanisms, seeing is most certainly linked with ruling. The structures that expose the world to the person of the sovereign are also the structures that represent the person of the sovereign to the world as legitimate ruler. Moreover, the verses also point to the specific qualities of seeing and ruling. The windows are an eye that brings the world into view, but not as a landscape of fields, waterways, mountains, and lakes. The world appears in the form of the subjects of an imperium, engaged in ceremonies and spectacles, and so not engaged, by contrary example, in commerce and warfare. The sovereign therefore sees, or rather oversees, normative performances. The windows, as instruments of the palace machine, bring a kind of world

---

tectural arrangement designed to instill an individualized discipline of behavior. As such, it was a model that could be used for the construction of prisons, barracks, schools, factories, or hospitals.

22. Necipoğlu 1991, 85. The verse is from Cafer Çelebi's "Heves-Name": *"Nedür her câm bir çeşm-i cihan-bîn / Temaşa itmeğe tertib ü âyîn. Nedür her küngüre ser-tâ kadem dil / K'ider medh ü senâ-yi şâh-ı âdil"* (Levend 1958, 72–73). Necipoğlu's translation appears to me to be an excellent rendering. A more literal, hence inelegant, translation would be, "What is every window but an eye on the world / for observing ordered ceremonies. What is every tower but from head to foot a tongue / for fulsome praise of the just shah."

into view, a world of propriety and sociability, pleasing in form and delightful to experience. So the sight of the sovereign, as mediated by the palace machine, has worked to compose the world it brings into view by sponsoring and supporting normative performances. The palace machine is both organizational and representational. Cafer spoke both brilliantly and succinctly as he put the spirit and logic of the palace complex into a score of words.

By the anachronistic terms "telescopes" and "megaphones," I have emphasized how the poet images the palace as an instrument of sovereignty. On the other hand, Cafer's tropes are more anthropomorphic than mechanical. He likens the palace windows to an eye and the palace towers to a tongue. Since these figures clearly do not refer to the sovereign himself, the poet is suggesting that the palace is an instrument of sovereignty that works through anthropomorphic rather than technical media, such as the scripts and documents of a centralized bureaucracy. As we shall see, the palace was indeed an instrument for extending and amplifying the personal presence of the sovereign by means of loyal and obedient officials who were something more than a centralized bureaucracy. This feature of the palace is indicated by another coordinated repetition of structures and functions, one that determined the overall layout of the palace complex (see fig. 7).[23]

A succession of three gates, leading to three courts, organized the grounds of the palace complex. The outer gate led to the outer court, from which the middle gate led to the middle court, from which the inner gate led to the inner court. This arrangement defined a series of thresholds leading to interiors, each standing in relationship to one another as "further out" or "further in" by reference to the person of the sovereign. At the same time, each instance of a threshold and interior was also associated with apertures and overlooks representing the personal presence of the sovereign, seeing but unseen, hearing but unheard. In this respect, the successive interiors defined by the gates and courts had the status of assembly spaces that were correlated with the increasing nearness, and hence intensity, of sovereign oversight. As the visitor to the palace complex moved through them, he experienced the progressive loss of his own will and purpose as he became more and more subject to ceremony and protocol. In this way, the visitor experienced his approach to the sovereign as an approach to a locus

23. The figure illustrates the ethical underpinnings of architecture and ceremony and is not otherwise an accurate representation of the layout of the palace complex.

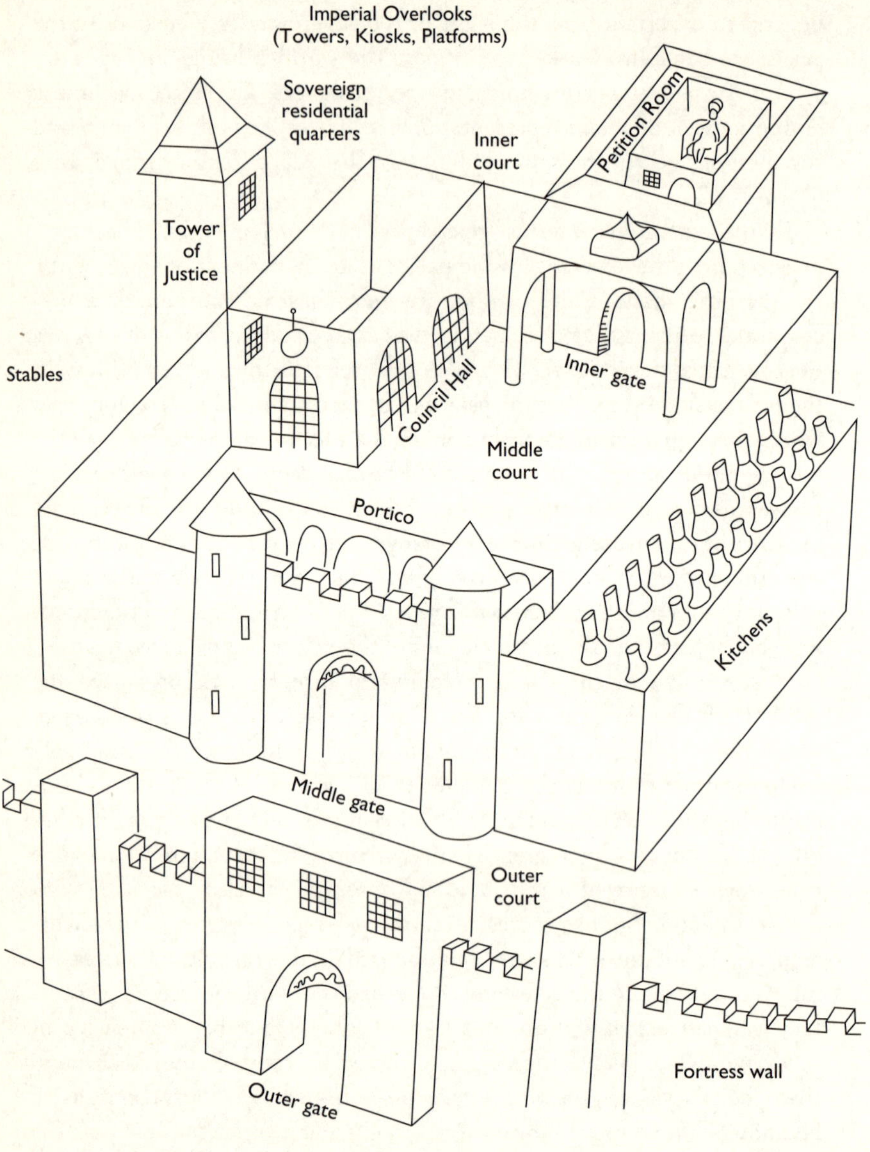

Figure 7. Schematic of Mehmet II's palace complex.

of normative regulations that otherwise radiated outward.[24] The series of thresholds and interiors therefore indicated the personal presence of the sovereign as a focal point of a world imperium. So an architecture of windows and towers was coordinated with an architecture of gates and courts.

An Omnipresent Personal Oversight

Following the lead of Cafer, let us begin with the Tower of Justice (*köşk-i 'adl*), a structure he may have had in mind when he composed his verses.[25] The base of the Tower of Justice was situated in the residential quarters of the sovereign located beyond the north corner of the middle court. The upper section of the Tower of Justice, fitted with a latticed window, rose above the rooftops of the other buildings so that it could be seen from afar. The sovereign was therefore able to mount the Tower of Justice and view the two continents of his imperium from the seclusion of his residential quarters. By its architectural prominence, this symbol of sovereign oversight, only one example of many, dominated the entire palace complex.

A Council Hall (*divan*) was situated before the Tower of Justice in the forward section of the middle court (see fig. 7).[26] Here, the highest officials of the ruling institution deliberated state affairs, reached administrative decisions, received petitions from subjects, and heard law cases.[27] At the base

24. The Ottoman sultans were represented at the portal of each gate by inscriptions, military guards, and victory banners. Pierce (1993) mentions the symbolism of inside and outside in the palace, as well as its incompatibility with contemporary concepts of public and private. Lewis (1988), cited by Pierce, observes that the language of power in Islamic societies, as opposed to the courts of western Europe, turns on spatial separations that are horizontal rather than vertical.

25. Necipoğlu (1991, 52, 54) confirms that the middle court was in existence early in the reign of Mehmet II. She also notes that its layout was identical to the administrative enclaves of the tent palaces of the Ottoman sultans (ibid., 53–54). Necipoğlu (1991, 84–85) concludes that the Tower of Justice was probably an early feature of Mehmet II's palace complex. She cites Cafer Çelebi's verses as evidence of this possibility and notes that royal buildings built before the New Imperial Palace featured similar structures.

26. The Council Hall and public treasury were located a short distance from the Tower of Justice during the reign of Mehmet II. They were moved to the base of the tower early in the reign of Süleyman I, sometime between 1525 and 1529 (ibid., 23, 79–80). For simplification, I am anachronistically referring to the latter arrangement, which Necipoğlu views as a refinement of the architecture and ceremony of the middle court.

27. Necipoğlu 1991, 56–58. In the time of Mehmet II, "Any male or female subject of the sultan, Muslim or non-Muslim, could petition the high court of justice to have his case heard and decided" (ibid., 76).

of the Tower of Justice, a little room was equipped with a curtained window that opened out into the upper wall of the Council Hall.[28] The sovereign could access the little room from the seclusion of his residential quarters and sit behind the curtained window. For all those present in the Council Hall, he was then always present, even when absent. Before the curtained window itself, hanging from the domed ceiling of the meeting room, a gilded globe represented the earth.[29] Round about the meeting room, large grilled openings at the entrances symbolized the availability of justice to all subjects.[30]

The window above, which overlooked two continents, was therefore punctuated by another window below, which overlooked the dispensation of justice by state officials. In the early years of his reign, and continuing for sometime thereafter but ever more rarely, Mehmet II had joined state officials in the Council Hall and participated himself in their deliberations. This practice, which was abandoned as the palace complex reached completion, points to the derivative and evolutionary character of the ruling institution. Once upon a time, it would seem, the sovereign had been more directly and routinely involved in the day-to-day matters of administration and adjudication. At a certain moment of dynastic history, one could presume, the device of the windowed overlook had begun to substitute for the personal presence of the sovereign.

The sovereign had ruled by his personal presence in accordance with a kind of justice that was interpersonal in character rather than abstract and technical. With the extension of his domains, however, the sovereign came to rely on his officials as stand-ins for his personal presence so that their eyes, tongues, heads, and feet were his representatives. And then with the further extension of his domains, his officials multiplied, so that they numbered in the thousands rather than the hundreds. The windowed overlook had then been adopted as a device for extending the personal presence of the sultan. Thus, the ruling institution retained its character as an interpersonal association even as it evolved into a world system. This had come about by a resort to an architectural instrument that preserved a founding principle but enabled its imperial amplification.

This "just so story" suggests that the Council Hall had first been fitted with a curtained window, and then a Tower of Justice with a latticed window had been added to the Council Hall. The windowed overlook would

28. Such an aperture, or window, was part of the old Council Hall of Mehmet II, as well as of the new Council Hall of Süleyman I (ibid., 79, 83).

29. Ibid., 59, 62 (fig. 41), 63 (fig. 42), 80, 86.

30. Ibid., 80.

have been first adopted as a device for supervising the ruling institution and then only later become a symbol of the ruling institution to be seen from afar.

A Spectacle of Interpersonal Association

In fact, the Tower of Justice also served as an internal device of the ruling institution as well as its external symbol. Its latticed window had been specifically constructed to provide a view of the core mediating segment of the palace complex, the middle court. From the seclusion of his residential quarters, the sovereign was able to mount the Tower of Justice, position himself before this latticed window, and observe an extraordinary scene of "ceremonies and spectacles" consisting of "praises and eulogies." Down below in the middle court, he could observe thousands of loyal officials who had assembled to show themselves to their sovereign, greeting and honoring him as they did so. In all probability, Cafer had these occasions in mind when he composed his verses describing the palace. He had sought to capture the wonder of a novel architectural structure by which personal oversight of normative performances had been translated into a world imperium.

In the early years of his reign, before the palace complex was completely finished, Mehmet II had not always mounted the Tower of Justice to view the assemblies down below. He had regularly joined his officials and troops in the middle court, appearing before them and hosting a meal.[31] Necipoğlu, relying on the description of a Genoese merchant, gives the following account of these gatherings, which occurred early each day at the break of dawn:

> On these occasions the courtyard was filled with eight thousand officials wearing "vests of brocade and silk of every color and type." The sultan appeared in glory under a magnificent portico (*lobia*) in front of the gate that led to the residential court. The ceremony lasted for a quarter of an hour, during which time servants offered food to the sultan on a gold tray and to those assembled on silver and copper trays, according to their rank. At the end of this banquet, at which not a word was spoken, the courtiers loudly acclaimed their ruler, extolling, praising, and glorifying his name. . . . Ambassadors were made to watch this ceremony of imperial glorification, after which they were conducted . . .

31. Observers report that Mehmet II regularly appeared before his soldiers to assure them that "he was still alive and that they were not threatened by a usurper" (ibid., 18). Such an explanation would be relevant to any dynast who removed himself from his officials and soldiers. Otherwise, it does not explain the elaborate symbolism devoted to the personal presence of the sovereign in the palace complex.

> to the sultan's seat. After bowing and kissing his hand, they were made to sit . . . until he rose to return to his private quarters. As soon as he stood he was again loudly acclaimed by the soldiers; then he sat and rose a second time to hear another acclamation, before entering his private apartment. After the soldiers left, the dignitaries of the [Council Hall] ate. Only then did [they] listen to the cases presented, which they subsequently reported to the sultan inside the private courtyard.[32]

The derivative and evolutionary character of the palace complex has once again come into view. Once upon a time, the sovereign had been more routinely present at the assembly of his officials, not only as they dispensed justice, but also as they congregated as a sovereign association. The windowed overlooks of the palace complex therefore appear as architectural replacements of the once-present sovereign.

At a certain moment, it would seem, Mehmet II had chosen to absent himself from his officials, substituting his participation in a sovereign association with the device of a windowed overlook. The intention of carrying out such a replacement can therefore be more or less precisely dated to Mehmet II's decision to build a new palace. It did not immediately follow the conquest of the Byzantine capital.[33] Mehmet II had first built another palace complex in Istanbul, later to be known as the "old palace" (*eski saray*). It was only after he had decided to launch an imperial project some years later that he undertook to build what would become formally known as the New Imperial Palace (*sarây-ı cedîd-i 'âmire*).

The Dynastic Court Tradition

Given its derivative and evolutionary character, the New Imperial Palace can be best understood in terms of its place in the history of the Ottoman dynasty. I shall here tell a second "just so story."

Osman, founder of the Ottoman dynasty, had been a chieftain of a Turcoman tribe of pastoral nomads in northwestern Anatolia. But during the course of his reign (1280–1324), he had also become a leader with follow-

32. Iacopo de Campis Promontorio, a Genoese merchant who served in the Ottoman court from 1430 to 1475, described the ceremony as it was held in 1475 (ibid., xii-xiii, 18–19). This was before the adoption of a new codification (*kanunname*) of court ceremony and protocol.

33. By this observation, I do not mean that the device of a windowed overlook was absent from earlier dynastic structures, whether buildings or tents. I mean to say that the windowed overlook became a fundamental principle of the ruling institution during the time of Mehmet II.

ers in the marchlands between the Byzantines and the Seljuks.[34] As such, he was the principal figure of a warrior association composed of individuals who came from many places and spoke many languages. This warrior association eventually came to represent a ruling institution legitimized by the extension of the lands of Islam at the expense of the lands of Christianity. So Osman was something other than a chieftain, and his associates were something other than tribesmen. But still, during this early period, they had participated in communal banquets more or less in accordance with the steppe traditions of the Turcomans.[35]

As successive Ottoman dynasts had fitfully risen in power and stature, these communal banquets continued as part of the dynastic court tradition. However, they gradually lost their tribal character and acquired a more Islamic character. The banquets therefore shifted from an occasion that reinforced tribal customs and habits to an occasion that celebrated the ruling institution as a normative association underwritten by the sacred law of Islam.[36] These banquets were then not mere expressions of royal hospitality and sociability that supplemented the otherwise separate business of implementing policy and applying justice. On these occasions, the leader appeared as the personal guarantor of an interpersonal association underwritten by the sacred law of Islam. So the banquets of the dynastic court tradition became at the same time disciplinary exercises and legitimacy performances.[37] The leader and his follower composed a ruling institution of Islam legitimized by the extension of the lands of Islam.

Accordingly, the holding of formal banquets prepared in the royal kitchens eventually determined the design of the grounds and buildings of royal palaces, just as they had also determined the layout of the royal tents during military campaigns. So long before the time of Mehmet II, the Ottoman dynast and Ottoman officials had joined in formal banquets in order to enact the normative performances of an interpersonal association. And

34. Kafadar (1995) examines the policies and followings of the early Ottoman dynasts.

35. See, for example, the depiction of more or less Islamized pastoral nomadic chiefs and tribes in *The Book of Dede Korkut* (Lewis 1974). The *Dede Korkut* stories have their origins among the thirteenth- to fourteenth-century Oghuz peoples of northeastern Anatolia. Meeker (1992) analyzes these stories as ethical representations of self and society.

36. Ibid.

37. Necipoğlu (1991, 19) refers to the commentaries of Aşıkpaşazade and Mihailovic, contemporary observers of the classical period who were of the opinion that the Ottoman sultan had personally appeared at communal banquets from the time of Osman, founder of the dynasty.

long before Mehmet II, such occasions had featured ceremony and protocol for the purpose of impressing, if not astonishing, subjects, participants, and competitors.[38] The palace complexes that preceded the New Imperial Palace were then likewise governmental residences that provided for a theater of state. They had also included assembly grounds, massive kitchens, and large staffs for this very purpose.

At this point, let us return to the middle court to consider what became of these formal banquets as the New Imperial Palace reached completion.

An Uncanny Discipline

During the later years of his reign, as the palace and mosque complexes were reaching completion, Mehmet II adopted new state regulations (*kanunname*) that decisively transformed his state system into an imperial system.[39] Afterwards, he entered the middle court to appear before the personnel of the ruling institution only twice each year, on the occasion of the two major Islamic festivals. Otherwise, he never again joined his officials to host them with food prepared in his royal kitchens. And yet the dynastic court tradition of the formal banquet still continued, but in a new "disarticulated" form.

After the adoption of the new state regulations the sovereign was still the focal point of the ruling institution, but the sovereign himself was more than ever inaccessible, even invisible. He retreated to his residential quarters within the palace, distancing himself even from the members of the official class. Meanwhile, the representatives of his ruling institution became more than ever a centralized and exclusive official class. The highest state officials were more and more often of "slave" status, individuals who had been separated from their families to be raised and trained within the palace.

Correspondingly, the dynastic court tradition changed in character to reflect the logic and sense of the new imperial project. The loyal and obedient officials now presented themselves before a sovereign who had come to resemble a divinity, seeing but unseen, hearing but unheard. Four times each week, thousands of officials came to the middle court to manifest the ruling institution as a normative interpersonal association through a dis-

38. Ibid., 69.
39. Ibid., 19.

play of ceremony and protocol.[40] Necipoğlu summarizes the intent of these so-called "Victory Councils" (*galebe divanı*) in the following terms:

> Ceremonial [of the middle court] served to create a visual diagram of this hierarchically organized military state that was immediately graspable at a glance. This diagram accentuated the omnipotence of the sultan together with the transformation of the centralized state into a bureaucracy and a great army at the personal service of the sultan.
>
> The perpetuation of ceremonial communicated a message of timeless order and stability, bestowing permanence and legitimacy on *an arbitrary social construct.* Its power lay in constant repetition, enacted in an eery silence, as if time had been temporarily suspended by an endless recurrence. It froze time in an eternal present and created the illusion of an *order transcending mere human experience.* [Italics mine][41]

A fragment of the old dynastic court tradition, a warrior leader hosting warrior followers, had been elevated to the level of an imperial project. But in the quote, which tells us a great deal, Necipoğlu has also uncharacteristically slipped past the most important point, which her study otherwise fully documents.

The imaginary potential of the displays in the middle court did not arise from the suspension of time through constant repetition. The witnesses of the ceremonies of the middle court, both insiders and outsiders, had an experience of repetition, but in the register of the uncanny, rather than the eternal.[42] The imperial theater of the middle court had distilled an interpersonal association, rooted in the dynastic court tradition, into its disciplinary essence. The ceremonial rested on an arbitrary social construct, but only in the sense that it revealed thousands and thousands of individuals whose being had seemingly been seized and compelled by such a construction. It was this conscious display of the unconscious that had lain behind the poet's image of the place complex in terms of body parts, eye (*çeşm*), head (*ser*), foot (*kadem*), and tongue (*dil*).[43] The display of a sovereign association had acquired the quality of an "order transcending human experience." The movements of its participants seemed governed by divine ordinances, by

40. Ibid., 61.
41. Ibid., 68.
42. Freud 1958 [1919].
43. During the earlier classical period, the sovereign might also observe executions of delinquent officials in the middle court below. In doing so, he opened the lattice to signal his presence while the condemned entreated his forgiveness (Necipoğlu 1991, 59).

their reduction to figures of loyalty and obedience. Such an imperial theater would not have been effective had it been arbitrarily staged and performed by casting directors and professional actors. Its power to seize and compel its witness relied on effects that could have only been induced by radical procedures of recruitment and training.

One did not have to "know" the meaning of the imperial theater in order to be impressed. Both foreign observers and official participants were struck by its representations. Fresne-Canaye, who witnessed one of the Victory Councils in the company of the French ambassador in 1573, noted its disciplinary essence, even as he could not conclude whether the sight was pleasurable, frightening, monastic, natural, civilized, or savage.

The Frenchmen had first passed through the outer gate into the outer court where they dismounted from their horses. They then passed through the threshold of the middle gate to enter into the open square of the middle court. Fresne-Canaye describes what they then saw:

> At the right hand was seated the Agha of the Janissaries [a high officer of the central army], very near the gate, and next to him some of the highest grandees of the court. The Ambassador saluted them with his head and they got up from their seats and bowed to him. And at a given moment all the Janissaries and other soldiers who had been standing upright and without weapons along the wall of that court did the same, in such a way that seeing so many turbans incline together was like observing a vast field of ripe corn moving gently under the light puff of Zephyr.[44]

The Frenchmen were then taken to the Council Hall in the forward section of the middle court where they were "courteously received" by the grand vizier and governors. Following this reception, they were then taken elsewhere in the middle court, where they were provided a generous dinner laid out under a portico. As they dined, they observed the officials and troops assembled in the middle court:

> We looked with great pleasure and even greater admiration at this frightful number of Janissaries and other soldiers standing all along the walls of this court, with hands joined in front in the manner of monks, in such silence that it seemed we were not looking at men but statues. And they remained immobile in that way more than seven hours, without talking or moving. Certainly it is almost impossible to comprehend this discipline and this obedience when one has not seen it. . . . After

44. Necipoğlu 1991, 64–65, Necipoğlu's translation. The original account is in Italian. I have consulted the French edition (Fresne-Canaye 1980 [1897], 62, 64).

> leaving this court, we mounted our horses where we had dismounted upon arrival [in the outer court]. . . . Standing near the wall beyond the path we saw pass all these thousands of Janissaries and other soldiers who in the court had resembled a palisade of statues, now transformed not into men but into famished wild beasts or unchained dogs.[45]

This representative of a country distant from the Ottoman Empire was both enchanted and frightened, but the nearer neighbors of the Ottomans came away with less ambivalent impressions. When the Safavid prince visited the palace complex in 1591, for example, his attendants were "exhausted" and "weakened" by what they saw in the middle court.[46]

According to the witnesses of this imperial theater, the crowds of officials did not behave as crowds at all. By the gravity of their movements and the silence they imposed on themselves, they took on the appearance of an exalted assembly under the governance of divine ordinances. The personal oversight of the sovereign was coupled with the enactment of a discipline of interpersonal association. The result was the manifestation of the ethical underpinnings of the ruling institution in the form of a body of loyal and obedient servants.

The Palace as Panopticon

The palace machine does indeed recall the panopticon of Bentham and Foucault. The guarantor of the discipline enacted by loyal and obedient servants was not himself present in the middle court, but positioned instead in the Tower of Justice up above. From behind its latticed window, the sovereign observed the middle court down below. And so by the device of the Tower of Justice, the sovereign retained his officials under his surveillance, even though he might not even be present. The windowed overlook was then a device of omnipresent inspection and regulation serving to inculcate self-control in each servant. But in this regard, there is something odd about the Tower of Justice, Council Hall, and middle court, at least by the measure of the nineteenth-century western European panopticon.

There is no compartmentalization of those subjected to surveillance, one of the most distinctive features of the panopticon.[47] On the contrary, regulation and inspection are invariably linked with assemblies and associations. The windowed overlook of the palace machine is therefore a device for internalizing a discipline that takes the form of an interpersonal ethic

45. Ibid., 65.
46. Ibid., 68.
47. Foucault 1975.

rather than a personal conscience. The eye of the sovereign up above is reinforced by others down below. Sovereign oversight therefore has no need of jails, workhouses, or barracks, because it is supported by the eyes and tongues of others. Sovereign oversight therefore takes the form of support and sponsorship of places of normative association, such as salons, coffeehouse, and mosques, rather than cells, exercise yards, and parade grounds.

The Tower of Justice, Council Hall, and middle court are not the panopticon of Bentham and Foucault because they refer oversight to "ethics" rather than "conscience." They are devices for instilling a discipline of interpersonal association, rather than a discipline of self-control by self-oversight. This is why apertures and overlooks indicate a *person* located within an *interior,* rather than a point of technical observation occupied by an anonymous warden. This is why the micro-forms of palace architecture are personalized, referring specifically to the location of the sovereign even in his absence. And this is why the personal presence of the sovereign can be projected through, and so has his counterpart in, the personal presence of others. And this is why the palace, insofar as it is imaged as machine, never escapes anthropomorphization. The windowed overlooks are insistently linked with the sovereign, precisely because he is not a machine, but a person who can be represented by the eyes, tongues, heads, and feet of others.

Disarticulation, Distribution, and Rearticulation

The architecture and ceremony of the palace complex would appear to have reduced the old dynastic court tradition to a disciplinary tactic of loyalty and obedience. The sovereign has left the banquet to become a figure of omnipresent surveillance. The servings of food have been removed, leaving nothing other than ceremony and protocol. The fellowship of the assembly has been transformed into a setting of individuals who have taken on the appearance of lifeless, marble statues. A windowed overlook is all that remained of the warrior leader who once hosted his warrior followers. But in fact, the totality of the old dynastic court tradition had remained in place in the palace complex. Mehmet II had not at all forsaken the old dynastic court tradition in the course of building his palace complex and launching his imperial project. He had rather disarticulated, distributed, and rearticulated it. The architecture and ceremony that supplemented the middle court illustrates this operation.

As we have seen, the layout of the palace complex consisted of a series of thresholds and interiors signaling an approach to the personal presence of the sovereign, but also by a reverse movement, the projection of the personal presence of the sovereign into world at large as an imperium. Tracing this double movement, we discover how the core mediating segment of the palace complex transformed the formal banquets of the old dynastic court tradition into a world empire. I shall start with the innermost approach and then conclude with its outermost projection.

The Inner Gate and Petition Room

When granted audiences with the sovereign, high officials and foreign ambassadors proceeded to the inner gate in order to enter the inner court. As they did so, they moved from the outer palace (*birûn*), a place that was subject to *devices* of sovereign oversight, to the inner palace (*enderûn*), a place that was subject to *actual* sovereign oversight. The difference appears in the official title of the inner gate: the Gate of Felicity (*bâb üs-saâde*). The approach to the sovereign is likened to an experience of happiness and delight. In this respect, an element of the scene of the warrior leader hosting his warrior followers—bountiful hospitality and engaging sociality—had been distilled into a figure of the pleasures of paradise.[48]

But paradoxically, having become an almost god in an almost cosmic setting, the sovereign was now unfit to engage in any form of reciprocity even as he remained a symbol of hospitality and sociability. In the inner court, his servants, forbidden to speak out or to reveal themselves, communicated in signs and hid behind columns. His personal assistants, eunuchs, mutes, and dwarfs, featured physical disabilities. His personal companions—youths who were not men, men without social origins, mothers who could not be wives, wives who could not be mothers—featured status debilitations.[49] The sovereign, as the fount and origin of an imperial normativeness, could not himself partake in horizontal social engagements, at least by the representations of official ceremony and protocols. The personal presence of a world ruler reduced every other being in his immediate environment to something less than fully human. No one "whole in being" was to be found close or near to him. The principle of sovereign oversight had in effect blasted away the imperial family. From the standpoint of ceremony and protocol, the sultan could not be a father, a son, a husband, a brother, a lover, a companion, or a friend. He could only be an ascendant or a descendant. The crossing from outer to inner palace was not a matter of entering a familial space and time, or a communal space and time. It was architecturally and ceremonially marked in order to symbolize the personal presence of the sovereign (see fig. 7).

48. Cf. Necipoğlu 1991, 90.
49. Cf. Pierce 1993, 39–45.

As the visiting official or ambassador passed through the inner gate, he stood before the Petition Room (*ʿarz odası*), where he would soon encounter the sovereign, but he was already under surveillance. The wall of the petition room was pierced by a large iron grating so that the threshold of the inner gate was exposed to the gaze of the sovereign. The visitor had therefore already come within the view of the sovereign sitting on his throne.[50] The visitor was then brought into the Petition Room, where he was presented to the sovereign in a manner that varied with imperial fashions and policies. The occasion might involve an exchange between the visitor and the sovereign, a ritual greeting and welcoming, but this was not the usual formality. More commonly, it was an exchange without exchange, submission without recognition, supplication without acknowledgment, or sentence without trial. The official or ambassador entered a room whose walls and carpets were encrusted with gold and jewels, in accordance with a solemn ritual, conducted in "the very silence of death itself."[51] The sovereign sat upon his throne, unflinching and immobile.[52] The ambassador, with eunuchs gripping both his hands, was then taken down to the knees of the sovereign to kiss his robes at his feet.[53] The official, standing before the sitting sovereign, might hear a clap of the hands, whereupon mutes might suddenly appear to carry out his execution outside the Petition Room before the grating.[54]

And yet the personal presence of the sovereign, in whose vicinity no man could compose his own will and purpose, had to be the foundation of a sovereign association that could be projected as a world rule. This was precisely the role of the palace machine, a monster of heads, feet, eyes, and tongues constituting the person of the sovereign as a world imperium. By

50. Necipoğlu 1991, 98.

51. Ibid., 90, 102 (quoting Miller).

52. Fresne-Canaye described the appearance of the sovereign as he was presented to him. "He did not look at us in the face, but with a troubled eye, mean and alarming, he held his head turned toward the fireplace, as though not really aware of those who came before him so humbly" (1980 [1897], 70).

53. See the plates representing the visits of European ambassadors in Necipoğlu (1991, 103–5). Fresne-Canaye described his ambassador being presented to the sovereign: "When the Ambassador had arrived at the door of the [Petition Room] where the Grand Turk awaited him, two aghas, superbly attired, took him by his two hands, and as soon as he had kissed the garment of the emperor, he was taken to a corner of the room" (1980 [1897], 68–69).

54. Necipoğlu 1991, 107–8. Fresne-Canaye writes, "All around the [Petition Room] there were hidden I don't know how many mutes, among whom are found the most faithful and proven executors of the atrocious orders of this tyrant" (1980 [1897], 70).

reversing direction, in order to move from Petition Room to the middle court, we can follow the path whereby personal presence was projected as world imperium.

The Petition Room is topped by a low roof in the imperial style, which extended beyond the walls of the structure itself. As in the instance of the coupling of an interior with an overlook, this feature of the roof symbolizes the projection of the sovereign's oversight of an interpersonal association into the world at large. The roof both covers an interior and extends beyond the limits of this interior. The symbolism is explicitly articulated by a feature of the overhanging roof that draws the Petition Room into a relationship with the middle court. On that side of the Petition Room facing the inner gate, the roof does not come to an end but penetrates the boundary wall in which the inner gate is placed. On the other side of the boundary wall, this same section of the overhanging roof reappears as a portico extending over and before the inner gate itself. Here, under a cupola set in the forward part of the projected roof, the sultan would sit on a throne to witness the ceremonies in the middle court on the occasion of the two annual Islamic festivals.[55] Otherwise, the throne and cupola served as symbols of the sovereign on the occasions of the Victory Councils four times each week.

So the inner gate represented an approach to an interior overlook (room and grating) even as it also represented the projection of an interior overlook (court and cupola). The micro-forms of palace architecture—the room and grating and the cupola and court—had disarticulated the old dynastic court tradition, then rearticulated it to link a sovereign, who was absent rather than present, with a sovereign association. However, the palace machine has not yet completed its operations. The placing of the inner gate before the Petition Room has its counterpart and complement in the placing of the middle gate before the middle court.

The Middle Gate and Middle Court

More than any other architectural boundary within the palace complex, the middle gate represented a transition from outside to inside. As such, it revealed what was composed on the inside (an interpersonal association) and

55. On the occasion of the religious holidays food was served from the kitchens, but apparently not while the sovereign appeared in the middle court. Uzunçarşılı (1984, 209) describes the celebration of religious holidays in the middle court during the early seventeenth century.

how this composition appeared on the outside (the sovereign power of a world ruler).[56]

The visitor arrived in the outer court crowded with the attendants and horses of all the officials and ambassadors who were to enter the middle gate and take part in the ceremonies of the middle court.[57] Approaching the middle gate, he was presented with what appeared to be a medieval stronghold (see fig. 7). The entrance was flanked by two stone towers topped by parapets and surmounted by a crenellated wall that joined the flanking towers together. The threshold itself was staffed by military officers and soldiers of the central army and festooned with banners, weapons, and armor commemorating imperial victories.

The external facade of the middle gate therefore represented the fortress of a ruler, and, in so doing, repeated the statement made by the watchtowers and gun emplacements of the high stone wall that surrounded the entire palace complex.[58] This restatement asserts the linkage between military force and victory on the outside with the discipline of interpersonal association on the inside. Accordingly, the threshold itself articulated the relationship force and ethics. It was the site of a court where two military judges (*kazasker*) tried military officers accused of malfeasance.[59]

In effect, the external facade of the middle gate is a remainder of the old dynastic court tradition of a warrior leader hosting his warrior followers. Now, however, all the symbolism of military capacities and formations has been exiled from the middle court by the logic of a disarticulation, distribution, and rearticulation. So passing through the threshold of the middle gate into the interior of the middle court, the visitor would discover the ethical "substance" behind the military "facade." The official name of this entrance, the Gate of Greeting (*bâb-üs-selâm*), contrasted with the official name of the Gate of Felicity behind it. The warrior leader hosting his warrior followers had been broken into pieces, consisting of military force and power (middle gate), ethical discipline (middle court), and hospitality (inner gate).

56. Cf. Necipoğlu 1991, 50.

57. Ibid. Before the completion of the surrounding wall, the palace complex consisted only of two gates and two courts.

58. Ibid., 32, 50–51. The exterior of the middle gate, as a segment of a fortress wall, could be regarded as a synecdoche of the surrounding fortress within which it was situated, making it a symbol of a symbol of sovereign power.

59. The two towers flanking the middle gate included a prison for those on trial. The court martials were held regularly following the ceremonies in the middle court (ibid., 76; Uzunçarşılı 1984, 21).

After the visiting official or ambassador passed through the middle gate, he was received under a "stately portico with ten marble columns attached to the gate's inner facade."[60] Before the portico itself, he saw a garden "paradise of peacocks and gazelles, cypress trees and other trees."[61] The visitor had left behind the crowds of attendants and horses in the outer court. He had also left behind the representations of the military force and power of the ruling institution. He now found himself welcomed by an assembly of officials whose dress and movement were regulated by ceremony and protocol.

The inner gate represented the personal presence of the sovereign as the guarantor of a discipline of interpersonal association. The middle gate represented the discipline of interpersonal association as an instrument of sovereign power in the world at large. The relationship of inner, middle, and outer courts was then a relationship of gaze, discipline, and rule.

The Never-Ending Banquet

And yet there would still seem to be one missing piece of the old dynastic tradition in the middle court. Mehmet II had seemingly suppressed the banquet itself, when the sovereign hosted his officials to food and drink. But this is not the case. The banquet had not disappeared at all, but it had rather become routine and perpetual.

I have already noted that the Tower of Justice rose prominently above the other buildings within the outer fortress wall. Similarly, twenty paired chimneys of the Imperial Kitchens had been designed as prominent marks on the skyline.[62] To the left of inner gate, the Imperial Kitchens comprised the transverse border of the middle court. Here thousands of "graded" meals were prepared each day in "graded" kitchens, for the sovereign, the staff of the inner palace, high officials of the ruling institution, and, finally, military officers and regiments.[63]

With the building of the palace complex, the warrior leader hosting warrior followers had become a master leader hosting slave followers, while

60. Necipoğlu 1991, 53.
61. Goodwin 1971, 132–3.
62. Necipoğlu (1991, 72) affirms the importance of the chimneys as visible architectural symbols. Both the Tower of Justice and Imperial Kitchens had been built by Mehmet II but were later either remodeled or replaced several times, during the classical period itself and also afterwards. But despite successive changes, they remained prominent architectural features of the palace complex. For early representations of the Imperial Kitchens, see ibid., 70–73, 84–86, plates 30a–b, 31a–c, and 32a–b.
63. Ibid., 71–72.

the banquet had become an everyday routine but no less charged as a symbol of loyalty and obedience. On campaign, military regiments were brought to shame by the loss of their cooking pots to the enemy, not the loss of their flags and banners.[64] And similarly, military officers and troops expressed their displeasure with the sovereign by overturning the soup cauldrons where their meals were regularly prepared.[65]

The elements of the dynastic court tradition had remained in place, as a warrior leader of warrior followers became the early modern sultan of a world empire. The symbol of personal presence (window), a normative oversight (tower), an interpersonal association (kitchens), and invincible sovereignty (fortress wall) were all the tropes of palace architecture as seen from afar. Each consisted of a disarticulated micro-form of a warrior leader hosting warrior followers. The elements were enduring because they represented something more deeply rooted in thought and practice than ceremony and protocol.[66]

We are now ready to accompany the sovereign on those occasions when he ventured from his residence in the company of his personnel. Where did they go and for what purpose?

THE MOSQUE COMPLEX: A DEVICE OF OFFICIAL ISLAM

So far as I have been able to determine, the ceremonies of the middle court did not include an occasion in which the sovereign appeared as a military commander leading a military formation.[67] Contrary to what one might expect—given the origins of the dynastic court tradition in an association of warrior leader and warrior followers—the Victory Councils represented the ruling institution as triumphant and invincible by virtue of its ethical underpinnings, rather than military organization or technology. However, the sovereign did routinely lead a procession of officials from the palace complex in parade formation. On such occasions, he came to the middle court where his attendants had brought his horse from the Imperial Stables

64. My reference for this is late. Ferrières-Sauveboeuf (1790, 220) noted that the worst thing that could happen to a unit of the janissaries was to suffer the dishonor of losing their cauldrons. They therefore assigned two "batteries of the kitchen" to prevent such a disaster.

65. Necipoğlu 1991, 72.

66. Indeed, the ethical underpinnings of the old dynastic court tradition are still to be found in the Turkish Republic, having been once again disarticulated and rearticulated. Meeker (1997) analyzes Atatürk's tomb and the Kocatepe Mosque as national monuments.

67. Returning military expeditions did sometimes enter the outer gate and parade in the outer court (Necipoğlu 1991, plates 33a–q).

opposite the Imperial Kitchens (see fig. 7). He mounted and rode through the middle gate in the company of officials and attendants on foot. In the outer court, he then joined a larger formation, which included both horsemen and footmen, and exited through the outer gate. They were on their way to perform the Friday prayers (*namaz kılmak*) in a great mosque of the imperial capital.[68]

Having arrived at their destination, sovereign and officials would perform their ablutions, preparing their minds and bodies for the religious observance. This done, they would enter the great mosque and assemble themselves in ordered ranks, the sovereign occupying a separate elevated compartment. Having oriented themselves in the direction of Mecca, the constituents of the ruling institution then performed the prayers, enacting a discipline of mind and body, in accordance with required formulas of speech and gesture. The staging and performance of a normative association before the sovereign, unseen and unheard, was therefore punctuated by the staging and performance of a normative association before divinity, unseen and unheard.[69]

Is it far-fetched to draw a parallel between sultan/palace and divinity/mosque? Is this merely a kind of free association of a ruling discipline with a religious discipline? Not according to western European observers of these ceremonies and protocol. Fresne-Canaye had noticed the parallel in his account of his visit to the Petition Room. As he waited his turn, he had observed high officials groom themselves before making their appearance before the sovereign: "And I saw the pashas . . . standing up straight and combing their beards with their hands: because they consider it meritorious to appear well groomed before God as they perform their prayers, and also in the presence of their emperor."[70]

68. Ibid., 24 (fig. 12). Fresne-Canaye (1980 [1897], 128) observed, "In this company and order, [Selim II] went off to the mosque of Sultan Beyazit, where an immense crowd had gathered, and he remained there a little more than an hour, then returned with the same people by the same procession."

69. One of my readers has criticized the use of the word "performance" in this paragraph as indicating that the ceremonies of the court and mosque were but superficial rituals, lacking in psychological depth. It is not my intention to suggest that this is so. I translate *namaz kılmak* as "perform the ablutions and prayers." I assume that these rituals are part of a range of rigorous disciplines that served to forge thought and behavior. For analysis of the discipline of religious belief and practice in terms of its power to create a psychological reality among contemporary believers in Cairo, see Mahmood (forthcoming). The example also serves to point out that discipline of religious belief and practice in the Islamic tradition can be used for various ends.

70. Fresne-Canaye 1980, 69.

And he had noticed the parallel again precisely on the occasion of the sovereign's procession to Beyazit Mosque in order to perform the Friday prayers:

> With the passage of the Great Lord, there was everywhere an extraordinary silence. One could say that his very look had the power to transform men, like Medusa, into marble or into mute fish; because they have the conviction that their lord is the shadow of the breath of God on earth, having learned nothing from their youth in the palace save obedience and respect for their emperor. And by that unique discipline, they are always going to increase their power, to the shame of all Christians.[71]

The impressions of foreign visitors are of course notoriously unreliable. However, Fresne-Canaye appears to be well informed. High Ottoman officials had not explained their thoughts and feelings to him, as his citations imply. Nonetheless, the ghost of Mehmet II could have been his "literal" informant, his calligraphers having left his "personal signature" all over the palace complex.

Two gilded inscriptions appear over the portal of the outer gate leading to the outer court. Necipoğlu is once again our guide to their significance. The lower of these is a foundation inscription that brings to mind once again the poet's verses. The solidity of the palace complex as an architectural structure is said to be the guarantee of social order and calm. Here, however, this accomplishment is attributed to a sultan who is both a substitute for and a favorite of divinity:

> By the help of God, and by His approval, the foundations of this auspicious Castle were laid, and its parts were joined together solidly for strengthening peace and tranquility, by the command of the Sultan of the two Continents, and the Emperor of the two seas, the *Shadow of God* in this world and the next, the *Favorite of God* on the Two Horizons [East and West], . . . may God make eternal his empire, and exalt his residence above the most lucid stars of the firmament, in the blessed month of Ramadan of the year 1478/883. [72]

The sovereign does more than acknowledge Islam. The palace is more than linked with Islam. The sovereign and his palace are a paragon of divine will

71. Ibid., 127.
72. Necipoğlu 1991, 34, 36.

and favor. When you approach the sovereign by entering the palace complex, it is as though you have crossed into the circle of divinity.

The upper inscription tells us just this. It is a Koranic quote that likens the threshold to the Gates of Paradise and the interior to the Garden of Eden:[73]

> But the God fearing shall be amidst gardens and fountains: "Enter you them, in peace and security!" We shall *strip away all rancour* that is in their breasts; *as brothers* they shall be upon couches set *face to face;* no fatigue there shall smite them, neither shall they ever be driven out from there. [Italics mine][74]

The inscription marks the portal of the outer gate, which is set in a surrounding fortress well. It stands over another inscription, which draws a relationship between the material structure of the palace complex and the eternal endurance of a world empire. Nonetheless, the material structure, that is to say, palace architecture, is but the frame or setting for an interpersonal association. You know you are crossing into the circle of sovereign power, the very shadow of divinity, when you encounter within these precincts the peace and security of a brotherly association and affection.

The palace was then explicitly analogous to the mosque. The throng of officials in the middle court assumed the quality of angels compelled by divine ordinances. The setting in which they were assembled seemed as though it was a landscape from paradise. The sovereign himself was represented as the epiphany of a divinity. The architecture and ceremony of the Tower of Justice, Council Hall, and middle court were directly associated with, if not embedded in, the legal tradition of Sunni Islam. In the middle court itself, the ceremony and protocol of a sovereign association, its disciplined gestures and movements, were the counterpart of other disciplined gestures and movements, the ablutions and prayers.

The sovereign and his palace were then affiliated with, even dependent upon, Islam. The former manifested and celebrated the ethical underpinnings of a world empire. The model for a discipline of interpersonal association was Islamic. The basis of the loyalty and obedience of the official class was Islamic. The legitimacy of such a world empire before all potential competitors within and outside the Ottoman Empire was based on its status as a paragon of Islamic authority and obedience.[75] Or is this exactly the

73. Necipoğlu 1991, 36. The Koranic citation is 15: 45–48.

74. Arberry's (1955) translation.

75. Unlike their Seljuk predecessors, the "countrified" Ottomans lacked a distinguished genealogical heritage. They therefore placed a special emphasis on sul-

way to express the relationship of power and religion? Did Islam have a claim on the palace? Or did the palace have a claim on Islam?

Mehmet II had built a mosque complex at a distance from the palace complex nearer the center of the capital city. As in other mosque complexes that would be built by his successors, its principal architectural feature was a great mosque. By its size and aspect, this mosque complex rivaled the Hagia Sophia, the still-existing basilica of the Byzantine emperors (but now a mosque memorializing the Ottoman conquest). Many observers have claimed that all the great mosques of the classical period seemed imitative and derivative, and, consequently, less effective as sacred buildings than the Byzantine "original." But as Aptullah Kuran has insightfully pointed out, the Ottomans had transformed Byzantine tradition, even as they drew from it, arriving at a distinctive and original architectural statement by means of a structure that is only at first sight similar to the Hagia Sophia.[76] What follows is my own elaboration of his conclusions.

From the outside, the great mosques of the classical period have a squat, frog-like aspect such that they appear to be among the most inelegant, if not unattractive, examples of mosque architecture in the Islamic world. But their ponderous arches and segmented domes are the price to be paid to achieve a specific representational objective. From the inside, the great mosques consist of an immense, virtually unobstructed interior space sheltered by a high dome.[77] The transparency and homogeneity of the interior represent a universal time and space for the assembly of Muslims who came from different lands, speak different languages, and live by different customs. The high dome that floats magically above this interior space confirms the role of sovereign power as the sponsor of this assembly.

The palace complex was therefore legitimized by a mosque complex. The sovereign was fit to govern all lands and peoples because his ruling institution represented a standard of ethical thinking and practice of cosmic import, valid for all times and places. However, such a reading of the great mosque is slightly askew, more in tune with popular contemporary interpretations of the classical Ottoman mosques in the Turkish Republic than with the intentions of Mehmet II.[78]

---

tanic sponsorship and support of the learned class of Islam, and, more specifically, ruling in conformity with the sacred law of Sunni Islam (Zilfi 1988, 23–24, 27–28).

76. Kuran 1968

77. Ibid., 198.

78. See Meeker (1997) on the nationalist features of contemporary mosques built in the classical Ottoman style.

Perhaps Mehmet II built his mosque complex in acknowledgment of the one and true world religion. Perhaps the vast domed interior of its great mosque could be seen as a place of worship for all the faithful of his imperial domains. But even if these points are conceded, and they are far from obvious, the sovereign also built the great mosque complex to stake a claim on Islam, to subject it and so command it.

The sovereign in his palace was entangled with a specific dimension of Islam, not the totality of this religious tradition. The ruling institution had a direct interest in the sacred law of Islam, which is a piece of Islam, and, however important, not all of it. And more exactly, the ruling institution had a direct interest in the legalistic and juridical side of the sacred law of Islam, which is a piece of the law, and, however important, certainly not all of it.

The Ottomans had invented and constructed mosque complexes (*imaret, külliye*) long before Mehmet II conquered the Byzantine capital. They were the means by which an Islamic dynasty had supported and propagated Islam among lands and peoples with Christian rather than Muslim majorities. They included schools, academies, dormitories, hospitals, kitchens, baths, shops, and warehouses situated in the immediate vicinity of the great mosque.[79] They served as "urban renewal projects" designed to created Muslim cores of what had been Christian towns and cities.

However, Mehmet II had set about to build a different kind of mosque complex just as he set about to build a different kind of palace complex. Now, the buildings and institutions of the mosque complex, together with their accompanying positions, salaries, meals, housing, and endowments, would become, more than ever before, the resources and instruments of a religious officialdom representing an official Islam. By this intention, the mosque complexes of the classical period served to support, hence to elevate, the learned class of Sunni Islam, but at the same time served to define the membership and formalize the activities of the learned class of Sunni Islam.

The judges of the imperial courts, drawn from the learned class, represented the first tier of officials of the religious establishment. The professors of the imperial academies, drawn from the learned class, represented the second tier of the religious establishment. The ladder of salaried appointments that led to the highest professorships was topped by another

79. See İnalcık (1973, chap. 15), for an account of the role of the mosque complex in the formation of Muslim towns and cities. See Ergin (1939) for an account of the activities that took place in the mosque complex. See Ayverdi (1973, 356–406) for an account of the buildings and endowments of Mehmet II's mosque complex.

ladder of appointments that led to the highest judgeships. This meant that the representatives of the state legal system had precedence over the representatives of the broader religious tradition. And this meant the broader representatives of the religious tradition were themselves oriented to the state legal system. So the judicial hierarchy was positioned over the academic hierarchy. The courts of the religious establishment placed an emphasis on that very part of the religious tradition that could best serve as the basis for the imperial legal system. And accordingly, the academies also placed an emphasis on that side of the sacred law of Islam that was most compatible and consistent with its role in the imperial legal system.

The gigantic domed interior was therefore the symbol of a centralized and exclusive religious officialdom, not the symbol of a single humanity united by a single true revelation. Accordingly, the gigantic domed interior was a place where the sovereign and his officials regularly assembled to subject themselves to Islam during the Friday prayers. But it was also routinely a site for the display of a religious establishment by which the sovereign had subjected Islam. Judges and professors, joined by attendants and students, regularly assembled in the interior beneath the dome, displaying themselves as the representatives of an official Islam. The assemblies of religious officials that appeared beneath the dome of the great mosque were then the counterpart of the assemblies of military officials that appeared in the middle court. The performance of authority and obedience in the mosque complex served as the foundation of the performance of authority and obedience in the palace complex. But by this logic, the palace had to hold Islam captive. If an Islamic discipline of interpersonal association was the basis of sovereign power, then the launching of an imperial project required that the palace complex had to command and control the mosque complex. The ruling institution of the classical period was subjected to Islam, but it was also the case that Islam was subjected to the ruling institution.

STATE SYSTEM AND STATE SOCIETY

Machiavelli had both understood and misunderstood the ruling institution of the new Ottoman Empire. The ministers of the Ottoman sultan, "being all slaves and bondsmen," were loyal and obedient servants of their master, but lacking any roots among the subject population, they could not "carry the people with them." Such a figure, that of a slave official, points to the exercise of sovereign power through an interpersonal association, but misidentifies an "ethic" as a "status." The actual Ottoman slave official (*kul*), a product of specific measures of recruitment and training, took his place in a centralized bureaucracy. All the personnel of this centralized bureaucracy, whether *kul* or not *kul*, were set apart from ordinary townsmen and villagers as an official class. The ethical underpinnings of this centralized bureaucracy, which constituted a tactic of sovereign power through interpersonal association, were otherwise fully transmissible, from inside to outside the imperial system. They could be the basis for training and recruiting segments of the subject population when the imperial system was in need of manpower and resources. And accordingly, they could also be appropriated and adapted by segments of the subject population determined to colonize the periphery of the imperial system. The classical imperial period therefore harbored a potential for dissemination that entirely escaped the attention of Machiavelli, as well as other western Europeans, right down to the twentieth century.

As we have seen from the outset of this chapter, the palace organized provincial government by relying on principles of bureaucratic centralism, that is to say, lower officials reporting to higher officials, ruling officials reviewed by judicial officials, and so on. However, it is now evident that these same principles of bureaucratic centralism were the rationalized and legalized expression of an imperial tactic: the exercise of sovereign power through a discipline of interpersonal association. The governors (*beylerbeyi*), the sub-governors (*sancakbeyi*), and their subordinate officers (*sipahi*) were the eyes, tongues, heads, and feet of the palace machine. In effect, they represented the body parts of the personal presence of the sovereign, the governors by reference to the sub-governors, the sub-governors by reference to the subordinate officers, and the subordinate officers by reference to ordinary townsmen and villagers. So each member of the official class was both ruler and ruled.

But this means that identification with and participation in the imperial system were not limited to the official class as such. Each governor, sub-governor, and subordinate officer was after all always more than a singular, isolated individual. He was a father of children, a master of a household, a relative among relatives, a friend among friends, a partner among partners, and a patron among clients. That is to say, each took his place in a world of nonofficial as well as official associations. So each was the representative of a discipline of interpersonal association as father, master, relative, friend, partner, and patron. And given that each was the subject of a discipline of interpersonal association, insofar as they were members of the official class, would it not also follow that adherence to such a discipline would also shape the ethics of families, households, patronage, kinship, partnership, and patronage? The state machine, a tiered hierarchy of bureaucratic centralism, was then conjoined with a state society, a tiered hierarchy of interpersonal associations. And moreover, the associational dimension of the regime always exceeded its official dimension. And by this fact, the associational dimension of the regime always exerted a constant pressure on its official dimension. Whenever the system of imperial regulations allowed some leeway, who would be favored and who would be disfavored? It would not be possible to answer this question without a thorough understanding of the system of interpersonal associations. And this being the case, to what extent could one be sure that the system of imperial regulations was not itself bent or warped, even corrupted and subverted, by the system of interpersonal associations? This very problem explains the precision and elaboration of the imperial system of regulations. It was built as a kind of dike against networks and connections that suffused the official class. And it was a dike that always leaked.

The problem of decentralization was then in place before, during, and after the classical period. The slave official had been conceived to contain and control such a tendency. The children of a subject population who became slave officials were outsiders to existing official circles of interpersonal association (theoretically if not in practice).[80] They were therefore recruited and trained in the Imperial College of the palace, married to women trained in the Imperial Harem, and then posted to governorships and subgovernorships. In this manner, the palace machine seeded the further reaches of the imperial system with creatures of its making, with individuals embedded in and compromised by official circles of interpersonal association. The eyes, tongues, heads, and feet of these individuals could therefore be relied upon to reconstitute the personal presence of the sovereign sitting in his tower, looking from a window, viewing the two continents of a world empire.

The palace machine was designed to hold in check the forces of decentralization that could only accumulate with the expansion and extension of the ruling institution. But the palace machine accomplished something far more general and enduring than what Machiavelli had estimated. By the work of Mehmet II, the exercise of sovereign power through a discipline of interpersonal association had been more perfectly and elegantly expressed as world rule based on a cosmic law. There was then, in principle, no limit to the number of individuals who might participate in the state society of

80. Kunt 1974.

the imperial system, only a limit to the efficiency and effectiveness of its bureaucratic centralism.

THE PERIOD OF DECENTRALIZATION IN THE PROVINCE OF TRABZON

As the central government grew weaker during the eighteenth century, provincial elites in the core Ottoman provinces assumed the status of sovereigns ruling extensive domains, passing their wealth and property, as well as their official titles and appointments, to their descendants.[81] The provincial elites lived in spacious mansions with many servants, including both male and female slaves. Their residences, often sited on promontories or hilltops, took the form of semi-fortified mansions (*konak*), which were like government buildings with receiving rooms, accounting offices, and prisons. They carried out all kinds of government functions, collecting duties and taxes, apprehending fugitives and enforcing court orders, assembling irregular troops, requisitioning military supplies, and maintaining roads and bridges by corvée labor. For this purpose, they maintained a certain number of administrative staff, and they moved about with retinues of armed supporters.

Since they were sometimes able to place tens of thousands of troops in the field, the provincial elites were in a position to resist, and even defeat, the central armies of the imperial system.[82] The Ottomans, that is, the state officials representing the palace in Istanbul, were therefore obliged to work with or against them, sometimes granting them titles and appointing them to offices, sometimes declaring them rebels and sending troops against them. The provincial elites were then both inside and outside the official class. As sovereigns of their domains, the provincial elites sometimes defied the central government, but they sometimes implemented imperial regulations and contributed troops to imperial campaigns. In most of the core Ottoman provinces, both higher and lower state officials were unable to carry out the

81. İnalcık 1977, 31; Sakaoğlu 1984, 10; Özkaya 1977, 67, 99; and Veinstein 1975, 1991. The local elites varied in their sociological character. This has led to disagreements among historians about the causes that brought them to prominence, the exact periods when they were dominant, and their most important social and political characteristics. Cf. Gould 1976; Nagata 1976; Skiotis 1971; and Uzunçarsılı 1975.

82. Akarlı 1988; Özkaya 1977, 8, 24–27, 67–68, 98, 111; Sakaoğlu 1984, 10; and Veinstein 1975, 1991.

most elementary governmental functions without their assistance. Accordingly, the Ottomans styled them in different ways at different times, for example, as "lords" (*derebey*) or as "usurpers" (*mütegallibe*), in accordance with an intent to accept or to question their legitimacy.[83] In many places, the provincial elites had risen to prominence by amassing vast farming estates worked by large peasant populations. They had done so in many cases by manipulating the tax-farming system, which had replaced the older system of military appointments and assignments. Acquiring the right to collect and forward tax-receipts, an individual could gain control over large tracts of land as well as large numbers of villagers who inhabited them.[84]

The local elites of the eastern coastal districts were of a different sort. Unlike their counterparts elsewhere, they did not own estates worked by peasants. Instead, they were able to assert themselves as sovereign powers—against their competitors or even against state officials—by their ability to mobilize large numbers of armed followers. But here, the foundation of their sovereignty, that is, large numbers of armed followers, has to be distinguished from the quality of their sovereignty. They were not gang leaders or warlords. Some of them appeared as such at least some of the time, and state officials and foreign consuls described them as such when they gave them trouble rather than assistance. They were also not exactly leaders of military formations, although they certainly manifested themselves in this form from time to time. More exactly, the local elites in their great mansions had a close kinship with the sultan in his palace. They were the principal figures of ruling associations based on a discipline of social thinking and practice. But unlike the sultan, their ruling associations were not closely linked with ceremony and protocol. The local elites in their great mansions were at the center of circles of interpersonal association. These circles were not formally constituted as corporate groups but rather as social networks. They were composed of agnates, affines, servants, friends, partners, and allies. They included a significant fraction of the rural population, even all of the rural population of Muslims, in theory if not in prac-

83. According to Sakaoğlu (1984, 5), the term "valley lord" (*derebey*) is a corruption of the phrase "recognized lord" (*derre bey*).

84. Akarlı (1988) discusses the rise of provincial magnates through the accumulation of agricultural lands. Sakaoğlu (1984, 10) remarks that Ottoman officials referred to them as simple landowners (*çiftlik ağası*), but they had in fact become provincial lords and rulers. See, however, Veinstein (1991) on the question of the extent to which the rise of local elites in the eighteenth century was linked with the control of land.

tice. In this respect, the makeup of these circles of interpersonal association directly reflected the largely Muslim makeup of rural society.

The local elites of the province of Trabzon were, much like the sultan in Istanbul, the overseers of circles of interpersonal associations. They maintained salons (*oda*) in their mansions where they received guests and visitors, and they sponsored coffeehouses (*kahve*) patronized by large numbers of partners and allies.[85] At the same time, they were wary of any signs of ambition or rivalry among their relatives or followers. They did not allow anyone within their domains to build new houses, to add rooms to existing houses, to open coffeehouses, or even to build mosques without their permission. Each of these steps could be a first move toward building local support and influence.

Since the sovereign power of local elites, no less than that of the sultan, was linked with a discipline of interpersonal association, they aligned themselves with a kind of Islam much like official Islam. Local elites arranged for the building of mosques in the market centers subject to their control.[86] They struck partnerships with representatives of the religious professors and students, even to the point of subsidizing them. With the assistance of these representatives, they took the liberty of intervening in the affairs of their followers, arranging marriages and settling disputes in the name of the sacred law of Islam. At the same time, they did not tolerate religious teachers and students asserting themselves as independent authorities in towns or villages.

When their collective interests were threatened by a provincial governor, the local elites of Trabzon joined in coastal coalitions that were able to raise thousands of men in arms and move them both by land and sea. But they were not generally interested in bringing down the sultan or the Empire. They were themselves the creatures of the imperial system. Having adapted and appropriated the imperial tactic of sovereign power, they had a stake in imperial legitimacy, that is, in official Islam. When they rose in

85. See Fontanier (1829, 13, 22) for coffeehouses in Sürmene and in Trabzon; Brant (1836) for comments on coffeehouses in the markets at Sürmene, Rize, Atine, Hopa, and Batum; Guarracino (1845) for coffeehouses from Batum to Artvin; Koch (1846, 3) for comments on a coffeehouse at Sürmene that was similar to those in Istanbul; and Decourdemanche (1874, 358, 360) for coffeehouses as places for travelers to stay and places for association. Also see Umur (1956, No. 89 1859/1275), which shows that the estate of Memiş Agha Muradoğlu of Of included a coffeehouse.

86. This claim is certainly true for the major mosques in the district of Of. I am assuming that the pattern holds for all the province of Trabzon.

revolt, they did so in order to defend or to extend their privileges and prerogatives within the imperial system. As a consequence, they could be partisans of the sultan and Empire, responding to call-outs for imperial campaigns, even as they also raised men in arms in order to force state officials to grant them titles and offices.

When French and British consuls arrived in the town of Trabzon during the first decades of the nineteenth century, they had no understanding of how the local elites of the coastal valleys had grown within the imperial system. Seeing that they were able to defy and threaten the governor of the province of Trabzon, the consuls concluded that the local elites were part of a "feudal system," an alternative political system entirely distinct from the central government.

Fontanier was among those consuls who so described the local elites; however, he eventually came to understand them in ways that directly belied his prejudices.[87] On two occasions, he inadvertently contradicted himself. The local elites were not the principals of a feudal system exactly like that of thirteenth-century Europe. He noticed instead that they bore an eerie resemblance to the sovereign in his palace.

In the first of the two passages, Fontanier was not describing the local elites but rather belittling the Ottomans. Momentarily "off-guard," he asserts that the sultan, the provincial governor, the district sub-governor, and the agha are all similar to one another:

> As we are ordinarily inclined to make judgments by analogy, we might guess that the Ottoman Empire is run by ministers with specifically defined abilities who are able to take the department assigned to them in whatever direction they might wish [as was supposedly the case in the existing monarchy in France]. This would be a serious misperception, because a ministry is nothing but the organization of each family applied to the state. Thus, the agha of a village, the bey of a district, and the pasha of a province all have their house set up *exactly like that of the sultan,* so that they are surrounded by officers who fulfill the functions analogous to those of the ministers. Just like the Great Lord, they have their own steward, judge, treasurer, etc., whom they choose from among *their relatives or their friends.* It's just the same in the case of the Imperial Divan itself. Accordingly, it is clear that the ministers are merely domestic servants without any particular standing in their own right whose power depends solely on the favor of their master. [Italics mine][88]

87. Fontanier 1829, 17–18, cited in chap. 1.
88. Fontanier 1834, 39.

Having forgotten the reversion from republic to monarchy in France, Fontanier condemns the Ottoman Empire because of a confusion of the official with the familial. At every level of political authority, sultan, pasha, bey, and agha, the family is applied to the state. However, in making this point, he recognizes that the ministers in question are not really members of a family at all, but rather "relatives" or "friends," and by analogy with the palace, one might add, "servants" or "slaves." So Fontanier has actually pointed to a specific tactic of linking sovereign power with interpersonal association. Furthermore, he has noted that this specific tactic was characteristic of every level of political authority, not just the sultan, but also the pasha, the bey, and the agha. That is, it was a feature of both officialdom and nonofficialdom.

In the second of the two passages, buried in a later chapter of his second book on the Ottoman Empire, Fontanier again qualifies his earlier expressed opinion that the aghas of the eastern coastal region represented a feudal system. The passage occurs once again at a moment when he is "offguard" as he considers the specific character of the local elites in the district of Sürmene.[89] Once again, he contradicts himself as he draws an invidious comparison; for he now judges the imperial system to be even lower in stature and quality than the feudal system of western Europe:

> The mode of administration [in Sürmene] was more or less the same as in Anatolia. The inhabitants put themselves under the protection of those whom they supposed to be wealthier or more powerful. This would have been a feudalism completely like that which once existed in Europe, if such a patronage were to accord positive rights, and if children were able to inherit power from their fathers. But far from that, the lord who is called a "derebey" [valley lord] is nothing more than the chief of a community. He can do whatever he likes when it comes to tormenting foreigners or pillaging neighbors, but his power over those he administrates is very limited. The democratic element is that on which *the society rests;* such that the society is nothing more than *a collection of little republics.* These are more or less *advanced in civilization* in accord with whether they have been more or less favored by *geographic, political, or commercial circumstances.* [Italics mine][90]

Here Fontanier recognizes that the agha is "nothing more than the chief of a community," but the phrase substitutes for an omission in his analysis. He never writes about the vertical and horizontal solidarities in which the

89. In this chapter, Fontanier is recounting the revolt against the government in the district of Sürmene in 1832.

90. Fontanier 1834, 321.

local elites were positioned. He does not take the trouble to point out that the community in question was not ethnic or tribal in character. But he understood nonetheless that the community in question was a kind of "society" constituting a sort of "republic." He even understood that the community in question was a protean one that could rise to the level of "civilization" if it were favored by "geographical, political, and commercial circumstances." Here, he could have pointed directly to the sultan in his palace. The failure in his analysis arises from a blindness. He is unable to recognize a distinctive imperial tactic: sovereign power through interpersonal association.

By the eighteenth century, the ethical underpinnings of the ruling institution had been disseminated among the populations of the core Ottoman provinces. The local elites of the eighteenth-century province of Trabzon were far removed from the ceremony and protocol of the classical period. And yet key features of the imperial tactic displayed by the middle gate, Tower of Justice, Council Hall, middle court, inner gate, and Petition Room reappeared among them. But it was not only the local elites who had assimilated the ethical underpinnings of the imperial system. Unlike elsewhere in the core Ottoman provinces, the rise of the local elites of Trabzon had been contingent on the assimilation of the imperial system by the provincial population, hence the ottomanization of the rural societies of the eastern coastal districts. So a classical imperial system—which Machiavelli had appreciated as a remarkable example of exclusivity and centralism—had resulted in the formation of "a collection of little republics . . . more or less advanced in civilization," as Fontanier was to put it.

5 Dissemination
Soldiers and Students

ETHNIC DIVERSITY AND IMPERIAL HOMOGENEITY

In this chapter, I examine the district of Of as a case study in the emergence of an ottomanist state society in the province of Trabzon. Documents transliterated and summarized by Hasan Umur, the local historian of Of, track three different phases of such a process: the Islamization of the district by conversion and immigration, the spread of soldiering and preaching, and the rise to prominence of local elites.[1]

Who are the Oflus? The question has often been posed by outsiders, and their answers are bewildering. The Oflus are Lezghis (Evliya Çelebi, a late-seventeenth-century Ottoman traveler who confused them with a remote Caucasian people). The Oflus appear to be Muslims but secretly subscribe to Christianity (an early-nineteenth-century French consul).[2] The Oflus

1. Hasan Umur described about 230 Ottoman documents, of which about 150 are dated to the period of decentralization (roughly from 1688/1100 to 1834/1250). His first book (1951) is the result of research in the Başbakanlık Arşiv Dairesi in Istanbul. It transliterates or describes 129 imperial edicts (*ferman*) that he located in the Trabzon complaints (*şikâyat*) and judgments (*ahkâm*) registers, dating from 1575/983 to 1875/1292. He culled these particular documents in the course of a search through hundreds of volumes for any material that related to the district of Of. Umur notes that he chose not to discuss twenty such documents because he felt it inappropriate to publish them. He also set aside many more documents relating to Of because they did not mention village or family names or they seemed uninteresting and uncharacteristic. His second book (1956) describes 100 documents from the Trabzon Şer'i court registers, which he located in the Topkapı Saray Museum. Of these, he examined Nos. 1815 to 2024, which covered the years from 1557/965 to 1880/1297. He reports that he examined 209 separate registers comprising about 30,000 pages, culling 100 documents from more than 500 relating to Of.

2. Fontanier 1834, 292–94. When travelers report groups of crypto-Christians in Of, they are usually referring to the Kurumlis or other groups who were not

are not like the Rizelis and Sürmenelis, but have distinct habits and customs (an early-nineteenth-century British consul).[3] The Oflus are a melange of Byzantine peoples like the Rizelis and Sürmenelis (a late-nineteenth-century British consul).[4] The Oflus are of Pontic Greek origin, but became fanatical Muslims (a late-nineteenth-century scholar of Greek dialects).[5] The Oflus are Muslims who keep Bibles, crosses, and other relics and would like to become Christians (a twentieth-century Greek churchman).[6] The Oflus are Çepni Turks who settled in the district sometime after its incorporation by the Ottomans (a twentieth-century Turkish historian).[7] The Oflus are Laz, like all the other inhabitants of the coastal region (the villagers of the interior highlands).

Despite all the confusion of outside observers, most of the Oflus I encountered in the district during the 1960s did not hesitate to say who they were. They were Turkish Muslims. This contemporary self-identification can be dated to the beginning of the nationalist period, but it is consistent with a much longer history of state participation. By the late seventeenth century, the district of Of had become a predominantly Muslim rural society and many, if not most, male Oflus were affiliated with imperial military and religious institutions. The claim to be both Muslims and Turks in the 1960s can therefore be regarded as an updating of this ottomanist legacy.

As Muslims and Turks, the Oflus represented a local state society that had come into being through a complex process of conversion, immigration, and transformation. Since the traces of this history had been pre-

---

resident in Of. Defner, whose assistant visited the district in 1876, does not refer to any crypto-Christians in Of. Among the Oflus, the residents of Ogene [Köknar, Karaçam], located in the upper section of the western valley of the district, have the reputation of having been stubborn holdouts against conversion. However, the Trabzon yearbook (*salname*) for 1888/1305 locates an official religious academy in this very village, and it is attributed with one of the highest enrollments of religious students in the entire district of Of.

3. Brant 1836, 191. The Rizelis and Sürmenelis have themselves been alternatively called Laz, Lazi, Greeks, Byzantines, Armenians (Bijişkyan 1969 [1817–19], 60–64), Çepni Turks (Şakir Şevket 1877/1294, 95–96; Sümer 1992, 83 ff.), and Akkoyunlu Turks.

4. PRO 526/8 "On the Lazistan Coast . . . ," Jan. 29, 1873, Palgrave.

5. Defner 1877.

6. Poutouridou (1997–98) cites a passage from the memoirs of Chrysanthos of Trebizond. Also see Asan's translation (1996, 44, 46) of the memoirs of an Oflu Orthodox priest.

7. Sümer 1992, 83 ff.

served in local habit and custom, the identity of the Oflus, like that of many other rural peoples in the eastern coastal region, has long been available for all kinds of polemical purposes. In the next section, I shall illustrate all the moving, remaking, and mixing by contrasting the distinctive features of the population in different sectors of the district. In this way, undercurrents of ethnic and linguistic diversity will serve to highlight the homogenizing process of imperial identification and participation.

TWO VALLEY-SYSTEMS

The district of Of is geographically divided into two systems of valleys, that of the Solaklı River and that of Baltacı River (see map 1). The villagers of each system of valleys interact more among themselves than they do with the villagers of the other valley-system. The major market centers of each valley are different, and the routes of seasonal movement up and down the valley are different.[8]

According to local tradition, which is probably correct, the large majority of the population in the district of Of has been Muslim since the mid- to late seventeenth century. Regional historians, western European travelers, and government records from the mid-nineteenth century all agree that the population was as much as 98 percent Muslim at that time.[9] Government documents from earlier centuries strongly suggest that such a situation came about no later than the close of the seventeenth century.[10] So almost all the inhabitants of the district have been Muslim for some time.

On the other hand, the villagers in different sectors of the district have a mix of ethnic backgrounds. The population in the eastern valley-system is (and, in local memory, has long been) almost exclusively Turkish speaking. The population in the western valley-system recently included a

8. Here the present tense refers to the period before the acceleration of rural to urban migration during the 1960s.

9. The Trabzon yearbook (*salname*) for 1869/1286 records 98 percent of the total population as Muslim (Emiroğlu 1993, 1: 141). Palgrave reports 5,300 Muslim and 83 Orthodox household in Of (PRO 526/8, "On the Lazistan Coast . . . ," Jan 29, 1873, Palgrave). Defner (1877) counts 10,000 to 20,000 Muslim and 150 Christian households.

10. Şakir Şevket (1867/1284, 98) dates the conversion of the district to two hundred years after Ottoman incorporation, that is, to about 1655/1065. He mentions that most of the priests accepted Islam. Defner (1877) dates the conversion of the Greeks to 180 years preceding the visit of his assistant, that is, the close of the seventeenth century.

large number of Greek-speakers and was not so long ago largely Greek-speaking.[11] This contrast correlates with the transit systems of the two valleys (see map 1). The eastern valley was open to settlement by peoples of the interior highlands. What was once the principal coastal market for the district, Eskipazar ("old market") was the terminus for a trade route that moved up the eastern valley, across the mountains, to reach the Anatolian town of İspir, and thence Erzurum.[12] In contrast, the western valley, lacking a natural trade route, was less conveniently connected with the Anatolian town of Bayburt. Its residents engaged in seasonal movements up and down the valley, but the valley was less accessible from the coast and from the interior.[13]

My interlocutors in Of drew conclusions about the social attributes of each valley that are consistent with their contrasting topographies. The villagers of eastern valley are said to be of "diverse" origins by virtue of their physical appearance and social behavior.[14] Many had accents that brought to mind the speech patterns of the people of Erzurum, across the mountains, suggesting that most immigrants had come from that area.[15] In contrast, the villagers of the western valley are said to feature older, non-Turkic cus-

11. This situation, the east being Turkish-speaking and the west being Greek-speaking, prevailed during the visit of Defner's assistant in 1876 (Defner 1877).

12. Günay (1978, 28–29) describes İkizdere, adjacent to the eastern valley-system of Of, as the focus of the dominant Turkic dialect in the province and proposes that this was an area of early Turkic settlement. Otherwise, the eastern valley-system may have consistently received settlers from Anatolia since ancient times (Bryer and Winfield 1985, 11, 54–55).

13. Bryer and Winfield (1985, 11, 55) do not believe that the contemporary road that connects Of with Bayburt, which was constructed during the Russian occupation (1916–18), was previously a trade route of any importance. In Of and Sürmene, it is asserted that it was previously a trade route.

14. When I asked individuals from leading families about their family history, they commonly told me stories of a migration from the interior highlands, or even from as far away as Iraq or Syria. For example, one of the Muradoğlu said the founder of his family came from Van during the time of Mahmut II, while his two brothers settled in Hopa and Vakfıkebir. One of the Tellioğlu said his ascendants came from Baghdad out of Arabistan, one branch settling in Of and another branch settling in Giresun. A Selimoğlu says that the family came from Tercan (about halfway between Erzincan and Erzurum).

15. Brendemoen (1987, 1990) has not discovered traces of a Çepni influence on coastal speech patterns east of Trabzon, although such an influence is clearly apparent west of Trabzon. However, like Günay (1978, 26), he says that the Turkish dialect in Rize is similar to the Turkish dialect in Erzurum. My Oflu contacts are also in agreement with this opinion. They say that the Turkish spoken in the eastern half of their district (which borders on Rize) is similar to the Turkish spoken in Erzurum.

toms and practices. Although many spoke Greek as their first language, they also shared dances, stories, and songs from village to village, regardless of their mother tongue. This conservatism suggested that the rural societies in the western valley had been less unsettled by arrivals and departures.[16]

Still, one cannot conclude that the villagers of the eastern valley were essentially of Turkic origin while the villagers of the western valley were essentially of Greek origin. More exactly, Turkish became the local language of assimilation in the eastern valley, while Greek became the local language in the western valley.[17] In general, both Turkish and Greek as spoken in Of obey the rule of ethnic fragmentation and imperial appropriation. They are simultaneously marked by archaic traits and yet responsive to contact with the outside world. Brendemoen has found old Turkish usages in the district of Of that have vanished in most other parts of Asia Minor.[18] Similarly, the Greek spoken in the district of Of is an old Pontic dialect unique to it and yet strongly influenced by Turkic, Arabic, and Persian.[19]

DOCUMENTING IMMIGRATION AND CONVERSION IN OF

The traces of past immigration and conversion in different sectors of the district are consistent with published descriptions of the four Ottoman registers compiled during the first and second century of Ottoman rule.[20] Hasan Umur carried out a study of three of these registers and summarized those portions that specifically referred to the district. Reorganizing his

16. See, for example, the comments of Umur (1949, 89–90). The dialect of Pontic Greek spoken by the Oflus is apparently indigenous to the valley (Defner 1877).

17. Some well-known families in both valleys are said to be of Turkic origin, but others of Kurdish origin, for example, the Muradoğlu, the Tellioğlu, and the Nuhoğlu. All the latter are located in the eastern valley, but there are also some families that are said to be of Kurdish or Turkic origin in the western valley-system as well. These new arrivals would have intermarried with the Greek-speakers, of course, and there are traditions of their having done so ("Fettahoğullarının Tarihi").

18. Brendemoen (1990, 49, 57) also notes that the same archaic Turkish usages are also found in the district of Tonya, another area where Muslim Greek-speakers were common.

19. Asan 1996 and Poutouridou 1997–98.

20. The three registers have not yet been exhaustively studied. See Gökbilgin (1962) for some general conclusions about the registers, Lowry (1977) for a study of that portion relating to the town of Trabzon, Umur (1951) for some of the details regarding the district of Of, and Bilgin (1990) for some of the details regarding the district of Sürmene.

Table 1. Number of Christian and Muslim Households, by Quadrant

	Christian and Muslim Households					
Register date	*1515/921*		*1554/961*		*1583/991*	
Valley quadrant	Christian	Muslim	Christian	Muslim	Christian	Muslim
Lower east	979	26	1,039	187	908	551
Higher east	—	—	61	7	200	16
Lower west	988	22	1,078	128	1,160	264
Higher west	288	2	427	27	646	95
Unlocated	97	—	124	10	201	50
Total	2,352	50	2,729	359	3,115	976
% Muslim	2		12		24	

SOURCE: Meeker (1971).

household counts by geographic sectors, one can detect the very beginnings of trends in migration and conversion that eventually led to the contemporary attributes of the population.[21] The results of this reorganization are presented in table 1.

The total Christian population in the district was increasing rather than decreasing during most, if not all, of the sixteenth century.[22] The Muslim population, still quite small in 1515—more than fifty years after the fall of Trabzon—becomes significant only in 1583, that is, well into the second century of Ottoman rule. Thus Ottoman incorporation of the district, which would have included the allotment of *tımars* and the assignment of *sipahis,* was not initially correlated with large numbers of arrivals of Muslims, departures of Christians, or conversions. At the time of the register of 1554, almost a century after the fall of Trabzon, the Christian population had risen slightly even in the lower valleys. On the other hand, there

21. Umur (1951) records the total number of households for each village locale and the number of households that were recorded as Muslim rather than non-Muslim. I have grouped the villages according to their location in a particular sector of the district. In those instances where I was unable to determine the location of a village, the household total is listed under "unlocated." These tabulations of Umur's data were first published in Meeker 1971.

22. The increase is about 15 percent from register to register.

are now indications that the Christian population was beginning to come under some kind of pressure. Since the compilation of the previous register there appear to have been a significant number of Muslim arrivals; moreover, a proportion of the Christian population has begun to resettle in the upper valleys, where new villages are being founded. At the time of the register of 1583, there is a clear indication of the onset of the Islamization of the district population by a combination of immigration and conversion. Since the compilation of the previous register, the Muslim population has significantly risen and the Christian population has significantly declined in the lower eastern valley. This was the sector where Turkish would eventually become the language of assimilation. One might estimate that the Christian population in this part of the district was already headed toward collapse by the close of the sixteenth century.[23] And since the Turkish spoken here now bears traces of an Erzurum dialect, arrivals of Turkic-speaking Muslims, coming directly or indirectly from the interior highlands of Erzurum, were already playing a role in the process of Islamization.[24]

The three sixteenth-century registers give us no exact information about the role of immigration as compared to conversion in bringing about the Islamization of the district. In all likelihood, both were equally important. Some of the new Muslims must have been Turkic-speakers by the evidence of contemporary linguistic studies. Some of the new Muslims must have been converts by the evidence of personal names recorded in the registers.[25] In other words, during the sixteenth century there was a gradual intrusion of Muslims and a gradual conversion of Christians, together resulting in an average increase of about twenty Muslim families a year from the second to the third register.

On the other hand, the registers point to the eventual establishment of Turkish and Greek as the languages of assimilation in the lower eastern and

23. Umur (1951, 20) reached a similar conclusion. The registers demonstrated to him that the lower reaches of the Baltacı and Solaklı rivers were being Turkicized and Islamized during the sixteenth century. He also acknowledged that Orthodox Greeks would have been converting to Islam and therefore joining the new Turkic settlers. In mentioning this he asked his readers to understand that no nation is completely pure but all are composed of a mixture of peoples.

24. Günay 1978, 26.

25. The name İskender, indicating a convert or a child of a convert (Lowry 1977), commonly occurs in the lists of Muslim residents of the villages of Of in each of the three registers, increasingly in the second and third. Since Umur gives only a few examples of the names for each village, the frequency of the name İskender cannot be determined from his study.

upper western sectors, respectively. In the former sector, the Muslim population was rising and the Christian population was faltering, while in the latter sector the Christian population was rising and the Muslim population remained small in number, although it too was rising. It is only the upper eastern sector that was inconsistent with the contemporary attributes of the population, since the formation of new Christian settlements did not lead to the persistence of Greek-speakers in this area. This inconsistency reinforces the point that the population of neither valley can be considered to have been exclusively of Turkic or Greek background.

The situation in the district of Of during the sixteenth century contrasts with what was taking place in the regional capital. Toward the latter half of the sixteenth century, the Ottomans had begun to move Muslims into and Christians out of the town of Trabzon.[26] Perhaps in response to these measures, large numbers of conversions had begun to take place among the Christians in the town. In any event, the Christians would have been inclined to convert for other reasons as well. The church hierarchy and institutions had declined, and the economic benefits of Muslim status were considerable. By the time of the registers of 1583, more than half of the population in the town of Trabzon had become Muslim, largely as a result of conversion rather than immigration, as evidenced by the fact that most of the citizenry still spoke Greek.[27] Judging from the example of Of, the advantages of both immigration and conversion were less immediate in the outlying districts than in the regional capital itself. Unlike the regional capital, the outlying districts were not the site of major emporia serving sea and overland routes. So the Ottomans were less concerned about the composition of their populations, Muslims were less motivated to immigrate there in the absence of opportunities, and Christians were under less pressure to convert.[28] Later, during the seventeenth century, the situation would change as the inhabitants of the eastern districts began to participate in imperial institutions as soldiers and students. The population of the eastern districts would become almost entirely Muslim, more so than the regional capital.

26. Lowry 1977.

27. Lowry (1977, 243–44) found that the population of the town of Trabzon, still largely Christian at the time of the Ottoman register of 1554/961, was more than 50 percent Muslim by 1583/991, and yet it remained about 70 percent Greek-speaking.

28. Since Rize was more like Trabzon than Of in this respect, it is possible that immigration and conversion were also already important there during the sixteenth century.

Christian conversion and Muslim immigration gradually gained ground in the district during the course of the seventeenth century.[29] An official document dated 1615/1024 indicates a substantial Christian presence in the district of Of.[30] Others, however, hint at steadily decreasing numbers of Christian households. One document dated 1631/1040 refers to 441 Christian households in the district of Of, while one dated 1673/1083 refers to only 90.[31] Probably there was no one moment of mass conversion among the Christians, but rather one or more occasions when a large number of people, and perhaps several villages, passed over to Islam *en masse*. But what did it mean when an individual or a group chose to be registered as Muslim rather than Christian? Does the fact of official registration as Muslim rather than Christian indicate anything about the relationship of an individual or group to the imperial system?

As we saw in the last chapter, the ruling institution of the classical period sponsored and supported the sacred law of Islam. However, this did not mean that ordinary Ottoman subjects, whether Muslim, Christian, or Jewish, were forced or encouraged to conform to official Islam. The sacred law of Islam accords legal standing to local customs and habits (*örf ve âdet*) of Muslims, just as it accords legal standing to the religious leadership and communities of Christians and Jews (*ehl-i kitab*). So, in terms of legal status and rights, the inhabitants of the eastern coastal districts did not need to become official Muslims, or, for that matter, to become Muslims at all. Nonetheless, those individuals whose family and commercial affairs conformed to official Islam would have enjoyed certain advantages. So at best

29. Poutouridou (1997–98, 57) has concluded that church organization in the district of Of probably collapsed sometime during the second century of Ottoman rule. Citing Vryonis and Bryer, she notes that the bishopric of Of was one of three remaining in Anatolia during the late fifteenth century, but had disappeared from the episcopal lists of the Patriarchate of Constantinople by 1645.

30. Umur 1951, No. 3 1615/1024. This document describes the desperate situation of the villagers in the district who may be forced by famine to abandon their villages. The writer observes that the Christian villagers were suffering even more because they were obliged to pay the special tax on non-Muslims, the *haraç*. Citing this document, Umur (1951, 20–24) concluded that the district would have been entirely Islamized and Turkicized at this date as a consequence of conversion or desertion of Christian villagers. However, the document only indicates the existence of hardship rather than actual desertions or conversions.

31. Umur 1956, No. 8 1631/1040 refers to 441 *cizye*-paying households of *zimmis* in Of; No. 25 1673/1083 refers to 90 such households. The *cizye* was a head tax on non-Muslims. The term *zimmi* refers to a non-Muslim subject. Since it is possible that the counts are partial rather than total, they can only be taken as the minimum number of Christian households remaining.

the imperial regime would have only exerted mild financial and political pressures on Christians and Muslims to move toward official Islam.

In response to such pressures, it is likely that villagers and townsmen in the province of Trabzon presented themselves as official Muslims when it came to their dealings with the state. Otherwise these same villagers and townsmen would have continued to follow religious beliefs and practices that did not conform at all to official Islam. The best example of this situation is those groups of villagers in Trabzon, such as the Kurumlis, who registered themselves as Muslim with the central government but otherwise followed Orthodox beliefs and practices.[32] And judging from the results of my fieldwork, I would expect that groups of heterodox Muslims also followed a similar strategy, presenting themselves as official Muslims before state officials, but then following Shi'i beliefs and practices when among themselves in their villages.

Thus the steady increase in the Muslim population during the seventeenth century is not in itself an indication of the emergence of a state-oriented society in the district of Of. It is possible that the local population featured all kinds of religious orientations even while the Oflus were officially registered as Muslims. But it is highly unlikely that this was in fact the case. The steady increase in the Muslim population was headed toward the disappearance of a Christian population, and this disappearance is associated with traditions of flight and apostasy. This suggests that the Oflus, both Muslim and Christian, were engaged in a transformation of their family and social lives, something far more drastic than adapting themselves to the state system by presenting themselves as official Muslims. The signs of such a transformation are clearly evident by the late seventeenth century. The Christians were converting and the Muslims were reforming, as both groups merged together to form a new kind of state society. The energy and conviction that went into this remaking of family and society was such that it soon became impossible for any of the Oflus to exempt themselves.

DOCUMENTING IMPERIAL PARTICIPATION IN TRABZON

Toward the close of the seventeenth century, the Oflus were most surely identifying with and participating in imperial institutions. One of the documents transcribed by Hasan Umur indicates the extent of this change. In

32. Bryer 1988. Cf. Janin 1912.

the year 1695/1106, the central government called on the people of the southern Black Sea coast to send 7,700 troops to report for an imperial campaign in Hungary. The interesting feature of this call-out is the distribution of troop assignments among the coastal districts. The further eastern districts, whose populations included large numbers of non-Turkic peoples, were expected to send the largest number of troops. In the document, each of fourteen districts, from Arhavi in the east to Şile in the west (beyond Bafra), were assigned a specific quota of recruits as follows (see map 2):

> 2,000 persons from the Kaza of Trabzon, 500 from Sürmene, 300 from Giresun, 1,000 from Of, 700 from Rize, 300 from Mapavri, 500 from Atine, 500 from Arhavi with Vetse, 250 from Keşap, 100 from Viçe, 500 from Ünye with Balya, 300 from Şile, 300 from Görele with Tirebolu, 100 from Pazarsuyu, 300 from Sinop, and, besides the total of 7,700 individuals, the resident aghas and sergeants (*ağa ve çavuş*) and house property owners and men of wealth, whoever they may be, are to unfurl the banners, appoint commanders (*üzerine başbuğ nasb*), and gather provisions for their appearance in the field at Edirne.[33]

The large majority of the troops were called from the districts that would have had the highest proportion of non-Turkic peoples descended from the Orthodox, Byzantine population, 5,500 of the total of 7,700. So that part of the coastal region, which had so recently had a large Christian population, was to send a much larger contingent than the western coast, which had been predominantly Muslim for centuries.

The district of Of was assigned the largest quota of troops (1,000), with the one exception of the district of the provincial capital (2,000). The quota of troops for Of surpasses the total number of Muslim households attributed to the district in the last Ottoman register compiled in 1583. At the same time, the quota of troops also represents a substantial fraction, about 25 percent, of the total number of households, both Christian and Muslim, recorded for the district. So, even taking into account that the population may have increased, the call-out for the imperial campaign indicates a substantial change in the character of the population. By this date, in all probability, the large majority of Oflus had become Muslim by virtue of the combined processes of immigration and conversion. And more than this,

33. Umur 1956, No. 38 1695/1106. The numbers for the districts add up to 7,650, not 7,700.

the central government clearly expected that these "new" Muslims would respond to the call-out in especially large numbers.

Two other court documents suggest that centers of religious study had also come into existence more or less at the same time as large numbers of soldiers began to be drawn from the district.[34] One of these, dated 1699/1110, records the following circumstances: On the complaint of one İbrahim of the learned class (*ulema*), one İbrahim Beşiroğlu of Paçan [*Maraşlı*] village in the district of Of, did sell property for a sum of money in the year 1689/1100, after which İbrahim the purchaser went to Istanbul for educational purposes (*tahsili ilm için*), whereupon İbrahim the seller did attempt to overturn the sale of the property, driving the wife and household of the purchaser from the premises and reselling it to another.[35] The document indicates that the residents of Paçan were already engaged in religious teaching and learning toward the close of the seventeenth century. The second document, which refers to an incident that occurred in 1737/1150, indicates that a center of religious teaching and learning, with a large library, was in existence in the upper western valley by that date. According to the document, to be discussed later in more detail, an individual had come to the court with a complaint against various persons who are described as brigands. They are accused of exacting retribution on the inhabitants and killing as many as forty teachers and students while stealing seven hundred books or registers.

By the middle of the eighteenth century, if not earlier, the district of Of had become famous for its many specialists in religious teaching and learning, to a degree that was almost unparalleled in any other rural area of Asia Minor. In his study of commercial conditions along the Black Sea littoral, M. de Peysonnel, referring to conditions in 1750, writes that the district of Of was famous for its "infinite number of Men of the Law known for their erudition."[36] Since the reputation presumably followed the fact by some

34. According to Uğur (1986, lx, lxxvi), the Ottoman religious academies were already in decline by the seventeenth century, troubled by "nepotism, simony, and favoritism."

35. Umur 1951, No. 20 1699/1110.

36. The relevant passage (1787, 70–71) is as follows: *"il y a sur-tout un nombre infini de Gens de Loi renommés pour leur érudition."* Peysonnel (*fils*) did not publish his treatise on commerce in the Black Sea until the year 1787; however, he explains in his preface that his information was based largely on material collected from Turkish, Armenian, and Greek businessmen in Izmir during 1750, supplemented by more information gathered when he served as a consul in the Crimea after 1753, then finally completed in 1762 while a resident of the kingdom of Candie. Acknowledging that the situation in the Black Sea had changed, he affirms that he

years, the remark indicates that large numbers of religious teachers and students were to be found in the district no later than the early eighteenth century.[37] By later memory and tradition, centers of religious study were distributed all over the district, both in the lower and upper valleys; however, they were especially concentrated in the upper western valley, where Greek was more commonly spoken than Turkish. Sermons were delivered in Turkish, but also commonly in Greek (in each instance with Koranic citations in Arabic). Koranic texts as well were discussed in Turkish, but also commonly in Greek.[38]

---

has presented his information exactly as he gathered it years before. For more on the Peysonnels, *père* and *fils*, both of whom served as consul in Izmir, see Veinstein 1975.

37. Other, more indirect evidence is consistent with the existence of a learned tradition in the district of Of from the early eighteenth century. Oflu Bilal Efendi of Paçan [Maraşlı] village is known as the "first poet of Of." Although his precise birth and death dates are unknown, he is thought to have lived in the first half of the eighteenth century, and one of his works is published in 1764. Hasan Umur (1951) transliterated a number of eighteenth-century court documents referring to disputes over the right to act as an official imam (*imam, hatip*) in this or that village in the district of Of (No. 22 1702/1114, No. 44 1719/1131, No. 73 1733/1146, No. 93 1770/1184, No. 94 1770/1184, No. 101 1780/1194, No. 109 1789/1203). Architectural evidence of religious buildings is fragmentary, since they were built of wood, and so most would have been reconstructed over the years. When a state official organized local brigands to raid the western valley of Of in 1711/1123, they are also said to have burned seven mosques in fifteen villages (Umur 1951, No. 35). A wooden mosque in Sürmene has the date 1785/1200 on its door (Bilgin 1990, 673). According to Umur (1956, 16–17), the death of the first preacher (*hatip*) in Yiğa [Yarlı] village is dated to 1798/1212, as deduced from a document dated in 1836/1251. Umur estimates from this (by the average life of a man) that the mosque was built 45 years before, that is, in 1737/1150. According to Karpuz (1989), there is a date of 1767/1181 on the door of the mosque in Alanomakot [Ağaçlı] village in the district of Of. He also mentions an eighteenth-century mosque in Çaykara, rebuilt in 1809.

38. The descendants of Greek-speaking Christians appear to have made an important contribution to the tradition of religious study in these villages. The Trabzon yearbook (*salname*) for 1888/1305 (pp. 127–30, 313–16) states that lessons in the religious academies of Of were sometimes given in Greek, although most of the population in the district was Turkish-speaking. In the 1960s, by the reports of my interlocutors, much of the population in the district of Çaykara still spoke Pontic Greek in their families and villages. Although the male population always spoke Turkish (many of the women did not), mosque sermons and religious instruction were said to be sometimes conducted in Pontic Greek. Also see Asan (1996, 121) and Poutouridou (1997–98, 62) for further documentation of the use of Pontic Greek by Muslim teachers and preachers. Paçan [Maraşlı] village, one of the most famous centers of religious study in the district and the site of the attack on teachers and students in 1737/1150, was among the Greek-speaking villages.

Pontic Greek historians of the last century believed that a mass apostasy eventually took place in the district of Of, provoking the flight of those who refused to convert to Islam.[39] They traced the cause for this mass conversion and flight to conditions of insecurity that followed the rise of aghas and agha-families (*derebey*). There is only a grain of truth in these otherwise erroneous traditions. The process of Islamization by conversion, which had probably begun during the first half of the sixteenth century, was gradual rather than abrupt.[40] Eventually, by incremental processes of both Muslim settlement and Christian conversion, the district of Of became almost completely Muslim by the late seventeenth century. But while no mass conversion and flight ever occurred, the close of the seventeenth century was a turning point in the eastern districts of the old province of Trabzon. Some considerable number of Christians, both Greek-speakers and Armenian-speakers, abandoned the eastern districts at this time in order to seek refuge in the province of Canık, significantly, that part of the coastal region that had not been part of the Greek Empire of Trebizond.[41]

These departures occur too early to be correlated with the rise of aghas and agha-families. More probably, the remaining Christians were pressured to convert or leave by a heightening of imperial identification and participation. The rural societies of the coastal districts were becoming not just Muslim but, more specifically, imperially Muslim toward the close of the seventeenth century. Large numbers of Oflus were making their way into the ranks of regular troops and irregular militia.[42] A smaller number

39. Orthodox Greek writers of the nineteenth century date this event to the mid- or late seventeenth century (Poutouridou 1997–98).

40. Umur (1951, 21–22), who knew the Ottoman documents relating to this question better than anyone, reaches this conclusion. So far as I am aware, there is no mention of mass conversion in any source earlier than the nineteenth century. Some such sources are of Muslim and some are of Christian origin (see chap. 8).

41. There is convincing evidence of a flight of Christians from Trabzon to Canık during the late seventeenth century. Biliotti encountered groups of Christian Armenians and Greeks in the latter province who had migrated there from Hemşin and Gümüşhane during the first part of the eighteenth century (PRO FO 195/1329, at Fatsa, No. 30, Aug. 1880; at Ünye, No. 32 and No. 33, Aug. 1880; at Çarşamba, No. 38 and No. 45, Oct. 1880; at Görele, No. 48, Oct. 1880). Janin (1912, 497–98) writes, without attribution, that the Christians of Rize and Of either fled to the Crimea and Moldavia or converted sometime around 1665. Also see Bryer (1970).

42. Reporting on his travels during the spring of 1835, James Brant (1836, 192) wrote of the district of Of: "The people are a hardy laborious and bold race, they are skilled in the use of a short rifle, which every man carries slung at his back wherever and on whatever occasion he moves, and they enjoy a high reputation as

were locally achieving appointments as janissary officers and soldiers.[43] A few were even able to advance themselves in the imperial military establishment, serving outside the district in various towns or cities.[44] At the very same time, in no less remarkable numbers, other Oflus were becoming religious teachers and students. And of these, some were also using what they had learned locally to propel themselves into the imperial religious establishment, financing their further education, when they could, in more prestigious institutions of the major Ottoman cities.[45]

There was probably some kind of correlation between ethnic background and imperial service. Individuals of Turkic and Kurdish background were probably more typically successful in military careers, while those of Greek background were probably more typically successful in religious careers, in view of the fact that the Greek-speaking villages of the district are so strongly correlated with religious teaching and learning. But given the large numbers of both soldiers and students in Of, and adding in the factor of intermarriage, such a correlation could not have been very significant. Local participation in imperial institutions transcended ethnic identity. With the new avenues of appointment and position that opened up during the later seventeenth century, there were new possibilities for both immigrants and converts. The two could join together in hopes of making a place for themselves in the imperial system, something that had not been previously possible.

DOCUMENTING THE ORIGINS OF AGHAS AND KONAKS IN OF

Since imperial participation was such an important factor in the district of Of, social changes in the district should be all the more closely correlated

---

Soldiers. A demand is always made on this country by the Porte, to supply a certain number of men for the Arsenal at Constantinople."

43. More and more janissary appointments were improperly granted by bribes during the eighteenth century (Özkaya 1977, 52–53). Janissary appointments were bought and sold like mortgage contracts (Bilgin 1990, 277).

44. For an early example, see Umur 1951, No. 79 1740/1153 and No. 81 1745/1158, which reports on a charge of murder where the victim is named as *"dergâhı muallâm yeniçerileri serdengeçti ağaleri emektarlerinden Piri Çavuş zade Mustafa nam ihtiyar kendi halinde iken Of kazası sakinlerinden."* For a late example, see Umur 1956, No. 75 1843/1259, which reports on a charge of land theft where the plaintiff is named as *"Of kazasında Baltacı deresinde vaki Konu karyesinden Tophane-i amire çavuşlarından Ömer Çavuş bin Mehmed."*

45. Umur 1951, No. 20 1699/1110. Also see the analysis of the learned class (*ulema*) in the district of Of in chap. 8.

with changes in state policies and structures. In other words, the history of social relations in Of should follow those changes in the central government that everywhere touched the populations of the core Ottoman provinces. Documents summarized or transliterated by Hasan Umur indicate that this was indeed the case.[46] Overall, the two hundred or so court cases and imperial decrees that he summarized are well coordinated with the major trends in the relationship of state and society. At the same time, the documents also point to the distinctive features of local elites in the province of Trabzon. When combined with local tradition, the documents suggest that imperial participation proceeded in a fashion that was not exactly duplicated in other Ottoman provinces, with results that also differed.

My interlocutors in the district of Of generally believed that the individuals who became aghas and established agha-families during the eighteenth century were often newcomers to the district of Of. I do not know of any definitive proof of this, but it is the overall opinion of both district outsiders and insiders.[47] Local tradition also holds that the different aghas and agha-families arose at different times during the period of decentralization, some of them very early and some of them very late. Most of them then endured right down to the present day, some declining and others flourishing.[48] The documents transcribed or summarized by Umur tell us something more than this. Given that some names that appear in the documents are unrecognizable, together with the fact that aghas and agha-families were always emerging, it seems likely that some individuals rose

46. At the time of my fieldwork, I had considered Umur's studies to be useless because it was impossible to establish his criteria for selecting documents. When reconsidering his books in the 1980s, I was surprised to discover that his documents regarding Of referred to events that correlated closely with the latest studies of provincial social history in the core Ottoman provinces. This is evidence of the reliability of his survey of documents since he would have been unaware of the results of the later studies.

47. Şakir Şevket (1877/1294, p. 249 ff.) comments that the ascendants of the Şatıroğlu family of Trabzon (prominent during the period of decentralization) first came to Trabzon at the time of the Ottoman conquest. Gologlu (1975, xxxxi [sic]) writes that the ascendant of the Selimoğlu family of Of is believed to have come to Trabzon as an *akıncı* (light cavalry raider) during the second half of the sixteenth century. According to Bryer (1970, 45), the names of the district and provincial lords (*derebey*) in the coastal region cannot be traced earlier than the seventeenth century. However, this may not be significant since it would not be possible to trace names until a family line had been established, that is, after the period of decentralization had already begun.

48. The Çapoğlu and the Ayazoğlu are said to have set down family lines very early. The Muradoğlu most certainly set down a family line very late.

to prominence but then failed to establish family lines. Furthermore, the documents also suggest that the individuals who did rise to prominence, whether or not they did set down a family line, had some kind of connection with the government, but were of no special official eminence. In this respect, they are usually mentioned in terms of personal names supplemented by an "official" patronymic in the "*oğlu*" or "*zade*" form.

Of the documents Umur reviews, the earliest mention of a patronymic that is eventually associated with aghas and agha-families appears in three separate documents that address the attack, theft, and pillage of a settlement in 1679/1090. A certain Hacı Ahmet Ayazoğlu is one of several individuals alleged to have participated in these aggressions.[49] Some of the other accused individuals also have patronymics, but I am unable to link them with contemporary family names. The names include some with various epithets of a military (*kanlı, bey*) or religious (*hacı, molla*) character, but no titles or ranks. Other epithets added to their personal names indicate that the individuals in the group were of different homelands (*Azaklı*) and different ethnicities (*Çerkes*). So the accused consist of a motley group of individuals of different familial, regional, and ethnic origins who have adopted low-level religious and military epithets. If the three documents are set in the larger context of state and society, they point toward a tentative conclusion.

During the final years of the seventeenth century, irregular troops and religious students without employment were commonly responsible for the kind of incidents described in the documents. For example, the group of individuals accused and convicted of the incidents in Of in 1679 would appear to have been so composed. So it would seem that some of the first aghas and agha-families in the district of Of arose from among individuals who were associated with the very lowest level of official military and religious activities. Alternatively, Hacı Ahmet Ayazoğlu may have been a black sheep from a more prominent family line. This possibility is unlikely when compared with the same pattern that appears in other documents. About thirty years after the above incidents (1708), Kanlı Hasan Ayazoğlu, acting together with brothers, a cousin, and associates, is accused and convicted of usurping the authority of the district janissary agha by appointing his son-in-law to that position. Then two years later this same individual, still other brothers, a cousin, and associates are named as well-known

49. Umur 1951, No. 9 1689/1100, No. 10 1689/1100, and No. 12 1689/1100. The documents all address the same incidents, which occurred in 1679/1090.

brigands who have been attacking marketplaces, committing homicides, and assaulting unmarried women for more than a decade.[50]

A second set of documents describes even more serious incidents occurring in the year 1737/1150.[51] A group of individuals is accused of hundreds of crimes, including assault, homicide, theft, looting, burning, rape, and kidnapping in the course of separate incidents. Among the names of the leaders one finds individuals who bear the patronymics Fettahoğlu, Çapoğlu, Selimoğlu, Hacıhasanoğlu, and Keleşoğlu, all of which are patronymics later associated with aghas and agha-families of the Five and Twenty-five parties.[52] In one of the documents, these individuals are described as brigands who act in concert with other brigands from the Sixty-fourth Regiment of Janissaries (also named) and from the Fifth Regiment of private soldiers (not named).[53] As in the previous documents, the individuals named have adopted various epithets of a military (*alemdar, deli, kanlı*) or religious (*hacı, molla*) character; however, there is no clear indication of diverse familial, regional, or ethnic origin. So the individuals in question are clearly of the lowest military and religious stations. This is especially significant since the targets of their aggressions are residents of Of bearing titles and ranks of the religious and military branches of government. Moreover, the crimes of which they stand accused are of such a serious character that it would appear they were attempting to annihilate the family lines and household organizations of prominent individuals.

In one incident, the brigands attack a retired janissary officer, Piri Çavuş zade Mustafa, kill him with a bullet not far from his house, then attack the house, seize the house and his wife, and then turn the house and the wife over to other outlaws. They later attack the house of the father of Mustafa, also an individual of some distinction, loot it of cash and valuables, and

50. One of my interlocutors, familiar with Umur's work, claimed that the Çapoğlu were the first aghas and agha-families in the district of Of, the Ayazoğlu the second.

51. Umur 1951, No. 29 1708/1120 and No. 32 1710/1122.

52. Umur 1951, No. 81 1745/1158, No. 85 1752/1165, No. 86 1753/1166, No. 87 1763/1176, and No. 88 1764/1178 refers to the assaults on members of the Piri Çavuşoğlu family. Umur 1951, No. 83 1748/1161 refers to the assaults on the religious teachers and students (*ulema ve talebe*) in Paçan village. All six documents refer to events that took place in 1737/1150.

53. Other patronymics listed in the documents are identical to family lines that were closely allied with the aghas and agha-families (e.g., Kalyoncu). Also see Umur 1951, No. 70 1732/1144 and No. 74 1735/1147, where incidents of brigandage are attributed to individuals with other patronymics, such as Ayazoğlu, Nuhoğlu, and Bektaşoğlu, patronyms associated with the Five and Twenty-five parties in the contemporary period.

then burn it down. They track down the father, who has fled to Rize, and they finally kill him as he leaves the mosque after completing his Friday prayers. Then they return to his residence in Rize, where they kill his wives and servants and burn the house. On yet another occasion, the same individuals are said to have caused considerable destruction in and around Paçan village while engaged in a battle with private soldiers. Attacking the village, they burn buildings and steal property, including seven hundred books or registers. After being taken to court and ordered to pay restitution, they refuse to pay and are declared to be in a state of judicial noncompliance. In the document transcribed by Umur, they are accused (but not convicted) of returning to the village, pillaging it once again, carrying off women and children to their "towers," and committing numerous homicides. They are accused, but not convicted, of having killed as many as forty among the religious teachers and students and as many as five hundred altogether.[54]

The last set of documents provides many indications regarding the social origins of the new local elites. First, the documents are a further confirmation that the individuals whose descendants later become aghas and agha-families are drawn from the milieu of irregular troops or local militias (*bölük*).[55] Second, they indicate these individuals began their rise to prominence by assaulting and threatening individuals with titles and ranks. Third, they show that individuals with different patronymics acted in concert with one another to challenge and intimidate prominent local residents. Fourth, they indicate that professors and academies were in existence in the district during the first half of the eighteenth century. Fifth, they suggest that the aghas and agha-families only arose after the professors and academies had already been established rather than in tandem with them. And sixth, the documents also point to tantalizing links between the regimental affiliations of irregular troops and the later emergence of the Five and Twenty-five parties.

54. The individuals with patronymics are among those accused as principals during the incidents. Given the character of the crimes of which they are accused, the combination of patronymics, and the composition of their followers, it is unlikely that they were renegades of their family lines. One of the accused, Hasan Agha Fettahoğlu, is also mentioned in the "Fettahoğullarının Tarihi." The writer of that document accepts that this man was a prominent ascendant and situates him in the family genealogy. However, see the following note.

55. The author of the "Fettahoğullarının Tarihi" claims that an enemy of his family, whom he names as "a hodja from the Kaltabanoğulları," assembled a group of false witnesses to bring trumped up charges against his ascendant.

The individuals with the aforementioned patronymics are described as brigands residing in Of who combine with brigands from the Sixty-fourth Regiment of Janissaries to act together with other known individuals of the Fifth Regiment of Soldiers.[56] By a report of Peysonnel, the province of Trabzon was troubled for many years by the rivalry of the Twenty-fifth and Sixty-fourth regiments of janissaries.[57] By combining the Umur documents and the Peysonnel report, one discovers an indication of the origins of the Five and Twenty-five parties in the district of Of: Members of the Fifth and Sixty-fourth regiments join in an attack in Of, while other members of the Sixty-fourth and Twenty-fifth regiments are bitter rivals in the province of Trabzon.[58] The patronymics attributed to the individuals who collaborated in the attacks in 1737/1150 eventually appear among the Five and Twenty-five parties. The Selimoğlu have become the leading agha-family in the Five Party just as their name is associated with the Fifth Regiment of Soldiers in 1737.[59] However, the Fettahoğlu and Çapoğlu are later associated with the Twenty-five rather than the Five Party. This change is consistent with a tradition that tells how the Fettahoğlu and Çapoğlu fell out with the Selimoğlu in the early nineteenth century and joined the Muradoğlu, who assumed the leadership of the Twenty-five Party.[60] So then, by a web of interrelated factual and hypothetical linkages, the regimental affiliations of the individuals involved in the attacks on prominent local residents point directly to the early origins of leading individuals, large residences, family lines, and district social formations.

Altogether eight patronymics that are eventually associated with aghas and agha-families during the period of decentralization are mentioned in the documents. These are Ayazoğlu, Bektaşoğlu, Çapoğlu, Fettahoğlu, Hacıhasanoğlu, Keleşoğlu, Nuhoğlu, and Selimoğlu. All of these names are consistently associated with regiments or janissaries, but in a way that

56. Umur 1951, No. 85.

57. Peysonnel 1787, 73.

58. Bryer (1970, 44) observes that the Twenty-fifth Regiment of Janissaries was headquartered in Trabzon. So it is possible that the Twenty-five Party was actually close to the level of a janissary regiment, while the Five Party was a regiment of private soldiers. Bilgin (1990, 312) associates the Five Party with the "*Cemaat-i Beşluyan,*" janissaries appointed to the castle force or town police of Trabzon, and the Twenty-five Party with the "*Yermibeşli,*" janissaries who were granted a tımar and assigned to the Twenty-fifth Regiment. Also see the discussion of the troop call-outs later in the text.

59. The Hacıhasanoğlu and the Keleşoğlu are associated with the Fifth Regiment of Janissaries and then later, consistent with this, the Five Party.

60. See chaps. 6 and 7 for further discussion of this issue.

confirms that they were individuals of the outer and lower fringes of the military establishment. The individuals with known patronyms are sometimes described as members of regiments, but only those composed of irregular soldiers or local militias (*bölük*). They are sometimes accused and convicted of attacking local janissary officers, but they never appear in the capacity of true janissary officers themselves. This pattern is supported by other incidents in which individuals accused of wrongdoing seem to be attempting to worm their way into the position of official janissaries. For example, individuals might carry out aggressions while falsely claiming to be acting as official janissaries. Or contrariwise, they are the victims of aggressions carried out by others who falsely claim to be acting as official janissaries.

So far the documents I have cited strongly suggest that the aghas who founded agha-families arose for the most part from lower-level regiments and militias. Some of them may have held janissary titles and ranks, since it became common for all kinds of individuals to do so. More typically, they belonged to regiments and militias that imitated and emulated the janissaries by their tattoos, insignia, and banners. Other documents offer further support for this same conclusion in a negative way by excluding the possibility that the aghas and agha-families were of other social origins.

One document, for example, describes how high state officials without appointments assembled groups of armed men from Of and then went about raiding and looting the villages of the district. During the year 1711/1123, the head steward (*kethüda*) of the former governor of Trabzon, in the company of close associates, is accused of raiding and looting villages in the district of Of. The head steward, leading a band of brigands recruited from various villages in the western valley-system, conducted a massive assault on fifteen villages (unnamed and unlocated). They burned and looted two hundred houses and warehouses. They destroyed seven mosques and raped eighteen girls. They shaved the heads of eight women and paraded them about, tied some of them to horses and dragged them, tracked down others and raped them. Fleeing in terror, many of the villagers subsequently died of exposure and starvation.[61]

The document illustrates how higher state officials, temporarily without positions or appointments, mustered a large band of brigands by recruiting

61. Umur 1951, No. 35 1711/1123. The villages from which the brigands were recruited are located all along the lower and higher reaches of the western valley-system, that is, the Greek-speaking areas.

soldiers in nine separate villages in Of.[62] It gives the names, patronyms, and villages of more than a score of Oflus who took part in the raiding and looting. On the other hand, among the accused Oflus there is not a single mention of a patronym that later emerges as an agha-family. If this and three other documents transcribed by Umur are representative, these kinds of incidents do not appear to have played a role in the origins of aghas and agha-families in the district of Of.[63] The individuals who are the ascendants of aghas and agha-families are not higher state officials without appointments, nor do they appear to have been followers of such higher state officials.

Another set of documents diminishes the possibility of a very different kind of social origin for aghas and agha-families. There are other individuals who organize the raiding and looting of villages but have no detectable connection at all with imperial institutions. They are not drawn from either high or low-level positions in the military or religious establishment. They are instead "tribesmen." The documents describe the following circumstances. During the year 1709/1121, the residents of seven villages in the upper western valley-system are accused of all sorts of crimes: They combined with the Ayaslo and Kolotlo tribes (*kabîle*), who came from outside the district and settled among the villagers. Acting in concert, tribesmen and villagers disturbed the peace of the main market in the district of Of. They attacked this market, making it necessary to move it to another place. They attacked houses, kidnapped women and girls, held them prisoner, sold them to one another, and married them as they wished. They attacked the house of the judge of Of and threatened him with death. They attacked individuals with knives. They did not pay dues to the fief-holders (*tımar* and *zeamat*) of their villages. They held the judge of Of in contempt, saying they had given him documents when he attempted to make a case

62. Barkey (1994) has recently called attention to these kinds of incidents, which were especially common during the seventeenth century. At that time, they were a direct result of the need for a large reservoir of officers and troops on the occasion of imperial campaigns. With demobilization, officers who had no appointments and troops without employment were obliged to extract their living by raiding and looting villages. When their activities became intolerable, state officials would take steps to suppress them, providing they had the necessary troops and resources for doing so.

63. The other three documents involve the following incidents: A man who had served as the district governor of Of (*mütesellim*) two years previously is accused of making war on the people of Of with the excuse that he holds an imperial decree (*ferman*) permitting him to do so (Umur 1951, No. 7 1689/1100). A man who had served as the district governor of Of is trying to recover a debt from certain Oflus (ibid., No. 6 1688/1099). A janissary and his associates are accused of attacking villages and committing all kinds of injustices (Umur 1951, No. 4 1665/1076).

against them. In punishment for all these violations, the order was given for the pasha of Trabzon to undertake the mass deportation of the two tribes and seven villages. They were to be rounded up and transported to Anakra Castle, where they would be settled at the Ottoman frontier with Georgia.[64]

The tribesmen organizing villagers are not named as individuals who bear patronymics. The names of their tribes do not appear among the patronymics of aghas and agha-families. The tribesmen are not associated with official titles and ranks, either truly or falsely. The tribesmen directly attack state officials and subvert the normal operations of the central government. Most telling of all, state officials are now capable of making a vigorous and ruthless response. Soldiers are sent to the seven villages, where they surround the villagers and descend on them like a flood.[65] Both the tribesmen and the villagers charged in these incidents are rounded up and deported to the frontier. The tribesmen, being from outside the state system altogether, were perhaps less able to retard or block the overzealous but effective response of state officials. In contrast, the cases lodged against the janissaries and soldiers who attacked prominent individuals in Of dragged on for three decades in the courts.

Of all the documents that Umur has assembled and discussed, about forty refer to incidents that can be plausibly linked with the emergence of local elites who challenged existing military, administrative, and judicial hierarchies. All of the documents date to the final decades of the seventeenth century or the first decades of the eighteenth century.[66] Usurpers or

64. Umur 1951, No. 43 1709/1121 [date corrected in Umur 1956, 13, n. 1]; Umur 1956, No. 45 1709/1121, No. 46 1710/1121, and No. 47 1710/1122. The seven villages are located in the western valley-system. They include some of the same villages from which the head steward had recruited soldiers for raiding villages in Of; see Umur 1951, No. 35 1711/1123. The deportation did not alter the prevalence of Greek as the language spoken in this part of the district. It is possible that not all the villagers were taken and removed, that some eventually returned from exile as was common in such cases, or that these seven villages were resettled by people from neighboring villages.

65. Umur 1956, 57.

66. Of 120 documents relating to incidents occurring between 1666/1076 and 1748/1161, about 40 refer to various kinds of social disorders that involve a challenge to the authority of district state officials (Umur 1951, 1955). About a third of the 40 cite individuals bearing patronyms that are the same as some of the agha-families that came to make up the Five and Twenty-five parties during the early nineteenth century. The 40 do not include about a dozen other documents that refer to "simple" incidents of brigandage involving various acts of destruction or spoliation. It should be remembered, however, that Umur specifically transliterated documents that mentioned well-known families in Of.

brigands are accused of having assaulted, robbed, intimidated, or assassinated individuals with military or religious titles. Military officials appointed by the central government are unable to exercise the authority vested in them by their office.[67] Men in arms who are "from among the usurpers and evildoers" (*mütegallibeden ve eşirrâdan*) and pretend to be janissaries descend on the market and battle one another with sword and shield, pistol and rifle. Committing many wrongs, they seize goods and attack the court.[68] They extort taxes from villagers, intimidate state officials, raid and loot village populations, seize the lands of non-Muslim subjects, and illegally arrest and punish people.[69] The documents that describe challenges to the authority of military officials occur in tandem with other documents that describe the subversion of judicial procedures. One individual with the title of molla, who acts in concert with another from Paçan village, is accused of improperly assuming the duties of court officials (*naip* and *kâtib*).[70] Other individuals who style themselves as notables (*âyan*), but are said to be "from among the usurpers" (*mütegallibeden*), are accused of putting pressure on the district judge (*kadı*), or his representative (*naip*), by receiving them in their houses and requiring they hear cases there.[71] Men in arms appear in the court carrying their weapons and disrupt the proceedings.[72] Men are accused of descending on the court while it is in session and freeing their confederates who are standing trial.[73]

DOCUMENTING THE AGHAS AND FAMILY LINES IN TRABZON

From the middle of the eighteenth century, Umur's collection of documents begins to change in character. The signs of conflict between new social elements and religious and military officials at the local level are no longer apparent. There are no reports of incidents involving attacks on state officials and brigands falsely claiming to be janissaries, and there are fewer cases that mention brigands and outlaws with the patronymics of agha-families.

67. Umur 1951, No. 26 1705/1117, No. 29 1708/1120, No. 30 1708/1120, No. 65 1730/1142, No. 72 1732/1144, No. 78 1740/1153, No. 79 1740/1153, No. 81 1745/1158, No. 85 1752/1165, No. 86 1753/1166, No. 87 1762/1176, and No. 88 1764/1178.

68. Ibid., No. 52 1724/1136.

69. Ibid., No. 21 1701/1113, No. 29 1708/1120, No. 30 1708/1120, No. 39 1716/1128, No. 42 1717/1129, and No. 56 1726/1138.

70. Ibid., No. 55 1725/1137.

71. Ibid., No. 54 1725/1137.

72. Umur 1956, No. 48 1723/1135.

73. Umur 1951, No. 72 1732/1144.

There are no further cases of mass assaults on villages, deportations of village populations, illegal land seizures, or the failure to pay taxes. All kinds of social disorders may have been occurring in the districts, but if so, they were infrequently brought to the attention of higher military and judicial officials. The local elites were perhaps usurping offices, interfering with the courts, improperly imposing taxes, refusing to forward revenues to the capital, and illegally confiscating property. But if they were, they were able to prevent the lodging of complaints against them.

Toward the close of the eighteenth century, a new order of aghas, mansions, family lines, and regimental parties was in place. This is indicated by three documents that call on local elites to muster troops. The earliest of the three, dated 1774/1188, was written by a military commander representing the palace. He calls on "the judges, religious officials, the righteous, officers, commanders, craftsmen, and community leaders" (*kadılarına, ûlema, sûleha, zabitan, serdarlar, iş erleri, söz sahiblerine*) of nine districts of the province to assemble and dispatch troops for participation in imperial military campaigns against the armies of Moscow.[74] However, in doing so, he reveals that the central government is unable to compel them to furnish troops, but entirely dependent on their willingness to do so. He chastises his correspondents for having failed to respond to previous orders to assemble troops for imperial campaigns. They have said they were ready to come and have unfurled their banners, but then, offering various excuses, have failed to mobilize. They have engaged in quarrels among themselves, a kind of behavior that cannot be called anything other than disobedience to the sultan. Begging them to mend their ways, the military commander exhorts his correspondents to assemble for liberating the Crimea from Moscow. Their previous faults will be forgiven. Their military service is a religious duty.

The other two documents, dated 1788/1202 and 1789/1204, provide more direct evidence that aghas from agha-families governed their districts more or less independently of the central government at this time. The earlier is written by a palace official.[75] It addresses the notables (*âyan*), officials (*mütesellim*), judges (*kadı*), and officers (*yeni çeri*) of the districts in the province of Trabzon, from Görele in the west to Hopa in the east. It calls on them to assemble troops and report for a campaign on the northeastern

74. Umur 1956, No. 71 1774/1188. The nine districts are Trabzon, Rize, Of, Sürmene, Pulathane, Vakfıkebir, Tirebolu, Keşap, and Giresun.

75. Ibid., No. 65. Also see Sümer (1992, 104–5). See Aksan (1999a, 1999b) for a general study of military recruitment in the Ottoman Empire at this time.

shores of the Black Sea (Anapa, Soğucak). The document lists 26 names of individuals or families in 16 districts, referring to them as "aghas" (*ağavat*). They are required to contribute either 100, 150, or 200 troops. About two-thirds of these names specify a patronymic, each in the "son of" (*oğlu*) format. Some of these add a personal name to the patronymic, as in "Tuzcuoğlu Hüseyin at Rize" and "Kuğuoğlu Süleyman at Görele."[76] Others merely list the patronymic alone without specifying an individual, as in "Bahadır oğlu at Büyük Liman" or "Hacı Hasan oğlu at Pulathane." In a number of instances, the patronymics listed in the document correspond with the patronymics of aghas who held official appointments and positions fifty years later, when European consuls began to report on the coastal region at the close of the period of decentralization. In other instances, the patronymics correspond with local traditions of aghas and agha-families during the nineteenth century.[77] The number of troops required from three families at Of are 150, 200, and 200, respectively. The total for the district of Of, 550, is larger than for any other district in the province. The total number for the three eastern districts of Rize, Of, and Sürmene is almost 40 percent of the total for the entire eastern coastal region.

The later document, dated 1789/1204, is a call-out for troops for a military expedition to the northeastern shores of the Black Sea (Anapa).[78] The troops are to be assembled in various ports of the Black Sea coast, including Samsun, Trabzon, Sürmene, Rize and others. The government will pay merchant ships to transport these troops, and these ships will be accompanied by galleons of the Imperial Navy. The document is divided into five sections, which refer in turn to the vicinity of Trabzon, the district of Of, the district of Rize, the aghas of the Laz, and the western districts. In the first four sections, there are lists of individuals and families, each of which is called upon to contribute a certain number of troops. The names are usually the same as those in the earlier document, but there are now more than forty names for the four mentioned areas. The total call-out for each of these areas is roughly 5,200 for the vicinity of Trabzon, 1,800 for Of, 2,300

76. Two are personal names without patronymics, as in "Mehmet Bey of Viçe [Fındıklı]" and "Mamoli Mustafa of Hopa."

77. Some of these correspondences that are known to me are as follows: Hacı Salihoğlu at Tonya, Kalcıoğlu at Trabzon, Hacıhasanoğlu at Pulathane, Eyyuboğlu at Maçka, Tuzcuoğlu at Rize, Ekşioğlu at Rize, Canoğlu at Of, Kıraçoğlu at Of, and Selimoğlu at Of.

78. Cevdet Asker 40224, dated 1789/1204. I am grateful to Mehmet Bilgin for providing me with a photocopy of this document.

for Rize, and 1,800 for the aghas of the Laz.[79] The individuals are usually labeled in accordance with their regimental affiliations, including the Sixty-fourth, Twenty-fifth, and Fifth. The document therefore confirms that the parties in Of were associated with janissary regiments, just as it also confirms the depth and breadth of local military affiliations.[80]

Taken together, the three documents indicate that the social changes taking place in the district of Of during the period of decentralization were consistent with social changes taking place in all the core provinces of the Ottoman provinces. By the late seventeenth century, large numbers of Oflus were serving as irregular soldiers or studying as religious students. Occasionally, some of these elements joined up with imperial elites who, while out of office or back from campaigns, extorted money from villagers and looted their farms. By the fourth decade of the eighteenth century, individuals with low-level military appointments were asserting themselves, sometimes by banding together to usurp the authority of local officials or to intimidate local villagers. At the same time, individuals with low-level religious qualifications had organized religious academies and were recruiting and training considerable numbers of religious students. But these teachers and students were eventually confronted with the emergent aghas and agha-families. Just as the palace had captured the mosque in Istanbul during the classical period, so too would aghas and agha-families capture the religious teachers and students during the period of decentralization, neutralizing them as alternative local sources of political legitimacy or social organization.

Aghas and mansions together with hodjas and academies were to be found in virtually every segment of the eastern coastal region. Coalitions of local elites constituting regional social oligarchies comprised the entirety of the province of Trabzon. However, some coastal districts of the province of Trabzon featured a broader and deeper participation in imperial institutions than others. In general, those coastal districts that had large Christian majorities and little Turkic settlement during the sixteenth century, such as Rize, Of, and Sürmene, are associated with broad and deep participation

79. The fifth section, devoted to the western districts, does not give the names of individuals. The places and quotas listed in the fifth section are as follows: Amasya (1,500), Ünye and Niksar (500), Tirebolu (500), Giresun (200), Karahisar Şarkı (3,000), and Canık (5,000).

80. The document mentions "Hüseyin Agha Selimoğlu of the 5th aghas." It does not mention an agha from the Muradoğlu in agreement with the family tradition that its founder arrived in Of sometime after 1800.

in imperial institutions. By contrast, coastal districts that had a sizable Muslim population and considerable Turkic settlement by the sixteenth century, such as Tirebolu, Giresun, and Ordu, were associated with narrower and shallower participation. It was then those populations that had a background in market and state participation that became part of the imperial system. To some degree, a legacy of participation in Byzantine institutions had helped their otherwise mixed populations to recognize and to exploit the opportunity for becoming part of the Ottoman state system and state society.

Two exceptions to the preceding pattern prove the rule. First, the hierarchy and institutions of the Orthodox Church had survived Ottoman incorporation precisely in that part of the coastal region where the Byzantine state system had been centered and developed, that is to say, the central districts around the town of Trabzon. According to Bryer and Lowry, the survival of these pieces of the older state system had been the basis for the survival of a large Greek Orthodox population in this same area. So an alternative to the imperial system had retarded conversion and immigration, and hence imperial participation, in this section of the province of Trabzon.[81] Second, one of the coastal districts in the west bears some resemblance to the district of Of in the east. The population in the district of Tonya included a large number of Muslim Greek-speakers, as well as broad and deep participation in imperial institutions (military rather than religious). But Tonya also stands as an exception among the western coastal districts. By its more isolated location, it did not receive as many Turkic settlers as other western coastal districts. So it is an example of a coastal district in the west that fits the pattern of the coastal districts in the east.

CONCLUSION

The Ottoman Empire is usually conceived in terms of a strict division between rulers and ruled. The rulers consisted of an official (*askeri*) class composed of military, administrative, judicial, and religious specialists. The ruled consisted of a diverse population of tribes, peasants, and townsmen. The rulers accorded legal status and rights to the ruled in various ways, one of the important ways being recognition of their religious leadership and communities.

81. Bryer 1975 and Lowry 1977. Also cf. Poutouridou 1997–98 and Vryonis 1968.

The district of Of, as an example of the rural societies of the old province of Trabzon, is not consistent with such an analysis. The Oflus, those of Muslim as well as those of Christian background, set aside their attachments to standing beliefs and practices as they oriented themselves toward an imperial project that claimed universal import. In doing so, they sought to organize everyday life in accordance with a system of ethical thought and practice as represented by authoritative texts and learned experts. What had always been said and done was discounted as degenerate and corrupt. What should be said and done was accessible only through literacy, teaching, learning, argument, and consensus. This reorientation of family life and social relations can be described as an effort to become good and proper Muslims, rather than remain ignorant and impoverished villagers. But it included a political dimension that exceeded piety and spirituality. The Oflus had set about to remake themselves in order to remake the world. They claimed a place in the state society of the imperial system, challenging the distinction between officials (*askeri*) and nonofficials (*reaya*). To do so, they acquired all kinds of military weapons, and they organized themselves in military formations. The idea of an empire of the future was perhaps more alive in the mansions and academies of Trabzon than in the great monumental centers of Istanbul.

The period of decentralization was the direct result of crises of state stability and competition. But the latter had been indirectly provoked by technological inventions and institutional disciplines occurring in the Euro-American sphere. Print, school, steam, factory, rifles, and barracks had led to new, more efficient forms of state power which lowered, rather than raised, the need for manpower and resources. In response, the Ottomans were pressed to respond to new rounds of imperial competition by expanding, rather than contracting, their ability to mobilize manpower and resources. The dissemination of the imperial project in the eighteenth century therefore anticipated the emergence of nationalism in the Euro-American sphere. Local consciousness in the province of Trabzon had become linked with state identification and participation at an earlier phase of the global modernizing process. This means that the period of decentralization was a preparation, and hence set the conditions, for the reception of national democracy.

PART III

THE OLD STATE SOCIETY AND THE NEW STATE SYSTEM

The Ottoman Province of Trabzon

6 A State Society
State Officials and Local Elites

A TIERED STATE SOCIETY

The rise of local elites in the coastal districts of the province of Trabzon came about through the appropriation and adaptation of an imperial tactic of sovereign power. Individuals from the lower ranks of military officers formed interpersonal associations with their lessers, equals, and betters. With this development, the structure of political authority came to feature a distribution of sovereign power with both vertical and horizontal cleavages. State officials no longer enjoyed a monopoly of military force as they once had during the classical Ottoman period. They were everywhere confronted with local elites in the coastal districts who were able to mobilize armed followings.

In this chapter, I shall describe the structure of political authority that emerged in the old province of Trabzon during the period of decentralization. As we shall see, it consisted of a hierarchy of leading individuals representing tiered circles of interpersonal associations. At the top, leading individuals consisted uniquely of state officials who were usually not from Trabzon. At the bottom, leading individuals consisted of local elites from the coastal districts. But the leading individuals in the middle range of this hierarchy held high titles and ranks in the state system precisely because they were eminent figures among the local elites of the countryside.

The two sides of the structure of political authority—official at the top and nonofficial at the bottom—reflect the two "pieces" of sovereign power in the imperial system: the mechanism of bureaucratic centralism and the tactic of disciplinary association. During the period of decentralization, the mechanism of bureaucracy had become less effective even as the tactic of association had become more generalized. Accordingly, the structure of political authority exceeded the state system so that local elites in the old province of Trabzon, together with all their relatives, friend, partners, and allies, comprised a very large fraction of the population. In effect, the dissemination of the imperial tactic of sovereign power during the period of decentralization had transformed the large majority of inhabitants of the coastal region into an ottomanist provincial society.

To analyze this structure of political authority, I shall rely on the reports of French and British consular officials who first began to reside in the town of Trabzon after 1800.[1] Although the quality of their insights is variable, they provide a wealth of information about specific individuals and incidents. Matching this information against other sources, I have been able to reach conclusions about the relationship of state officials and local elites, as well as about the breadth and depth of popular participation in the imperial system.[2]

For the most part, I shall not directly examine the observations of the consuls in this chapter. Instead, I rely on the information in their reports to understand the narrative of a Frenchman who briefly visited the provincial capital a few years before the beginning of the consular era.[3] Citizen Beauchamp was one of the last western European visitors who was able to contemplate the relationship of state officials and local elites from a position of curiosity. A few years later, the consuls who followed him would come to believe that the success of their mission depended on the eradication of the local elites (see chap. 7).

CITIZEN BEAUCHAMP AND THE PROVINCIAL CAPITAL

In the summer of 1796, a French scientific expedition set out for the province of Trabzon in order to collect specimens of the unique flora of the eastern Pontic Mountains.[4] After arriving in Istanbul, the party duly applied to

1. There were French consuls in the coastal region through most of the nineteenth century. Dupré, the first consul in Trabzon, arrived in 1803, and Fourcade, the first consul in Sinop, arrived in 1802. Brant, the first British consul in Trabzon, did not arrive until 1830.

2. For another approach, see Aktepe (1951–52), who examines the relationship of state officials and local elites through official correspondence, thereby revealing the web of interpersonal relationships in which both were enmeshed. In contrast, the early French and British consular reports refer directly to civil disorders, and in so doing indicate cleavages of political authority.

3. There was already a Russian consul in both Trabzon and Sinop at the time of Beauchamp's visit. From the reports of both Dupré and Fourcade, it would appear that the Russian consuls had extensive contacts and agreements with both state officials and local elites. See MAE CCCT L. 1 and MAE CCCS, *passim.*

4. Whatever the unannounced motives of the expeditions, the French had a long-standing botanical interest in the eastern coastal region. Tournefort (1717, 240–41) had led a scientific expedition to Trabzon almost a century earlier. See his

the central government, requesting permission to proceed. Beauchamp, one of the members of the expedition, explains how they were initially refused. "The first intermediary (*drogman*) had responded in the name of the Porte [Ottoman government]. The Laz were savages, wild and virtually independent. It [the Porte] did not wish to compromise itself in the eyes of our government should some kind of accident take place."[5] Most likely, the request for permission had been denied without comment; nonetheless, the intermediary had fulfilled his function by explaining official motives otherwise left unstated. Although the explanation is probably accurate, the characterization of the residents of the coastal region is tendentious and misleading.

The so-called Laz were outsiders to the high official circles of Istanbul. They were rough-and-tumble country people who had grown up in mountain villages. Their speech and manners featured all kinds of infelicities. Their costumes and appearance were inappropriate, if not unacceptable. Nonetheless, the Laz were also insiders of the imperial system. They comprised an ottomanist population whose presence and influence were palpable not only in Trabzon, but also in Istanbul. The local elites of this population had contacts and influence in the palace to such an extent that they were able to thwart provincial governors. The local elites had participated in military campaigns as leaders of militias and regiments, most recently in the Crimea and the Caucasus. Its tradesmen and craftsmen were also to be found as residents of the imperial capital, just as its professors and academies represented official Islam in many modest urban and rural quarters. Beauchamp probably never had the slightest inkling that the Laz were such an ottomanist population, rather than a specific people speaking a specific language. But he was fully aware of the difference between what he had been told in Istanbul and what he was soon to observe in Trabzon. This is why he includes this episode in his account, to illustrate the gross inconsistency between official formalities and governing practices.

Persisting with their request, the French are at last granted an imperial decree (*ferman*) addressed to the governor, but warned that his capital is in a state of insurrection at that very moment. They set sail for Trabzon accompanied by one of the janissaries who had been assigned by the Ottoman government to the French legation. Not far into their voyage, the boatman who was hired to take them begins to insist they bypass the provincial capital and proceed further eastward to the vicinity of Rize (see map 2). The

---

description of the conditions of insecurity in the interior highlands of northeastern Anatolia at this time.

5. Beauchamp 1813, 265.

boatman was himself from Rize and enrolled there in a janissary regiment, while the "Laz" in the town of Trabzon were enemies of this regiment, making it impossible for him to land there.[6] The French eventually learn that the objections of the boatman are little more than a pretext aimed at diverting the expedition.[7] He wants to take on cargo in his homeland for his return trip to Istanbul, so he tells the French plausible lies.

Although the claims of the boatman are false, they are nonetheless revealing. The rural societies of the coastal districts were affiliated with military formations, militias, and regiments that were linked with the central army (janissaries).[8] These military formations included ordinary traders, craftsmen, and boatmen. They were associated with district alliances and coastal coalitions that spread throughout the old province of Trabzon from Batum to Ordu. As such they functioned as fraternal organizations, providing hospitality to visiting members from other communities.[9] On some occasions, they responded to call-outs for troops by state officials who summoned them to participate in imperial campaigns alongside the central

6. See Fontanier's (1829, 5; 1834, 286) comments on similar experiences with boatmen who are reluctant to land at ports for fear of rival militias or regiments.

7. One of the sailors then tells them that they should not agree to the diversion, since the country of the boatman would not suffer any Christians there, much less Europeans. The warning of the sailor is consistent with the "fanatical" reputation of the eastern coastal districts. It is such warnings that incline almost all the European visitors who follow Beauchamp to avoid the districts of Rize, Of, and Sürmene.

8. The number of individuals affiliated with the janissary institution in the eastern coastal districts appears to have been large. Fourcade encountered "Laz" janissaries who had participated in the revolt against Selim III (MAE CCCS folio 191). Fontanier writes:

> When the great lord became determined to annihilate this fearsome corps, he gave the order to forbid the entry or exit of all Turkish vessels from the coast of Anatolia. He was not unaware that it was this part of the empire [the Black Sea region] from which those of his subjects who came to the capital were most prone to insubordination. Almost all of them were affiliated with the janissaries and were found in large numbers among castle guards. The government was afraid that a revolt might ensue in those provinces where they had numerous chiefs if the news of the massacre arrived there before appropriate measures could be taken. As well, the pasha of Trabzon set to sea in the fleet and menaced the coast as the first fugitives began to arrive." (1829, 25–26)

Consul Brant reports that many janissaries fled to Trabzon after June 1826, and thereafter kept alive the spirit of this party among the people (PRO FO 524/1 p. 23, Aug. 23, 1832). See also Fontanier (1829, 27–28, 29–30) for other interesting observations on janissaries as a civil opposition to the government.

9. This is suggested by a tradition in Of whereby a visitor to a village would first determine if a particular house featured the insignia of his party (Five or Twenty-five) before asking to be received there as a guest (see chap. 1). As was determined in chapter 5, the Five and Twenty-five parties were regiments or militias.

army. On other occasions, they mobilized to challenge state officials and the central army or to confront rival alliances and coalitions. Accordingly, the members of a military formation associated with one social network hesitated to travel to towns and districts that were dominated by a military formation associated with a rival social network.

The French anchor at the provincial capital of Trabzon, learn the town is actually at peace, and forward their imperial decree to the pasha of Trabzon. This document includes a request that they be given assistance to mount an expedition for the purpose of gathering botanical specimens. Beauchamp reports the response as conveyed to their messenger:

> The governor, after having read the decree, told him that he regretted he was not able to fulfill its requirements as the chiefs of the town [*les chefs de la ville*] had assumed authority, and so it was for them to receive us. Our janissary then went to find the two ayans [chief notables], Osman Agha and Memiş Agha. The latter, having learned of the orders that were in our possession, arranged for a house to be prepared for us at once and sent two riflemen aboard our boat for our debarkation. For a moment, we thought that we were going to be led away to prison.[10]

Beauchamp has been led to expect insurrection and savagery, but he finds instead a working arrangement among three competing political authorities. Every other visitor who follows him will discover a similar situation until the close of the period of decentralization (1830s). The provincial governor (or a representative in his absence) is consistently matched by two (and more rarely three) leading individuals with followings.[11] The exact relationship

10. Beauchamp (1813, 268–69).

11. Shortly after his arrival in 1803, Dupré describes the situation as follows: "The town is governed by a *mütesellim* [district governor] nominated by the pasha, and then there is a *kadı* [judge], a janissary agha [district military commander for the central army], and *dizdar agha* [military commander of the fortress for the central army], and finally three derebeys [commanders of valleys] who have the greatest influence in the countryside, and who are the chiefs of parties during periods of dissension" (MAE CCCT L. 1, No. 11, 2 Nivôse An XII [Dec. 1803]). In later years, Dupré refers to only two chiefs in the town, but others in the near vicinity. "Two derebeys are present with the governor, but not allowed to speak" (MAE CCCT L. 1, No. 15, Floreal An XII [May 1804]); "two derebeys have united with one another in fear of Yusuf Pasha, who had deposed Tayyar Pasha" (No. 37, Brumaire An XIV [Oct. 1805]); "the two derebeys of the city, who are sworn enemies, have taken sides" (No. 65, July 1807); "the chiefs of the factions have agreed to a request for armistice after six months of civil war and the foreigners (outsiders) have retired, but the two principals have made it known that their animosity continues" (No. 78, Aug. 1808); "a rapprochement of the two derebeys has occurred upon the occasion of the marriage of their son and daughters" (No. 81, Oct. 1808). Fontanier

of the provincial governor and the chiefs of the town is never exactly the same.[12] The governor does not always defer to the two chiefs. The two chiefs do not always defer to one another.

The relationship of the three political authorities varies because each is in effect a sovereign power occupying a stronghold and able to mobilize military force. The provincial governor occupies the citadel and commands contingents of janissaries and mercenaries. The two chiefs occupy fortified residences within the city walls and command large numbers of armed followers such that their forces normally outnumber those of the governor. Sometimes the chiefs fill the streets of the town with men in arms, forcing state officials to retreat into their fortress within the city walls. Sometimes they conduct skirmishes with one another from their separate residences or lay protracted sieges around one another's residences. Since the town was at peace during his visit, Beauchamp does not witness any such events, but he sees the clear signs of them in the appearance of the town itself:

> The town is built on a rise of a hillside at the coastline in an attractive setting. It forms an imperfect square: Its walls are high, crenellated, and badly maintained. At the center of the town, there are two fortified mansions that are closed each night with double doors of iron. It is there where the two chiefs reside. The narrow streets are paved. Except for one part of the town, near the sea, all the rest is nothing more than large gardens enclosed by walls. The commerce of Trabzon is currently not very active. It consists of linen cloth, copper, hazelnuts, and slaves from Georgia.[13]

The doors of iron are but one feature of the chiefs' fortified residences; they are also equipped with secret underground passages for the purpose of receiving supplies or permitting escape during sieges.[14] The walls of the gar-

---

(1829, 18, 20) writes of fortresses in the town belonging to private individuals as though there were several such buildings, not just two.

12. The chiefs of the town are described by different terms according to context. The Ottomans refer to them as squire (*ağa*), notable (*ayan*), lord (*derebey*), usurper (*mütegallibe*), or brigand (*şaki*). The French and British consuls refer to them as chief, agha, ayan, bey, derebey, derebey ayan, and valley lord. When these individuals with followings hold formal appointments, they then may appear in the guise of state officials.

13. Beauchamp 1813, 274–75.

14. A few years later, Dupré describes the suburbs of the town as follows: "The houses of the suburbs consist of a single story and those of the Christians are enclosed with a wall of around eight to ten feet in height, such that one moves through the streets without being able to see the crossroads, or nearly so. They say it is the internal wars to which this town has always been subject that brought about this manner of building" (MAE CCCT L. 1, No. 11, 2 Nivôse An XII [Dec. 1803]). On

dens are so high that it is impossible to see from one street to another. They have been constructed as defenses against the pillaging that occurs during military invasions from the countryside. Strife between the governor and the chiefs, and, more commonly, between the chiefs themselves, periodically reduces the level of commercial activity. This may have been the case during the last few years of the eighteenth century.

Having contacted first the governor and then the two chiefs by messenger, the French are taken to a dilapidated residence, which they are allowed to use as their quarters. They are then separately visited by attendants of all kinds of officials and notables (*tant du pacha que des ayans*). The next morning they send timepieces in the customary manner (*alaturka*) to the two chiefs and coffee and sugar to other officials, the pasha, the kadı, and the janissary agha. After these preliminaries, they proceed to visit the principals (*les grands*), first the two chiefs in turn and then the pasha. The first chief, Memiş Agha, receives them with gravity, serves them coffee, and offers them pipes. He asks why the French have abolished all the churches in France. When they reply that religion is free in their country, so that he can himself come and pray in a mosque if he likes, he only smiles. After a quarter of an hour, he says there are no wild plants at Trabzon (that is, in the town itself), but he would send them with an escort of horsemen into his own lands at a distance of thirty leagues, that is, about one hundred kilometers. Refusing his offer, saying they fear the Laz, the French take their leave and visit the second chief, Osman Agha. The latter has a more agreeable countenance and makes them more at ease. He recommends they look for plants in his territories at a distance of six leagues, that is, about twenty kilometers, and he offers to take them there himself. Again they refuse his assistance, but they do later make an excursion to his lands (to the south of town along the trade route). Taking their leave, the French next pay a visit to the pasha. They are well received (*avec beaucoup d'aménité*), but the governor does not offer them a full reception, withholding pipes, since they lack any official diplomatic capacity. Beauchamp here explains they had not requested appointment as official consuls for fear this might infuriate the Laz,

---

the occasion of his visit in 1827, Fontanier comments on the same architectural features of the town: "The citadel is held by a pasha who also occupies a fortress within it. As I have already noted, several lords each dwell in a kind of château-fort. As well the town has a military appearance to it that renders it cheerless. The houses of private parties are built low and in large stones. They are connected with one another by secret passages that are for the purpose of assisting the flight of the owners who might be attacked" (Fontanier 1829, 20).

so the imperial decree given them describes them only as travelers.[15] Nonetheless, in the evening the pasha sends them musicians who play for them in their lodgings. Beauchamp and his companions do not like the music, but they are reassured by the pasha's attentiveness.

This last section of Beauchamp's observations is rich in clues to the relationship of officials and nonofficials as competing sovereign powers. The French are received by all three principals (*les grands*) in an almost identical fashion. They are visited by representatives of all three. They are obliged to send presents to all three. They are invited by all three to a social occasion where they meet, share refreshments, and converse with one another. On the other hand, the reception of the governor follows ceremony and protocol, while the receptions of the two chiefs are more informal. For example, the governor is referred to only by his title while the two chiefs are known by their first names. The governor withholds pipes since the French lack diplomatic standing, but the chiefs offer them coffee and pipes. The governor has the means to embellish his reception of official visitors with an elaborate table and skilled musicians in the style of the court. The two chiefs are content to meet their visitors, offer refreshment, and engage in conversation. All three receive the French in accordance with a discipline of an interpersonal association. In the instance of the governor, this discipline has been formalized in accordance with the rules and aesthetics of the imperial court. In the instance of the two chiefs, the discipline is less adorned and more simply expressed. The logic of a sovereign power based on interpersonal association is the same for each, but it is expressed in two different registers.[16]

After their meetings with the two chiefs and the pasha, the French visit the chief judge (*kadı*) and the military commander (*yeniçeri ağası*). The military commander has been posted to the town by the central government and has no connection with the two chiefs, even though the latter are associated with janissary-like militias and regiments. He speaks at length about the lack of authority of the pasha and himself in the city. He hopes

15. When they learn that there is a Russian consul in Trabzon, they realize their mistake.

16. Other visitors with diplomatic status provide better accounts of the ceremony and protocol during a reception by the pasha of Trabzon. See Rottiers's (1829, 217–28) description of his elaborate reception at the court in 1818 and his conversation with Hüsrev Pasha, successor to Süleyman Pasha. See Fontanier's (1834, 98–108) description of the court of Osman Pasha Hazinedaroğlu. By way of contrast, see Morier's (1812, 323–24) description of his less elaborate reception and entertainment by Emin Agha, district governor of Erzurum in 1809.

that one day the pasha of Erzurum might come and take the heads of the two chiefs. The military commander offers the French his house and his garden, but they refuse, even though they are so badly quartered. They fear a close association with him might alienate the "rebels" of whom they believe themselves in need. Nonetheless, the French find the military commander cheerful and engaging, "without any of the Oriental gravity of his nation." Here Beauchamp touches on the tendency of foreigners to miss the principle of sociability underlying official procedures. The military commander has chosen to host the French as his personal guests, rather than to treat them as visiting officials. His behavior therefore illustrates a discipline of interpersonal association in its register of gaiety and warmth, rather than protocol and ceremony.

THE STRUCTURE OF POLITICAL AUTHORITY IN THE CAPITAL

In the summer of 1796, Beauchamp had encountered the pattern of divided political authority characteristic of the later period of decentralization. There were two kinds of sovereign power. That of the provincial governor appeared to represent state institutions and organizations. That of local elites appeared to rely on a local base of allies and supporters. But Beauchamp, and the other western Europeans visitors who followed him, could not so easily perceive the basic similarity and close relationship of the two kinds of authority.

On the one hand, the political authority of high state officials was primarily based on their position in the state system. The provincial governor, for example, was the head of a more or less effective centralized bureaucracy composed of military and judicial officials. He had at his command officers and soldiers from the central army and, perhaps as well, some private officers and troops. He had at his disposal funds that were raised by tax collections, not only from the eastern coastal region, but also from farms and estates outside the province of Trabzon. At the same time, his position in the state system had a social component that was just as important, perhaps even more important, than its bureaucratic dimension. But this social component involved the provincial governor's contacts with other state officials in other parts of the Empire, outside the province of Trabzon. His household was organized in accordance with imperial ceremony and protocol. His staff and servants were recruited and trained in accordance with official thinking and practice. Like other members of the official class, he might move his household, his family, servants, and staff, from town to town or from region to region. In this respect, his political authority was not directly dependent on his position and influence in the social networks of the inhabitants of Trabzon (even if some of its local elites were his allies and others were his enemies). Instead, he was more directly dependent on his position and influence among members of the imperial official class, such as other governors and sub-governors in other provinces, or the highest officials of the palace in Istanbul. Accordingly, the souring of his social standing in official circles could lead to his immediate downfall, while a serious revolt of the local elites in the coastal districts could drive him from the capital but not deprive him of the provincial governorship.

On the other hand, the political authority of local elites, such as the two chiefs of the town, was primarily dependent on their local position and influence in some specific territory of the eastern coastal region. The two chiefs lived in large mansions and had large households that were functionally equivalent to those of state officials (see fig. 8). They even had staffs and servants who performed governmental functions, legally or illegally, just like the staffs and servants of state officials. So it was that they had the capacity to displace or replace state officials and govern districts in their stead. But the households of local elites were otherwise not organized in accordance with imperial protocol and ceremony, and their personal dependents and armed supporters were not recruited or trained in accordance with official thinking and practice. Rather, the local elites were creatures of a system of leaders and followers that was based on a discipline of interpersonal association. They were therefore dependent on their social networks among the inhabitants of a particular place somewhere in the eastern coastal region. They were Trabzonlus, not Ottomans, and by that fact they did not move in official circles. Nonetheless, they were able to defy, if not defeat, the provincial governor by mobilizing large numbers of men in arms because of their place in a regional social oligarchy that composed a major fraction of the rural population. When they lost favor with the provincial governor, this might have no effect whatsoever on their position and influence so long as they retained the support of clients, friends, partners, and allies.

For a century, from 1740 to 1840, these two kinds of political authority, one official and the other nonofficial, confronted one another in the town of Trabzon. The relationship of the provincial governor to the two chiefs of the town was not institutionalized but the subject of negotiation and renegotiation. In 1796, the two chiefs of the town had assumed authority ([*ils s'étaient*] *emparé de l'autorité*) from the provincial governor, reducing him to a mere symbol of the state system. In 1803, the two chiefs of the town

Figure 8. A mansion (early to mid-nineteenth century).

were included in the official receptions of the provincial governor but were not allowed to speak.[17] In 1827, the two chiefs of the town had not been granted any official recognition by the provincial governor and were excluded entirely from his official receptions.[18]

During some periods, either state officials or local elites prevailed over the other for a period of time. When the provincial governor was in a much stronger position than the chiefs were, he was able to force one or both of them to abandon the city altogether, exiling all their dependents and supporters to one of the outlying coastal districts.[19] When the two chiefs were in a much stronger position than the provincial governor was, they might force him to take refuge in the citadel, or even to abandon the capital or province altogether.[20] Still other kinds of alignments occurred when no party was in a dominant position. During periods of political crisis, for example, the relationships of the governor and the two chiefs were entirely fluid,

17. MAE CCCT L. 1, No. 15, Floreal An XII [May 1804].

18. This appears to have been the case when Fontanier (1834, 96–108) was received at the court of Osman Pasha Hazinedaroğlu during his second visit.

19. Aktepe (1951–52, 39–43) and Gologlu (1975, 154–55), in regard to the exile of Osman Agha Şatıroğlu, circa 1825.

20. See the note 33, below, citing eight known occasions between 1758 and 1833.

changing from month to month, if not from week to week. Sometimes the governor allied himself with one of the chiefs against the other, and then a short time later allied himself with his former enemy against his former ally. Sometimes the two chiefs joined together and called in reinforcements from their friends and partners in the countryside in order to force concessions from the provincial governor. Sometimes the governor called on allies among the local elites in the outlying coastal districts to force the compliance of one or both of the chiefs.

So the government was divided between state officials and local elites during the later period of decentralization. And yet this division cannot be understood as a centralized "state system" ranged against a localized "social system," since the latter was both structurally and functionally related to the former. All leading individuals with armed followings, whether or not they held official appointments, were essential to the carrying out of the most elementary functions of the provincial government. So state officials were dependent on the regional social oligarchy. On the other hand, local elites were always interested in penetrating the state system in order to consolidate and legitimize their political authority. So the local elites were dependent on the imperial system.

During the later period of decentralization, a few of the local elites of Trabzon gained entry into the circles of state officials, acquiring high titles and offices and cultivating social networks that reached up into the palace.[21] The two chiefs whom Beauchamp accords the title "ayan" appear not to have held high titles and offices at the moment of his visit.[22] The term "notables" (*âyan*) referred generally to persons of wealth and influence in a town or district, but it also designated a specific, officially recognized, social position. On the other hand, the term also referred to specific leading individuals who had been appointed as chief notable (*âyan başı*) by virtue

21. Memiş Agha Tuzcuoğlu was repeatedly able to block attempts by provincial governors to restrain him. Later, Tahir Agha, his son and successor, was able to do the same. Bilgin (1990, 311) infers that his son had influence in the palace. Consul Brant confirms that Tahir Agha had "powerful friends at Court" since the "Kapidan Pasha and Kapidan Bey are both Rizeli" and the "Serasker [of Erzurum (?)] likes him" (PRO FO 524/1 p. 29, Jan. 15, 1833).

22. Casual foreign visitors like Beauchamp commonly use the term "ayan" but did not always have a good understanding of it. Some years later, however, Dupré confirms Beauchamp's account. As a long-term consular resident, Dupré would have been well acquainted with its meaning. He sometimes refers to the two chiefs of the town as the "first ayan" and "second ayan," indicating that they are ranked as first and second chief notable (MAE CCCT L. 1, No. 86, Apr. 1809).

of their capacity to represent all the notables of a village, town, or area. The chief notable was not a state official, but he did assist in the carrying out of certain governmental functions.[23]

The principals among the local elites in the town of Trabzon and in the outlying coastal districts were often so appointed.[24] Otherwise, the two chiefs in the town sometimes acquired titles and offices usually reserved for state officials, such as district governor (*mütesellim*), military commander (*kaymakam*), military general (*paşa*), and provincial governor (*paşa, miri mîram*).[25] It was also the case that the most prominent of the local elites outside the provincial capital sometimes held such titles and offices, and probably did so on the occasion of the French expedition. The provincial governor, or his superiors in Istanbul, granted such official titles and offices in response to shows of force, as a means of mollifying or manipulating troublemakers. This being the case, it is not surprising that leading individuals with armed followings moved into state offices with greater frequency during periods of political crisis. Correspondingly, they were less successful in retaining such appointments during periods when the provincial governor was in a position to confront them. A strong provincial governor would dismiss those local elites who held state offices and replace them with as many of his own personal associates as possible.[26] Still, even the strongest provincial governors never alienated the local elites entirely from the state system but merely curbed the worst of their illegal practices and scaled back their official titles and offices, usually by relegating them to the position of chief notable.

23. See the Muradoğlu document dated August 14, 1834, for an example of such an appointment in the instance of Memiş Agha Muradoğlu, son of İsmail Agha, founder of the family line. This late document describes the chief notable as an "official" (*memur*); nonetheless, I think it best not to regard this position as a state office.

24. Sometimes Dupré writes of a certain individual as a valley lord (*Dere Bey* [sic]) and then later reports that this same man has been appointed as chief notable (*Ayant* [sic]). Sometimes he describes a valley lord (*Dere Bey*) as one of the "notables" (*Ayant*) of a certain place. So he implies that valley lords are a category apart from notables but also that some valley lords are notables and that some of them become chief notables. See MAE CCCT Ls. 1 and 2, *passim*.

25. I have discovered instances in which a man described as a chief, agha, or valley lord is appointed to the following offices or ranks: chief notable (*âyan başı*), agent (*mübaşir*), military commander (*kaymakam*), district governor (*mütesellim*), castle keeper (*muhafaza*), door keeper (*kapıcıbaşı*), general (*paşa*), and governor (*miri mîram*).

26. Sometimes the provincial governor would himself assume the positions of both district governor and military commander in the provincial capital.

CITIZEN BEAUCHAMP AND THE COASTAL DISTRICTS

With the benefit of these summary conclusions, I shall now return to Beauchamp's account in order to consider what his observations tell us about the relationship of the provincial government to a regional social oligarchy composed of local elites with armed followings. From his remarks, we can glimpse a pattern of vertical and horizontal alliances and oppositions.[27]

According to Beauchamp, the two chiefs, Memiş Agha and Osman Agha, were not natives of the town. They hailed instead from outlying rural areas of the province of Trabzon.[28] So the provincial capital had been invaded and occupied by leading individuals with armed followings who came from very different parts of the coastal region. This was indeed the "normal" situation. More or less the same pattern appears to have prevailed during the entire period of decentralization.

Why did some of the local elites from distant parts of the province set themselves up in the capital? How were they positioned among the local elites of their homelands? Each of these questions points toward a pattern of alliances among local elites who were sometimes attempting to stabilize and sometimes attempting to destabilize the provincial capital.

From the clues Beauchamp gives us, checked against other sources, we can assess the position of each of the two chiefs in these alliances. Following is my summary of the evidence about each of them.

The chief who was known as Osman Agha most likely came from the rural mountain areas to the south of the provincial capital. Later, the French expedition proceeds in this direction and visits an Orthodox convent that was said to be situated in his territory. This means that the homeland of the chief is in the vicinity of the principal route and pass that link the anchorages of the town with the major trade routes of the interior plateau. Thus we can conclude that Osman Agha was associated with the central areas of the province where a substantial Orthodox population remained in place.[29]

27. My reading of his account is informed by a review of the consular reports of Dupré and Fontanier.

28. Some years later, when Dupré was residing in the provincial capital (1807–9), an Osman Agha and a Memiş Agha were chiefs of the town, enemies of one another, sometimes engaged in hostilities with one another, and now and then appointed as chief notable by the provincial governor, as well as to other offices, such as district governor and military commander (MAE CCCT L. 1, Nos. 22–94, *passim*). For my estimate that these were the same men that Beauchamp had encountered, see the footnotes that follow.

29. This man was almost certainly an individual named Osman Agha Şatıroğlu. A call-out of troops (Cevdet Asker 40224, dated 1789/1204) confirms that Osman

The chief who was known as Memiş Agha most likely came from, or was associated with, the vicinity of Rize. This would fit the distance to his lands, his offer of an escort on horseback to reach them, his interest in questions of church and state, and the association of his homeland with the Laz.[30] If this is correct, Memiş Agha was from the local elites who were associated with the eastern districts, each of which enjoyed its own combination of ports, routes, and passes linking with the major trade routes of the interior plateau.[31]

These inferences are highly probable, even if not completely certain. And in any case, even if not entirely correct, they conform in their pattern to circumstances that prevailed in the town of Trabzon both before and after Beauchamp's visit.

During much of the period of decentralization, one of the factions in the town was more or less consistently linked with the Tuzcuoğlu family line of Rize. The Tuzcuoğlu coalition was largely composed of a coalition of local elites from districts beyond the central district of Trabzon, in particular, the districts of Rize, Of, and Sürmene. This coalition was usually opposed

---

Agha Şatıroğlu was a leading individual who commanded a large number of soldiers in the vicinity of Trabzon (*nefs-i Trabzon*). In 1804, Dupré tells us that Osman Agha Şatıroğlu was a *"Dere Bey et Ayant"* who replaces Hasan Agha as district governor (MAE CCCT L. 1, No. 22, 4 Vendémiaire An XIII [Sept. 1804]). As we shall see, he remained a leading individual in the vicinity of the provincial capital until the 1830s. If Beauchamp's Osman Agha is this man, then these conclusions would be further reinforced.

30. The contemporary roadway connecting the towns of Rize and Trabzon is 75 kilometers, so it would make sense that the distance to the interior of Rize would have approached 100 kilometers in 1796. As I have explained, the population in this part of the old province of Trabzon was oriented toward official Islam, and was therefore sensitive to issues of religion and state. As always, any mention of the Laz should be understood with respect to the situation of the speaker using the term. Although all the peoples of the province were considered Laz in Istanbul, the peoples of the further eastern sectors, Rize, Of, and Sürmene, were considered Laz in Trabzon. The Lazi-speakers of the coastal region inhabited the valleys still further east of Rize. Memiş Agha is most probably not from among the Lazi-speakers, since their homelands would have to be reached by boat, not horseback.

31. This Memiş Agha is most likely not Memiş Agha Tuzcuoğlu, a leading individual who commanded a large number of soldiers in the district of Rize. But he is almost certainly one of his allies, since the Rizeli was usually allied with one of the chief notables in the provincial capital, and he sometimes came there himself, as was the case in March of 1807 (MAE CCCT L. 1, No. 58, Mar. 1807). He may rather be Memiş Agha Kalcıoğlu. See Goloğlu (1975, xxxi), who lists this man as a chief notable (*ayan*) of Trabzon during the year 1807. Bilgin (1990, 282) claims the Kalcıoğlu family line hailed from the western coast. Nonetheless, Memiş Agha Kalcıoğlu was a son-in-law of the Rizeli and a part of his coastal coalition. So he could have had a secondary, or even a primary, mansion and base somewhere in Rize even if his ascendants had been from the western coast.

to the pasha of Trabzon. The other faction in the town was more or less linked with a coalition of local elites from the immediate vicinity of Trabzon. Often led by a representative of the Şatıroğlu family line, this coalition was usually allied with the pasha of Trabzon. Given the distribution of sovereign power during the period of decentralization, this pattern makes perfect sense.[32]

If the passage of commerce through the town of Trabzon was disrupted, then the transit trade was diverted to other land and sea routes of the coastal region. This meant that civil disorders in the town of Trabzon could have a direct effect on the balance of power between state officials and local elites, as well as between different coalitions of local elites. For if trade declined in the town of Trabzon, both the pasha of Trabzon and the local elites in the vicinity of the town were weakened by a fall in tax receipts. And when trade declined in Trabzon, the local elites of the outlying coastal districts were strengthened since commerce was diverted to the outlying ports, markets, routes, and passes, resulting in a rise in tax receipts.

In general, it was the local elites of Rize, Of, and Sürmene who had the most to gain from disruption of commerce in the capital, given the proximity of their transit valleys to the land routes of the interior highlands (see map 2). Thus the pasha of Trabzon, as well as the local elites in the vicinity, such as the Şatıroğlu family line, had a common (but not identical) interest in peace in the town. And the local elites of the outlying coastal districts, but especially the Tuzcuoğlu family line and its backers in Rize, Of, and Sürmene, had no compelling interest in peace in the town. That is to say, there was peace in the town of Trabzon only if the provincial governor struck a partnership with the Şatıroğlu family line in central Trabzon and at the same time made concessions to the Tuzcuoğlu family line in Rize, Of, and Sürmene.

Otherwise, civil disorder in the provincial capital increased or declined in accordance with different strategic combinations of officials and nonofficials.[33] The provincial governor might ally himself with the local elites of

32. The western coastal districts of the province also had their local elites with armed followings, but they did not challenge the provincial government so frequently as the local elites in the eastern coastal districts. This is probably explained by the fact that the ports and valleys of Rize and Trabzon are potentially in direct competition for the transit trade into northeastern Anatolia, especially the market center of Erzurum.

33. On at least eight occasions between 1758 and 1833, state officials were forced to close the gates of the city and shut themselves up in the citadel as the walled city was surrounded and the suburbs were sacked. The dates of the invasions are 1758–59 (Peysonnel 1787); 1807 (MAE CCCT L. 1, No. 65, July 1807); summer of 1808

the central districts, a common circumstance that usually kept peace in the town. If the local elites of the central districts became too strong, however, he might ally himself with the local elites of the outlying districts, a less common circumstance. On the other hand, the local elites of both the central and outlying districts sometimes joined together to foment civil disorders in order to weaken a strong provincial governor. And occasionally, the central and outlying elites combined to keep peace in the town of Trabzon for their mutual benefit, holding the provincial governor as their virtual hostage. The provincial governor might also face enemies other than the local elites of the coastal region. For if the provincial governor succeeded in gaining the upper hand over the local elites, usually by bringing in reinforcements from outside the province, the palace might begin to take steps to drive him from office, lest he use his position of strength in the coastal region to force concessions from the central government.

The situation in the provincial capital, as I have described it, can be more or less exactly correlated with the onset of the period of decentralization. The evidence for this appears in Peysonnel's account of commercial conditions along the Black Sea littoral. In a site-by-site description of the commerce of the eastern coastal region, Peysonnel writes:

> The town of Trabzon was once much more flourishing than it is today [text revised and completed in 1762]. Internal warfare caused by the old quarrels of the Twenty-fifth and Sixty-fourth Regiments of Janissaries has reduced this town to the most deplorable condition. In succession Ömer Pasha Üçüncüoğlu [governor of Trabzon 1741–45] and Ali Pasha Hekimoğlu [governor of Trabzon 1751–54] were successively able to pacify these troubles by the most terrifying kind of examples and the severest kind of discipline; but in 1758 and 1759 the disorders began once again worse than ever to the point that the commerce of this place has been completely disrupted. The inhabitants did not dare leave their houses, grass was growing in the streets and markets, and a large number of the inhabitants, especially the *reayas* [here, the Christian population], were forced to abandon the town, and to go in search of tranquility and security at Jaffa and in other places.[34]

As we know from other sources, the "janissary regiments" that are mentioned in the quote were associated with the aghas and agha-families of the coastal districts, and their membership consisted of local residents who

(No. 76, Aug. 1808); fall of 1808 (No. 81, Oct. 1808); 1816 (MAE CCCT L. 2, No. 26, Aug. 1816); 1827 (Fontanier 1829, 19; Bryer 1970, 44); 1830 (Bryer 1970, 44); and 1833 (PRO FO 524/2 p. 25, Feb. 1833).

34. Peysonnel 1787, 72.

were associated with the alliances and coalitions of the aghas and agha-families.[35]

Understood this way, Peysonnel's account links the rise of lower military officers and soldiers in the coastal districts, as established in the previous chapter for the district of Of, with the onset of civil disorders in the provincial capital. Early in the period of decentralization, before local elites and state officials had fully worked out the arrangements of their "ordered anarchy," commercial activity had declined and grass grew in the streets of the provincial capital. Even at this early date, however, the misfortunes of Trabzon were the basis of prosperity in Rize. Peysonnel writes, "All the maritime commerce of the province of Trabzon takes place at Rize when the internal quarrels are ravaging the former principal city. If duty is paid at Rize, it counts at Trabzon, and if it is paid at Trabzon, it counts at Rize."[36] Peysonnel duly informs his merchant audience that their duty would "count" at either Rize or Trabzon, presumably as far as the palace in Istanbul was concerned. Locally, however, it did not "count" for the same individuals and groupings when it was collected at one or the other of the two ports. For during this same period, the local elites of the coastal districts often refused to forward receipts to state officials in the provincial capital.

With this understanding of the background of civil disorders in the provincial capital, we can now piece together a clearer picture of the local elites in the outlying coastal districts.

THE STRUCTURE OF POLITICAL AUTHORITY IN THE COASTAL DISTRICTS

Just how many of the local elites, that is, how many aghas living in mansions, representing family lines, and backed by armed followings, were to be found in the coastal districts of Trabzon? On the occasion of the call-out for troops in 1788/1202, Ottoman officials cited twenty-six personal or family names in sixteen coastal districts, almost all of them in the vicinity of Trabzon and further east to Hopa.[37] On the occasion of the call-out for troops in 1789/1204, the officials cited more than forty personal or family

35. See note 8 above citing Fourcade, Fontanier, and Brant on janissaries in Trabzon.

36. Peysonnel 1787, 53–54.

37. See the official document that calls on certain individuals and families in the coastal district to send troops (Umur 1956, No. 65 1788/1202, pp. 65–67; Sümer 1992, 104–6).

names in the vicinity of Trabzon and further east to Hopa.[38] During a political crisis in the summer of 1807, Dupré despaired that "the government of the province was in the hands of fifty despots . . . who did not even listen to the sovereign."[39] When Osman Pasha had momentarily pacified the local elites in 1831, Fontanier listed seven family names of chiefs as he (erroneously) declared the province of Trabzon "disencumbered of that crowd of little despots."[40]

The common denominator of each of these assessments is an assumption that one, two, or three leading individuals are to be found in each of about sixteen districts; however, these one, two, or three were simply the principals among the local elites whom the central government had appointed as their intermediaries. In other words, they were the "chief notables" among still other "notables" much like them. So provincial state officials and western European consuls recognized only a fraction of the aghas, mansions, family lines, and followings in each of the coastal districts. Nonetheless, provincial state officials, if not the western European consuls, were fully aware that the principals represented social networks that reached out "by twig and branch" into the rural societies of the coastal districts.[41] Taken altogether, some twenty-five to fifty "little despots" represented but the uppermost, visible tier of a regional social oligarchy that included a substantial segment of the population.

The accounts of my interlocutors in the district of Of confirm that a segment of the local elites was more or less invisible to the residents of the provincial capital. Official documents, consular reports, and travel narratives usually don't mention more than two or three family lines in the district, but there were far more than two or three aghas from agha-families in its two valley-systems.[42] As we have seen, my interlocutors were able to list twenty-two aghas and agha-families of the nineteenth century and sort them according to their affiliation with the Five or the Twenty-five Party.[43]

38. Cevdet Asker 40224, dated 1789/1204.
39. MAE CCCT L. 1, No. 59, June 1807.
40. MAE CCCT L. 3, No. 11, Jan. 1831.
41. The arboreal metaphor is borrowed from Aktepe (1951–52). See the quote in note 44, below.
42. The names of the two principal family lines are not always the same: Garaçoğlu and Selimoğlu in 1788, Cansızoğlu and Selimoğlu in 1832, Muradoğlu and Selimoğlu after 1834.
43. See chap. 1. My interlocutors in Of were also able to describe the places where the mansions of the aghas of each agha-family were located before they were destroyed by Osman Pasha.

Each of the twenty-two aghas and agha-families were also linked by kinship, friendship, and partnership with other lesser and greater individuals from other family lines.[44]

For example, the author of a family memoir ("Fettahoğullarının Tarihi"), probably written in the early twentieth century, begins by listing those family lines that had been comrades of his family line during the eighteenth and nineteenth centuries. He mentions two patronymic groups that had been the principals of the Twenty-five Party (Muradoğlu and the Cansızoğlu), but he also mentions six other patronymic groups that my interlocutors did not include among the aghas and agha-families of either party. This implies that each agha and agha-family would have been associated with still other individuals and families. Taking this into account, one reaches the conclusion that social networks in the district of Of alone included thousands of individuals who hailed from scores of families. By analogy, one could also reasonably conclude that social networks in the old province of Trabzon included tens of thousands of individuals and hundreds of families.[45] These conclusions are consistent with the official callouts that summoned the most prominent of the local elites to assemble from one to two hundred men each. They are consistent as well with consular reports that describe occasions when coalitions of local elites mobilized ten to twenty thousand men in arms in order to set siege to the provincial capital.

44. Aktepe (1951–52, 28–29) notes that the Tuzcuoğulları, by virtue of their various relationship with other families, "spread by twig and branch over a considerable region." See also Bilgin (1990, 310–11), who gives numerous examples of intermarriage among the agha-families during the late period of decentralization. For example, Memiş Agha Tuzcuoğlu, leader of a coastal coalition that eventually challenges the provincial government, is eventually related to most of the other principal figures of the late period of decentralization. Osman Şatıroğlu of Trabzon and Gümüşhane is his son-in-law (MAE CCCT L. 1, No. 59, June 1807; PRO FO 524/2 p. 39, Jan. 1834, Suter). Memiş Kalcıoğlu of Trabzon and Sürmene is his son-in-law (Bilgin 1990, 282). Memiş Büberoğlu of Of is the father-in-law of his son, Ahmet (Bilgin 1990, 311). Arslan Bey of Batum is his son-in-law (PRO FO 524/1 p. 35, July 1833, Brant). Note that the above-mentioned individuals are sometimes rivals of one another, even though related, some supporting and some opposing the Tuzcuoğlu coastal coalition.

45. Without accounting for overlaps among the allies of the principals, the number of family lines in the district social networks of Of can be calculated as follows: 22 agha-families each allied with 6 non-agha-families equals 132 patronymic groups. Estimating 20 households per patronymic group, 132 times 20 equals 2,640 households in the district social network. This is the same order of magnitude of the number of households in the district of Of at this time (estimated at 6,000 in the census of 1869/1286; see Emiroğlu 1993, vol. 1, 141).

The existence of an extensive regional social oligarchy, comprising a major fraction of the population, may not have had its exact counterpart elsewhere in Asia Minor. The dissemination of a tactic of sovereign power had occurred everywhere in the core Ottoman provinces, but it followed a specific course with specific results in the province of Trabzon. First of all, and most importantly, the inhabitants of the coastal region were inclined to become participants in the imperial system by reason of both their ecology and history (see chap. 3). In addition to this, there was a relative absence of towns and estates, and hence wealthy merchants and magnates who might succeed in centralizing political authority. This entailed the proliferation of vertical and horizontal cleavages of political authority, but also, in response to this, the elaboration of district alliances and coastal coalitions. A different leading individual with an armed following was associated with virtually every point in the landscape that was of some strategic importance (anchorages, crossroads, passes). However, no local leading individual with an armed following was able to stand alone by virtue of the importance of transport and commerce for all the local economies. Every local leading individual with an armed following therefore participated in social networks, district alliances, and coastal coalitions. These circumstances explain why French consuls and Ottoman officials could look upon the eastern coastal districts of the period of decentralization with such contradictory expectations. The former could not "imagine a more complete anarchy," but the latter could hope to call out its inhabitants for mass participation in imperial campaigns.[46]

Combining the evidence from consular reports, official documents, and fieldwork, the distribution of sovereign power in the coastal districts can be spelled out in terms of the following patterns:[47]

1. Commercial Centers and Leading Individuals. Wherever economic activity was concentrated, there one also found a leading individual with an armed following. An anchorage associated with sea or land routes, a market center in a densely settled patch of a coastal valley, or a choke point through which the movement of people and goods were funneled would all

46. Fontanier 1829, 18. Also see Dupré, MAE CCCT L. 1, June 1807.

47. Aktepe (1951–52) has carried out the most systematic study of local elites in Trabzon during the later period of decentralization. Other important works based on Ottoman and Turkish sources are Ahmet Cevdet Paşa (1892/1309), Şakir Şevket (1867/1284), Umur (1951, 1956), Gologlu (1975), Bilgin (1990), and Sümer (1992). The most important works based on Greek sources are Bryer (1969, 1970) and Bryer and Winfield (1985). There are probably significant Armenian sources that have not yet been addressed by scholars.

be associated with a kind of local "government," consisting of a leading individual, a large residence, a household organization, a family line, and an associated body of allies and followers. The concentration of trade, manufactures, and farming meant that large numbers of people had a common interest in security. They were inclined, if not obliged, to submit to a leader with a following who collected revenues "off the top" (as some combination of goods, services, and cash) in return for his protection.

2. The Hierarchy of Commercial Centers. The centers of economic activity in the province of Trabzon varied widely in their commercial function and position. For example, the more important markets in the coastal valleys were located near transit points where overseas and overland routes intersected, near areas of high population density and more productive agriculture, or near choke points that funneled the movement of people and goods through the precipitous terrain. Some centers of economic activity were therefore "feeders" to others that were "collectors." The feeder markets were always destined to remain byways of regional trade, manufactures, and produce, but some of the collector markets had the potential to emerge as the principal emporia of the coastal region.

3. Coordinated Hierarchy of Authority and Commerce. The relative economic importance of commercial centers was correlated with the relative eminence of its associated leading individual with an armed following. For local elites (as opposed to state officials), the function and position of the commercial center may have been more important than the absolute volume of trade. For example, an individual with a following who controlled a major "collector" market in a coastal valley was in a position to dominate other individuals with followings who dominated its "feeder" markets. In this fashion, a hierarchy of leading individuals reflected a hierarchy of collector and feeder markets. However, there was never one perfectly integrated politico-economic hierarchy either at the level of the district valleys or at the level of the provincial region. Rather, the precise character of the politico-economic hierarchies of valleys and regions was the focus of some degree of factional competition, both locally and regionally.

Leading individuals with armed followers arose from within the state system wherever there was commercial activity, compromising centralized government. But this disintegrative principle was countered by an integrative principle. A hierarchy of local elites tended to crystallize around any hierarchy of commercial centers. The interdependency of authority and commerce explains the alignments of local elites in the coastal districts. Each transit valley was potentially a single politico-economic hierarchy. Its villagers followed a transhumant way of life that required the periodic movement of families and herds from the lower coastal foothills to the upper mountain pastures. They also needed to move products and manufactures, both exports and imports, through the valley from coast to mountains. Thus the local elites of a transit valley (who were associated with its anchorages, markets, roads, and passes) all had an interest in the secure movement of both people and goods from the shoreline to the highlands. On the other hand, the local elites of neighboring transit valleys did not necessarily share the same interests and so might be competitors.

The district of Of illustrates such patterns of intravalley organization and intervalley competition. There were two major valley systems in the district of Of. An agha of the Muradoğlu led a "party" that prevailed in the eastern valley, and an agha of the Selimoğlu led another "party" that prevailed in the western valley. While each of the two parties (*fırka*) appears to have dominated one of the transit valleys, they were also rivals. Furthermore, the membership of the Five and Twenty-five parties was not completely segregated territorially but interspersed between the two valleys, both in the lowlands and in the highlands. For many decades, the local elites of the district of Of were divided by disputes over the location of the principal market near the shoreline. At the same time, by virtue of their local rivalry, they each allied themselves with different groups of local elites in districts to the east and west.[48]

In the instance of some of the principal transit valleys, their anchorages, roads, and passes also constituted an attractive transport system for overseas and overland commerce. This provided yet another incentive for local elites to form district alliances among themselves and cultivate social networks based on hospitality, friendship, partnership, and intermarriage. On the other hand, the diversity of the trade, craft, manufactures, and cash crops did not match up in any one way with the multiplicity of anchorages, markets, routes, and passes in the coastal districts. Different combinations of political authority and commercial activity were always possible at both the district and the regional levels. The bouts of civil disorder, if not civil war, among the local elites of the coastal region were generally struggles to

48. There are always local details that do not exactly fit the models I am using. For example, the eastern valley in Of was primarily a route for reaching the interior highlands, while the western valley was primarily a migration route toward high mountain pastures. There was perhaps a measure of cooperation between the elites of the two valleys for this reason, since the residents of each would want to trade and to migrate in both.

establish one rather than another of these politico-economic hierarchies. If the local elites might squabble among themselves over such issues, so they might also squabble with state officials. As we shall see later, the most serious revolts of coastal coalitions were actually challenges to the politico-economic hierarchy associated with the provincial government.

For the reasons I have just mentioned, state officials were not neutral parties in the rivalries of local elites in the districts. On one occasion they might have an interest in supporting one alliance of local elites at the expense of their competitors, and then on a later occasion supporting the second at the expense of the first. On the other hand, state officials did not invariably adopt a policy of divide and rule. They more typically took steps to consolidate the authority of one particular individual in this or that valley. For example, one of the local elites was usually able to dominate the entry point of the transit valley near the coastline where a major market was typically located. The leading individuals in such strategic locations had a better chance of being appointed chief notable, if not district governor, and thereby becoming preeminent among the local elites of a transit valley. And once having become preeminent, they also had a better chance of perpetuating their family line so that their descendants would also be appointed chief notable. This appears to have been the case in the instance of the aghas of the Selimoğlu family, who were settled at a choke point of the western valley and then later at its coastal entry point.

Alternatively, the provincial governor might attempt to gain control of or manipulate an alliance of local elites by inserting one of his own followers at the entry point of a transit valley and confirming him as chief notable or district governor. The local elites of the transit valley might then be obliged to recognize him as the principal representative of their alliance by virtue of his occupation of an anchorage, market, route, or pass of strategic importance for the transit valley. It is probably by just such an appointment that İsmail Agha Muradoğlu set down a family line in the district of Of during the second decade of the nineteenth century. He appeared out of nowhere. He was of Kurdish origin and had no family line. But within a few years he had built an immense mansion to rival that of any state official in the most productive agricultural area of the district.[49] It was aghas of the Selimoğlu type and Muradoğlu type whose family names appear in official documents and consular reports. They entered the field of vision of state officials and foreign consuls in different ways, either by cashing in on their

49. The date of 1822/1237 is inscribed on one of the hearths in the great mansion.

local position to enter the state system or by cashing in on the state system to establish a local position.

After the provincial governor had dispatched one of his own personal followers to one of the coastal districts (as perhaps in the case of İsmail Agha Muradoğlu), he might discover some years later that this person had himself risen to a position among local elites and so refused to submit to the governor's authority and could not be recalled.[50] The former *protégé* would have built a mansion, enlarged his household, founded a family line, and assembled a following. So the local elites were not a fixed and invariant class. Some had become deeply entrenched in district social networks during several generations of succession. Others coupled their sponsorship from a provincial governor with efforts to establish themselves by building a following and extending their associations within the district. The local elites always included both newcomers and long-time residents since state officials planted their *protégés* in the coastal districts.

The provincial governor could never know exactly in what measure his appointed clients in the coastal districts, or even his own subordinates in Trabzon itself, had been drawn into the local networks of friendship, marriage, partnership, and alliance in the coastal districts. For example, Fontanier reports that one of the local elites in Sürmene, having declared his support for the provincial governor, secretly dispatched reinforcements to assist an ally who had remained in a state of revolt against the provincial governor. He writes, "They had sent proposals for accommodating the pasha, made magnificent promises of submission to him, and assured him that they would pay their taxes. At the same time, they placed on the very boat that was to carry these dispatches some fifteen men under the command of the nephew of their agha who were intending to go to the assistance of the chief who was in revolt."[51] Then on another occasion, also during the "strong" governorship of Osman Pasha, British consul Guarracino described how government troops, dispatched to suppress rebels in one of the coastal districts, dutifully engaged them in what was merely a mock battle, since they were in fact their friends and allies:

> Uzunoglu Mehmet Agha, the commander of Osman Pasha's troops, came to Miruvet; it was agreed between Kior Hussein Bey and Uzunoglu

50. Dupré comments that Yusuf Pasha "appears resolved to force a *derebey* to come back to the town. The latter is his protégé, in possession of various villages, which for some time he has usurped from those who were first to acquire them and who now defend their supposed property with force of arms" (MAE CCCT L. 1, No. 65, July 1807).

51. Fontanier 1929, 14.

> that a feigned engagement from the opposite bank of the river should take place, but that neither party should direct their fire on their opponents. The men maintained a constant fire for two days, and of course without a shot taking effect. The troops, who were apparently enemies during the day, crossed the river in boats in the night, and feasted together.[52]

There was an inescapable, decentralizing logic to a tactic of sovereign power based on interpersonal association. The provincial governor had his own circle of dependents and followers in the imperial rather than the local style. He could project his political authority by sending out a close friend or partner into the coastal districts. But once the latter found himself in the milieu of the countryside rather than the capital, he transformed himself from state official into one of the local elites.

A SINGLE GOVERNMENT OF STATE OFFICIALS AND LOCAL ELITES

My analysis has examined the cleavages between state officials and local elites, as well as among the local elites themselves. This puts a spotlight on the instability of the structure of political authority. Similarly, the available sources, consular reports, travel accounts, official documents, and local traditions, all emphasize moments of crisis, since periods of peace were deemed less interesting and significant. So it is necessary to recall that state officials and local elites sometimes, if not usually, worked together for months, if not for years, without coming into conflict. There were two different situations in which state officials and local elites tended to cooperate. A strong provincial governor, one who was able to draw on manpower and resources from outside the eastern coastal region, was able to intimidate the local elites. For example, he might make examples of a few of the aghas and ayans, burning their markets or mansions or even arresting or executing them. The other aghas and ayans would then fall into line, declaring their loyalty and obedience to the governor and taking their places in the provincial government as intermediaries and assistants. Alternatively, a provincial governor who lacked manpower and resources could establish a working relationship with the local elites. For example, he would make concessions to the most powerful of the local elites in order to establish a negotiated peace. Then, relying on the assistance of the latter, he could move against

52. Guarracino (1845, 298) heard this story while on a journey that probably took place during the summer of 1841.

any of the less powerful of the local elites who opposed the terms of the negotiated peace. From the comments of Dupré, it could be inferred that provincial governors sometimes assumed office by the first technique and then gradually shifted to the second technique as they became more experienced.

Given the means by which provincial governors imposed or negotiated peace, it should come as no surprise that the prospect of the dismissal, resignation, disgrace, flight, or death of a provincial governor usually entailed a period of civil disorder at least until the arrival of his successor. On such occasions, the cleavages among state officials and local elites came out into the open. Accordingly, conditions in Trabzon were also directly affected by instability in the central government. For example, a strong provincial governor was in place when Consul Dupré first took up his post, but some years later political crises in Istanbul began to have repercussions in Trabzon. From 1807 to 1811, nine different individuals served as provincial governor, resulting in recurrent episodes of civil disorder in the town.[53] Consul Dupré sometimes wrote with desperation:

> The two parties [of derebeys] who were joined in an alliance are again in arms and the city is in a state of civil war. . . . There is veritable anarchy in the city. [The governor] Ahmet Pasha is powerless. The undisciplined troops of [Osman Agha] Şatıroğlu commit disorders, brigandage, thefts, assassinations with impunity.[54] (June 6, 1807)

> Civil war continues in the country and rekindles daily more and more. It was formerly only in the neighboring villages, but with the arrival of reinforcements for Memiş Agha [Kalcıoğlu] from [Memiş Agha] Tuzcuoğlu [of Rize], it is now occurring in the city itself.[55] (Aug. 20, 1808)

Even so, one has to recall that civil disorder in Trabzon did not necessarily mean that there was also civil disorder in all or even most of the outlying coastal districts. Indeed, trouble in Trabzon was sometimes the sign of peace in the outlying coastal districts, just as peace in Trabzon was sometimes the sign of trouble in the outlying coastal districts. The disintegrative effects of the decentralization of sovereign power were countered by the integrative effects of the existence of a state society counterpoised to the state bureaucracy.

The other factor to bear in mind is the sometimes-gratuitous character of civil disorders. Oftentimes, they were merely a show of force not unlike

53. Gologlu 1975, 304.
54. MAE CCCT L. 1.
55. Ibid.

the marriage celebrations that I witnessed in the district of Of during the 1960s. There was a great deal of gunfire, but it might be no more than a demonstration of numbers and firepower rather than actual combat. Fontanier suggests as much by his description of the town of Trabzon in 1827. At the time, Osman Pasha Hazinedaroğlu had just assumed the provincial governorship only months after the abolition of the old janissary institution:

> It is difficult to imagine a more complete anarchy. In the town itself, there are fortresses that belong to private parties who make war on one another. For several days while this is going on, one hears nothing but rifle shots as they fire from one house to the other. It is true that these fights are more noisy than murderous because at the conclusion of a battle it is often the case that no one has been killed or even wounded. A few days after my departure, I was told that the entire population had taken up arms and set siege to the pasha in his fortified mansion. Then, weary of war, they had allowed him to re-assume his position of authority. As a result of this state of affairs—that the inhabitants have always to be in arms—the collection of taxes is difficult, and not in correspondence with the fertility of the soil or the variety of its productions.[56]

This point having been made, it must also be said that there were also episodes of serious destruction and suffering. Such episodes generally occurred when a provincial governor undertook to alter the balance of power between state officials and local elites.[57] There are two late examples. Süleyman Pasha Hazinedaroğlu (1811–18) assumed the provincial governorship with the intention of implementing the so-called "New Order" (*Nizam-i Cedid*).[58] This measure entailed the organization of a new central army and hence the weakening of the old central army, as represented by the janissary

56. Fontanier 1829, 18–19.

57. As we have seen in chap. 5, there was destruction and suffering during the early period of decentralization, when local elites first began to assert themselves against state officials. Canıklı Ali Pasha (1772–79, 1781–84) sent 10,000 troops to Of, but they had to return without accomplishing anything (Karadenizli 1954, 46; Şakir Şevket 1867/1284, 94). Süleyman Pasha sent 2,500 troops against Memiş Agha Tuzcuoğlu in Rize in 1816 after retaking the capital (Bilgin 1990, 290). Süleyman Pasha sent 25,000 to 30,000 for the invasion of Of in 1816 (ibid.). Tayyar Pasha sent 6,000 troops not far from Trabzon to try to suppress a valley lord (MAE CCCT L. 1, No. 71, Mar. 1808). Süleyman Pasha invested and destroyed Görele in 1811 (Bryer 1969, 191). Süleyman Pasha took a military expedition to Batum (MAE CCCT L. 1 [1801–11], No. 92, Sept. 1809; No. 94, Nov. 1809).

58. Dupré wrote that the pasha is once again to attempt to establish the new military organization, having failed previously to do so (MAE CCCT L. 2 BPMT, Dupré, No. 9, Oct. 1812).

institution. Before he left office, the aghas and ayans of the outlying coastal districts had sacked the suburbs of the capital, and the government had responded by dispatching tens of thousands of troops for the invasion and occupation of the district of Of.[59] Ten years later, Osman Pasha Hazinedaroğlu (1827–42) assumed the provincial governorship just after the abolition of the janissary institution. He then proceeded to carry out a program of pacifying the aghas and ayans, intending to reduce their military capacities. Once again, the aghas and ayans set siege to the capital, and in response, the government flooded the district of Of with tens of thousands of troops.

I shall conclude by comparing and contrasting three prominent individuals as examples of the relationship of state officials and local elites. The three examples will also make it possible to diagram a "tiered" state society consisting of higher and lower state officials merging and combining with greater and lesser local elites.

STATE OFFICIALS AND LOCAL ELITES

Memiş Agha Tuzcuoğlu of Rize, Osman Agha Şatıroğlu of Trabzon, and Süleyman Pasha Hazinedaroğlu of Canık were the principal figures in a crisis of political authority in the province of Trabzon (1814–17). Each of these individuals was from a family of provincial state officials. Each of them had a regional base that provided him with resources in the form of cash income and armed followers. Each of them came to serve as a district governor and aspire to powers equivalent to a provincial governor. All three were rivals, and two became bitter enemies.

Memiş Agha Tuzcuoğlu and the Regional Elite

Memiş Agha Tuzcuoğlu is said to have been born in the eastern coastal region sometime during the early eighteenth century, perhaps as early as the year 1715. His father was one of the "notables" (*eşraf*) of Rize, where he was perhaps engaged in trade. One of his uncles held the rank of pasha and served as provincial governor of Erzurum.[60] By the 1780s, Memiş Agha

59. On the sack of the suburbs, see MAE CCCT L. 2, No. 26, Aug. 1816. On the invasion of Rize, Of, and Sürmene, see Aktepe (1951–52, 33) and MAE CCCT L. 2, Nos. 43, 47, 49, and 50.

60. Aktepe (1951–52, 20–21) estimates his year of birth as 1715 by the tradition that he was more than 100 years of age at the time of his execution in 1817. Also see Bilgin (1990, 282), who reviews Aktepe (1951–52) and Ahmet Cevdet Paşa (1892/1309).

had risen to prominence in the coastal districts of the eastern province of Trabzon by a combination of government, financial, and commercial activities. He was somehow involved with the manufacturing and shipping of flax and linen, which had become an important industry in the vicinity of Rize.[61] He advanced villagers cash for their future produce so that they might be able to make tax payments. He collected funds to be forwarded as tax receipts to the provincial governor, taking some varying share for himself in proportion to his own position of strength.[62] He was then all at once a social oligarch, an entrepreneur, a moneylender, a tax-collector, and, eventually, a provincial state official.

By no later than 1788, Memiş Agha was regularly serving as chief notable, if not district governor, of Rize. This means he was a principal figure among the local elites of the eastern province of Trabzon by this date. Just a few years later, he held an imperial rank commonly granted to eminent provincial notables, gate-keeper (*kapıcıbaşı*). Afterward, he also occasionally served as military commander (*kaymakam*) of Rize and castle-keeper (*muhafaza*) of Faş.[63] By the 1800s, if not earlier, he was the leader of a coastal coalition that included aghas and ayans distributed across the eastern coastal districts.[64] The coastal coalition in question consisted of what I

61. The "Fettahoğullarının Tarihi" mentions the connection of local elites with the transport of locally manufactured linen.

62. According to tradition, Memiş Agha was a tall and fat man. On the days when he collected taxes, he would ride a great mule, leading a second carrying a small cannon. When the villagers heard the shot of the cannon, they knew he was coming. They would gather around him as he remained seated on his mule, and he would tell them to pay this or that amount in taxes. There are stories that tell of his kindness, but others tell also of his cruelty; both probably contain a grain of truth. Bilgin (1990, 283, n. 2) writes, "An old man complained to Memiş Agha that his son was not behaving properly to him and asked if would he please help to reform him. Memiş Agha thereupon ordered the son to be hanged. The old man pleaded that he did not ask him to kill but to 'reform' (*ıslah*) his son. 'This is the way I reform people,' he replied and rode away." In contrast, Umur (1949, 20–22) writes that Memiş Agha was close to the people and enjoyed their support. Stories of his mistreatment of the people were slanders spread by Süleyman Pasha and his representatives in their attempt to undermine local confidence in him and also to discredit him with the palace. Favoring the view of Umur, at least in regard to the family line in general, Consul Suter reports that Tahir Tuzcuoğlu, his son and heir, was "loved by his people" by reason of "his influence and wealth" (PRO FO 524/1 p. 40, Mar.–Apr. 1834).

63. See Bilgin 1990, 285.

64. For an indication that Memiş Agha Tuzcuoğlu was the leader of such a coalition no later than 1788, see the official documents that call on certain individuals and families in the coastal district to send troops (Umur 1956, No. 65 1788/1202; Cevdet Asker 40224, dated 1789/1204).

have termed a hierarchy of authority and commerce, centered on the districts of Rize, Of, and Sürmene and controlling the transit trade from the coast to the interior.[65]

From 1814 to 1817, he had raised the ayans and aghas of the coastal districts of Rize, Of, and Sürmene in revolt against the provincial governor, Süleyman Pasha Hazinedaroğlu. At the time, his enemies accused him of intending to form a separate state. More probably, he was hoping to maintain, if not enhance, his prerogatives and privileges within the imperial system, perhaps by establishing himself as a provincial governor of a separate "province of Rize."[66]

I shall describe Memiş Agha as one of the "regional elite," thereby distinguishing him from lesser local elites of the coastal districts. I use this term to designate the limited number of local elites who held higher state appointments and imperial ranks. There would probably have been somewhere between twenty and fifty representatives of such a regional elite at any one time.

Süleyman Pasha Hazinedaroğlu and the Imperial Elite

Süleyman Pasha Hazinedaroğlu was not a native of Trabzon, and he did not reside there until later in his career. According to an undocumented tradition, he came from an old family line that had long been associated with the western province of Canık.[67] However, his position in the western coastal region was not comparable to the regional elite of the province of Trabzon. He was instead the owner of vast estates worked by sharecroppers reduced to the status of serfs.[68] So he was not linked with a coalition of aghas and

65. This does not mean that all the ayans and aghas of Rize, Of, and Sürmene were followers of Memiş Agha. For example, Dupré reports that the Rizeli was unable to respond to a call for troops by the provincial governor in 1808 because he had already sent six thousand men to set siege to a valley lord occupying a fortified castle among the Laz to the northeast of Rize (MAE CCCT L. 1, No. 71, Mar. 1808; No. 72, Mar. 1808; No. 73, June 1808).

66. Perhaps a third hierarchy of authority and commerce existed among the local elites of the western coastal districts, where the rural economy was based on a different combination of ports, routes, products, and manufacturers. According to Bryer (1969, 197), Süleyman Pasha called on eastern local elites to make war on the western local elites in the first year of his appointment to the governorship (1811).

67. Gologlu (1975, xxix) describes the Hazinedaroğlu family as a well-known and very old family of the coastal region.

68. The western coastal region could be economically exploited as large estates farmed by life tenants. By this fact, it was a potential reservoir of cash and men that could be used to gain control of the sometimes-lucrative trade route at Trabzon. The provincial governors who were able to import manpower and resources into Tra-

ayans in any section of the coastal region, and therefore he was not dependent on the support of the population of any particular place. He controlled the lands and peoples in the province of Canık by the mechanisms of the state system rather than by a coalition of aghas and *ayans*. Thus, he was able to bring troops and supplies into the "ungovernable" eastern coastal region from the "governable" western coastal region.[69]

When Süleyman Pasha first arrived in the town of Trabzon, he held appointments as military commander of Canık and district governor of Trabzon, but he expected to be appointed provincial governor of Trabzon.[70] When he rose to that position soon afterward, he did so by bidding for the office and then paying a large fee for his governmental concession. That is to say, he counted on his ability to force the local elites of the coastal region to forward tax receipts to the provincial government. This was consistent with his intention of implementing the so-called "New Order" (*Nizam-i Cedid*), which would have had the effect of curbing the military strength of the aghas and ayans. So Süleyman Pasha hoped to reinforce the formal state system in the province of Trabzon at the expense of its local elites, and, in particular, the coastal coalition led by Memiş Agha Tuzcuoğlu.

I shall describe Süleyman Pasha as an "imperial elite," thereby distinguishing him from the local elites of the province of Trabzon. As such, he conducted his provincial governorship in accordance with state ceremony and protocol.[71] His various households (he came to have more than one) were composed of numerous dependents, servants, and slaves, many of

---

bzon from the western coastal region (Canık) were in a good position to intimidate local elites. At least four such provincial governors can be cited: Canıklı Hacı Ali Pasha (1772–78, 1781–84), Canıklı Tayyar Mahmut Pasha (1801–5), Süleyman Pasha (1811–18), and Osman Pasha (1827–42).

69. During his tenure as governor, Süleyman Pasha repeatedly brought troops from Canık to deal with uprisings of the local elites. See, for example, MAE CCCT L. 2, No. 25, July 1816; No. 32, Nov. 1816. He also sometimes used his mansions and estates in the province of Canık as a kind of refuge, especially during the bouts of plague or rebellion in the capital (MAE CCCT L. 1 BPMT, No. 3, Nov. 1811; L. 2, No. 125, Jan. 1812; BPMT, No. 23, Feb. 1814; No. 27, Sept. 1816; No. 54, Nov. 1817). Hüsrev Pasha, successor to Süleyman Pasha, also went to Canık to raise troops to deal with a rebellion in Sürmene (MAE CCCT L. 2, No. 75, June 1818). He, too, transported his household to Canık as a precaution in the face of an imminent rebellion in Trabzon (MAE CCCT L. 1, No. 82, Aug. 1819).

70. See MAE CCCT L. 1, No. 110, Nov. 1810.

71. Reports on the household of Süleyman Pasha are meager, but see Hamilton's (1842, 282–92) remarkable description of his son's mansion and household at Çarşamba. Hamilton meets Osman Pasha late in his tenure as governor of Trabzon. He describes him as a man of impressive wealth who had adopted European dress and lived in greater state than anyone he had ever encountered in Turkey. He de-

whom would have been raised and trained in accordance with official conventions and procedures. He had at his side state officials and military officers who were not from Trabzon but were themselves associated with the formal state system. He was associated with still other higher state officials by kinship, friendship, and alliance.[72] He was backed by a certain number of paid regular or irregular soldiers in his capital and was able to raise and transport large numbers of regular and irregular soldiers from the province of Canık.[73] He joined with other high state officials to launch imperial campaigns in the Caucasus. When faced with revolts in the eastern coastal region, he was able to call on high state officials in neighboring regions, and they supported him by dispatching military reinforcements.

Given his position in the formal state system, Süleyman Pasha was not obliged to consider the tranquillity and prosperity of any particular settled population. He could afford to sacrifice the welfare of the inhabitants of the province of Trabzon in the interest of mobilizing troops and requisitioning supplies for military campaigns.[74] Unlike the local elites, he therefore enjoyed the advantage of a relative freedom from any sympathy for, or loyalty to, a land or a people. At the same time, he appears to have had a money problem, understandably so since his governorship relied on payment for services rather than the support of a circle of aghas and ayans. He had been forced at some time to borrow funds from Memiş Agha Tuzcuoğlu. So he

---

scribed his house as "a gay straggling building" with a large harem, many wives, ladies, and slaves, and a household staff that included European experts and doctors.

72. During the Tuzcuoğlu rebellions of the 1810s and 1830s, for example, first Süleyman Pasha and then Osman Pasha depended on officials in Adjaria, Bayburt, Canık, Erzurum, Gümüşhane, Kars, and Sivas for the invasion and occupation of Rize, Of, and Sürmene, as well as for the arrest and execution of members of the Tuzcuoğlu family. For the Tuzcuoğlu rebellion of 1814–17, see MAE CCCT L. 2, Dupré, No. 32, Nov. 1816; No. 33, Jan. 1817; No. 41, Feb. 1817; No. 43, June 1817; No. 47, July 1817; No. 49, July 1817. For the Sürmene revolts of 1831–32, see PRO FO 524/1, Brant, p. 23, Aug. 1832. For the Tuzcuoğlu revolt of 1832–34, see PRO FO 524/1, Brant, p. 29, Jan. 1833; p. 35, July 1833; Suter, p. 42, Oct. 1833; p. 43, Mar. 1834; PRO FO 524/2, Brant, p. 24, Dec. 1832; Suter, p. 56, p. 41, Apr. 1834; p. 46, Apr. 1834; p. 46, May 1834; p. 56, Aug. 1834.

73. In 1815 Süleyman Pasha was also appointed provincial governor of Canık, so that he was the putative ruler of the entire northern coast of Asia Minor (MAE CCCT L. 2, No. 12, Apr. 1815).

74. Süleyman Pasha had a direct interest in the town of Trabzon as the means for dominating and controlling the regional overseas and overland trade routes. Still, he was willing to let its residents suffer in order to address a larger problem of the state system. For example, he disrupted the commerce of Trabzon for months on end in the course of assembling a large body of troops for the purpose of carrying out an invasion of the Caucasus (MAE CCCT L. 1, No. 117, May 1811, Dupré).

was indebted to a man who should have been his subordinate, and, as well, a subordinate who was asserting his independence by withholding tax receipts.

The Contrast Between the Imperial and Regional Elite

When Süleyman Pasha moved decisively to restrict his independence, Memiş Agha responded by raising the ayans and aghas of districts east of Trabzon in revolt (1814–17). The manner in which Süleyman Pasha was at last able to suppress this revolt serves to illustrate the uprooted and mobile character of the imperial elite as opposed to the rooted and immobile character of the regional elite.

Süleyman Pasha had long sought to obtain a warrant for the arrest and execution of his rival, but this had proven a difficult task by reason of the Rizeli's influence in palace circles.[75] When the warrant was issued in 1816, Memiş Agha proceeded to march on Trabzon, occupying its suburbs with thousands of soldiers and forcing Süleyman Pasha to flee his capital.[76] From this position of strength, Memiş Agha initially attracted the allegiance of still more of the ayans and aghas in various parts of the coastal regions.[77]

Süleyman Pasha was later able to return to Trabzon after receiving military support from other members of the imperial elite, that is to say, other high state officials with whom he had contacts. At the time, a combination of forces, supported by ships from the imperial navy, moved on the province of Trabzon from different directions. These included the armies of Ali Pasha of Kastambol [sic], Mehmet Pasha of Erzurum, the pasha of Sivas, and the military commander of Gümüşhane.[78] Like Süleyman Pasha, all of these individuals were uprooted and mobile in that they commanded some considerable number of salaried and conscripted troops. As these different

75. Turkish local historians usually mention the tradition that Süleyman Pasha and Memiş Agha had long been personal rivals and had quarreled over a large debt that the former owed the latter. Nevertheless, the historians have also recognized that the personal animosity of the two was fueled by their leadership of two competing hierarchies of authority and commerce. See Aktepe (1951–52, 23), Goloğlu (1975, 143–45), and Bilgin (1990, 287) on this point.

76. The revolt of Memiş Agha Tuzcuoğlu was the forerunner of other revolts by his sons, Ahmet Agha (1818–21) and Tahir Agha (1832–34). In each instance, the same conflict between hierarchies of authority and commerce is evident, one centered on Rize and the other centered on Trabzon.

77. See Aktepe (1951–52), Goloğlu (1975), and Bilgin (1990, 287).

78. MAE CCCT L. 1, No. 32, Nov. 22, 1816; No. 33, Jan. 10, 1817; No. 41, Feb. 18, 1817; No. 43, June 12, 1843; No. 47, July 21, 1817; No. 49, July 30, 1817, Dupré.

armies moved on the province of Trabzon, many of the ayans and aghas, especially those in the western districts of the province, then reversed themselves, declaring their allegiance to Süleyman Pasha.

Once Süleyman Pasha had reinstalled himself in the provincial capital, he dispatched 2,500 troops to set siege to the residence of Memiş Agha Tuzcuoğlu in Rize. This led the latter to flee to Of, where he was able to find refuge among the local elites of that district. Süleyman Pasha then sent representatives to the district of Of hoping to persuade its ayans and aghas to turn over Memiş Agha. After months of fruitless negotiations, Süleyman Pasha gathered twenty-five to thirty thousand troops from the vicinity of Batum and dispatched them to the district of Of, where they engaged in a two-month battle with the local ayans and aghas. Although no eyewitness accounts of this particular invasion are available, we can reasonably assume that the troops adopted the same measures they followed on earlier and later occasions. They burned and looted mansions, shops, warehouses, and residences. They destroyed or seized crops, stores, and stock. They impressed villagers into military service, and they extorted exceptional taxes from them. In other words, Süleyman Pasha succeeded in forcing the surrender of the population by terrorizing and impoverishing them.[79] Eventually the local elites and their followers submitted, and the soldiers were at last able to capture and execute Memiş Agha Tuzcuoğlu in October 1817.[80]

Less than six months after his victory over Memiş Agha, Süleyman Pasha fell into disgrace and a few days later suddenly died. The provisions of the "New Order" would never be implemented in the province of Trabzon, and his successor would soon face revolts by alliances of local elites in the outlying coastal districts.[81]

79. The governor dispatches warships and troops to Rize (MAE CCCT L. 1, No. 32, Nov. 1816). State officials seize goods without payment (No. 33, Jan. 10, 1817). State officials raise new taxes, terrorize the population, place hundreds of men in chains (No. 41, Feb. 1817). Rize is occupied by government troops for five months (No. 47, July 1817). The forces of Süleyman Pasha enter Of by sea (No. 49, July 1817). Bilgin (1990, 287 ff.) and Gologlu (1975, 148) report that tens of thousands of troops invaded the district of Of on this last occasion and battled with its residents for two months.

80. See Aktepe 1951–52, 33.

81. Aktepe 1951–52, 33–39. Hüsrev Pasha, successor to Süleyman Pasha, was rumored to have poisoned him on orders of the palace (Fontanier 1834, 98–99). A "slave official" (*kul*) of the palace, this man became the guardian of his predecessor's three sons, sending them to Istanbul after the death of their father. The oldest son, Osman, became a page of the sultan (Fontanier 1834, 98), and then later returned to Trabzon to serve as provincial governor. The middle son, Abdullah, served his older brother as a state official once he had become provincial governor,

By way of contrast with Süleyman Pasha, and the state officials who sent him reinforcements, the aghas and ayans of the province of Trabzon were rooted and immobile. They were obliged to serve the interests of extensive social networks and ensure the security of trade and commerce in the transit valleys. It is true that they favored their dependents and allies at the expense of the general population. It is also true that they were sometimes drawn into protracted and destructive conflicts with one another. Nonetheless, they did not carelessly wreak havoc on the very populations from which they drew their followings.

Memiş Agha Tuzcuoğlu exemplifies how the regional elite were also rooted and immobile since they were leaders of district networks and coastal coalitions of local elites. He had built a large mansion, founded a family line, assembled an armed following, and was able to mobilize a coastal coalition. If his household included many servants and slaves, it was not organized in the imperial manner. Removed from the context of the social networks and commercial interests of Rize, Of, and Sürmene, he would have been reduced to a figure of inconsequence.

Keeping in mind the differences between Süleyman Pasha and Memiş Agha as representatives of the "imperial" and "regional" elite, we can now turn to Osman Agha Şatıroğlu.

Osman Agha Şatıroğlu and the Local Elites of the Central Districts

Osman Agha Şatıroğlu represented the local elites in the vicinity of the town of Trabzon, just as Memiş Agha Tuzcuoğlu represented the local elites of Rize, Of, and Sürmene. They were in some respects of similar background and position, and they were even related to one another through the marriage of their children.[82] On the other hand, they can be distinguished by fine differences that point to two different strategies that were adopted by the regional elite. Some (like Memiş Agha) relied on a coastal coalition of

---

then later succeeded him as provincial governor. It is also interesting that Süleyman Pasha may have himself taken extreme measures to bring about a succession in the Tuzcuoğlu family line. When Fontanier visited Rize circa 1833, İzzet Agha Tuzcuoğlu was serving as the military commander of that district. Then about thirty years old, he had "at sixteen years of age, on orders of the pasha, killed his uncle with two shots of a pistol" (ibid., 298). The shooting would have taken place sometime around 1817, that is, during the revolt of Memiş Agha Tuzcuoğlu.

82. In 1807 a dispute between Memiş Agha and Osman Agha had been settled when the former gave his daughter in marriage to the son of the latter (MAE CCCT L. 1, No. 58, Mar. 1807).

ayans and aghas to assert themselves against state officials. Others (like Osman Agha) relied on a narrower base of *ayans* and aghas to vault themselves into the state system, where they formed close alliances with some but not all higher state officials.

The first members of the Şatıroğlu family line are reputed to have arrived in the coastal region at the time of Ottoman incorporation.[83] Whatever the case, various members of the family line appear as prominent individuals (chief notables) and state officials (district governors) in the province by the later eighteenth century, usually in the vicinity of Trabzon or Gümüşhane.[84] While members of the family line often served as state officials, they were also named as "valley lords" (*derebey*) and "usurpers" (*mütegallibe*). In all these respects, Osman Agha Şatıroğlu continued the tradition of his forebears.

Osman Agha Şatıroğlu was probably one of the chiefs of the town when Beauchamp arrived in 1796. He was most certainly among the local elites who served as state officials about a decade later. Dupré initially calls him "Osman Agha" and describes him as a "notable and derebey" who has been appointed district governor of Trabzon (1804). In later consular reports (1804–9), Dupré alternately names him as chief notable or military commander or district governor.[85] The terminology of the French consul probably did not keep pace with his career. After Süleyman Pasha Hazinedaroğlu

83. Bilgin 1990, 294; Gologlu 1975, 153.

84. Mehmet Şatıroğlu was appointed as Trabzon chief notable in 1768, and in the 1780s was a noted "valley lord" against whom Abdülhamit I issued a *ferman* condemning him for brigandage (Bilgin 1990, 294). İbrahim and Ömer Şatıroğlu were associated with the government of Canıklı Hacı Ali Pasha, serving as tax collectors in the vicinity of the town of Trabzon in 1777, in the vicinity of Gümüşhane in 1778, and in Trabzon in 1782–83 (ibid.).

85. Dupré reports that Osman Agha Şatıroğlu, "*Dere Bey et Ayant,*" has been appointed "commandant" of the town (MAE CCCT L. 1, No. 22, 4 Vendémiaire 13 [Sept. 1804]). Dupré reports that Osman Agha, "*Dere Bey et Ayant,*" is appointed as military commander (*kumandan*) of the town by Yusuf Pasha at the time of a revolt in Canık (MAE CCCT L. 1, No. 48, Aug. 1806). Dupré reports that he is the enemy of Yusuf Pasha in 1807 (MAE CCCT L. 1, No. 53, Jan. 1807; No. 55, Feb. 3, 1807; No. 68, Apr. 15, 1808; No. 69, Apr. 15, 1808; No. 75, Aug. 1809; No. 92, Sept. 30, 1809). Dupré reports that Osman Agha has been appointed military commander and district governor of Trabzon (MAE CCCT L. 1, No. 98, Mar. 1810). From 1807 to 1810, Dupré reports that Osman Agha is repeatedly at odds with a certain Memiş Agha, who is sometimes military commander or district governor in his place. Their rivalry includes land and naval warfare. Described as the two derebeys of the town, they attempt to settle their differences on one occasion by arranging the marriage of their son and daughter, but to no avail since they are soon once again at loggerheads (MAE CCCT L. 1, No. 81, Oct. 1808). This Memiş Agha,

had assumed the governorship (1810), Osman Agha attained the imperial rank of gate-keeper (*kapıcıbaşı*). A few years later, he appeared as one of the principal supporters of Süleyman Pasha during the revolt of Memiş Agha Tuzcuoğlu (1814–17). He eventually acquired other titles and ranks, such as castle-keeper (*muhafaza*) and finally governor (*miri mîram*). During the 1820s, he served as sub-governor of Trabzon, ruling the town for four years in the absence of a provincial governor. Then, with the appointment of a new provincial governor (a former ally of Şatıroğlu, now a rival), he left Trabzon to take up residence in Sürmene, where he was accused of fomenting brigandage in the eastern districts, conspiring with the sons of Tuzcuoğlu, and rising in rebellion against the governor.[86]

The composition of Osman Agha Şatıroğlu's household and followers was probably mixed, so that they resembled those of Memiş Agha in some ways and Süleyman Pasha in other ways. He would certainly have around him all kinds of relatives, friends, associates, and dependents, but there are also indications that he also had paid mercenaries and professionals in his service. He was therefore always obliged to gain appointments to state offices, since the form of his political authority required a higher level of cash flow given that his support was not entirely drawn from a coastal coalition. By way of contrast, Memiş Agha Tuzcuoğlu was required to work against the provincial governor to enhance the prerogatives and privileges of dissident elements among the local elites, since otherwise the latter would have no reason to support him.

We can now draw some conclusions from all the details that have been reviewed above. Just as the contrast between Memiş Agha Tuzcuoğlu and Süleyman Pasha Hazinedaroğlu reveals differences in the political authority of the imperial and regional elite, so the contrast between Memiş Agha Tuzcuoğlu and Osman Agha Şatıroğlu reveals two types of political authority among the regional elite. In terms of his social background and personal career, Osman Agha Şatıroğlu was most certainly one of the ayans and aghas of the coastal districts. He was the descendant of an old family line that was linked with a certain area and had large numbers of followers from that area. He participated in district social networks and coastal coalitions, and he occasionally rose in revolt against the provincial government at the head of local elites with armed followings. On the other hand, Osman Agha Şatıroğlu consistently insinuated himself in the formal hierar-

---

who is otherwise unnamed (see note 31, above), is also an ally of Memiş Tuzcuoğlu (MAE CCCT L. 1, No. 73, June 31, 1808; No. 86, Apr. 1809).

86. Goloğlu 1975, xxxiii, 153–58; Bilgin 1990, 294–95.

chy of authority and commerce of the state system. This is why his family line was more or less closely linked with the trade route of Trabzon and the silver mines at Gümüşhane. Both the route and the mines represented aspects of the coastal region that were closely associated with the state system rather than with dissident elements among the local elites.

Osman Agha Şatıroğlu was sometimes without any official appointment and so out of the government. In these circumstances, he sometimes appeared as one of the valley lords, participating in the civil wars of the coastal region or rising in revolt against the provincial governors of Trabzon. Still, his interests and inclinations were close to those of the provincial government that he supported most of the time. Accordingly, he was one of a certain number of the regional elite who enjoyed a degree of uprootedness and mobility, similar to that of the imperial elite. At different times, he lived and ruled in Sürmene, Trabzon, Gümüşhane, and Görele, and on exceptional occasions he briefly held official appointments in Erzurum and Van.[87] In the course of his career, when he was simply one of the local elites, he was addressed as "Agha" and described as an ayan and derebey. Later in his career, when he was one of the regional elite, he was addressed as "Bey" and described as a district governor or military commander. Still later, for a few years in the mid-1820s, he was the *de facto* provincial governor of Trabzon, after which he was addressed as "Pasha."[88]

The three individuals just reviewed indicate the essential difference between the imperial and regional elites. The former were able to draw on manpower and resources generated by the state system without any dependence on a local following. The latter were also able to draw on the manpower and resources of the state system, but they were more directly dependent on their position in a regional social oligarchy. In this regard the

87. Osman Agha was mobile like the imperial elite but normally only within the confines of the province of Trabzon. He was appointed to state offices outside the province of Trabzon, but only briefly, probably at the instigation of provincial governors who hoped to remove him from the coastal region for a time.

88. Sometime around 1832, Fontanier met with Osman Agha, who was then an aged man, living in the coastal town of Araklı, not far from Sürmene. He describes him as the "lieutenant of the provincial governor," having recently acquired the title "Pasha" and the rank of "Mirimiran" all for his services in putting down the Sürmenelis. Nonetheless, Fontanier spoke with him more or less freely and openly, as though without ceremony. At the time, Osman Agha maintained a large household and enjoyed a handsome income, but only a small fraction of that of the then prospering provincial governor, Osman Pasha Hazinedaroğlu. Nonetheless, the latter was obliged to rise in order to salute him (Fontanier 1834, 288–90). Interestingly, Consul Brant refers to Osman Agha as "Osman Pasha, an ayan of the town [of Trabzon]" (PRO FO 524/2 p. 25, Feb. 21, 1833; p. 39, Jan. 22, 1834).

Table 2. Elites of the Province of Trabzon, Early Nineteenth Century

Attributes	*Imperial Elite*	*Regional Elite (Type 1 and Type 2)*	*Local Elites (Greater Aghas)*	*Local Elites (Lesser Aghas)*
State appointments	In and out of higher state offices	In and out of state offices	Agha, ayan, mütesellim	Agha, ayan
	Pasha of Trabzon	Agha, ayan, mütesellim, kaymakam, muhafaza		
Household organization	In the imperial style	Large residence(s)	Large residence	Large residence
	Multiple large residences	Large family and/or large following	Large family and/or large following	Large family and/or large following
	Large retinue			
	Mobile	One or two coffeehouses	One coffeehouse	Immobile
		Type 1 more mobile, Type 2 less mobile	Immobile	
Social milieu	The imperial elite in other parts of Asia Minor, Caucasus, Crimea, eastern Europe, Middle East	The regional elite, local elites of the coastal districts, and a local social network	Local elites of other districts and a local social network	Local elites of other districts and a local social network

Higher social connections	Connections with the palace	Type 1: Connections with the palace and with the pasha Type 2: Connections with the palace but not with the pasha	The regional elite and greater aghas of his locale	Greater aghas of his locale
Lower social connections	Weak to strong connections with regional elite	Type 1: Narrower connections with greater aghas Type 2: Broader connections with greater aghas	Lesser aghas, traders, and farmers	Lesser aghas, traders, and farmers
Strategy	Dominate the ports and routes of the provincial capital with the support of Type 1 regional elite	Type 1: Allies himself with the pasha in order to control commercial centers Type 2: Allies himself with local aghas in order to control commercial centers	Allies himself with Type 1 or Type 2 regional elite in order to control his locale	Allies himself with a greater agha in order to control his locale
Examples	Süleyman Hazinedaroğlu Osman Hazinedaroğlu	Type 1: Osman Ağa Şatıroğlu Type 2: Memiş Ağa Tuzcuoğlu	Muradoğlu aghas Selimoğlu aghas	Fettahoğlu aghas Ayazoğlu aghas

imperial and regional elites represent the top tiers of a state society. The characteristics of individuals in each of these two tiers are represented in columns 1 and 2 of table 2, respectively. Each tier of the state society is differently positioned in the official state system, just as each tier refers to a different level of interpersonal association.

As we have also seen, the regional elite were the principals among a much larger number of local elites of varying prominence. In recognition of this, it is necessary to add two more tiers of the state society. Some were usually appointed as chief notables and sometimes appointed as district governors in the outlying coastal districts. Others are seldom mentioned in official documents, although they were sometimes recognized as the aghas or ayans of their respective areas. The characteristics of the leading individuals in each of these two tiers are represented in columns 3 and 4 of table 2.

7 Blindness
A Feudal Past Without a Modern Future

CONSULS THEORIZE THE STATE SOCIETY OF TRABZON

In 1796 Citizen Beauchamp had noticed that the Muslims of Trabzon were "different" from the Muslims of Istanbul:

> The inhabitants have a wild look about them at first appearance. Their dress consists of pants and coat of Capuchin cloth. They all walk about armed with pistols and a rifle, even within the town itself. They are not as fanatic as the Muslims of Constantinople.[1] During the three hundred years the [latter] have encountered Europeans, they have always preserved the custom of insulting them and mistreating them as unbelievers. During our stay at Trabzon, we didn't hear a single bad word; we were not even an object of curiosity for children.[2]

Beauchamp's comparison of the citizens of the imperial and provincial capitals is an exceptional one. Other French and British visitors usually found the Muslims of Trabzon to be more fanatical and less polite than the

1. Here Beauchamp is in disagreement with most other western European visitors to Trabzon, who remark on the mistreatment of Christians in the town (but see the following note). In MAE CCCT L. 1, No. 12, Nivôse An XII [Dec. 1803], Dupré writes that he is threatened and insulted in public. The Muslims cannot tolerate the way he dresses. The pasha issues an order that anyone who insults a Christian will have his nose and ears cut off. Later, Dupré complains about mistreatment on the part of the followers of Osman Agha Şatıroğlu; see No. 75, Aug. 1809, No. 86, Aug. 1809. Fontanier describes aggressive attitudes toward Christians and their subjection to forced labor in Sürmene (Fontanier 1829, 9–10). He also comments that Christians are treated worse in the town of Trabzon than in other parts of the Empire (ibid., 22).

2. Beauchamp 1813, 276–77. One might also wonder if the botanists were simply more circumspect in their dress and manners than the consuls who follow them.

Muslims of Istanbul. Nonetheless, Beauchamp accurately points to a characteristic for which the Laz are still famous. They can be exceedingly grim on first encounter, so it is surprising that they later prove to be remarkably polite. What Beauchamp noticed was a sharp contrast between an "outside" countenance that was intentionally intimidating and "inside" countenance that was no less intentionally sociable. These two contrasting demeanors of the Laz bring to mind the middle gate of the Ottoman palace. From without, its twin towers and fortress wall symbolized invincible sovereign power. From within, its painted portico and garden vista symbolized harmonious fellowship. The analogy is not coincidental. The Muslims of Trabzon were the creatures of imperial undertakings and accomplishments, not a marginal people at the fringe of the Ottoman Empire. The character of the Laz is then the product of the palace machine.

Beauchamp was not in a position to see how this was so. During his brief visit he had not had sufficient opportunity to learn how the Muslim population had come to compose a state society through participation in imperial military and religious institutions. More interestingly, however, the first French consuls, who resided in the coastal region for many years, also failed to understand the place of its Muslim population in the imperial system. In their very first reports, Consul Fourcade in Sinop and Consul Dupré in Trabzon addressed the relationship of state officials and local elites, and each of them reached the same mistaken conclusion: There were two different kinds of authorities in the coastal districts, and they represented two different kinds of government, one based on bureaucratic centralism and the other on interpersonal associations. Fourcade and Dupré had dissected the imperial system, then reconstituted it as two pieces, each with a separate and independent entity. A formal system of state officials representing bureaucratic regulations and procedures was the basis of one government. An informal system of leading individuals with armed followings was the basis of another government.

It is altogether possible that Fourcade and Dupré were simply repeating what was already the fixed opinion of other western European officials in the Ottoman Empire.[3] But whatever the case, they never qualify their initial impressions in order to develop a more nuanced understanding of the relationship of officials and elites. On the contrary, they and their successors come to insist ever more categorically that the coastal districts were subject to two alternative governmental systems. But neither the initial

3. See, for example, Veinstein's (1975) analysis of the reports of Peysonnel *père* and *fils,* consuls in Izmir during the middle of the eighteenth century.

misperception nor the later exaggeration is especially surprising. As I have already suggested in the last chapter, the French consuls were not in a good position to understand the place of the state society of Trabzon in the imperial system due to their official standing, their personal background, and their diplomatic interests.

The consuls were themselves French officials, and, as such, the counterparts of Ottoman officials. They therefore had contacts with the upper tier of the state society of Trabzon, where procedures were more visibly bureaucratic and less visibly interpersonal. The consuls represented a country where the state system had been used as a weapon to defeat inherited privilege and wealth, even if the Jacobinic revolution had recently come to an end. They would have naturally assumed that state officials of Trabzon were distinct from and opposed to its local elites. The consuls were assigned the task of implementing the terms of commercial treaties and agreements that had been negotiated between higher state officials of the two centralized governments. This task became meaningless, however, insofar as political authority worked through interpersonal association rather than through rules and procedures.[4]

But these were not the only reasons the first consuls drew a contrast between state officials and local elites. Unlike the French scientific expedition that preceded them, they had arrived in Trabzon after the Napoleonic invasion of Egypt, and with diplomatic credentials.[5] For the Muslims of Trabzon, the first consuls therefore represented a foreign power with a record of intervention. Moreover, shortly after their arrival, a series of political crises unsettled the agreements between state officials and local elites in the coastal region.[6] From the third or fourth year of their residences, the first consuls began to witness civil disorders in the town, skirmishes in the

4. In an earlier period and in a different province, however, Peysonnel *père* and *fils* preferred to reach agreements with local elites whom they found more reliable than representatives of the palace (Veinstein 1975).

5. The invasion had been noticed both by the Muslim majority and the Christian minority. Rottiers (1829, 179–80) reports in 1818 that the career of Napoleon had also provoked a lively and keen interest on the part of the Lazi of Arhavi, who were militantly anti-Russian. In MAE CCCT L. 2, circa Feb. 1814, Dupré reports that the Christian minority anticipated a great reconquest by a Christian king.

6. The arrival of the scientific expedition in the town of Trabzon had actually caused a stir in all the cafés. It was said that the French had been sent as an advance party to scout the coastal region in preparation for an invasion. Nonetheless, their hosts had chosen to set aside their suspicions and receive them correctly. The French learned of these rumors through their barber, the only Christian with whom they were allowed to have contact.

countryside, sieges of strongholds, and naval gun battles during the course of which they were sometimes subject to reprisals.

In reaction to these harrowing experiences, it would seem, they came to adhere ever more rigidly to the theory of two "alternative" governments, passing along their convictions to their successors. As we shall see, neither the French nor the British consuls were able to recognize the existence, let alone analyze the structure, of the state society in the coastal region by the close of the period of decentralization.

FOURCADE'S THEORY OF TWO GOVERNMENTAL SYSTEMS

In 1802 Consul Fourcade had been pleased to encounter and cultivate the agha of Sinop even before leaving the imperial capital to take up his post in that town. Congratulating himself on his good fortune, he had patiently explained to his superior the principle of two separate governmental systems, one prevailing in Istanbul, another in the eastern Ottoman provinces. He wrote, "These Asiatic provinces are governed as were those of France during the period of high feudalism. Their customs, their lands, their manufactures, their money, are all in the hands of these aghas whose enmity or friendship can either bring ruin to our commerce or cause it to flourish."[7] By these remarks, Fourcade was repeating, if not inventing, what was to become the dominant "consular theory" of the period of decentralization. The aghas were feudal lords as formerly existed in France. As such, they were sometimes a mere nuisance and sometimes a real danger, but one could understand how to manage them by recognizing them for what they were.

Two years later, Fourcade's enthusiasm for working through local elites had dimmed as a consequence of their unpredictability. Once again ahead of his time, he articulated what was to be the dominant "consular practice," writing "One cannot say it often enough. The regime of little aghas here is not suited for commerce. . . . [We] the French are therefore interested only in what might increase rather than decrease the power of the pasha and will assist him with all [our] means and all [our] influence. But we should also expect reciprocity, and this leads us to speak of England and Russia."[8] Fourcade follows these remarks with complaints about his Russian counterpart, whom he suspected of conniving with the agha of Sinop against him.

7. MAE CCCS No. 3, Brumaire An XI [Nov. 1802].
8. MAE CCCS No. 16, Prairial An XIII [June 1805]. This conclusion stands in sharp contrast to the approach of both Peysonnel *père* and *fils* (Veinstein 1975).

To remedy such ills, he called for an explicit diplomatic policy whereby the representatives of foreign powers would work together. They would prop up the central government so that state officials might prevail over local elites. A coherent theory had matured into coherent practice.

But Fourcade had miscalculated. Consular theory and practice were contingent on the assumption of two governments, one a decentralized feudalism and the other a centralized bureaucracy. But no such division existed, so there was no possibility of lending support to the latter without in some way also lending support to the former.

Fourcade had first met the agha of Sinop in Istanbul. The latter had been obliged to travel there in order to address the court intrigues by his rival and neighbor. So at the time of this very first encounter, the agha of Sinop was as much enmeshed in a politics of laws and courts at the level of centralized government as in a politics of local rivalries and alliances among provincial leaders and groupings. Similarly, two years after writing the above assessment, Fourcade would discover that French policies with regard to the Ottomans would be noticed by provincial leaders and groupings, precisely because their political fortunes were directly dependent on the structure and processes of the centralized government.

In 1807 a revolt of janissaries in the imperial capital brought the reign of Sultan Selim to an end. Soon afterward, the revolt had reverberations in the town of Sinop:

> Because of unfavorable winds, several ships from Trabzon, Rize, and Phasis have been obliged to anchor at Sinop. The ships were coming from Constantinople. They were stuffed with these barbarians known as the Laz, driven out of the capital by reason of their insolent behavior and drenched in the blood of the ministers of the unfortunate Sultan Selim. Dispersed in the coffeehouses of Sinop, these miserable characters constantly abused the French, whom they accused of having subjugated their [Ottoman] government and sold out Rumelia to the Muscovites. The district governor [of Sinop] manifested the greatest indifference to all this, and his behavior has encouraged this foreign rabble.[9]

By his stylization of them, Fourcade clearly did not know what to make of these "barbarians known as the Laz." He consequently stumbled whenever

9. MAE CCCS folio 186, Oct. 1807. Sultan Selim III was deposed by a revolt of janissary auxiliaries (*yamaks*) on May 29, 1807 (Shaw 1976, 273–74).

he attempted to name them, describing them at one point as "drunken fanatics," and then at another point as "foreign rabble" (*canaille étrangère*). But if Fourcade did not understand the Laz, they understood him perfectly. It was as though they had been reading over his shoulder when he composed the consular report recommending a conspiracy of the French, British, and Russians on behalf of the sultan. A few days after their arrival, a group of them expressed their displeasure with the French directly, attacking and beating one of the consular staff in the street before Fourcade's house. When the latter bravely attempted to intervene, he was himself assaulted, receiving serious injuries that left him partially paralyzed. Having a keen sense of justice, Fourcade thereupon lodged a complaint against specific individuals among the Laz who were subsequently arrested and held. In reprisal, their companions united to lay siege and set fire to the consul's house, a technique strangely reminiscent of the attack on Paçan village in 1737/1150. Fearing further attacks, the consul was forced to intercede on behalf of those he had accused and withdraw his complaint. The Laz whom he had charged were then released on the condition that they and their companions set sail for the east the following morning.

Fourcade's concept of two governments, a decentralized feudalism in the provinces and a centralized bureaucracy in the capital, had been overtaken by events. A motley group of men from a variety of coastal districts could somehow identify their interests in terms of bringing down a sultan, then later come together to challenge the representatives of a foreign power who had sought to manipulate the imperial regime. So there was something broader and deeper than a collection of aghas in some of the Asiatic provinces, and certainly in the eastern coastal districts of the province of Trabzon. But the consul lacked the stamina to decipher the meaning of his experiences. Unable to make a full recovery from his wounds, he soon retired from the consular service.

During the years that followed, as other French and British consuls took up residence and learned more about the coastal region, it became harder for them to see what Beauchamp had just barely noticed. As the later consuls became more engaged in manipulating the balance of power in the imperial regime, so they were more inclined to see "grimness" rather than "politeness" in the countenance of the Laz. Their disability would prove to be more than a failure to appreciate the civilized conventions of otherwise uncivilized ruffians. It was also the basis for a misevaluation of what could be accomplished by governmental reforms relying on western European methods and technologies.

Fontanier provides a striking example of this misevaluation. He was perhaps the most experienced and intelligent of all the foreigners who described one of the core Ottoman provinces during the period of decentralization. His two books on his travels in the Empire contain remarkable insights and rare information. And yet, as we shall see, he too came under the spell of consular theory and practice. In the instance of Fontanier, we can see more clearly how consular contacts with local elites raised existential questions. What is the character of the moment in which we live? The answer turns upon what we can say has come before us and so what can be expected to come after us. But what if we should have an experience that shuffles our notions of before and after? What if the elements of the past should suddenly acquire a vitality that suggests they might hold the power to shape the future?

Consular contacts with the rural societies of the coastal districts provoked this kind of disorientation. For all the consuls, sovereign power through interpersonal association was a thing of the past, not the future. When they misidentified it with the feudal regime of thirteenth-century France, they were not simply drawing an analogy. They were also making an existential assertion. They assumed that reform of the state system would inevitably lead to the demise of the local elites.

Fontanier was no different than the other consuls in this regard, but he was exceptionally informed and intelligent. This means he was intellectually vulnerable to experiences that would have upset his consular colleagues, but otherwise left their thinking unaffected. Being a writer, that is, someone with a taste for reflection and representation, Fontanier reveals that the consuls were obliged to misunderstand the imperial system if they were retain a clear sense of who they were.

FONTANIER EXPERIENCES AN UNACCEPTABLE SOCIABILITY

In 1827, the sixth year of his residence in the Ottoman Empire as an attaché of the French legation in Istanbul, Fontanier and a companion sailed from Redut-Kaleh to Trabzon on a boat with a cargo of Indian corn.[10] The "Turkish" captain (*un batelier turc*) and five crew members all hailed from the district of Sürmene. Fontanier recounts the story of their setting sail, voyaging across the southeast bight of the Black Sea, and finally reaching the port of Trabzon. But what he recalls and relates was determined by only

10. Redut-Kaleh was to the north of Poti, in what is now Georgia.

one of the voyage's episodes, an occasion when he found himself fearing for his liberty, if not his life, in the marketplace of Sürmene. He begins, "Before the anchor was raised, all of them performed their prayers [ablutions, recitations, exercises], and we crossed the depths at the mouth of the Copi River to the cries of 'Yallah! Yallah!'"[11] Fontanier describes the departure by referring to the ritualized acts and words of the Sürmenelis, which they performed in unison as Muslims. As he begins his tale, Fontanier recalls the captain and crew as "Turks," just as he was himself something else, that is, not Turkish. Confined to close quarters with the crew on the boat, Fontanier could not but notice the otherness of the sociability of the Sürmenelis; however, it was his later experiences in Sürmene that led him to condemn and ridicule it.

As the boat approaches the coast of Lazistan, Fontanier is anxious to go ashore to find relief from his cramped quarters, and perhaps also relief from the captain and crew.[12] To his annoyance, he learns that they are unable to disembark at Batum because the Sürmenelis are in a state of war with its inhabitants. A little further on in their journey, they encounter a storm that halts their progress for two days. Still, he is advised that they cannot leave the boat for fear of whom they might encounter on shore: "Such is the state of these miserable lands that the four or five districts of which they are composed, from Batum to Trabzon, are most of the time in a state of hostility such that the nationals themselves cannot approach without danger." Fontanier, trapped in the hold of a ship filled with corn, blames his predicament on the defective sociability of all the natives of the coastal region in general. At long last, the crew is finally forced to go ashore in order to repair the broken mast, but only after a careful reconnoitering. Fontanier is not permitted to accompany them. He is told that he would almost certainly be taken prisoner and held for ransom.

Afterward, they continue on their way toward Trabzon, passing one of the most beautiful coastal landscapes one might observe anywhere in the world. Fontanier is struck by the houses perched on hilltops and surrounded by thick vegetation, but he discounts their welcoming appearance, writing "A group of country houses well situated on the slope of a hill gives the landscape a cheerful appearance, but this would no doubt vanish as soon as

11. Fontanier 1829, 3. The citations that follow in this section appear in the same place between pages 5 and 16. All italics are my own.

12. The first French and British consuls use the term "Lazistan" to refer to all the eastern coastal segment of the old province of Trabzon, roughly comprising Batum, Gönye, Arhavi, Atine, Rize, Of, and Sürmene.

one put one's foot on the land." He is anticipating the moment when he will be able to leave the boat in order to visit the marketplace in Sürmene. He is recalling how he at last escaped his shipboard prison, only to find he could not bear what he found ashore.

Concluding the paragraph that summarizes the voyage across the coastline, he sees before him a landscape of great wealth spoiled by the anarchic tendencies of its inhabitants. "No country could be more productive than these shores of the Black Sea, if only they were not *the scene of utter barbarism and ceaseless war.*" And just at this moment (in the text, but not in the voyage), the coastal district of Sürmene, cherished by the Turkish captain and crew, incongruously comes into view. He writes, "Sürmene, which came into view after Rize, was the country of our captain and his crew. It was *for them the promised land.*" The story of Fontanier's visit to Sürmene follows. It will include references to destruction, murder, kidnapping, pillage, and enslavement.

For Fontanier, the coastal region is a scene of utter barbarism and ceaseless war, in other words, a kind of hell. For the captain and the crew, it is the promised land. How is it possible that the visitor and the natives should have such opposed perceptions of the same place? What could the Sürmenelis find at all rewarding and enjoyable about their homelands? Fontanier will actually give us an answer to this question in the very terms that one might already predict. That which makes Sürmene a promised land for its inhabitants, their experience of sociability, is exactly what makes Sürmene a hell for the outsider. He begins to focus on their sociability, but only to belittle and discount it, consistently and systematically.

As they reached the wide bay of the district of Sürmene, a small boat with a welcoming party aboard is launched from the coast to meet them. The leader of their hosts "had a rifle on his shoulder, pistols, a dagger, and an enormous powder horn suspended from his belt." This man is a friend of the captain of the boat. Fontanier composes a parody of their exchange of greetings, using the familiar form of address (*tutoiement*):

> Oh, Ali Reis [the captain], welcome! Mahmut, Selim [the crew], welcome! Who are these infidels [Fontanier and his companion]?—They are sons of Frankish lords who are our guests and whom we are taking to Trabzon.—Welcome! [addressed to the infidels]. —What is new in the countryside? —Nothing at all. The son of the agha of Rize [Tuzcuoğlu] has killed his cousin out of jealousy and is in hiding with us. He's a nice kid. Ah! I forgot to mention that Hussein put gunpowder under the house of his neighbor and blew it up. Five people were killed. —That's astonishing! But what can one do? They are just children.

While ridiculing the Sürmenelis, Fontanier nonetheless describes a discipline of interpersonal association. They boisterously hail one another, but by customary phrases and formulas (greeting/response: *selamün aleyküm / aleyküm selam, hoş geldiniz / hoş bulduk, merhaba / merhaba*). The welcoming party learns the infidels have the status of guests (*misafir*) and so extend their greetings to them. The captain and the crew are eager to rejoin friends and associates whom they have not seen for so very long (two weeks? a month?).

The captain and crew prepare themselves to accompany the welcoming party and go ashore. Fontanier introduces the theme of anarchy once more, but now the weapons and explosions are unmistakably the expression of an enthusiastic and vigorous sociability. He writes, "During this exchange, others were preparing the little boat, our captain and crew armed themselves, and all took themselves to the shore, as though at the conquest of an enemy country. Soon we heard a lively round of gunfire that, however, was not at all threatening. It was the greetings to which our people were responding." Even though the captain and crew have gone ashore, Fontanier is obliged to remain on the boat waiting for the return of the captain and crew. They do not soon reappear. Despite his desire to "get out of this hole in which I had been living for four days," he is obliged to spend another night on board. He does so in a state of fright and confusion, thinking "I simply could not easily understand how, in such a wild country, the captain could dare to leave his boat and cargo in the charge of no one but two foreigners who in the event of a robbery could not make any resistance." When he later mentions this, the captain is astonished at his concern. No such robbery would ever occur, he is told. The boat and cargo were under the protection of the local inhabitants the moment the anchor was dropped, so that no surveillance of any kind was necessary. Fontanier adds the remark, "What a singular mixture of honesty and barbarism!" Where, according to Fontanier, all manner of violations are endemic, there is nonetheless an entire range of violations that are not permitted.

The next day Fontanier and his companion are abruptly awakened by the crew, who have returned with a large number of their compatriots who are interested in buying some portion of the cargo of corn:

> As soon as [the Sürmenelis] saw us, they came to us and began to examine the different pieces of our dress. One of them, who had just come from his work as a dyer, took hold of my eyeglasses and, seeing my cheeks displayed the imprints of his fingers, found it amusing to continue the operation he had accidentally begun, and so set himself to daub my face in blue. He was more than a little surprised when I dared

> to push him away, and more especially when the captain intervened to side with me against him. "Isn't this fellow an infidel?" he said. "And do I not have the right to paint him, to do him harm?" These justifications appeared self-evident to him, so that the captain was obliged to plead with him at length in order to convince him of the difference between a Frank and a *reaya.*

Again the description is a parody of the event itself, but it is nonetheless indirectly revealing. The dyer is intrigued by the Frenchman's eyeglasses, a technical instrument for the observation of others. The eyeglasses appear to the dyer as something strange, comical but also perhaps invasive. They reveal that the Frenchman is inspecting and analyzing, that is to say, mentally "depicting" the Sürmenelis. In response, the dyer "depicts" Fontanier by daubing his face with the blue dye on his fingers. If the Frenchman is to characterize him by means of an instrument of observation, so he will characterize the Frenchman as a Christian, that is, as morally deficient and hence socially contemptible.

But the eyeglasses have a different meaning for Fontanier. By his own account, he has just despaired for lack of a framework for understanding what he was seeing, that is, a mixture of honesty and barbarism among the Sürmenelis. Now, his eyeglasses are the instrument by which he is able to see, and therefore to describe, but also to judge. And so for Fontanier, the dyer's ignorance and effrontery are reassuring, at least in retrospect. Fontanier feels himself to be in possession of instruments that enable him to perceive and portray the "Turks," even as they are unable to perceive and portray themselves. He, by his own self-perception, represents a scientific and technological future. They represent a past condemned to anarchy by their ignorance. And so accordingly, just a few pages later, he will repeat the dictum of Fourcade, affirming that the "Turks" represent the feudalism of thirteenth-century Europe.

But on the occasion itself, when actually faced with the dyer, Fontanier is disturbed and confused. The dyer, by his own self-perception, also feels himself to represent the future, one based on an ethical rather than an instrumental relationship of self and other. He is a believer whose own social thinking and practice are in accordance with a divine truth and law. By this universal and transcendent standard, he is able to recognize Fontanier, the observer, as an unbeliever who espouses a corrupt, hence inferior, version of that divine truth and law. He therefore makes fun of Fontanier, removing his eyeglasses and daubing his face with dye, portraying him as he sees him, as an unbeliever deserving humiliation. So, then, Fontanier has found himself in a land and among a people who associate with one another on terms that confirm he is both different and inferior. This would hardly be troubling in itself, save that the Sürmenelis exclude and diminish Fontanier by principles so closely resembling those by which he would affirm they are different and inferior to him. Fontanier is shaken by the question of who it is that holds the future. It is perhaps the memory of this existential question that so terrifies him. As if to confirm that this is so, the story of his encounter with the dyer is followed by another encounter during which he feared for his personal safety.

Later that same day, the agha of the coastal settlement comes aboard. He is in the company of the young man who is the son of the agha of Rize (Tahir Agha Tuzcuoğlu) and who had assassinated his cousin two days before, thereby meriting a place among the bodyguards of the agha of the coastal settlement. The latter lectures Fontanier about the "indisputable superiority of Turkey over all other sovereign powers, not failing to indulge in abuses of the Russians." He receives a lesson and an example of how the form of sociability of the Sürmenelis, which is also that of all the Trabzonlus, is the basis of an indomitable sovereign power. He has been told exactly where the local elites and their social formations fit in the Ottoman Empire, but Fontanier does not register this information. He tells his story of course as a joke. The "Turks" are so badly informed, so seriously overestimating their world position. But the joke is also a kind of self-reassurance provoked by a moment of powerlessness.

Following their meeting, the agha gives Fontanier and his companion permission to enter his territories. They leave the boat and visit the marketplace of Sürmene.[13] During his tour, he repeatedly mentions the signs of underlying civil disorder and social injustice. The traders keep guns at their side in anticipation of an alert. The thick walls of the houses serve the purpose of defense. Toward the end of his tour of the market, he witnesses a scene that once again unsettles him. The Christian shopkeepers, unlike the Muslim shopkeepers, are not permitted to carry arms. Unable to defend or assert themselves, they must submit to forced labor in the fields of the agha. Fontanier next describes an "observation" that instills terror: the arrest of one of the Greeks who has failed to report for such duties. Identify-

13. Fontanier (1829, 12) describes a marketplace that is part of a wider state and market system of the Black Sea (see chap. 3). There are local cash crops, fruits, olives, and nuts, some of them exported "to a great distance," while other items are imported from elsewhere, including rye from Bayburt and lemons from Rize. The inhabitants praise their local cornbread, but the corn to make it must sometimes be imported from Redut-Kaleh.

ing for a moment with his co-religionist, he fears he too might be seized and impressed. Immediately following this statement, he returns to the subject he can neither comprehend nor forget:

> I was able to observe [*faculté de remarquer*] the order with which this operation [of forced labor in the fields] was carried out, not without fearing, however, that I too might be required to take part.
>
> None of the Turks [sic] who dwelled in this country resided during the daytime in their houses; all were in the bazaar where they smoked and conversed with one another. They joined their families only during the evening.

He is surrounded by males who congregate in the bazaar. But he and his companion are not one of the group. They do not subscribe to the right beliefs. They do not dress the right way, and so they have become a spectacle. Fontanier and his companion feel themselves alone and isolated in a crowded marketplace. This moment of exclusion is coupled with one of abandonment:

> Our captain, so as not to seem too much in a hurry to see his wife, had his children sent to him the day of his arrival. Then he spent the night with one of his friends. It was the following day before he took himself to his family and house. He did not invite us to accompany him there, even though he should have considered that it was not very agreeable for us to traipse about in this kind of forum where all the male population had come together and where our foreign dress attracted an excessive amount of public curiosity. We resigned ourselves to returning to the boat, where at least we were left in peace.

Fontanier now complains of desertion by the captain and crew, whose company seemed so oppressive only the day before. Seeking relief from a sociability that excludes and diminishes him, he and his companion return to their lodgings in the hold of the boat. He prefers bobbing up and down in the bay of Sürmene to the stares of the crowd in the market.

What was heaven for the Sürmenelis, to associate with others, had for a moment been the hell of Fontanier. Confronted with the threat of another kind of future, he had for a moment lost confidence in his own faculties that positioned him in relationship to the future. After two more days in the hold of the boat, about which we learn nothing, he leaves for Trabzon. When he arrives, the first thing he will seek is an antidote to the alien sociability of the Sürmenelis. He concludes the chapter, "I took myself to the consulate over which floated the French flag, and I found there M. Beuscher, whom I had come to know at Constantinople, and in whose company I could forget the exhaustion and dangers of my trip." Fontanier instinctively knows the remedy for his experiences in Sürmene, even as he cannot exactly name or recognize that other kind of sociability that had so disturbed him.

THE END OF THE PERIOD OF DECENTRALIZATION

Fontanier's account of his visit to Sürmene in 1827 casts light on an otherwise puzzling report he wrote some years later, after he had returned to Trabzon to serve as a consular official (see chap. 1). On January 27, 1831, more than three years before any such event could have plausibly taken place, he declared the triumph of Osman Pasha Hazinedaroğlu, writing to his superior in Istanbul:

> In these countries, which of all were the most difficult to bring to submission, even the chiefs [in the coastal districts] that I have cited for Your Excellency *no longer exist.* The most terrible of all, Fatzanoğlu, has been beheaded. The others have been either dispersed or employed by diverse pashas; resistance has vanished, and the country, now rid of this crowd of minor despots, enjoys a perfect tranquility. [Italics mine][14]

The "chiefs" would have been astonished to learn that they no longer existed, and perhaps amused by the qualifying euphemism, "dispersed or employed by diverse pashas." Almost all the local elites of the coastal districts still held the positions to which Osman Pasha had himself appointed them when he first assumed the governorship of Trabzon.[15] And soon enough, they would find cause to assert themselves once again, eventually rising in full revolt against the provincial government. Before exploring the reason for Fontanier's misassessment, and how it might be linked with his visit to Sürmene, I shall summarize the series of events that prove how seriously he had been mistaken.

14. MAE CCCT L. 3 (1825–35), No. 11, Jan. 27, 1831.

15. British consul Brant had also reported the end of the feudal order just a day earlier but in more cautious terms, writing "[Osman Pasha has] induced most of their beys [of the eastern coastal districts] to put themselves in his power [although the agha of Atine still had three thousand men in arms]. . . . The people of Surmeneh and Ophis have agreed to build barracks and furnish their Contingent of regular troops required. Lazistan [the coast from Batum to Sürmene] never before was in so perfect a state of submission and so tranquil" (PRO FO 524/1, Jan. 26, 1831).

When Fontanier was writing his report, the political situation in the province of Trabzon was not that much different from what it had been before the abolition of the janissary institution five years earlier. Indeed, it was as though the clock had been turned even further back. The very same triangle of leading individuals and coastal coalitions that had led to the revolts of 1814–17 was in place, save that two sons were now standing in for two fathers. Osman Pasha Hazinedaroğlu, like his father Süleyman Pasha before him, had assumed the provincial governorship in the conventional manner, re-appointing many of the local elites to their former positions as district governors and chief notables in the coastal districts. Osman Agha Şatıroğlu, formerly the ally of Süleyman Pasha, now the ally of Osman Pasha, led a coalition of local elites in the central districts. Tahir Agha Tuzcuoğlu, like his father Memiş Agha before him, was district governor of Rize, where he led a coalition of local elites in the districts of Rize, Of, and Sürmene.[16] Moreover, the same bitter quarrel that divided the two fathers—the degree to which the eastern coastal districts would be obliged to submit to the provincial government at Trabzon—now divided the two sons. In this respect, the revolts of 1831–34 would be re-enactments of the revolts of 1814–17.

Just a few months after Fontanier submitted his report, there were fresh disturbances in the eastern coastal districts. The Oflus and the Sürmenelis, still suffering from the combined effects of poor harvests and the Russo-Ottoman War of 1828, balked when called upon to pay higher taxes and send more troops to the central government.[17] Then, toward winter, news came of the rebellion of Mehmet Ali Pasha in Egypt, and sporadic civil disorder in the eastern coastal districts blossomed into full-scale revolt.[18] By the summer of 1832, the Oflus and Sürmenelis were categorically refusing to accede to the new tax and troop levies. Meanwhile, the residents of the provincial capital slipped into panic with the spread of alarming rumors.[19]

16. See Gologlu (1975, 159–60); Aktepe (1951–52, 21–22, 44–45); MAE CCCT L. 1, No. 58, Mar. 1807; No. 71, Mar. 1808.

17. See PRO FO 524/1 p. 14, Sept. 1831, on lack of grain, continuing plague, and the disruption of caravan trade; and p. 18, Feb. 2, 1832, on general dissatisfaction with higher tax and troop levies, and how the district governor had been driven away from Sürmene.

18. Fontanier 1834, 320.

19. MAE CCCT L. 3, No. 21, June 1832. The French consul reported that the news of the rebellion of Mehmet Ali Pasha in Egypt had created a panic in Trabzon, giving the provincial governor an opportunity to crush his opponents.

There was one report that the aghas of Of and Sürmene had received letters from Mehmet Ali Pasha promising his support.[20] There was another that the janissary institution had been revived among the villages of Of and Sürmene.[21] At this point, Osman Pasha adopted harsh military measures in order to force the local elites of these districts into submission.[22] His brother led seven thousand troops in an attack on Sürmene from the west. The governor of Adjaria led another seven thousand troops in an attack on Of from the east. A third force was dispatched from Bayburt to attack these same districts from the south. The result was massive destruction of houses, shops, crops, and flocks in the two districts.[23]

The military invasion during the summer of 1832 inflicted a terrible devastation on the districts of Of and Sürmene. And yet, the crisis of political authority remained unresolved. Tahir Agha Tuzcuoğlu, assisted by three brothers, was still the district governor of Rize, and he was more than ever intent on defying Osman Pasha in Trabzon.[24] Toward the fall of that

20. Bilgin (1990, 300) cites an official document. The aghas are said to have received letters from Mehmet Ali Pasha in which he assured them his armies would support them when they invaded Anatolia.

21. In MAE CCCT L. 3, No. 21, June 1832, the consul reports a general sentiment among the Muslims for restoring the "old order." He believes the reports of the revolt by the Sürmenelis and Oflus, as well as the restoration of the janissariat there, are pretexts for sending a large force there.

22. Fontanier (1834, chap. 23) believed that Osman Pasha had invaded Of and Sürmene in order to avoid having to confront the armies of Mehmet Ali Pasha, which eventually invaded Anatolia.

23. In PRO FO 524/2 p. 19, May 1832, Brant anticipates invasion of Sürmene and Of; in PRO FO 524/1 p. 23, Aug. 1832, Brant reports:

> it is stated that about three thousand houses have been burnt and destroyed, as many cows and oxen captured, as well as everything the Surmenehs could not carry away—There was no fighting of any consequence. The people had transported their flocks, moveables and families to the mountains. They refused to give up the leaders of the Revolt or to make their submission and nothing seems to have been gained by the Expedition. On the other hand, it has distressed the inhabitants of this place by the Contributions required to pay the Expenses—it has caused a great destruction of property and incalculable misery to the Revolted without either inducing them to order or rendering them obedient and useful subjects and it is most probable they will become Robbers and dangerous neighbors.

Also see Bilgin (1990, 299; n.d. b, 9) and Bryer (1969).

24. In the paragraphs that follow, I summarize the events that led to the end of the period of decentralization, as they were reported by Brant and Suter. The circumstances themselves, involving a group of men caught up in a web of friendship and enmity, were of course far more complicated than such a summary suggests. Cf. the accounts of Aktepe (1951–52), Gologlu (1975), and Bilgin (1990), who rely on official documents (Ahmet Cevdet PaŞa 1892/1309; Şakir Şevket 1877/1294).

year, there was a report that the forces of Mehmet Ali Pasha, then occupying parts of Anatolia, had made contact with the Tuzcuoğlu brothers. Using the report as an excuse, Osman Pasha charged Tahir Agha with conspiracy and obtained a writ for his execution.[25] Thereupon Tahir Agha rose in full revolt, bringing two of his three brothers with him. By January 1833, the Tuzcuoğlu had assembled an army of twelve thousand men from Rize, Of, and Sürmene and defeated a military force that had been led against them.[26] By February 1833, they were advancing on the town of Trabzon, sending word to its minorities and consuls that they had nothing to fear.[27] Osman Pasha first moved his furniture into the citadel as a precaution, then chose to leave his capital and province altogether.[28]

Having mounted a convincing show of force, Tahir Agha contacted the palace to declare himself a faithful servant of the sultan, but demanding the rank of pasha and the office of governor, that is, the independence of Rize, Of, and Sürmene.[29] The palace acceded to these conditions at the urging of Tuzcuoğlu's friends in court (the high admiralty was said to be a Rizeli), but with the requirement that he send a brother and three hundred followers to Istanbul for service in the arsenal. Thus Tahir Agha had reconstituted the hierarchy of authority and commerce first put into place by his father in the second half of the eighteenth century. The eastern districts from Sürmene to Batum were to become a separate province. Its governors would be appointed from the Tuzcuoğlu family line. Its capital would be the town of Rize.

Later during the year of 1833, however, Osman Pasha returned to his provincial capital, then appointed Osman Agha Şatıroğlu as district governor of Sürmene, intending to deprive the Tuzcuoğlu of that district.[30] By the spring of 1834, the Sürmenelis, fearing the burden of Osman Agha's occupation, demanded the right to appoint their own governors, "as in other districts under Tusgioglu [sic]." But now the crisis involving Mehmet Ali Pasha was concluded, and the palace was no longer inclined to accommodate Tahir Agha. Toward summer, Osman Pasha declared Tahir Agha and two

25. PRO FO 524/2 p. 24, Dec. 1832.

26. PRO FO 524/1 p. 29, Jan. 15, 1833, Brant.

27. In PRO FO 524/2 p. 25, Feb. 21, 1833, Brant discounted the number of troops as an exaggeration, estimating no more than six thousand men.

28. PRO FO 524/2 p. 25, Feb. 21, 1833. Osman Pasha had taken up residence in Tokat but was later driven from there by an army of "Kurds" led by Seyyid Agha, "governor of Sivas" (PRO FO 524/1 p. 32, Apr. 5, 1833; p. 32, May 15, 1833).

29. PRO FO 524/1 p. 29, Jan. 1833, Brant, to the end of the paragraph.

30. PRO FO 524/2, p. 40, Mar. 1834, Brant, to the next note.

of his brothers to be fugitives, and both sides began a series of troop movements along the coast from Atine [Pazar] to Sürmene. The brother who had been sent to Istanbul, but had returned to participate in the revolt, was apprehended and executed.[31] Tahir Agha and another brother took refuge in the district of Of, after which that district was subject to yet another invasion by fifteen thousand troops.[32] Tahir Agha and his brother finally surrendered, and were later exiled to Varna (on the Black Sea coast of Rumania).[33] The inhabitants of the district of Of, who had given them sanctuary, were subjected to a punitive level of taxation for an indefinite period.

Osman Pasha had much in common with other strong provincial governors of the period of decentralization. He had a good knowledge of the local elites of Trabzon since he was the son of a previous provincial governor. He was supported by two brothers who were willing to do his bidding and served him well as subordinate officials. He had a good knowledge of palace circles, having been sent to Istanbul to become a page to the sultan after the death of his father. He had great wealth since he had managed to recover the land holdings that had been confiscated from his father, and by this great wealth, he had the ability to bring both manpower and resources into Trabzon from the western province of Canık.[34]

From all that can be gleaned from the consular reports, Osman Pasha used these advantages to deal with the local elites of Trabzon in much the same manner as other strong provincial governors during the period of decentralization. Both before and after 1834, he never attempted to suppress all the local elites in all the coastal districts, and it seems likely that he never even considered such a possibility.[35] During his entire tenure in office,

31. Aktepe 1951–52, 47, 50.

32. Aktepe 1951–52, 49; Bilgin 1990, 303; Gologlu 1975, 162; PRO FO 524/2 p. 41, Apr. 1834, Suter.

33. Gologlu 1975, 163. PRO FO 524/2 p. 46, Apr. 1834, Suter. Other followers of Tuzcuoğlu later appear in Egypt as bodyguards of the Mehmet Ali Pasha family (personal communication of descendants in Istanbul and demonstrated by court documents concerning land claims).

34. Fontanier 1834, 98–99. Hamilton (1842, vol. 1, 270, 282) reports that Osman Pasha owned three hundred farms in Canık. He observes three hundred men engaged in constructing a boat at the site of Osman Pasha's mansion in Fatsa. In PRO FO 195/1329 No. 38, Aug. 1880, Biliotti reports that many of the native settlers east of Samsun had become landowners by "getting title from sipahis but 50 years ago they were reduced to serfage by Osman Pasha."

35. Fontanier did not have the opportunity to re-declare the suppression of the old feudal system in 1834, since he left Trabzon in the midst of diplomatic and financial difficulties (Hoefer 1856 [1965], vol. 17, 118). However, Brant (1836) erroneously declared in 1835 what Fontanier had erroneously declared in 1831: "Oph

from 1827 to 1842, he moved to "rectify" and "improve" (*ıslah*) those local elites that resisted the provincial government, in accordance with standing official procedures. He appointed as many new district and provincial officials as possible from a narrow circle of his supporters, sometimes dismissing or demoting local elites. He made examples of the most troublesome of the local elites, dispatching forces to take them prisoner and disperse their followers. But even in these instances, he sometimes re-appointed other members of their family lines to succeed them.

During the revolts of 1831–34, moreover, Osman Pasha had used the "classic" methods of the period of decentralization in putting down the revolt of the Tuzcuoğlu. He cannonaded and demolished many of the mansions of the aghas of Of and Sürmene. He burned and relocated many of the markets they had dominated. He executed one of the three brothers who had led the revolt, and he exiled the other two along with many of their followers.[36] But while other provincial governors before him had applied the very same measures, he had done so with more consistency and severity, thereby confirming a decisive shift in the balance of power.[37] The local elites of the eastern coastal districts would never again rise in revolt against the provincial government.[38] Osman Pasha had indeed brought about a divide in the political history of the province of Trabzon by 1834.

and Lazistan were formerly governed by Dere Beys, or feudal chiefs who exercised absolute authority in their own districts, carried on petty warfare with each other, did not owe allegiance to a superior and never paid contributions to the sultan. This state of insubordination has been put an end to by Osman Pasha."

36. Osman Pasha, through the intercession of Osman Agha Şatıroğlu, a relative even if also a rival of the Tuzcuoğlu, accepted the exile of Tahir Agha and Abdülaziz Agha. The execution of Abdülkadir Tuzcuoğlu was carried out by the governor of Erzurum (PRO FO 524/2 p. 46, Apr. 1834, Suter). A fourth brother, Reşit Agha, was somehow not implicated in the revolt, and so remained in favor (PRO FO 524/2, p. 41, Apr. 1834, Suter).

37. By the 1840s, the town of Trabzon was reached by regular steamboat service with connections to the major ports of the Black Sea and Mediterranean (Hamilton 1842, 158). By 1864 the town of Trabzon, as well as several of its coastal districts, was linked by telegraph line to Istanbul (MAE CPCT L. 3, No. 24, Feb. 1864).

38. More or less minor incidents occurred in the years to follow. Cafer Agha Cansız went into hiding after the collapse of the Tuzcuoğlu revolt in 1834. On the occasion when the aghas of Of were planning to refuse to forward the taxes in 1837, he informed Osman Pasha of the conspiracy in hopes of regaining his good graces (PRO FO 195/101 Sept. 12, 1837, Suter). In the district of Of, a minirevolt occurred in 1842 when a local group lay siege to the residence of the district governor. The incident took place upon the arrival of the news of the death of Osman Pasha. So it could be considered a test of his brother, Abdullah Pasha, who succeeded him (PRO FO 195/173, June 17, 1842, Stevens).

In retrospect, this divide can be described as the end of the period of decentralization all along the coastal region. However, he did not restore centralized government, and he did not abolish the local elites. After the end of the period of decentralization, the local elites of the eastern coastal districts—if not they themselves, then their descendants—continued to serve as appointed government intermediaries.[39] The inhabitants of the coastal districts had not been disarmed, and most of the men continued to move about with their rifles. They still served as soldiers in the central army, perhaps in larger numbers than ever before.[40] Likewise, the local elites continued to play a role in gathering and dispatching recruits to the central government.[41] So the local elites must also have retained the capacity to mobilize armed followings against rivals.[42] Henceforth, the responsibilities of local elites were more minutely defined than they had previously been, but these definitions were not necessarily respected.[43] The readiness of lo-

39. In the district of Of, Osman Pasha recognized an agha from the Muradoğlu and an agha from the Selimoğlu as the chief notables of the eastern and western valleys of the district, respectively, from 1834 until about 1847. For the Muradoğlu, see the "Muradoğlu documents," which confirm that Memiş Agha Muradoğlu, son of İsmail Agha, founder of the family line, had emerged from the last Tuzcuoğlu revolt as the principal agha and ayan of the eastern valley of the district of Of. For the Selimoğlu, see the local traditions cited by Bilgin (1990, 303) and Goloğlu (1975, 163), which report that Ömer Agha Selimoğlu went over to the side of Osman Pasha after his mansion was surrounded by government troops. He is said to have been rewarded by appointment as a government intermediary of a number of villages. Also see the "Fettahoğullarının Tarihi," which indicates that members of this family were accorded the title *ağa* and granted *ağalık* through the nineteenth century, except during the governorship of Kadri Bey (1893–1903).

40. PRO FO 195/101, July 7, 1835, the pasha sends eight hundred recruits from Trabzon and Lazistan and eight hundred from Canık to Istanbul, Suter; June 12, 1838, the pasha to send three thousand men to the Arsenal in Istanbul, Suter; June 5, 1839, a levy of twelve thousand men imposed on Lazistan and Canık for service in Malatya will "create great distress and misery throughout the pashalik"; June 19, 1839, the preceding levy has proceeded, and four hundred men are to be taken from the capital and the same number from each of the districts of Sürmene, Of, Rize, and Lazistan (here meaning the vicinity of Batum). The levy is in anticipation of a war with Egypt.

41. This would apply to those local elites who held district state offices, but also to the aghas who were appointed to non-official government positions (*ağalık*). See the Muradoğlu documents dated September 24, 1846 and April 21, 1847. For an indication of the character of the role of nonofficial government intermediates, see the reference to the position of *ağalık* in the Muradoğlu documents dated August 14, 1834, March 16, 1847, and April 15, 1847.

42. During the Russian invasion of the coast during 1916, the aghas of Of apparently played a role in mobilizing armed forces and setting up a front to resist the Russian advance (Yiğit 1950).

43. I have drawn this conclusion from the Muradoğlu documents.

cal elites to challenge district officials, hold back tax collections, and interfere in the courts was most certainly diminished, but not eliminated.

CONSUL FONTANIER ANTICIPATES THE FUTURE IMPERFECTLY

We can now address the question of Fontanier's erroneous report of the extinction of the local elites in the coastal districts. Upon his return to the town of Trabzon, probably sometime in 1830, Fontanier had been impressed by the change in the political situation. Osman Pasha had been able to consolidate his provincial government since his last visit, especially his hold on the provincial capital. There were no longer two "chiefs" who resided in fortress mansions within the city walls, set siege to one another's residences, and forced the governor to appoint them to state offices. The "complete anarchy" that he had described on his first visit was no more, such that the transit trade that passed through Trabzon was already increasing. By his western European background and experience, Fontanier could read this situation and look clearly into the future. He understood that the balance of power would inevitably shift to the advantage of the central government and to the disadvantage of the local elites.[44] And by this understanding, he correctly anticipated the end of the period of decentralization. At the same time, he incorrectly expected that the end of the period of decentralization would also lead to the abolition of the local elites. That is to say, his knowledge of what was possible in terms of the technology of bureaucratic centralism was matched by his refusal to think through the relationship of society and state in the province of Trabzon. Fontanier believed that the aghas, mansions, family lines, and parties represented a feudal system, and by that assumption, no feudal system could continue to exist alongside centralized government. In effect, he viewed society and state in Trabzon through a lens of past, present, and future that could not bring into clear focus the political situation in Trabzon.

Let us now read the passages that follow and conclude his declaration that the local elites no longer existed. Immediately, we seem to hear echoes

44. Fontanier's misunderstandings of the imperial system appear as inconsistencies. Writing as a consular official, he applauds the abolition of the janissary institution as a necessary step in the abolition of the local elites. In his first book (1829, 25–31), however, he describes the janissary institution with some admiration as a civil opposition to the government and expresses guarded optimism about its abolition. In his second book (1834, iv, 35), he complains that the abolition of the janissary institution failed to improve the position of the people in general, and he deplores its absence as a check on the arbitrary power of the sultan and high state officials.

of his sojourn in the marketplace of Sürmene. The topic is the "imagination" of the residents of the province of Trabzon:

> It would appear, Monsieur le Comte, that a people who pass so quickly from arrogance in the extreme to intimidation in the extreme, such that a pasha with practically no means at all might subdue them, must be endowed with a great mobility of imagination, thereby making them fit more than others for becoming civilized. I do not think that one should sustain such a hope in the case of the Turks. Although it is the case that one finds a natural happiness among them [the captain and crew who saw Sürmene as the promised land], religion is an invincible obstacle such that civilization will never make any progress. Perhaps its forms might be acquired, but it will never exist in itself. It is impossible that the religion of Muhammad should be in accordance with any other, it is impossible that those who follow it should adopt the customs and habits compatible with those of other people [the experience of an another threatening sociability in the marketplace of Sürmene].[45]

The Muslims of Trabzon are beset by an imaginative deficiency. They are imprisoned within the rigid existential frames of Islamic belief and practice. Fontanier seems to recall a moment when he glimpsed the rigidity of his own imaginative capacities, precisely because he became aware that others thought and acted altogether differently. His response is characteristic of someone who has been thrown off-balance by such an encounter. Unable to compose the experience of difference, Fontanier moves to suppress his failure. It is not myself but these others who are hopelessly imprisoned within the existential frames of their perceptions.

When Fontanier defensively observes that the Muslims have an imaginative deficiency, he disjoins Islamic belief and practice from aghas, mansions, family lines, and parties. Islam, the locus of a disturbing sociability, is deemed irrepressible but ineffective. The aghas, mansions, family lines, and parties were deemed effective but evanescent. He thereby splits the state-oriented social formations of Trabzon into a political anarchy that cannot endure and a social nullity that cannot change. As his report continues, however, Fontanier draws the logical conclusion of this illogical analysis:

> All the appearances of civilization will take the form of an autocratic and monopolistic government (*se tourneront en monopole*); the sultan, following the example of Mehmet Ali Pasha, will make himself master of the fortunes of his subjects, that will be the limit of his innovations. Without doubt this state of affairs gives an advantage to foreigners;

45. MAE CCCT L. 3 (1825–35), No. 11, Jan. 27, 1831.

> without doubt nothing is better for trade than a country that provides raw materials and consumes manufactured products. For security is a necessary condition for trade, and I believe that it now exists in Turkey more than ever, and that the time has come to engage in speculation in these countries. These speculations will be favorable, Monsieur le Comte, insofar as the most absurd despotism does not manage to strip its inhabitants of all their resources.[46]

Fontanier refused to consider how local society and the state system were fused together. This allowed him to imagine the state system as a bureaucratic centralism unconstrained in any way by society, hence entirely autocratic and monopolistic.

But society and state were, for better or worse, inseparable in the province of Trabzon. So the autocracy and monopoly of centralized government would never come about. Leading individuals with large followings still inhabited the new state system, just as they had inhabited the old state system. Through the later nineteenth century, right down to the collapse of the Ottoman Empire, they continued to participate in the most elementary functions of government. But they did so through adapting themselves to the mechanisms of the new technology of bureaucratic centralism.

If Fontanier had failed to understand the future of Trabzon, he was clairvoyant in another sense of that term. Three years before the end of the period of decentralization, he had formulated what would become a general dictum among consular officials. Osman Pasha had restored the authority of the centralized government (a feat he never exactly accomplished), and in doing so, Osman Pasha had suppressed the aghas, mansions, family lines, and parties (a feat he never even attempted to accomplish). Like Fontanier, the later consuls would also reach these conclusions through the lens of a past, present, and future. Unlike him, they would do so by simple inattention, rather than in reaction to their encounters with another kind of sociability.

After the end of the period of decentralization, British and French consuls would no longer be obliged to curry the favor of local elites, fret about their rivalries, or fear their challenges to the provincial government. Instead, the consuls were able to devote themselves to the speculative opportunities that accompanied the new technology of bureaucratic centralism. Accordingly, their consular reports address customs regulations, port facilities, import and export tonnages, overland and oversea haulage fees, wage

46. Ibid. Note that Fontanier is able to promote the idea of absolute governmental centralism for Turkey even while acknowledging the absurdity of such a proposal.

levels, official regulations, court procedures, and so on. Incidents of civil disorder are still occasionally mentioned, but only if linked with major market centers or trade routes. For the consuls, the regime of aghas, mansions, family lines, and parties was henceforth entirely a matter of history.

By the 1860s, the western European diplomats, soldiers, and explorers who pass through the coastal region sometimes mention the local elites, but only as a thing of the distant past. As such, they were said to be exactly what the first French consuls had declared them to be. They were the "lords of the valleys," the representatives of a "feudal system," much like that of Europe during the high medieval period.[47] Some travelers occasionally encounter some of the old "valley lords," describing them as reduced to penury but still holding out in their decaying mansions. But the same travelers never mention the existence of local elites, large followings, or a regional oligarchy. It was as though the aghas, mansions, family lines, and parties had vanished into thin air.

Consul Palgrave (1868–73) was to travel all over the coastal region by horseback, risking his life by encamping near malaria-infested marshes. Nonetheless, he somehow never noticed the local elites who were still very much in place. Thus, Palgrave was able to reminisce in later years, "Beys and Aghas, good masters in their days, spending in the land what they took from it, not like the Osmanlee leeches."[48] In this fashion, he commemorated the valley lords who had been so bitterly denounced by Dupré and Fourcade for the purpose of delegitimizing the imperial government. The "Beys and Aghas" possessed all the virtues that bureaucratic centralism lacked. They had been benevolent rulers, close to their peoples, sponsors of public works, and protectors of local interest.

The local elites of coastal districts, who had taken their proper place in the imperial government, had become virtually invisible. As we shall see, however, they would reappear toward the 1880s, suddenly and unexpectedly, as an inexplicable phenomenon.

47. Hamilton (1842, vol. 1, 253) and Koch (1855) perceive the descendants of the old valley lords as the remnants of a feudal order that had been suppressed by the central government. Still later, Palgrave (1887, 12; PRO 195/812, No. 19, Mar. 1868), Decourdemanche (1874, 363), and Biliotti (PRO 195/1329, No. 32, Aug. 1880) refer to the "old system" of the valley lords as a suppressed feudal order that was no more.

48. Palgrave 1887, 17. Idealizations of the valley lords on the part of the British and French begin to appear almost from the moment of their suppression. See, for example, Slade (1833), whose views on valley lords are in my opinion far too one-sided, but compare the assessment by Lewis (1968).

8 Scandal
Aghas and Hodjas

CITIZENS, NEWSPAPERS, AND MISGOVERNMENT

The first constitution of the Ottoman Empire was promulgated toward the close of 1876, the same year in which Sultan Abdülhamit II began a thirty-three-year reign.[1] The constitution had been prepared and adopted under the auspices of Mithat Pasha, one of the most prominent of the Ottoman reformers. It provided for the selection of representatives who would assemble as a legislative body. The spring of the following year, the deputies of the new parliament took their seats and began their deliberations. Not quite one year later, Abdülhamit II dissolved the parliament, but claimed to preserve the constitution. The election of deputies and the convening of another parliament would not occur again until the Young Turk revolution of 1908.

During its brief life, the parliament accomplished very little as a legislative body, but it did play an important role in shaping public opinion. In the course of their deliberations, the deputies soon became aware that their own personal experiences of misgovernment were not singular, but a general condition of the Ottoman Empire. The shock of this discovery was then transmitted in turn to a new audience of newspaper readers in the capital.[2] However, the scandal of misgovernment that came to light in 1877 was not entirely contingent on the existence of these new channels of communication.

The government of the core Ottoman provinces had almost certainly improved since the end of the period of decentralization.[3] It seems almost

1. My account of the first constitutional period follows Lewis (1961, 160–64).
2. See Lewis's (1961, 164–65) quotation of the Istanbul correspondent of the *Daily News.*
3. Cf. Hourani 1974, 73–74.

certain, then, that the scandal of misgovernment was as much a matter of perception as of information. A new kind of public life was taking shape in the towns and cities of the Ottoman Empire. Those who were part of it had outlooks and interests that led them to expect a different kind of governing institution. For an emergent Ottoman citizenry—including both Muslims and Christians—what had once been entirely normal now appeared as grotesque and outrageous.

At the time of the first constitutional period, such an emergent Ottoman citizenry was only somewhat less developed in the province of Trabzon than in the imperial capital.[4] A new military and bureaucratic infrastructure had put an end to the unstable political conditions that had prevailed during the period of decentralization. If some of the eastern coastal districts remained unsafe for foreigners, the trade route from Trabzon to Erzurum had been made secure and the transit trade to Persia had greatly increased.[5] As the volume of trade reached its height during the late 1860s, further administrative and judicial reforms extended the scope of centralized government. Just three decades earlier, higher state officials in the province of Trabzon had been tax-farmers backed by private armies.[6] But gradually the provincial governors, and some limited number of their staff, had become instead professional bureaucrats, fluent in French and trained as public administrators. For the first time in almost three hundred years, the eastern coastal districts were subject to systematic administrative surveillance by the central government. More or less reliable censuses were being taken, including counts of shops, mosques, professors, academies, students, houses, cows, sheep, and goats.[7] The centers of each of the coastal districts were incorporated as municipalities with mayors and councils chosen from among the local residents.[8]

4. The first printing press in Trabzon was established by the provincial government in 1869. The government printing house published official yearbooks (*salname*) and an official newspaper from that date. The first private newspaper did not appear in Trabzon until 1908 (Odabaşıoğlu 1987; Birinci 1989).

5. See Issawi 1970. The transit trade at Trabzon begins to decline after the opening of the Suez Canal (1869) and the completion of the railroad from Tiblis to Teheran (circa 1870).

6. In PRO FO 195/261, Jan. 1846, Fr. Stevens anticipates application of the Reordering (*Tanzimat*) in Trabzon. Bilgin (1990, 164) dates the application of the *Tanzimat* in the province of Trabzon to 1847.

7. Beginning with the first in 1869 and continuing into the 1900s, Ottoman yearbooks regularly described an array of public representatives and institutions that reached out from the provincial capital into these district towns.

8. See the Ottoman yearbook of 1869/1286 (Emiroğlu 1993, vol. 1).

By chance, I came across a reverberation of the scandal of misgovernment in the province of Trabzon, in the course of reading reports of one of the British consuls. Alfred P. Biliotti was the son of a family of Italian origin linked to the island of Rhodes, apparently his birthplace. He first entered the British consular service in 1856, at the age of twenty-three, on the island of Rhodes, his residence at that time.[9] He was assigned to Trabzon in 1873, where he remained as a consul until 1885. By his Levantine background, he could himself be described as a member of the new Ottoman citizenry, and so entirely familiar with its multiethnic and multireligious societies, despite his affiliation with the British.

During the first seven years of his residence in Trabzon, Biliotti dedicated most of his attention to questions of commerce. But then in 1880 his reports suddenly turn to the scandal of misgovernment.[10] Once they did so, he would discover, to his astonishment, what he later professes to have always known. The province of Trabzon was burdened by conditions of injustice and oppression as a consequence of the collusion of local elites and state officials, at all levels of government.

Biliotti first mentions this kind of misgovernment as he was addressing another more specific policy issue. In the spring of 1880, he was writing a report that approved of recent proposals of the central government to regulate the distribution of firearms. However, in the course of referring to local elites with armed followings in the district of Ordu, he was carried away by this larger problem.[11] With a degree of moral passion uncharacteristic of consular reports, he declares that district officials systematically colluded with local elites to exploit the population, both the Muslims and the Christians.

9. Biliotti would have almost certainly known Italian, French, and Greek as well as English. He should have known Turkish, too, but I am less certain of his fluency. He also served as a consular official in Crete from 1885 to 1899 and in Salonica until his retirement to Rhodes in 1903. David Barchard tells me that Wyndham Graves, Biliotti's consular successor in Crete, considered him to be a native of Rhodes.

10. The British government favored institutional change as a means for protecting the interests of the Christian minorities as well as for insuring the stability of the Ottoman Empire. The Foreign Office had been displeased when Sultan Abdülhamit II exiled Mithat Pasha and dissolved the parliament. Subsequently, the Foreign Office had probably instructed its representatives to gather information about injustices so that a case for reform might be pressed upon the Hamidian regime.

11. Biliotti initially attributes the problems in the district of Ordu to a specific cause, the Laz immigrants who had been newly settled there after the conclusion of the recent war with the Russians. But then he goes on to broaden his remarks to apply to all the "Beys and Aghas" of Ordu (PRO FO 195/1329, May 12, 1880).

However, his remarks feature a certain inconsistency, if not a blatant contradiction:

> The measure [regulating the carrying of firearms] would be a great comfort to the Muslim and Christian population which seems to be cowed down, and to have lost all characteristics of honorable manhood under the terrorism which has oppressed them, and still continues to oppress them, and which the local Beys can ill conceal behind the Mashattas and Shahadnames [judicial dispositions] which they exact from time to time from interested Tsorbadjis [toughs] and corrupted priests who bear false witness [in their favor] [and] are certainly more to blame than those feudal chiefs [Aghas and Beys], *who have inherited these abuses* from their forefathers. The oppression is now felt incomparably more than former ages, for not only the contact with the outside world through traveling, commerce and the wars, has made it manifest to both Moslem and Christian that their condition is abnormal, but the Beys themselves are not Beys of old of whom one heard and read, *those rich magnanimous, hospitable Lords,* whose patriarchal government was naturally and thoroughly submitted to; with few exceptions the Beys and Aghas of the present day are *abject instruments* in the hands of a corrupt Government for oppressing a population which tyranny has rendered vicious and submissive. The Beys would fain be independent and exercise all those inequities to their own advantage, but they are *obliged to council with officials trained to duplicity and cunning.* Some of them [local elites (?) or district officials (?)] are accused of tolerating, if not authorizing brigandage in their domains and as to their morals, it is useless to say anything. They [local elites (?) or district officials (?)] are certainly the lowest dissolute beggars. [Italics mine][12]

In this passage Biliotti describes how local elites ("Beys and Aghas") combined with district officials to subvert the administration of justice. However, he appears to be confused about the exact relationship of the former to the latter. Have the aghas and beys only now oppressed the population that they formerly protected? Or have they always oppressed the population? Do the aghas and beys oppress the population only because they have now become instruments of district officials? Or do they strive to oppress the population independently of district officials as they have always done? The passage reveals that the source of Biliotti's confusion lies in a certain assumption.

12. Ibid. Biliotti also discusses abuses at Pir Aziz in this same report, and abuses at Giresun and its sub-district, Bulancak, in a subsequent report (PRO FO 195/1329, May 14, 1880).

Although the evidence is all to the contrary, Biliotti is inclined to believe that the problem is essentially one of misgovernment. That is to say, if district officials were to behave correctly, in accordance with administrative and judicial law, all would be well. This is why he attempts to make the district officials, not the aghas and the beys, the culprits. At the same time, Biliotti is well enough informed to know that there was a larger problem of local elites that exceeded the question of official misbehavior. This is why he keeps contradicting himself in his remarks about the aghas and the beys. But being well informed about specific incidents and being able to theorize and analyze a general problem are two entirely different matters.

In the spring of 1880, Biliotti holds fast to the idea that state officials were primarily responsible for general conditions of injustice and oppression in the province of Trabzon. He never considers the possibility that the local elites and district officials might be intimately linked (as they were), or might even in some instances be one and the same (as they were). His stubborn conviction is a direct reflection of the scandal of misgovernment that had come to light during the first constitutional period. If there were local elites in provincial society who mistreated the population, this was only because a bad government had allowed or encouraged them to come into existence. If, then, a good government were put in place to regulate provincial society, these local elites would not be able to oppress the population. The ponderable problem for Biliotti was how to replace bad government with good government. The imponderable problem was a relationship of state and society that underlay a certain kind of governmental structure.

Biliotti was thinking in the same terms as the emergent Ottoman citizenry, as he indirectly reveals in the passage above. Both Muslims and Christians, he tells us, now saw conditions of injustice and oppression as "abnormal" by virtue of two kinds of comparison. First, the general population in Trabzon now felt abused as never before by virtue of their "contact with the outside world." That is to say, they had come to assess political conditions in terms of new concepts of government. Second, the general population in Trabzon had "heard and read [of] those rich magnanimous, hospitable Lords" of the old feudal system. That is to say, they were no longer able to recognize existing political conditions as the legacy of old concepts of government. The collusion of local elites and district officials was both unacceptable and incomprehensible. An underlying principle of the imperial regime since the beginning of the decentralization, even the beginning of the classical period, could no longer be understood as a normal feature of the governmental structure.

The spread of new concepts of government, hence also misgovernment, had transformed long-standing practices into a scandal. The amnesia of the general population was now coordinate with and parallel to the ignorance of the foreign consuls, not to mention the ignorance of their superiors in London and Paris. A tactic of sovereign power based on interpersonal association had continually reproduced the collusion of local elites and district officials generation after generation. An ottomanist state society had come to occupy a place and play a role in the governmental structure of the westernized imperial system. Local elites and district officials were not representatives of two different political systems, but rather still part of a single governmental structure.

BILIOTTI'S REPORTS ON THE WESTERN COASTAL DISTRICTS

In the summer of 1880, some months after writing the passage cited above, Biliotti set out by horseback from Samsun intending to reach Trabzon several months later. As he slowly worked his way back toward the capital over the course of several months, he carried out inspections of each of the coastal districts, pausing for weeks at a time to gather information and conduct interviews. Judging from the consular reports that he wrote during his travels, he had undertaken the expedition for the express purpose of gathering evidence of misgovernment.[13] The reports include case study after case study of local political and social conditions, often mentioning individuals and villages of no special commercial importance or diplomatic significance.[14] Sometimes illegible, packed with details, and occasionally ram-

13. The later British and French consuls did not normally undertake such expeditions. They had little interest in the coastal districts after the "pacification" of the local elites during the 1830s. As the treatment of the minorities became a diplomatic issue, they began to think once again of the coastal districts, but very few consuls submitted themselves to the ordeal of visiting the more remote rural areas by horseback. William Gifford Palgrave, Biliotti's predecessor, was, however, another exception among the later consuls. He also left the provincial capital, traveled extensively throughout the coastal region, and submitted lengthy, heavily documented descriptions of the coastal region (PRO FO 195/812, Jan. 1868, "General Report"; No. 19, Mar. 20, 1868; PRO FO 526/8, Jan. 29, 1873, "On the Lazistan Coast . . ."; Palgrave 1887). Palgrave's consular reports include a wealth of statistical information, gleaned from official Ottoman documents, but very little reliable information about political and social conditions in the coastal districts. They are marred by prejudice against both the Muslims and Christians. For doubts about Palgrave's accounts of Trabzon, see Bryer 1969, 193, and especially Bryer 1988.

14. However, Biliotti eventually writes a report that presents an overview of the province of Trabzon in which he reaches general conclusions about its social conditions (PRO FO 195/1329, No. 64, Dec. 1880).

bling, his consular reports are more like "field notes" than official communiqués. As such, they provide a mass of details from which it is possible to glimpse the patterns of government or misgovernment that prevailed in different sections of the coastal region.[15]

During his travels, Biliotti discovered that local elites and district officials were almost everywhere linked by ties of kinship, friendship, and partnership. Usually they worked together for exploitative, if not criminal, purposes, but this was not always the case. Here and there, competent officials administrated certain districts in accordance with the new regulations of the central government.[16] Here and there, benevolent local elites took a genuine interest in the welfare of the population and the maintenance of public order.[17] However, such circumstances were exceptional. More typically,

15. Biliotti's consular reports, written from 1880 forward, are consistent with three major sociological patterns in different parts of the coastal region. The patterns and their sources follow: 1) Along the coast to the west of Ordu toward Samsun (the old province of Canık) he found vast farming estates, some of them spin-offs of the lands of the Hazinedaroğlu. Here the local elites were often large landowners who formed a kind of government by themselves. Their sharecroppers were often "life tenants," little more than serfs who were bought and sold with the land. See PRO FO 195/1329, No. 38, Aug. 1880 at Çarşamba, describing eastern Çarşamba; No. 30, Aug. 1880 at Fatsa, describing the coast from Fatsa to Ordu; No. 32, Aug. 1880 at Ünye, describing Fatsa; No. 33, Aug. 1880 at Ünye, describing Ünye. 2) Along the coast east of Trabzon toward Hopa, which Biliotti knew about only indirectly, his reports indicate that local elites were members of large family groupings who were positioned in district social networks. State officials were often more or less completely dependent on such individuals, even for carrying out the most elementary tasks of government. See PRO FO 195/1238, Jan. 23, 1879; 195/1381, No. 54, Sept. 1881; 195/1381, No. 33, Nov. 1881; 195/1420, No. 27, June 1882. 3) Along the intermediary coast, from Trabzon to Ordu, the local elites were more variable in their character. In those places where there were plains along the coastline, local elites resembled the landowners of the western coast, while the conditions of their sharecroppers were sometimes better and sometimes worse. In other places, the local elites were from large family groupings that combined to dominate rural areas as along the eastern coast. In still other places, local elites were prominent townsmen who had been able to permeate district governments with their friends and relatives. See PRO FO 195/1329, No. 34, Aug. 1880 at Çarşamba, describing Terme; No. 30, Aug. 1880 at Fatsa, describing Ordu; No. 45, Oct. 1880 at Çarşamba, describing Pir Aziz, sub-district of Giresun; No. 45, Oct. 1880 at Çarşamba, describing Bulancak, sub-district of Giresun; No. 48, Oct. 1880 at Görele, describing Tirebolu; No. 49, Oct. 1880 at Vakfıkebir, describing Görele.

16. Also see his comment on the district officer (*kaymakam*) at Ünye (PRO FO 195/1329, No. 33, Aug. 1880 at Ünye, describing Ünye, and PRO FO 195/1329, No. 48, Oct. 1880 at Görele, describing Tirebolu).

17. See Biliotti's comments on Mithat Bey at Sürmene (PRO FO 195/1238, Jan. 23, 1879).

local elites and district officials manipulated the new government regulations for the benefit of their relatives or friends. In some instances, local elites exerted pressure on district officials who were unable to resist them. In other instances local elites had managed to have themselves appointed as district officials. In still other instances, district officials used the local elites rather than the other way around. And there are indications that it was still possible to begin as a district official as a first step toward becoming a local elite. Whatever the exact pattern in any district, local elites and district officials commonly combined to defeat any administrative or judicial reforms undertaken by the central government. The individuals in question were sometimes descendants of the old family lines that had been prominent throughout the later period of decentralization. But they were sometimes the descendants of new family lines that had displaced older local elites after the period of decentralization.

Taken together, Biliotti's reports reveal that the political situation in some places resembled that of the period of decentralization. The local elites were leading individuals with armed followings. They collected illegal taxes, extorted state funds, imposed forced labor, confiscated land and goods, forced women into marriage, exacted fees for marriages, subverted the court, suborned officials, and intimidated opponents. In some places the local elites represented large family lines and large followings, engaged in all kinds of illegal agreements with district officials, and joined in alliances with their counterparts in neighboring districts. In other places the town or the district was divided into two camps of local elites in competition with one another, each side striving to suborn district officials and subjugate the population. So to some considerable degree, the practices of the period of decentralization had continued, years after the reforms of the Reordering (*Tanzimat*) had been applied to the province of Trabzon. The local elites no longer dared to challenge the government militarily with thousands of men in arms, but otherwise little else seems to have changed.

But indeed there had been changes. The relationship of the state system and the state society was not the same as it had been at the beginning of the nineteenth century. The new, westernized system of centralized government had eased some of the harshest of the old official exactions, but it had also introduced all kinds of new bureaucratic regulations. If a trader, craftsman, or laborer wished to travel, then he needed a passport. If a young man wished to postpone military service, pay another to serve in his place, or claim an exemption by virtue of his religious training, then he needed a government certification of such a privilege. If a man or woman wished to register some piece of property, a house, a mill, a garden, or a farm, then it was necessary to acquire a deed. If two fathers wished to marry their children, then they needed a license. If a man with religious training wished to lead the mosque prayer, deliver a sermon, or perform a circumcision, marriage, or burial, then papers bearing the correct seals and signatures were necessary. If an individual wished to construct a warehouse in a marketplace or if a group wished to build a village mosque, then this or that approval was necessary, from municipal, district, or provincial officials. Biliotti informs us that local elites were almost everywhere the key to obtaining such official certifications and instruments. They performed such services for a fee that had no basis in law whatsoever, and the fees they charged could be exorbitant.

Biliotti was not the only one to be surprised by his discoveries. In the course of his journey eastward toward Trabzon, he happened to encounter Yusuf Pasha, who had served as provincial governor of Trabzon in 1878 and had briefly held that office again in 1880. Biliotti considered him one of three recent provincial governors who were men of exceptional probity, training, and ability.[18] He therefore hoped that Yusuf Pasha would be able to address the problems that he had been encountering and deal with them effectively. Biliotti writes, "Yussuf Pacha unites in his person all the qualities required for the efficient fulfillment of this special duty. He is an incorruptible upright functionary, he is known as such to the populations of the province, he has a rank which while overawing the oppressors, will inspire confidence to the oppressed, and he is fresh from his recent experience in Armenia in dealing with similar questions."[19] Biliotti immediately informed Yusuf Pasha of the conditions of misgovernment, only to find that he had not the slightest inkling of the problems of injustice and oppression that Biliotti had been encountering during his travels:

> The latter wondered at the many abuses which I summarily related to him, and of which he had heard nothing while he was Vali [governor] in this Province. I had no more heard myself of these before I went on the spot. The populations fear to speak and the Kaimakams [district governors] and Mudurs [district administrators] consider useless to report thereon. However the facts are undeniable, but the Porte is in complete darkness on the subject, and in the meantime abuses continue to the detriment of the population.[20]

18. The other two governors he mentions are Ahmet Rasim Pasha and Giritli Sırrı Pasha. See Deringil (1998) for an in-depth study of the political outlook of high Ottoman officials during this period.

19. PRO FO 195/1329, No. 50, Oct. 1880.

20. Ibid.

Official and consular ignorance of political and social conditions in the outlying coastal districts was nothing new. I have already given many examples dating from the period of decentralization. The Porte (central government) was always kept in the dark about certain matters by provincial governors. Provincial governors were always kept in the dark about certain matters by chief notables and district governors. No doubt the chief notables and district governors were also kept in the dark by the greater and lesser aghas of the outlying villages. All centralized bureaucracies work by filtering out information as it passes upward. Still, a centralized bureaucracy vertically segmented by tiered circles of interpersonal association could be expected to filter out information even more reliably and consistently.

BILIOTTI'S AWARENESS OF A STRUCTURE OF MISGOVERNMENT

Shortly after his encounter with Yusuf Pasha, Biliotti found himself back in his consular residence in the town of Trabzon. It was now time for him to write a summary report for his superiors, one that would set out general conclusions and recommendations instead of dwelling on specific instances of injustice and corruption. Before he undertook this task, however, he would be able to reconsider the coastal region in the light of all that he had learned about the prevailing social and political conditions. Strangely, facts he had always known about the provincial capital itself now acquired a new significance. He now realized that the problem of misgovernment involved something far more serious than collusion between district officials and local elites.

As he began to write the last of his reports, Biliotti understood that the best representatives of the reformed state system were powerless. A new governor, Sırrı Pasha, had just replaced the old governor, Yusuf Pasha. Biliotti admired the capability and integrity of the former no less than the latter. Nonetheless, he now saw both as victims of a governmental structure that they were unable to control or to change in any way:

> The same spirit [of defiance of the provincial governor by subordinate state officials] prevails down to the native official of the lowest rank. There are families that monopolize Government employments at Trebizond; the same thing happens in the districts. These families are connected to each other by blood or interest, but even when they are not, there is a kind of solidarity between native officials, who whatever the

> personal spites between them may be, unite to fight the power of the Vali, whom they consider an intruder.[21]

The same collusion of local elites and district officials that existed in the coastal districts also prevailed in the provincial capital. But now in the town of Trabzon, where he had been a resident for more than seven years, this problem appeared in a new light. Local elites and state officials were one and the same. It was not that the latter had succeeded in corrupting the former; rather, it was that the two were one within a structure of misgovernment.

To demonstrate the full extent of the problem, Biliotti described how a single family had penetrated the provincial government. He listed fifteen individuals from this family holding fifteen different governmental positions: five members of various courts, four chief administrators of provincial bureaucracies, three clerks to chief administrators, and three members of various councils. In addition to holding these offices in the provincial capital, other members of this same family held the position of government secretary in Gümüşhane and government treasurer in Rize.[22]

Biliotti now understood that a regional social oligarchy of families and friends spread by "twig and branch" outward and downward into the coastal districts, but then also upward and inward into the highest circles of imperial officials. This regional social oligarchy had a kind of sovereign power of its own, apart from that of the westernized, that is, rationalized and institutionalized, state system:

> It is easy to comprehend that with the influence that all these officials, severally and collectively, can command in the Capital of the Province, and with the support which they give or receive from their relatives or friends in the districts, the power of the Vali is more nominal than real. . . . Not only this, but several natives of this Province holding important appointments in the Capital [of the Empire] they naturally always enlist their influence in favor of their countrymen, friends, or relatives.[23]

He concludes that the governor had almost no control over major segments of the coastal region. His subordinates, the sub-governor of Rize in the east and the sub-governor of Samsun in the west, were virtually independent, regularly disregarding his orders. Furthermore, it was reported that the

21. PRO FO 195/1329, No. 64, Dec. 1880.
22. Ibid.
23. Ibid.

sub-governor of Rize was attempting to have his sub-province separated from Trabzon so that he might be appointed governor of this new province. This was exactly the situation that divided Memiş Agha of Rize from Osman Pasha of Trabzon in 1814–17, and then later divided Tahir Agha of Rize from Süleyman Pasha of Trabzon in 1832–34!

Provincial governors were oftentimes upstanding, well-educated, and capable administrators, that is to say, accomplished representatives of the new westernized state system. But there was nothing they could do about misgovernment, even though they had good intentions and were determined to make a difference. Biliotti writes, "Sirri Pacha who has worked very hard since his appointment here 20 months ago, will, I expect, soon break down, as broke down before him, Ahmet Rassim Pacha and Yusuf Pacha, also two first rate Valis, and as will break down all those that may succeed him."[24] Eventually the new professional bureaucrats would be defeated by a government subverted by a regional social oligarchy whose leading individuals used the law to favor their own interests.

Biliotti's new awareness of the subversion of the westernized state system by local elites had led him toward a moral judgment of conditions in the coastal region. Good government was dependent on good character. The province of Trabzon seemed to him to be awash with bad characters, and for that reason its provincial government was corrupt and abusive. His new perception was, however, incomplete. He was still unaware that another kind of morality, different from the morality of professional bureaucrats, underpinned what appeared to him as misgovernment.

Here I must comment further on Biliotti's perception of both ordinary and elite Muslims in the province of Trabzon. His consular reports always include assessments of the general condition of both the Muslim and Christian populations. He remarks again and again that local elites and district officials treated ordinary Muslims even worse than they treated ordinary Christians. He repeatedly cites instances in which leading individuals among the Christian minorities participated in the exploitation of both ordinary Muslims and Christians. Still, he knew more about the Christians than the Muslims, and he assesses the circumstances of the former in more detail than the latter. In all probability he always resided with Greeks and Armenians during his travels, and his hosts were most probably the chief sources of the information he gathered.[25]

24. Ibid.

25. David Barchard, quoting the memoirs of Wyndham Graves, has recently given me evidence of Biliotti's close contacts with Christians during that later period.

In mentioning these features of Biliotti's consular reports, I do not wish to cast any suspicion on the accuracy of the information he provides, or even to suggest that it was one-sided. He was perhaps the most open-minded of all the British and French consuls. Nonetheless, his consular reports are in a certain sense unreflective. Unlike other exceptional and accomplished consuls, Biliotti never pauses to theorize or analyze the character of the ottomanist state society of the province of Trabzon. This is partly because he was personally inclined to cite facts and incidents rather than offer generalizations. Still, his consular reports are curiously skewed. They include an impressive body of ethnographic details, more than are found in the reports of any other British or French consul. And yet he never attempted to describe in structural terms the local elites from family lines or the social formations that backed them.

BILIOTTI'S REPORTS ON THE EASTERN DISTRICTS

Biliotti's failure to theorize and analyze is perhaps linked to his Levantine background. Unlike some of the other British and French consuls, he never writes as though he feels uncomfortable or threatened by Muslims. Having perhaps been born and raised among Muslims, he was able to take them for granted rather than search for some way to interpret them. As an "Oriental," he found it impossible to be an "Orientalist." So Biliotti consistently perceives the collusion of local elites and state officials as misgovernment and therefore never as a structural legacy of an ottomanist state society. He consistently assesses social and political conditions as a consequence of corrupt and abusive practices and therefore never as an alternative governmental morality.[26] We can see how this is so by considering how he addresses the differences between the western and eastern coastal districts.

Biliotti had chosen to carry out an inspection of western rather than eastern Trabzon for several reasons. The commercial interests of the British were more important in the western than the eastern coastal districts. The reforms of the state system had been applied earlier in the west than the east. There were large, concentrated populations of Christians in the western districts, but not in the eastern. And then, perhaps most importantly, the eastern segment of the province of Trabzon had once again become a dangerous place for state officials let alone foreign consuls. This was

26. The consular report cited above, in which Biliotti expresses his confusion about the role of the feudal lords in old Trabzon, indicates how little attention he had given to provincial Muslim society during seven years of residence in the coastal region.

a direct result of Russo-Ottoman War (1877–78), which had seriously disrupted the political and economic arrangements that had linked the rural societies of eastern Trabzon with Anatolia and the Caucasus. So for all these reasons, Biliotti did not have the opportunity to observe that segment of the province of Trabzon. When his attention was drawn to the coastal districts to the east, however, we find he was entirely aware of their peculiar features that set them apart from the coastal districts to the west.

In the year following his trip by horseback from Samsun to Trabzon (1881), Biliotti wrote at some length about an incident in the district of Sürmene, still famous for its civil disorders. Writing with the benefit of his fieldwork in the western coastal districts, he was now able to understand the larger implications of the fragmentary pieces of information that arrived in the provincial capital. A state official, Hüseyin Bey, had set out for Sürmene with "a score of zaptiyes [policemen]" in order to investigate an attack by brigands on villagers that had occurred during the annual return from the high summer pastures. Having arrived in the district center, Hüseyin Bey had immediately sent back an urgent request for reinforcements, saying that even ten score men would not be sufficient. Biliotti pauses in his account of the incident to provide his superior with background information, writing "The district of Surmeneh and indeed the whole country between Trebizond and the Russian frontier [which had newly become the Çoruh River after the loss of Batum] is in a state of anarchy and insecurity beyond description. No traveller is safe on the roads, and I have from time to time reported cases of plunder and murder in villages."[27] The "state of anarchy," to which Biliotti refers using the standard consular phrasing, was directly related to the recent loss of territories to the Russians. The outbreak of brigandage was the predictable result of the weakening of the centralized government, the westward flight of large numbers of Muslim refugees, the breakdown of customary trade across the Çoruh River, and the return of demobilized soldiers.

Having oriented his correspondent, Biliotti returned to the incident in question, explaining why Hüseyin Bey required a force of hundreds of men just to apprehend a few outlaws who had robbed some villagers:

> [In these eastern districts where a state of anarchy reigns] there are Beys or Aghas who command influence and are the abettors of brigands. Sometimes moved by a feeling of jealousy against each other they assist the Police in capturing criminals. . . . But if there is no feud between

27. PRO FO 195/1381, No. 54, Dec. [or possibly Sept.] 1881.

> the brigands the police are quite powerless. Hussein Bey . . . reckons that there are only at Surmeneh [alone] about 5,000 Martini rifles with plenty of ammunition in the hands of the population, which is very warlike, and considers that nothing can be done without the assistance of some local Bey. He states that a certain Bazoglou Djafer Aga is all powerful, and that through him the culprits may be apprehended. It may be so, if they do not belong to his clan, but I doubt that he will ever give up relatives or friends.[28]

By this account, we can be sure that Biliotti understood that the "Beys and Aghas" in the east were not exactly like the majority of the townsmen and landlords he had described in the western districts.[29] Although he does not closely compare the two, he refers to the features of the local elites in the eastern districts that distinguish them from those in the western districts: (1) They had armed followings ("brigands"). (2) They provided essential assistance to state officials ("capturing criminals"). (3) Their assistance to the government was directly related to their local rivalry ("moved by a feeling of jealousy"). (4) They were the representatives of large family groupings ("clans"). (5) They were positioned in broad and deep social networks ("relatives or friends"). (6) The extent of these social networks reached impressive levels, that is, thousands of men in arms. The situation in the district of Sürmene differed from that in the western districts by the greater breadth and depth of the structure of misgovernment.

Biliotti knew that the "Beys and Aghas" in the eastern districts were of a special character in that they enjoyed a more substantial backing of the local populations. Still, he could not identify their significance as the representatives of an alternative governmental morality. For Biliotti, collusion of state officials and local elites was everywhere a manifestation of the same scandal of misgovernment, even if it took a somewhat different form in the east and the west. And it is his knowledge of another, seemingly unrelated, scandal that confirms this prejudice.

THE SCANDAL OF CHRISTIANS WHO WERE MUSLIMS

The proliferation of country hodjas and medreses was another peculiar feature of the eastern districts. So the excess of hodjas and medreses was a characteristic of precisely those districts where collusion between local elites and state officials was backed by a substantial cross-section of the

28. Ibid.
29. See note 15, above, summarizing the sociological patterns of local elites, which can be inferred from Biliotti's consular reports.

population. But Biliotti felt no compulsion to ponder this correlation. It was just another isolated fact rather than a piece of a puzzle that might be deciphered. He never considered a possible connection between aghas and agha-families, who appeared to subvert the centralized government, and the hodjas and medreses, who represented the official Islam of the centralized government.

Biliotti had occasion to mention the hodjas and medreses in 1885 in a study of the system of education in the province of Trabzon. The following excerpt is given without *lacunae:*

> The number of medressés [higher religious academies] is especially great eastward of Trebizond.
>
> The majority of the inhabitants of these districts are the descendants of Byzantines who began to embrace Islamism about 150 years since [1885 − 150 = 1735].
>
> Numerous medressés may have been necessary at that period for the purpose of instructing proselytes, but their usefulness is no longer apparent. One of the present undeniable results of these institutions is to enable the youths attending them to evade conscription. Another probable result is to entertain a feeling of hostility toward Christians at large, for hardly any live in these districts. Furthermore no progress seems to be made in good moral[s], as the native population eastward of Trebizond is more addicted to brigandage and murder than in any other part of the Vilayet.
>
> Not withstanding their so thoroughly learning the Turkish language, they continue to use in familiar intercourse, a corrupt Greek dialect called Lazico, of which I shall speak later.
>
> Another *remarkable fact* is that with all their fanaticism they still stick to Christian Customs and traditions, and that the families that furnished Christian priests in bygone time, are those in which the greater number of mollahs [hodjas] are to be found.
>
> They preserve with reverence their sacred books, the sacerdotal vestments and emblems of their forefathers and put the greatest faith in their healing power. They impose the former on sick persons and to drink in a communion cup is reserved as the last hope of recovery in desperate cases of disease. Pilgrimages with offerings in a renowned Byzantine monastery, that of Soumela, at 8 hours distance from Trebizond, dedicated to the Virgin, are not unknown occurrences. But in spite, or perhaps, because of all this, the Mussulmans Eastward of Trebizond, especially those of Off, are the most fanatical in this vilayet. [Italics mine][30]

30. PRO FO 195/1521, "Report on the Schools in the Vilayet of Trebizond," May 1885.

These are indeed remarkable facts, for the account seems almost to explode from the tension of contrary tendencies. According to Biliotti, the populations in the eastern districts were almost all Muslim, in contrast to other parts of the coastal region. On the other hand, this had not always been the case, since they still spoke older Byzantine languages among themselves and still preserved Christian scriptures, vestments, and relics. And yet, at the same time, they were now among the most "fanatical" of the Muslims in all the province, having come to know Turkish thoroughly and to specialize in Islamic teaching and learning. On the other hand, these accomplishments notwithstanding, the many hodjas and medreses that existed in the eastern districts had no apparent effect on morals whatsoever, since the peoples of the eastern districts specialized in robbery and homicide. All told, these signs of having used their former accomplishments as Byzantines for the purpose of new accomplishments as Ottomans were to no avail. For one could not say what the function of hodjas and medreses should have been, save to enable the residents of the eastern districts to avoid conscription (in that part of the province, which had always provided large numbers of soldiers for the Porte) and to encourage hostility toward Christians (which, however, were virtually nonexistent in their district). If Biliotti's superiors believed this section of his consular report, they would believe anything.

At the time he was writing, Biliotti was completing the final year of a long tenure of service in the Trabzon. So he was as fully informed and experienced as he ever would be during his residence there. The incoherence of his remarks can therefore be taken as a measure of how little he had reflected on the character of society and state in the province of Trabzon. In this respect, he was no different from other British and French consuls of the later nineteenth century. The local elites of the outlying coastal districts had not posed a serious military threat to the central government for decades. Consular officials therefore had no reason to pay attention to either the aghas or to the hodjas. Accordingly, with the passage of time, they understood less and less, rather than more and more, about the ottomanist provincial society of Trabzon.

On the other hand, Biliotti was not an ordinary consul, and he was not submitting a routine report. He was exceptionally well informed about the coastal districts, and he was writing a lengthy treatise on the system of education in the province. Even if he was never inclined to analyze the general character of Ottoman society, he usually gave examples of incidents or individuals to illustrate specific points. So the incoherence of his account of the eastern districts deserves closer attention; for, despite its internal contradictions, the cited passage does feature a certain consistency. Biliotti pretends to be reporting on all the eastern districts, but he is actually passing along a collection of rumors and slanders regarding the district of Of alone. Moreover, these rumors and slanders would have been most current among the Christian minorities, and especially the Greek Orthodox minority. The clearest indication of this is his reference to a mass conversion that resulted in Greeks becoming Muslims.[31] This clue requires that I qualify my preceding remarks.

While the consuls had ignored the rural societies of the province of Trabzon for decades, the eastern coastal districts had recently captured public attention once again. I have noted that new concepts of government were spreading among an emergent Ottoman citizenry during the last decades of the nineteenth century. Among the Christian minorities, and especially among the Greek Orthodox minority, these new concepts included nationalist ideologies. From the mid-nineteenth century, the Orthodox Greek population in the old province of Trabzon had prospered and expanded, partly as the result of immigration into the coastal region from the Aegean. And given the existence of an independent Greece, nationalist sympathies and movements had naturally gained ground in Trabzon, stirring memories of the Ottoman conquest of the Greek Empire of Trebizond. Inevitably, the existence of Greek-speaking Muslims in the district of Of became a subject of nationalist reflection.

How could a Christian majority ever come to abandon their religion and become a Muslim majority? The question had always bothered the Christians in Trabzon. For a very long time, perhaps for centuries, they had explained every instance of a large Muslim population of Byzantine background by a specific mythic formula. Some eminent leader in this or that district must have turned away from Christianity, and led his unfortunate followers into Islam, for the sole purpose of enjoying a personal advantage, that is, to gain official Ottoman favor. In the instance of the Lazis between Atine and Hopa, it had been "Prince Lazerew."[32] In the instance of the

31. Another indication is Biliotti's reference to brigandage and murder, charges that were usually leveled against the Oflus. In MAE CCCT L.2 (1812–24), No. 74, Feb. 1819, "Off, the refuge of brigands"; Fontanier (1834, 293–94) writes, "its inhabitants as well as those of Sürmene are reputed to be great robbers, but have the advantage over the latter of being fearless pirates as well." Koch (1855: 110–11) writes, "In all the mountains, the land of Off is the most feared and avoided because of brigandage."

32. Fontanier (1834, 299) mentions the tradition of Prince Lazerew for Mapavria.

Greeks of Of, it had been "Bishop İskender."[33] So a concept of high apostasy and perfidy, referring back perhaps to the traumatic surrender of the Byzantines of Trebizond to Mehmet II, had also required a thesis of mass conversion. But now in the later nineteenth century, when Biliotti was writing, the question of how Christians had become Muslims had begun to disturb the minorities in a different way. How could peoples who were not really "Turks," but rather Greeks or Armenians or Georgians, become Muslims? Such questions were provoked by a nationalist rather than a religious anxiety. For the minorities, this was also a scandal, no less than government corruption.

From the later 1860s, western European observers, and more notably their informants from the Greek Orthodox minority, attempted to minimize or controvert the relationship of the district of Of to the Ottoman system, especially in regard to the matter of Islam. They did so at the very moment when information about the extent of religious teaching and learning in the district was newly available as a matter of public record.[34] According to the Trabzon yearbook (*salname*) for 1869/1286, there were 82 professors (*müderris*) and 2,364 students (*talebe*) in the district of Of.[35]

33. Fontanier (1834, 299) mentions the tradition of Bishop İskender for Of but does not give his name.

34. For the first attestations of many professors, academies, and students in the district of Of, see chap. 5. Attestations from the nineteenth century are abundant. Şakir Şevket (1877/1294, 98) notes that the district of Of was known for having produced many men of the learned class (*ulema*). See Karadenizli (1954, 45), more readily available, for a translation of Şakir Şevket's passage on the district of Of. British consul in Trabzon W. G. Palgrave writes, "It is curious that no district of Anatolia furnishes so large a number of Mollas and Muftees that is of Professors and Legists as Of, nor I must add such ignorant and narrow mindedness" (PRO FO 526/8, Jan. 29, 1873, "On the Lazistan Coast. . . ."). Trabzon yearbooks, including the first published in 1869/1286, state that the district of Of was famous for its many professors, academies, and students.

35. The Trabzon yearbook for 1869/1286 (Emiroğlu 1993, 1: 150–51) lists the total number of students (*miktar-i talebe-i ulum*), academies (*medâris-i ilmiye*), prayer-leaders (*eimme*), sermon-givers (*huteba*), and professors (*müderrisîn*) for each district of the province of Trabzon. For the district of Of, these numbers are 2,364, 350 [?], 98, 137, and 82, respectively. By way of comparison, the corresponding numbers for the sancak of Trabzon (coastal districts from Rize to Giresun) were 4654, 435, 576, 946, and 170, so that Of made up more than half of the total number of students. The number of academies listed for Of is presumably a clerical error since it exceeds the total number of villages by severalfold. The number 35, rather than 350, would be in line with the other figures given in this and later Trabzon yearbooks. This would mean there were 35 academies in Of out of a total of 85 in the sancak of Trabzon, again roughly half.

These numbers are completely out of proportion to its relative population. The district is recorded as having about five percent of the Muslim population (six thousand households) living in all the villages and towns of the entire coastal region from Batum to Bafra, that is, the combined subprovinces (*sancak*) of Trabzon, Canık, Lazistan, and Gümüşhane. Nonetheless, more than half of all the religious academies, more than a quarter of all the religious teachers, and more than a third of all the religious students of the entire region are officially attributed to this single district.[36]

By the logic of the new nationalist ideologies among the Greek Orthodox minority, all these professors, academies, and students became evidence of alienation from, not connection with, imperial institutions (see fig. 9). In 1885, Biliotti referred to the two most popular interpretations of this alienation, both of which had been current among the minorities for years: (1) The hodjas and medreses of Of were evidence of a past Byzantinism, not a present ottomanism, since they were to be found among families that had once produced Orthodox priests and still preserved Christian sacred books and sacerdotal instruments. By this interpretation, the hodjas and medreses, which were so strongly associated with a strict and literal version of official Islam, are transformed into evidence of the vitality of an underlying Christianity.[37] (2) The extraordinary number of hodjas and medreses in the district of Of were evidence of the evasion of military service, hence a sign of the lack of commitment to the Ottoman system on the part of the population. By this interpretation, the hodjas and medreses, which were predominant in those districts known for contributing large numbers of troops to imperial campaigns, became evidence of disaffection from imperial military projects and ideals.

36. The Trabzon yearbook for 1888/1305 also lists the numbers of students, the official academies, and the names of the professors in each of the districts of Trabzon. On pages 127–31, the thirty-nine academies in the old district of Of are listed in order of their official number, from No. 134 to No. 172. Of these, eleven were in villages in what is now the district of Of, twenty-three were in villages in what is now the district of Çaykara, three were in the "Holo" villages that are now attached to Sürmene, and two are of unknown location. The total enrollment in the academies was given as 2,800. Umur (1949: 25–33) writes that there were probably about three to four thousand students in the academies of the old district of Of during the late Ottoman period. He lists nineteen villages with academies in the valley of the Baltacı River alone (most now in Hayrat sub-district), only five of which appear on the official lists in the Trabzon yearbook for 1888/1305. He also names a professor who was associated with each of these academies and provides a short biographical sketch.

37. The nineteenth-century reports of crypto-Christians generally refer to the Kurumlis—Christians officially registered as Muslims—who were settled in the

Figure 9. One of several imperial mosques decorating a village mosque.

Of the two ways of distancing the Oflus from the Empire, the charge that hodjas and medreses were merely devices to avoid conscription has to be taken seriously. Toward the close of the seventeenth century, large numbers of Oflus had become either irregular soldiers or religious students, and, probably in many instances, both at the same time. So from an early date there was always a connection and coordination between the military and religious engagements of the populations in the eastern coastal districts. The intimate and necessary connection between aghas and hodjas, however, was not without tension and conflict. The relationship of the officials of the imperial military and religious establishments was institutionally regulated. The relationship of the aghas and hodjas in the coastal districts, both of them interlopers in the imperial military and religious establishments, was less regulated and more competitive. In other words,

upper districts of Sürmene and Trabzon rather than in Of (see chap. 5). The contemporary Oflus, like other Trabzonlus, believe in the curative powers of Christian priests and preserve Christian relics that they used as charms for cures. In the 1960s, during my residence in Of, I met observant and knowledgeable Muslims who showed me small interlocking silver ornaments, said to be useful as prophylactic devices, that they had purchased from Christian priests.

the colonization of the military and religious establishments worked by a logic entirely different from the institutional integration of the two establishments within the imperial system.

For example, the Oflus who identified themselves with the imperial military establishment were different from the Oflus who identified themselves primarily with the imperial religious establishment. Those villagers who became irregular soldiers participated in the social networks and coastal coalitions of the aghas and agha-families. Those villagers who were engaged in religious teaching and learning were potential migrants interested in escaping the aghas and agha-families. So the relationship of aghas and hodjas was always variable, and, in some respects, always troubled. As the documents transcribed by Umur demonstrate, a newly emergent complex of aghas and mansions came into direct and tragic conflict with an already existing complex of hodjas and medreses, most dramatically in Paçan village during the year 1737/1150. This was the occasion when irregular soldiers, led by individuals who would eventually establish family lines, were accused of murdering forty religious professors and students and destroying large numbers of books and registers. From this date, it would seem almost certain that the system of aghas and mansions had dominated and subjugated the hodjas and medreses in all the eastern districts.

But this situation began to shift in 1826 with the abolition of the janissary institution. According to Hasan Umur, official registers show an immediate change in the district of Of that is directly correlated with the abolition of the janissary institution. During the course of two decades (1826/1240–1844/1260), prayer-leaders and sermon-givers are granted appointments (*berat*) to serve in mosques in virtually every village in the district.[38] Umur interprets the flurry of permits as a sign of increased security brought about by the central government's Reordering (*Tanzimat*) of 1839–76. Although his information seems significant, his conclusion does not necessarily follow. It is doubtful that there was much change in security within the district of Of itself. After all, the Reordering was not applied to Trabzon until 1846 or 1847, that is, after the flurry of permits.[39] The aghas would continue to give patronage to armed followings, and the villages would continue to bristle with Martini rifles throughout the nineteenth

38. Umur (1956, 16–17) fixes the period when many new permits were granted from 1825/1240 to 1844/1260.

39. See note 6, above, referring to the application of the Reordering (*Tanzimat*) to Trabzon.

century. Thus, it would seem that the flurry of permits is a harbinger of the reorientation of the population away from military and toward religious occupations.[40] Probably from the time of the abolition of the janissary institution, imaming had begun to take the place of soldiering as the principal mode of imperial involvement and participation in the district of Of.

After Sultan Abdülhamit II ascended the throne, an imperial policy of pan-Islamism further served to stimulate religious teaching and learning in the district of Of. By the report of British consul Palgrave, resident of Trabzon during the 1870s, the hodjas and medreses in the district of Of, like the sultan himself, had come under the influence of the Wahhâbî movement in Arabia.[41] And by a contemporary tradition in the district itself, the Oflus were first contacted by representatives of the Nakşibendi and Kaderi religious orders sometime during the Hamidian period.[42] This was the period when the Oflus turned to religious teaching and learning by the thousands. They did so not only to exempt themselves from military service, but also to take advantage of new career prospects. The Oflus had less to gain from a military profession or hobby and so, evading conscription, directed their attention toward a religious profession or hobby.

40. My interlocutors in Of knew that registration as a religious teacher or student was a tactic for avoiding conscription, but they insisted that the main motive for such activities was social prestige and economic advantage rather than evasion of military service. However, Umur (1949, 28) mentions that the abolition of examinations during the later Ottoman period turned the religious academies into asylums for military deserters.

41. Palgrave (1872, 130) writes, "Not the common people only, but many of the highest and best educated classes, even the Sultan himself among the number, are distinctly inclined toward the stricter school, and so are the principal doctors and teachers throughout the Ottoman East, as he will find who visits the 'Medresehs' at Of, Koniah, Damascus, Gaza, and even Mosool."

42. See Cansız (1948, 13) who also states that there were never any meeting places for religious brotherhoods (*tekke*) in Of; however, one such a meeting place is officially recorded in the Trabzon yearbook for 1869/1286. The number of meeting places for religious brotherhoods is unusually low in all the coastal districts east of Trabzon. The Trabzon yearbook for 1869/1286 lists none for Lazistan (Batum to Arhavi), twenty-six for Trabzon (from Rize to Bucak), and forty-eight for Canık (Ünye to Bafra). Of the twenty-six in Trabzon, there were only three in the district of Rize, one in Of, and none in Sürmene. Cuinet (1890–95: vol. 1, 55, 64) counted only two *tekke* for all of the *sancak* of Trabzon, one each in Giresun and Tirebolu. Noting the low number of *tekke* in the coastal region, Bryer (1975: 141) concluded that the energies of the early missionary dervishes of Anatolia had been spent by the time that Trabzon was incorporated by the Ottomans. Alternatively, the low number of *tekke* might be interpreted as a sign of the preference for "official" as opposed to "charismatic" Islam by all the population of the coastal region.

Table 3. Individuals Listed among Ottoman Learned Class, by District and Region

Eastern Black Sea		*Western Black Sea*		*Mediterranean Sea*		*Capital*	
Batum	53	Trabzon	12	Akseki	25	Istanbul	252
Arhavi	31	Görele	3	Ibradı	82		
Hems¸in	18	Tirebolu	4				
Pazar	21	Giresun	13				
Rize	39	Ünye	13				
Of	23						
Sürmene	8						

THE LEARNED CLASS FROM THE EASTERN DISTRICTS

A recent study indirectly tells us something more about the distinctive orientation of the Oflus toward religious teaching and learning during the late nineteenth century. Sadık Albayrak, an independent scholar from the district of Çaykara, published a four-volume work consisting of transcriptions of the official biographies of the Ottoman learned class during the final years of the Empire.[43] Using his index, which lists the birthplace of each individual, I was able to arrive at a count of the number of individuals who were listed among the Ottoman learned class for particular locations. Table 3 presents the counts for the principal coastal districts of Trabzon, for two mountain districts of Antalya (Akseki and Ibradı), and for Istanbul. The counts provide a rough indication of how many individuals from each location had become officially recognized as members of the Ottoman learned class. The locations are grouped in order to illustrate how the counts vary in different regions: eastern Black Sea, western Black Sea, Mediterranean Sea, and the capital.

By the counts, the number of individuals born in the district of Of who appear among the learned class is relatively high, but not as high as for

43. The title of his study can be translated as "The Last Period of the Ottoman Learned Class" (1980–81). It is based on the biographies of hundreds of officials whose birth dates usually occur sometime during the nineteenth century. The biographies themselves sometimes add further details about educational background. Albayrak notes that he was unable to consult all the biographies since many had been destroyed or were in poor condition. Thus, the counts in table 3 are only a rough indication and cannot be considered definitive.

other eastern Black Sea coastal districts. Since the numbers of religious professors, academies, and students in Of would have surpassed all the other districts cited by far (save for the imperial capital itself), this means that a relatively small number of those Oflus who took up religious studies were able to rise into the Ottoman learned class.[44]

The contrast between the districts of Arhavi and Of illustrates how the inhabitants of coastal districts with fewer religious professors, students, and academies than Of produced more members of the learned class. From Albayrak's study, we discover that some fraction of the learned class born in Arhavi did receive their early education in its local centers of religious studies. On the other hand, many others did not begin their early education until after they left Arhavi to reside in Istanbul.[45] In effect, the Arhavilis were more successful than the Oflus in leaving their mountain homelands and seeking their fortune in the capital.

Comparing the eastern and western districts of the Black Sea coast, we see that the inhabitants of the former were far more successful than the latter in rising into the Ottoman learned class. This is consistent with the relative differences in the relationship of society and state in these two regions. To the east, the Muslims consisted more nearly of a melange of peoples of Turkic, Lazi, Kurdish, Greek, and Armenian background. Although their districts had been almost entirely rural in character until the late nineteenth century, a more continuous history of local participation in the imperial system resulted in large numbers of individuals among the ranks of the Ottoman learned class. To the west, the Muslims consisted of a larger proportion of Turkic peoples of pastoral background. Even though there were a number of sizable towns, the Muslims in these districts did not have the same history of local participation in the imperial system and so they were less prominent among the Ottoman learned class.

A further comparison casts still a different light on this matter. Akseki and Ibradı are districts nestled in the upper valleys of the Toros Mountains,

44. The counts might conceivably underestimate the extent to which centers of religious study in Of contributed to the religious education of members of the Ottoman learned class, wherever they may have been born. Some of the learned class may have in fact received some of their religious education in its centers of religious study even though they were not born there. This would probably not have been a significant number, however, since the Oflus themselves were not able to rise into the learned class in large numbers.

45. Some went to Sürmene, where the teacher in the local religious academy would probably have been an Oflu. Some of those who went to Istanbul may have also received lessons from an Oflu teaching in one of the great mosques.

which run along the southern tier of Asia Minor.[46] The landscape in which the villages are located is hilly and forested, and historically there were no farming estates or land magnates in this area. The district centers were stops on the caravan routes running from the shoreline through the mountain passes to the important provincial center of Konya. Many of the inhabitants of these districts became migrant traders and craftsmen, leaving their villages seasonally to work in towns and cities. In other words, Akseki and Ibradı were much like Of, save that they were located in the Mediterranean province of Antalya rather than the Black Sea province of Trabzon. Like their eastern Black Sea cousins, the residents of Ibradı and Akseki were propelled by circumstances to seek their fortunes beyond their rural homelands. As in the eastern Black Sea districts, these two Mediterranean districts once produced large numbers of professors, academies, and students.[47]

And yet, there is a striking difference between the Mediterranean and Black Sea districts in this regard. The number of the Ottoman learned class who declare Akseki and Ibradı as their birthplace or homeland is very high. The numbers involved are comparable to all the learned class of all the eastern Black Sea coastal districts taken together, or even to all the learned class of Istanbul. Ibradı and Akseki are then two striking additional examples of provincial participation in the state society and system, only by a different path and in a different way.[48] There were large numbers of professors, academies, and students in Akseki and Ibradı during the late nineteenth century, to a degree that was comparable to Of.[49] Still, the Aksekilis and Ibradılıs were far more successful in entering the ranks of Ottoman religious, military, and administrative officials.[50] The reason for this appears to lie in their very early contacts with the imperial center, a fact Evliya Çelebi took the

46. These two districts have usually been part of a coastal Mediterranean province, such as Alanya or Antalya. Ibradı is now a sub-district (*nahiye*) of the district (*kaza*) of Akseki in the province (*vilayet*) of Antalya.

47. So far as I can determine, Ibradı and Akseki were never known as recruiting grounds for irregular soldiers as were Rize, Of, and Sürmene.

48. I was able to visit the town of Akseki very briefly during 1967 and 1968. Although it was a remote mountain district, I was particularly impressed with the gracious appearance of its houses and streets. In fact, I chose not to use this town as a site for a second study because its residents seemed so educated and sophisticated. This was a mistake that I have since sorely regretted. The comparison of Of and Akseki would have been a fascinating exercise.

49. In the census of 1878/1295 there were fifty religious academies attributed to the district of Akseki, which included the sub-district of Ibradı (Özkaynak 1954, 43).

50. Özkaynak (1954, 123–79) mentions that they were as successful in becoming military and administrative officials as religious officials.

trouble to point out. From a very early date, no later than the classical Ottoman period, the inhabitants of these two small Mediterranean districts were unusually well connected in the ranks of Ottoman officialdom, despite their remoteness.[51] Over time, moreover, they were able to preserve and cultivate these connections so that the two towns, even though agriculturally impoverished, were recognized as centers of both learning and wealth by state authorities during the eighteenth and nineteenth centuries.[52] These long-standing connections with individuals in high imperial positions were probably essential for maintaining the quality, if not the quantity, of local educational activities. And, of course, they must have also played an important role in providing access into high imperial circles as one generation of successful Ibradılıs and Aksekilis gave assistance to the next.

The peoples of the district of Of, like those in the districts of Akseki and Ibradı, were also obliged by their circumstances to seek their fortune through participation in a state society and system. On the other hand, their situation was very different from their Mediterranean cousins. The district of Of had remained outside the realm of the Turco-Islamic dynasties of Asia Minor for a much longer time. Its inhabitants included many newly converted peoples during the seventeenth century. As newcomers, they were at a disadvantage. They would not have had contacts among circles of higher imperial officials. They therefore would have had more difficulty working their way into circles of higher imperial officials. So they did not have what the Aksekilis and Ibradılıs had: representatives among higher imperial officials who endowed local religious establishments and sponsored local youths of promise. What the Oflus had instead was collective experience in penetrating a state system from its margins.

During the post-classical period, the Oflus set about colonizing imperial institutions wherever and whenever they could do so. As a consequence of this mode of entry, the Oflus were remarkably successful on the ground floor of imperial institutions, so to speak, in the same measure that the Aksekilis and Ibradılıs were successful at the top floor. In the district of Of,

51. Evliya Çelebi refers to a connection between Ibradı and one or more Şeyh-ül-İslâm in Istanbul during the later seventeenth century (Özkaynak 1954, 10, 100; Selekler 1960, 82). There is also a tradition that the Şeyh-ül-İslâm Minqârî-zâde Yahya Efendi was associated with Akseki. Uğur's (1986, xliv, 450–52) summary of the official biography of this man includes no mention of this; however, he does note that he sponsored many individuals wishing to enter the upper ranks of the *ulema*.

52. Özkaynak 1954, 100–101. A number of large mansions were built in the town by individuals with official connections at this time.

one discovers all the ways in which people at the margins of the Empire could better themselves through a strategy of identifying with a state society and system rather than resting content with purely local communal identities and occupations. Religious teaching and learning were therefore popular activities in the district of Of precisely in the measure that involvement in the outside world was the local way of life. Religious teaching and learning were fused with the practice of trades and crafts precisely because acquisition of the former was the precondition for the exercise of the latter in the towns and villages of a state society and system.

Through the nineteenth century and beyond, the local elites of the eastern coastal districts adapted themselves to the westernizing state system. The aghas and agha-families remained essential to the state system since they were still necessary for carrying out the most elementary governmental functions at the local level. The hodjas and medreses remained essential to the state system given the policy of building an Islamist population for the support of the imperial regime. By this combination, the military and religious foundations of an ottomanist rural society remained in place until the very end of the imperial regime. Again, it is the district of Of, homeland of so many soldiers and students, that provides one of the best examples of how this was so.

MEMOIRS OF GÜNDAY

The problem of misgovernment by local elites and district officials was probably especially severe in the early 1880s, as a consequence of the recent Russo-Ottoman War. A little more than a decade later, when Biliotti had left Trabzon for an assignment in Crete, a new provincial governor appears to have reigned in the regional social oligarchy. Kadri Bey (1893–1903) did not bring about a definitive change in the structure of political authority. Rather, by the classic measures of a strong provincial governor—reprisal and intimidation, combined with appointments and concessions—he "rectified" and "improved" (*ıslah*) the local elites and district officials.[53] But then, upon his sudden death in office, there was a deterioration of governmental authority, just as there had been upon the death of Süleyman Pasha (1818) and Osman Pasha (1842).

At the time, British consul Longworth described conditions in the town of Trabzon in terms that bring to mind the consular reports of Fourcade and

53. See my summary of Osman Pasha's reforms (*ıslah*) of the local elites during the early years of his governorship (chap. 7).

Dupré a century earlier. The town of Trabzon, he tells us, is divided into factions led by two family lines, the Kahyaoğlu and Hacıoğlu, such that "lawlessness has become rampant." There are "rowdies in the streets" who "fight wherever they meet." They use "their firearms freely to the danger of those around." A young Kahyaoğlu who had shot a policeman was "freed by the gendarmes," and "no one will bear witness" against the troublemakers.[54] These civil disorders were not entirely restricted to the province of Trabzon. The Ottoman Empire was drifting toward the Young Turk revolution of 1908. The repeated failure to address the problem of misgovernment was leading Ottoman officials and citizens to draw more radical conclusions about the steps necessary for governmental reform. One such Ottoman official and citizen would eventually cite the district of Of as a case in point.

When the revolution of the Young Turks occurred in 1908, it was accompanied in the province of Trabzon by demonstrations against governmental corruption and incompetence. Large crowds assembled before government buildings in each of the coastal districts to express their outrage. Fearing for their personal safety, district officials deserted their posts, leaving much of the province of Trabzon without any kind of governmental authority. Faik Hurşid Günday was an advisor to the governor and resident of the capital at the time. As he recalled years later in his memoirs, he was asked to investigate and resolve an especially serious incident in the district of Of, where two local parties were on the brink of armed conflict.

According to reports, the district officer (*kaymakam*) of Of was supported by one group of local aghas, while the municipal mayor of Of, Hasan Efendi Selimoğlu, was supported by another group of local aghas. Each of the two opposed parties had called on their followers to assemble in the district center (*kasaba*), and some seven or eight hundred men in arms from the villages had responded.

Günday had been asked by the governor to mediate between the two parties and restore the peace, just as countless other state officials had been obliged to mediate among the competing local elites during the period of decentralization. In his memoirs, he describes how, in the company of just two gendarmes, he set out from the capital by horseback and reached the district after a half-day's ride:

> I went to the government building and entered the office of the district officer. The government building was a rented house in a state of ruin

54. PRO FO 195/2136, Apr. 1, 1903.

> with stairs that were broken down, dirty, and disgusting. Afterward I received the aghas from the two sides. I told them I had no idea that there were *armed characters such as they* in the district of Of and that they should *put their affairs in order in accordance with their position.* When the news of my arrival and the resignation of the district officer spread, the two opposed sides sent all their men back to the villages. [Italics mine][55]

Günday had come to the district of Of to "rectify" or "improve" (*ıslah*) the aghas, that is, to put them back in their proper places, not to suppress or disperse them. He lectures them specifically on the point of having taken up arms against one another and orders them to "put their affairs in order in accordance with their position" as local elites who represent the peoples of the district. There will be no mention of criminal charges or proceedings during his visit, most assuredly not by an official who had but two gendarmes at his side in a district that had only recently mobilized as many as eight hundred men.

Günday provides a sketch of the district such as he came to know it during two and a half months residence as acting district officer. The following citation is given without *lacunae*:

> I saw that the dominion of "agha-ness" (*ağalık*) was everywhere in existence in Of, in a stronger and more powerful form [than elsewhere].
>
> Of these, the Solaklı Valley aghas were from the Selimoğlu, the most powerful family in Of. In the second place, there were the Baltacı Valley aghas from the so-called Muradoğlu, as well as other aghas like Osman Vehbioğlu and Tellioğlu.[56]
>
> The villages of these aghas were in places distant from the district center (*kasaba*), but all of them had salons (*oda*) in the district center, and all of them resided in these salons.
>
> In these salons they were all as it were in the position of being like a [nonofficial] government (*hükümet*) for each of their separate areas (*mıntıka*). The aghas served as intermediaries between the official government and the villagers who belonged to them, such as in the instance of the marrying of boys and girls. The aghas exacted charges and bribes in accordance with the means of each man or the task in hand. I also established that they collected an "agha-ness" contribution (*ağalık aidatı*) each year in their villages.

55. Odabaşıoğlu 1990, 4–13.
56. In the 1960s, the Vehbioğlu and the Tellioğlu families were considered allies of the Selimoğlu.

The conditions Günday was describing were a more or less corrupted version of the form of local government officially instituted by Osman Pasha. The illegal practices of the aghas of Of were not really that far from legal practices in force from 1834 to 1847.[57]

Günday next mentions the existence of seventy medreses in the district of Of, adding that almost everyone was a student. He then goes on to describe the collusion between the local aghas and almost all the district officials, including the head of the accounting office, the head of the census office, and the judge's representative, in the following terms:

> In Of, with the intervention of these aghas, and including almost all the civil servants, there was a battle over these bribes. The two-headed revolt that had broken out in the affair involving district officer Celal Bey was precisely because of these bribes.
>
> I also learned other things. Except for the mayor of the municipality, Hasan Efendi Selimoğlu, and his supporters . . . , a very sizable association collected money from every businessman who came to the government. This association included . . . the district officer Celal Bey, the administrative assembly members, Ferhat Selimoğlu, and Hasan Efendi Muradoğlu, along with a number of civil servants like the census official. Acting together in this matter, they then divided the money among themselves.

Günday gives specific examples of the way that an "embezzlement commission" (*irtikap komisyonu*) extracted money in the instance of fees paid for exemption from military service, the registration of deeds, and so on. We can assume that the "embezzlement commission" was probably standard practice both before and after the period of decentralization. It was one more way in which practices of the central government had been locally appropriated and adapted.

Hoping to abolish these practices, Günday ordered the salons of some of the aghas to be closed and the bribery to cease. In response to these measures, one of the aghas told him he was going to the British consul for assistance.[58] Another agha told him that the bribes were the "bread" of the aghas, and he was taking their "bread" from them. Eventually the mayor, Hasan Efendi Selimoğlu, showed Günday an order sent down by a previous

57. See the Muradoğlu documents.

58. During the later nineteenth century, it became common for British, French, and Russian consular officials to act as the protectors of the Christian minorities. When the agha proposed seeking the help of the British, he was seeking to emulate this practice, seeing himself as an abused minority.

provincial governor (Kadri Bey) calling for the salons of the aghas to be shut and the aghas themselves banished to their respective villages (that is, removed at a safe distance from the government but otherwise not punished).[59] So Günday was doing in Of what Kadri Bey had done in Of just a few years before. And Kadri Bey had done in all of Trabzon more or less what Osman Pasha had done in all of Trabzon before him. Get the aghas out of the district government. Destroy their mansions or close down their salons. Send them back to their villages. Require them to serve the government as they should: "Put your affairs in order in accordance with your position."

Günday concludes his remarks with a negative assessment of what he or anyone else could have accomplished under the imperial regime. After the declaration of the Constitution of 1908, he tells us, there were no real changes, either in Of or in any other of the coastal districts of the province of Trabzon. All along the coastal region the old local elites (*eşraf*) and usurpers (*mütegallibe*), such as he had encountered in the district of Of, stayed in place by registering themselves as members of the new dominant party of the new constitutional revolution, the Union and Progress Committee.[60] In other words, his mission to the district of Of was inevitably a failure. He had temporarily "rectified" or "improved" (*ıslah*) the aghas of Of, but no real structural change had taken place.

Some years later, Günday would participate in the nationalist movement. He served as the governor of the province of Sivas. He represented the army in the National Assembly. His memoirs were written still later, sometime during his retirement in the 1950s. His account of the aghas and agha-families of Of should therefore be read as a retrospective account. When Günday points to what could not be accomplished in the district of Of in 1908, he is almost certainly thinking of what he felt had been accomplished later during the first decades of the Turkish Republic. He insisted on the failure of an imperial policy of reform, for which he himself had worked, because he was convinced of the success of the nationalist movement and revolution in which he had become so deeply involved some years later. By the later prescriptions of Kemalism, which Günday would have most certainly espoused, it would not be enough to westernize the state system while hoping that social thinking and practice would follow along. It would be necessary to reinvent both the state and social systems at the same time.

59. See my comments on the strong governorship of Kadri Bey (1893–1903) in chap. 7.
60. Odabaşıoğlu 1990, 13.

PART IV

OLD MODERNITY AND NEW MODERNITY

The Republican Town of Of

9 Revolution
Amnesia and Prohibition

NATIONAL PUBLIC CULTURE AND IMPERIAL PUBLIC CULTURE

The official history of the Turkish Republic begins on May 19, 1919, with the arrival of the Ottoman military commander, Mustafa Kemal Pasha, in the Black Sea port of Samsun.[1] Under the terms of an armistice, the Ottoman sultan had accepted the disbanding of what remained of his armies, as well as military occupation by Britain, France, and Italy. Having left Istanbul under orders to implement the armistice, Mustafa Kemal, later to become known as Atatürk, instead set about coordinating a national resistance in defiance of the imperial government. Just days before his departure, a Greek army had landed at the Aegean port of Izmir with intentions of annexing western Asia Minor. In time, however, Mustafa Kemal was able to rally imperial commanders and troops in Anatolia and assume leadership of a National Assembly meeting in Ankara. The Independence War (1921–22) that followed concluded with the defeat and retreat of the Greek army. In the aftermath of this victory, Italy, France, and Britain came to terms with the nationalist movement, whereupon the imperial government collapsed. The declaration of the Turkish Republic followed soon thereafter (1923).

From the moment of military victory, the National Assembly, urged along by Mustafa Kemal, began to move toward radical revisions of the state system. By 1925, the Sultanate and Caliphate had been replaced by a president. The sacred law of Islam had been entirely abandoned in favor of the Swiss civil code and the Italian penal code. Religious schools and institutes had been closed in order to emphasize secular education. The Gregorian calendar and the international clock had replaced Islamic dates and times.

1. See Zürcher (1993) for an assessment of official history as it took shape during the one-party period of the Turkish Republic.

From their inception, these changes in governmental institutions anticipated nothing less than a revolution, the replacement of an imperial by a national public culture. Certain kinds of religious speech, script, dress, and manners in public life were legally proscribed. Other kinds of secular speech, script, dress, and manners in public life were officially approved. There would be a new Turkish writing, a new Turkish language, a new Turkish history, and a new Turkish folklore. Scholarly institutes would be founded, academic research would be sponsored, and a core of schoolteachers would be trained for the purpose of propagating new national norms that would take the place of old imperial norms.

The effects of this revolution were not restricted to the greater cities, even during the early years of the Turkish Republic. Many district officers, public prosecutors, and gendarmes in towns and villages were zealous nationalists. They were ready, if not eager, to use their powers to arrest and prosecute anyone who defied the secular reforms. In addition to legal enforcement, provincial state officials also conducted propaganda campaigns aimed at disgracing local representatives of the imperial system, that is to say, aghas and hodjas. By the later 1930s, anyone who wished to take part in public life was obliged to do so in accordance with the new national norms. Indeed, even direct descendants of aghas and hodjas took care to appear in public life as Turkish nationalists rather than Muslim ottomanists. It is true that not everyone in the towns and villages of Anatolia changed their everyday habits. But any villager or townsman who wished to receive the respect of a state official was obliged to reform himself or herself.

The revolution would not have been so successful, and perhaps not successful at all, without the coupling of repression with enjoyment. Contrary to a stereotype of provincial Ottoman society, the villages and towns of Anatolia were anything but inert sociopolitical entities, even if the population had been impoverished and exhausted by decades of warfare by the 1920s. The top-down project of modular nationalism therefore required that citizens be drawn into the new public life of the Turkish nation by a process of self-discovery and development. Of the various steps taken, one of the more effective in provincial Turkey was the encouragement of local celebrations of local engagements in the Independence War, which became known everywhere as Liberation Day (*Kurtuluş Günü*). Sometime during the early years of the Turkish Republic, the towns in the western Aegean provinces began to commemorate the exact day of the year when foreign troops withdrew. The result was a series of rolling Liberation Days that progressively marked the westward advance of the nationalist forces toward Izmir.

By analogy, the towns in the eastern Black Sea provinces also began to commemorate their own series of rolling Liberation Days, but in reference to the end of an earlier military conflict. The Russian army had initially invaded and occupied the eastern coastal region in 1916, but then withdrew in 1918 as a consequence of the Bolshevik Revolution. This means that the Liberation Days in the Black Sea towns commemorate events that predate the landing of the Greek army in Izmir, Mustafa Kemal's arrival in Samsun, the rise of the nationalist movement, the subsequent Independence War, and the concluding declaration of the Turkish Republic. That is to say, they refer to events that occurred "anachronistically," in the context of an imperial rather than a national struggle.

In the next four sections of this chapter, I shall consider the way in which two Oflu authors attempted to understand this dislocated periodization during the later 1940s. At the time, the new national forms of speech, script, dress, and manners had thoroughly displaced the old imperial forms in the district of Of. Indeed, the revolution in public culture was as thorough and complete as it would ever be. Nonetheless, a state society of imperial origin was already colonizing nationalist institutions and organizations. As a result, the new public culture was beginning to feature splits and divides that challenged some of the most experienced and knowledgeable of the Oflus. National ideology and institutions had indeed brought about a change in consciousness in the district of Of, but in such a way as to make the relationship of present and past difficult to decipher.

THE BATTLE FOR OF

The celebration of Liberation Day in the district of Of does not really mark the final withdrawal of foreign troops, as is the case elsewhere, but resistance to their initial assault two years previously. In this respect, the first event of local nationalist history occurs at a moment when the imperial government was anticipating victory. The district of Of therefore offers a striking example of a dislocated periodization, exceptional even for the towns along the eastern Black Sea coast. To explain, I must first briefly mention the larger context of military conflict in the late winter of 1916.

The Germans and Ottomans had been at war with the British, French, Italians, and Russians for a little more than a year. A great Ottoman victory, credited to Mustafa Kemal, had recently been achieved at Gallipoli. But all kinds of disasters were looming in the eastern provinces of Erzurum, Van, and Trabzon. Already, the imperial government had begun to deport the

Armenian minority into the Syrian desert, where many would die without provisions or shelter. Very soon, the Muslim majority would also suffer massive casualties and extraordinary hardship as a consequence of Russian offensives followed by Ottoman counteroffensives.[2]

The Russian advance on Trabzon began in February, when a land army supported by naval gun ships occupied the town of Rize.[3] Avni Pasha, regional military commander of Lazistan, decided to gather the remnants of his retreating forces and make a desperate stand at the Baltacı River in the district of Of (see map 1). Arriving in one of the interior villages of the district, he proceeded to summon to his side a number of the local leaders, asking them to rally the population in support of his army. The response he received seems to have exceeded anything he might have expected. For the next two or three weeks, several thousand Ottoman troops, reinforced by thousands of irregulars and assisted by thousands of civilians, succeeded in halting the forward movement of a formidable Russian force.[4] During a brief but terrifying interval, the twentieth century arrived in the district of Of in the form of machine guns, naval bombardment, trench warfare, and civilian refugees.[5]

As a popular effort involving great danger and sacrifice, the Battle for Of rightfully came to be remembered as the dawn of a new kind of political identity and participation. It was the local instance of a Turkish nation that was coming into existence even before the prospect of the extinction of the Ottoman Empire. Some twenty-five years after the declaration of the Turkish Republic, as the country was moving from a one-party to a multiparty system, two little books appeared that explored the meaning of the Battle for Of. Each of their authors pondered the early spring of 1916 as they considered the identity of the inhabitants of the district of Of. Each of them posed the question of how the Oflus had been able to manifest themselves as a Turkish nation, already in the twilight of the Ottoman Empire.

2. See Zürcher (1993) for an assessment of the massive losses among the civilian population, both Armenian (pp. 119–21) and Muslim (pp. 170–72).

3. Yiğit 1950, 88.

4. Yiğit (1950, 96) estimates the number of troops at five thousand regular soldiers, three thousand Oflu irregular soldiers, and another three thousand regular infantry who arrived on the tenth day of the battle.

5. The Russian army occupied the eastern segment of the province, including the town of Trabzon, for about two years. Failing to control the Zigana Pass, which connects the port of the provincial capital with the highlands, the Russians undertook to build a road from Of to Bayburt. Many Oflus eventually worked on the road, but the money given them as wages soon became worthless.

The first of the books to appear, in late 1949, was a memoir based on first-hand experience. It was written by Hasan Umur, student of the hodjas during the later Empire, participant in the Battle for Of, activist in the nationalist movement, and local politician in the early Turkish Republic. The second to appear (early 1950) was a research project based on personal interviews, official documents, and authoritative sources. It was written by Altay Yiğit, a young teacher in a primary school, native of the new district of Çaykara, and an intimate of leading individuals from large family groupings. I shall begin with their contradictory reports of what Avni Pasha, regional commander of Lazistan, said and wrote soon after he arrived in the district of Of, on February 28, 1916.

Umur was among the local leaders who responded to the summons of Avni Pasha. He tells us that his party found the military commander sitting in a chair in the garden of a village residence sometime after midnight:

> Upon introducing himself to us, he said: "I am going to engage the enemy in battle here. I will give weapons to those who wish to join *our soldiers* in the battle. If there are those who do not wish to engage in the battle, let them carry munitions for *our soldiers.* And if there are those who are unable to do this, let them dig trenches for *our soldiers.* And if there are still those who say they cannot do this, let them say prayers for *our soldiers.* And if as well there are those who say they cannot do this, by God I shall hang them, and so help me God I shall hang them." And then he excused himself [from our presence]. [Italics mine][6]

Umur goes on to explain what he took to be the meaning of these remarks. Avni Pasha was saying that no one would be forced to take part in the battle, and no one who fled the front lines would be arrested. Given that the situation was so desperate, he had no alternative but to appeal to the patriotism (*vatan aşkı*) of the Oflus.

Umur recollected that an imperial military officer had delivered a speech that resembled a nationalist exhortation of the republican period. Avni Pasha had called for a popular rising of a total society in support of "our soldiers," constructing an image of a division of labor that implicitly included young and old, male and female, well and infirm. In doing so, he had attempted to inspire his audience to identify themselves with the imperial troops, rhetorically insisting that he would hang anyone who refused to say prayers in support of their efforts. But Umur was citing utterances that he

6. Umur 1949, 46.

had heard thirty years earlier, before the collapse of the Empire had been followed by the founding of the Republic. This raises the possibility, if not the likelihood, that his memory was playing tricks on him. There is good evidence that this was the case.

Avni Pasha had also sent communiqués to district officials in late February, delegating to them the authority to organize support for the war effort. Yiğit discovered one of these documents in the archives of the müftü of Of and published a transliterated version in his own account.[7] In his communiqué, Avni Pasha uses terms that correspond to Umur's recollections, but their meaning is entirely different. He addresses the müftü with respect for his person and his office, recognizing his devotion to state and religion. So he does appeal to a kind of patriotism, but it is an "official" patriotism limited to those individuals who held titles and positions in the imperial system. He orders the müftü to send him everyone, whether residents or guests, including all army deserters, absentee conscripts, and soldiers on furlough "capable of contributing to the war effort, for fighting, attacking, transporting, and constructing." So he does refer to his need for a division of labor, but not to a total society composed of individuals with different abilities and inclinations. He also calls for extreme, punitive measures to be applied to anyone who refused to support his troops, but he does not do so merely by way of rhetorical emphasis. On the contrary, he delegates full authority to the müftü "to rain down the most terrible kind of worldly punishments and afflictions on anyone who opposed him." And to this end, he recommends "destruction and burning of their households, and the deportation and torture of their relatives and descendants." In other words, Avni Pasha was licensing the harshest treatment of the Muslim population, just as other state officials had already licensed the harshest treatment of the Armenian population.

7. Yiğit 1950, 91:

> *Lâzistan Havalisi Kumandanlığı / Bismillahirrahmanirrahim; / Müftü kazayı Of Hüseyin Sabri efendiye / Mektup velâi selâhiyetimdir. / Bu kerre kazayı Of'da [mukim] ve misafir harp ve darbe veya nakliyat veya inşaatı ceriyyeye kudreti vafir [bilumum] firarî, bekaya ve tebdilhava efradının nezdi fazilânelerine yollanan ve emir ve kararımıza terfik olunan Hacı Haşım ağanın sây ve gayreti ve sizin din ve devlet uğrundaki fedakârane faaliyetiniz ile cem ve tarafıma sevk olunmalıdır. [Müfrezede] ve kapısı önünde çalışmaktan ve emrinize itaatten [istinkâf] edecek kimseler üzerine dünyanın eşeddi ceza ve mesaibini yağdırmağa sana selâhiyeti tamme verdim. Bu gibi kimselerin hanelerini ihrak ve tahrip ve evlât ve ahfat ve [akraba] ve [tallükatını] nefy ve tazip hususundaki icraatınızı görmek isterim. / Veminellahitevfik. / 28 — Şubat — 1331 / Lâzistan Havalisi kumandanı / Mirliva Ahmet Avni.*

In contrast to the oral quote, the communiqué is consistent with state policies that had been repeatedly applied to the district of Of at moments of extreme political crisis during the post-classical imperial period. The governors of the province of Trabzon had often called on local elites to assemble and dispatch troops in support of the central armies of the Ottoman Empire. In doing so, they had often appealed to their identification with and participation in the imperial system, that is, their readiness to fight for state and religion. On the other hand, the governors of the province had also on some occasions carried out punitive expeditions against local elites. In doing so, they had burned houses, destroyed crops, hanged leaders, and deported families in order to force the submission of local elites at the head of local followings.[8] In his message to the müftü, Avni Pasha therefore wrote in these two conventional registers of the post-classical imperial period. He acknowledged the "devotion to state and religion" of his official respondent even as he licensed "worldly punishments and afflictions" for anyone resisting his orders.[9] So he in no way indicated any inclination to rely on the "patriotism" (*vatan aşkı)* of the general population in the district of Of.

Avni Pasha may have adjusted the two conventional registers to suit his audience, drawing the line here when speaking to local leaders and drawing the line there when issuing orders to district officials. By such an estimation, the military commander would have spoken with respect for those who came to meet him at midnight in the garden, just as he also mercilessly

8. The provincial government subjected the district population to such measures on at least four occasions. Troops surrounded and deported seven villages in 1710/1121 (Umur 1956, Nos. 45, 46). Canıklı Ali sent about ten thousand troops into Of sometime around 1775 (Gologlu 1975, 44–45). Süleyman Pasha sent twenty-five thousand troops into the district of Of and Sürmene in 1817 (Aktepe 1950–52, 33; MAE CCCT L. 2, Nos. 43, 47, 49, 50, Dupré). Osman Pasha sent twenty-five thousand troops into the districts of Of and Sürmene in 1832 (PRO FO 524/2 p. 19, May 1832; PRO FO 524/1 p. 23, Aug. 1832, Brant). Houses are burned and men are hanged (PRO FO 195/101, July 17, 1839). A large force is dispatched to punish the Lazes (PRO FO 195/101, Sept. 9, 1839).

9. Umur (1949, 47) and Yiğit (1950, 104) relate other anecdotes that suggest that Avni Pasha was not among the most progressive Ottoman military commanders. They describe how he dispatched his soldiers to the front promising to reward them with a silver coin for each enemy hat and a gold coin for every enemy rifle, a practice reminiscent of payment for each head of an enemy soldier, still an official policy during the eighteenth century. Umur also recounts how Avni Pasha flew into a rage when he received the report of one of his cavalryman, striking him on the head with his horsewhip and threatening him with execution. After intercession on the part of another military officer, the cavalryman was allowed to explain that he had failed to remove telephone lines before the arrival of the enemy out of fear for his life.

threatened those who would not support the troops. When Umur recalled what he said, more than thirty years later, he may have further adjusted the two conventional registers, unconsciously redrawing the line between respect and threat. It was by this final edition that Avni Pasha had come to speak as a nationalist of the republican period.

Even if it is possible to soften the jarring contrast between the oral and written versions of Avni Pasha's remarks, the fact remains that Umur had mis-remembered. He had recalled that Avni Pasha did not intend to arrest anyone who fled the front lines but relied instead on an appeal to patriotism. The communiqué flatly contradicts this interpretation, and in doing so casts doubt on the reliability of Umur's memory. But there is also another reason to doubt Umur's recollection. If the overall design of his little book is considered, we can see that the words of the military commander are cited for a literary purpose. They confirm the presence of a certain "nation-thing" during the experience of the Battle for Of that was otherwise absent at the time of its recollection in writing. For the point of Umur's little book is that a national relationship of state and people, which had become palpable during the Battle for Of, had not afterwards been fully realized by the Turkish Republic. This is a strong indication that the memory of Avni Pasha's statement had been unconsciously reformulated as the singular moment of a pure national origin to be contrasted with an impure national aftermath.

HODJAS AS THE FOUNDERS OF THE NATION

Following the Battle for Of, Umur left the district of Of as a refugee, never again to return as a permanent resident. Sometime later he became an activist and politician in the nationalist movement, and so came to embrace the idea that the state should represent the people. However, by the later 1940s he had come to think of all the ways in which the people (*halk*) as defined by nationalist ideology and institutions, were not the people (*millet*) as measured by his own background and experience.

Umur was having such thoughts in anticipation of the possibility of free and direct elections. The prospect of a sounding of public opinion had probably brought to his mind the gap between the nation-state and the nation-people, the gap that should not have existed by the measure of his nationalist conviction and commitment. Accordingly, he had begun to reconsider who the people really were and therefore what the state really should be. And in doing so, he had followed his memories back to the moment of a pure national origin, back to the Battle for Of. There, he discovered an answer that stood in direct contradiction to revolutionary ideology and institutions. His little book, *Of and the Battles for Of,* is the result. It is an effort to explain what would have been unconscionable to the large majority of secular nationalists.

Umur begins with a brief essay on the importance of patriotism in human history, revealing his preoccupation with questions of the nation, as a people bound to a homeland. He then reviews the history of the district of Of, about which he was singularly informed.[10] And what he brings to light for his readers, as he sifts through legend and rumor, is a people who are a people only as a consequence of the local religious professors and academies. It was they who had brought about the Islamization of the district of Of, making a place of many peoples speaking many languages into a place of one people with one religion.

His discovery had come to him from what he had personally learned and experienced in the district of Of; nonetheless, he concluded that his homeland could be taken as but a small part of a larger whole. The professors and academies that were once to be found in the district of Of, but that also existed throughout the core Ottoman provinces (*bütün yurttaki medreseler gibi*), had "laid the foundations of the Turkish nation."[11] They had forged a common moral outlook and hence a communal solidarity among the people, not only in the district of Of, but in the rest of the country as well. Such a claim was not an original one at the time it was published; nonetheless, it was far from innocuous in its specific formulation.[12] Umur was not just saying that religion had played an important role in the history of the Turkish people, as would have been acknowledged even by the most radical secularists. He was saying that no such thing as a Turkish people would have ever existed without the local representatives of the imperial religious establishment.

Knowing that his conclusion would prove controversial, Umur provides his readers with a historical and sociological account of the professors and academies. He discusses what was good and what was bad about religious education, consistently deriving its virtues from the personal character of the professors and its vices from inept policies and regulations. So he admits

10. He would be even better informed several years later, after completing a program of archival research (Umur 1951, 1956).

11. Umur 1949, 29–30.

12. Cf. Barkan 1942a, 1942b.

the deficiencies of the imperial religious establishment, but he consistently traces them to the state system, while otherwise lauding the religious teachers and students. As proof of their accomplishments, he includes a series of short biographies of the district's most distinguished representatives during the last years of the Empire and the first years of the Republic. His readers would be able to remember one or more of these men as their own personal teachers. In doing so, they would recall them as individuals who had been respected, if not cherished. It is this larger argument that explains why Umur had mis-remembered exactly what Avni Pasha had said in the midnight meeting in the garden. He was recalling the Battle for Of as a moment when the moral qualities of the people, put in place by the professors and academies, had been called forth by a state official.

Now Umur was completely correct with regard to the accomplishment of the professors and academies. They had indeed done exactly what he claimed they had done, at least in the context of the history of the district of Of. They had constituted the dominant form of ethical thinking and practice. Without them, the Oflus would be a hodgepodge of ethnic, if not tribal, groupings with little or nothing in common. But he was altogether incorrect to identify the Battle for Of as a moment of a perfect relationship between people and state. Indeed, the Battle for Of featured a gulf between the state and the people, as Avni Pasha's communiqué to the müftü clearly demonstrates. And this disjunction between state and people in 1916 was structurally similar, although not strictly identical, to the disjunction that had stirred Umur to question national public culture in 1949. To see more clearly what troubled him, we must examine the second account of the Battle for Of.

AGHAS AS FOUNDERS OF THE NATION

Altay Yiğit intended his little book, *Eastern Black Sea Battles in the First World War*, to be used in classrooms so that the children of the district would know local history. He had therefore conceived and constructed his story of the Battle for Of in an impeccable Kemalist format, the essential precondition for its adoption by a state school. The narrative of the little book is the result of research based on participant testimonies, official documents, and published histories. In other words, it is a nationalist history that conforms to scientific criteria. Nonetheless, the narrative is also interspersed with poetry composed by the most famous and eloquent authors of the early nationalist period. It joins authoritative methods and facts with an impassioned patriotism.

Yiğit also begins by explaining the importance of patriotism in all of human history in his introduction. This leads him to the example of Kemal Atatürk, the founder of the Turkish Republic. Here he cites the accomplishments of the Eternal Leader (*Ebedî Şefß*), and he concludes with a quotation of his "Speech to Youth" (*Ey Türk Gençliği!*). The first two chapters that follow then examine the imperial period as a run-up to the national period. They bear the titles "Our Relationships with the Russians Through History" and "The Collapse of the Ottoman Empire and Its Causes." Yiğit then turns to his main topic, an account of local residents who joined troops of the imperial army in order to resist Russian military invasion and occupation. Before mentioning specific incidents and individuals, however, he briefly explains the general significance of the Great War.

Because it was a modern military conflict, the Great War took the form of "total warfare" (*topyekun harb*). By this fact, the Ottoman Empire had to rely more than ever before on a people, all the more so because of the weakened condition of the state system. And of course, the only people it found to rely upon, at least in Asia Minor, were the Turkish people. As a consequence, the Great War brought to light the qualities of the Turkish nation (*ırkımıza has kahramanlık*). And so it was that the Russian advance in 1916 locally took the form of a struggle for national existence (*bütün varlığı ile savaşmak zorundadır*). An imperial army, which had been transformed into a national army (*Türk ordusu*) by total warfare, would require the assistance of the local population—not only its local militias, but all the residents of what was already in effect a national homeland (*Karadenizin evlâtları*).

By these textual moves, made in three short paragraphs, Yiğit set the Battle for Of in the framework of the age of nations: A state had come to represent a people because the state was obliged to depend on the people. He immediately follows this opening argument with a list of the names of those volunteers who were known to have first rushed to the front lines between Batum and Hopa, even before the Russian advance. The list includes forty-five names of militia members from Rize, Of, and Sürmene. Next, he briefly describes three successive battles that occurred as the Russians advanced westward beyond Batum toward Rize, estimating in each instance the number of casualties on both sides. He then describes the Battle for Of in more detail. In the course of this account, he tells how soldiers and civilians worked together to organize a front at the Baltacı River.[13] Here he

13. Yiğit explains that an organization (*teşkilat*) was set up to assemble volunteers for the battle (1950, 91–92). The individuals who participated in this organi-

again gives lists of names of the volunteers who were part of this endeavor, but he also tells his readers about their words and actions. In doing so, he usually recounts how a military officer (his name is given) gave orders to one or more local residents (their names are given).

This account of the Battle for Of is remarkable in its tacit features, meaningless to anyone but an Oflu. The names that appear in the lists are in romanized characters, but they otherwise appear in their old imperial form. This being the case, the personal names of individuals are sometimes accompanied by a title, such as agha, bey, or pasha. When the individual is a local resident, the personal names are almost always preceded by a family name in the form of a patronymic (always if titled), such as Nuhoğlu Ahmet Agha. The exact distribution of the names in the lists is significant. Of the forty-five names of volunteers who rushed to the front lines at Batum, a third have the title agha as well as the patronymic of an agha-family from Rize, Of, or Sürmene.[14] As for the lists of names associated with the Battle for Of, they always begin with a large cluster of individuals whose personal names are accompanied by the title agha and whose family names are those of agha-families. As for the accounts of the interactions of military officers and local leaders, they almost always involve well-known aghas from well-known agha-families.

Now, Yiğit's lists of names are in no way false or even biased. On the contrary, they appear to be a reasonably accurate version of the Battle for Of, even if not an exhaustive and definitive one. Leading individuals from large family groupings had always provided the leadership for local militias and regiments. The aghas from agha-families had assembled and accompanied soldiers on imperial campaigns, at home and abroad, for centuries. One would therefore expect that aghas from agha-families would be in the forefront of popular support for the imperial troops on the occasion of the Russian invasion in 1916. What is more significant is the placement of the aghas and the agha-families in a nationalist frame. The volunteers from among the local residents are presented as representatives of a Turkish people. The military officers and troops are representatives of a Turkish state. So the aghas from agha-families are given pride of place in the relationship of the nation-people and the nation-state. However, there is still

zation are then listed for each of the principal areas of Of (pp. 93–96). Here we find the names of the old aghas from the principal agha-families of the old Five and Twenty-five parties, including the Selimoğlu, Muradoğlu, Nuhoğlu, Tellioğlu, Bektaşoğlu, Cansızoğlu, and so on.

14. There are also one pasha, two beys, and one efendi among the names.

more to the matter than this. By the lists of names, aghas from agha-families act as the representatives of the people of Of as the latter manifest themselves as a Turkish nation coming to the assistance of a Turkish state. But in the details of the account, aghas from agha-families are not depicted as assembling and directing volunteers (as they must have done in fact during the Battle for Of). They are depicted as receiving and fulfilling the orders of military officers. So for Yiğit, as for Umur, the nation once again becomes visible through a relationship of state and people, but in a different form. For Umur, the relationship of state and people manifested a moral solidarity (a state official evoking the support of a local population), but for Yiğit the relationship of state and people manifested a hierarchy (state officials directing local leaders who then direct the local population).

To understand this difference, we must return once again to the time the little book was written. Leading individuals from large family groupings had once again become intermediaries between state officials and the local population by the later 1940s. This had come about as state officials of the Kemalist period followed a governmental practice of the imperial period, turning to leading individuals from large family groupings for assistance, even though this contradicted nationalist ideology and institutions. As a consequence, an imperial state society at the local level had gradually but efficiently reoriented itself to become a national state society at the local level. Leading individuals from large family groupings, the descendants of aghas from agha-families, now appeared as nationalist rather than ottomanist in behavior, speech, and dress.[15]

Yiğit's account of the Battle for Of therefore confirms that the old modernity, which could now be described as the "old republic," had inhabited the new modernity, which could now be described as the "new republic." According to this reorientation, the consequence of official practices if not policies, it was no longer possible for the Oflus to identify leading individuals from large family groupings as an unwelcome imperial legacy. Consequently, the ascendants of leading individuals from large family groupings, the aghas from agha-families, began to appear in memory as a nationalist leadership, even in the mind of a young Kemalist teacher in a primary school.

15. As we shall see in chap. 10, it was not always a question of their descendants. There were also a few examples of the old aghas of the later imperial period (Reşat Agha, Harun Agha) who re-emerged as leading individuals during the later Turkish Republic.

The confusion of the present with the past is clearly apparent from other formal features of the little book. It includes photographs of places and individuals associated with the battles of 1916 but that clearly date from after the declaration of the Turkish Republic. One of the five photographs of places shows a battle site (the high pastures in the Sultan Murat Mountains), but the other four show contemporary scenes of government buildings in the towns of Rize, Of, and Çaykara, one of them being identified as "headquarters." The four photographs of individuals include two individuals with the title "agha." One is a leading individual from the Muradoğlu (Harun Agha), and the other a leading individual from the Selimoğlu (Ferhat Agha). These two men are identified as participants in the Battle for Of, but they would also be among the most conservative, if not reactionary, of the local elites during the early Republican period.[16]

But I have not yet mentioned the most striking of all the ironies that result from all these crossovers by which the local imperial was embedded within the local national. Yiğit could have *plausibly* described the aghas as the actual leaders of the people during the Battle for Of. After all, they were members of a regional social oligarchy, positioned in district networks, surrounded by large numbers of agnates, relatives, friends, partners, and followers. And indeed, for the very same reasons, their descendants could also *plausibly* be described as leaders of the people during the later 1940s. However, to so describe either group, it would be necessary for Yiğit to position them in circles of interpersonal association that were linked with Islamic belief and practice. But in the meantime, between 1916 and 1950, the Kemalists had disestablished Islam, thereby de-legitimizing the regional social oligarchy of the old province of Trabzon. So Yiğit could mention Islamic belief and practice as a feature of the Turkish nation (as he does in his introduction), but he could not describe aghas from agha-families as leaders of the people. He could only describe them as leaders of the people by virtue of their connections with officials of the nation-state, the latter having monopolized the legitimate representation of the nation-people.

In this regard, Yiğit is strangely silent when it comes to the professors and academies of the district of Of that were not only in existence legally in 1916, but also still in existence illegally in 1950. In this regard, his silence has all the earmarks of a prohibition. For example, of the more than a hundred personal names on his lists, only two have official religious titles (*müftü, müderris*), and only a few more indicate any kind of religious ac-

16. The other two are individuals from well-known family groupings, but they are given the title "educated gentlemen" (*efendi*).

complishment (a number of *hafız,* but not a single *hacı*).[17] Instead, the most common title affixed to a personal name after that of agha is efendi. Such a title would have indicated an "educated gentleman," hence by implication a graduate of a secular state school (*rüşdiye*), even though at least some if not most of these efendis had once been religious students, or even religious teachers.[18]

Now Yiğit was a schoolteacher somewhere near the town of Of, but he was also himself from Çaykara, that part of the old district of Of so famous for its professors and academies. This means he would have not only been well informed about hodjas of Of, but he would also have inevitably had connections with such persons. It is even likely that he was a descendant of a line of hodjas, as was the case for many men and women who became schoolteachers, and certainly for most men and women who became writers or scholars. But Yiğit tells us nothing of this. Instead, he obliquely informs his readers that he is both a close relative and close friend of leading individuals from large family groupings.[19]

Yiğit was most certainly withholding important information from his readers. But he was not intentionally attempting to trick or deceive. He was writing as an Oflu/Çaykaralı and Kemalist. He wished to pay homage to the bravery of local residents in 1916, but he was obliged to so do by imposing on himself the revolutionary prohibitions that had made possible the move from Empire to Republic. He had therefore obliged himself to remain silent on this point or to disguise that point, and in the process of accepting such prohibitions, he progressively developed amnesia. By the time he had finished writing his book, he was no longer conscious of the relationship of the aghas to the hodjas. And because he was no longer conscious of this relationship, he could no longer understand who aghas had been or why the agha-families existed.

His citation of an official document in his little book confirms this conclusion. Yiğit had explicitly recognized one instance of the cooperation of a kind of agha and a kind of hodja. It occurs precisely in his citation of the

17. Some of the family names include the titles *hacı* and *molla,* but these were of historical rather than current significance.

18. For example, the two other photographs of individuals are of "Boduroğlu Hasan Efendi" and "Hacıbektaşoğlu Ömer Efendi," both of whom are wearing a Kemalist tie but also sporting the beard of a *hacı.* Hasan Efendi, who is shown bareheaded, is none other than Hasan Umur, who studied under a distinguished religious professor as well as in secular institutions. Ömer Efendi, who is shown wearing a fez, probably also had such a mixed religious and secular education.

19. The dedication of the book and its place of sale provide indications of these connections.

communiqué that I have as yet only partially translated. Avni Pasha writes to the müftü that he was sending Haşım Agha to assist him in carrying out his orders "to rain down the most terrible kind of worldly punishments and afflictions on anyone who opposed [them]." So his citation of the communiqué ever so slightly lifts the veil on the partnership of aghas and hodjas in the old regional social oligarchy, which is otherwise damaging to his case. And his citation of the communiqué also lifts the veil on official readiness to license the regional social oligarchy to inflict all the horrors of imperial sovereign power on the local population, which is also damaging to his case.

Yiğit was attempting to show that the imperial troops had emerged as a "Turkish army" just as the local population had emerged as a "Turkish people" in 1916. Nonetheless, he chose to include a document that reeks of the "imperial" and so directly contradicted the "national" significance of the Battle for Of. Why did he not "suppress" this most embarrassing official instrument? In my opinion, Yiğit cites the communiqué because it stood as concrete evidence of the readiness of state officials to delegate full sovereign power to local elites. It therefore stood as substantial confirmation that local elites were a nationalist leadership, at least in the terms of his argument. But it could only serve as confirmation if he simultaneously forgot that the communiqué otherwise wildly contradicted nationalist ideology and institutions. It revealed that an imperial state official was ready to use sovereign power to threaten and coerce the general population, and it revealed that local elites, consisting of aghas and hodjas, were ready to lend their assistance in such an effort.

In effect, Yiğit was himself unconsciously moving to reconstitute the hierarchy on which Avni Pasha was depending when he wrote his communiqué. He was at the time a schoolteacher who did research and wrote books, but he was doing so in a way that made him a "nationalist hodja." His account of the Battle for Of confirmed that nationalist aghas occupied a proper place in the state system. The result was the legitimization of a nationalist empire in which local elites assisted state officials to manage, and if need be to coerce, the general population. The old pattern by which state power captured religious revelation was reappearing as a new pattern by which state power captured secular history.

This puts Hasan Umur in a different light. Since he dared to reflect on the role of the professors and academies, and so defy secularist prohibitions, it would seem that he should have had a clearer vision of the past, and hence a clearer understanding of the present.

AMNESIA AND PROHIBITION

By all accounts of the Battle for Of, and they include a large body of songs and stories, Avni Pasha had no need to threaten the local population with burning, destroying, torturing, and deporting. Caught between two armies, the local residents would have had more to gain by siding with the Russians, who were advancing, and more to lose by siding with the Ottomans, who were retreating. And yet, for reasons that should be clear from previous chapters, a very large number of Oflus chose to join or assist "their" imperial troops.

Part of the response of the Oflus would have most certainly involved aghas directing local militias in accordance with the orders of imperial military officers. And yet, the popular response would not have been limited to such a process. Accordingly, Hasan Umur was able to provide an account of the Battle for Of that makes virtually no mention of aghas.[20] This is evidence that the rising of the Oflus against the Russian invasion was general and popular in character, rather than limited to the circles of local elites, their agnates, relatives, friends, and partners. Umur's account of the Battle for Of as a popular rising therefore has to be regarded as a reasonable and accurate version, even if it, too, cannot be said to be exhaustive and definitive.[21] The inconsistency in the accounts of Umur and Yiğit are therefore not wholly matters of "construction." They indicate that the events of the Battle for Of were of a complex and variegated character, which is exactly what one would expect during a conflagration.

And yet there are also signs of prohibition and amnesia in Umur's *Of and the Battles for Of*. As we saw in chapter 1, Umur does refer to aghas in the introductory historical section of his book. He describes the "time of the aghas" (*ağa devresi*), a period he restricts to the half century between 1790 and 1840. In doing so, he associates the aghas and agha-families with conditions of civil disorder that he attributed to the decline of the classical

20. In his account of the Battle for Of, I have discovered only three instances of personal names with the title. They all occur in the same sentence, where they refer to one, and only one, agha taking part: "According to Genç Agha Nuhoğlu, as many as sixty people took part in the battle [on a certain hill near a certain village], among whom were found Ali Agha Nuhoğlu, the son of Esat Agha, and İzzet Demircioğlu" (Umur 1949, 55).

21. Since he regarded this popular rising as a manifestation of the work of professors and academies, his book otherwise features numerous references to personal names with the titles *müderris, hoca, molla,* or *hacı.*

imperial system. He thereby disconnects them from the later Empire just as he disconnects them from the early Republic.[22] So for Umur, the aghas were the pathological effects of a weakened and ineffective state system. Otherwise, he makes no other explicit reference to them.[23] Umur's omission of the aghas is no less suspicious than Yiğit's omission of the hodjas.

During his youth, Umur would have been among that segment of the Ottoman public who had come to believe in a new kind of governmental institution. So it is very likely that he would have seen the aghas, intermediaries between the state and the general population, as a problem of misgovernment. If this were the case, he would have had a sense of *déjà vu* during the later 1940s. Once again, leading individuals from large family groupings had begun to play a prominent role in public life. And once again, in the opinion of the majority of local residents, there were severe problems of misgovernment.

If Umur was so apprised of the situation in the district of Of during the 1940s, his silence is entirely understandable. He would refuse to recognize that the aghas had played a role in the Battle for Of. He would not give them an important place in events that he otherwise had conceived as the first signs of a Turkish state that effectively and genuinely represented a Turkish people. Instead, he would foreground all those ways in which the injunctions of a military officer had stirred a popular rising against the Russian invasion and occupation. And as a way of explaining how it had been possible for the state to represent a people at this moment, he would turn to the work of professors and academies.

And of course he was justified in doing so, as I have already noted. By virtue of the efforts of the professors and academies, the Oflus enjoyed a common moral outlook that enabled communal solidarity. They therefore enjoyed a capacity to form all kinds of circles of interpersonal association, not only in the form of leading individuals at the head of armed followings, but in all kinds of other, more entrepreneurial ways, along the lines of my friends in the Crystal Palace Hotel and Teahouse. And so, Umur appropriately praised the professors and academies. But in doing so he not only con-

22. It is true that he gives a favorable report on Memiş Agha Tuzcuoğlu, but only as an instance of the cruelty and corruption of imperial state officials, such as Osman Paşa Hazinedaroğlu. It is perhaps significant that Memiş Agha was also a merchant and financier, like Hasan Umur himself during his later years.

23. Later, of course, he would publish the results of his archival research (Umur 1951, 1956), which would cast the aghas and agha-families in a highly unfavorable light.

sciously chose to remain silent about the aghas, but he also forgot about them precisely by way of a thought that was forbidden to him.

The descendants of aghas had once again inhabited the state system, controlling nationalist institutions and organizations by the later 1940s. They were ready and able to monopolize sovereign power at the local level by virtue of a discipline of interpersonal association. And this was itself a legacy of an imperial tactic, one by which state power held official religion as a captive. But Umur could not see how this was so because the descendants of aghas represented themselves as a national leadership. They wore hats, trousers, and shoes rather than turbans, baggy pants, and slippers. They were represented by schoolteachers who wrote authoritative histories of their close connections with the nationalist movement. All this being the case, it was not easy to recognize (even if it was otherwise easy to see) that they were positioned in a regional social oligarchy rooted in the imperial history of power and religion. In his account of the Battle for Of, just after his quote of Avni Pasha, we find a confirmation of this second instance of amnesia born of a prohibition.

Just a day or so before Avni Pasha arrived in the district, the campfires of Russian troops had began to appear along the western banks of the İyidere River, the border between Of and Rize (see map 1). Umur hoped that a front might be organized there, sparing the villages of central Of from the worst of the fighting. To assess this possibility, he had set out from the district center in the company of a policeman (*zabit*), intending to reach one of the villages near the western banks of that river. On their way, the two of them came across an older hodja, blissfully unaware of all that was happening. Umur describes their meeting as an incongruous scene of pastoral serenity:

> While ascending just at the point of passing the Baltacı River, in the fine air of a cool spring day, we saw Hurşit Efendi, professor of the Eskipazar religious academy, reclining in a sheltered spot in a meadow just above the road. Every time I encountered this man I gave him a greeting [1st pers.: *selamün aleyküm;* 2nd pers: *aleyküm selam, hoş geldin;* 1st pers.: *hoş buldum;* 2nd pers: *merhaba;* 1st pers.: *merhaba;* 2nd pers: *nasılsın?;* 1st pers.: *iyiyim,* sen de *nasılsın?,* etc.] "Where are you going?" he inquired. After briefly explaining the situation, I said, "We are going to battle. We will not let the enemy into the country." [Thinking Umur was going to fight the imperial government] the hodja said in reply, "I grant all of the district of Of to you. If you don't struggle and become a man, what good is there in it?" I understood what he meant, but my policeman friend did not and asked me, "What is the hodja saying?" To which I replied, "The hodja doesn't understand the affairs of

> this world. He is talking about something else again." Immediately I set out on the road, and of course the policeman followed along. The hodja had a grudge against the [imperial] government. He was alluding to the possibility of setting up a new government that would replace the existing government, which did not know how to direct the people. [24]

The fact of interpersonal association (the exchange of greetings) was enough to sanction the hodja's engagement in a revolutionary initiative aimed at seizure of sovereign power. Such a revolutionary initiative would have the purpose of bringing the state into proper alignment with society. It was therefore inspired by the old imperial modernity in which interpersonal association was the foundation of sovereign power. Umur could not formulate the connection of aghas and hodjas any more successfully than Yiğit. Even though he dared to challenge a prohibition, he, too, was afflicted with amnesia. He could not understand that aghas and hodjas came in the company of one another as the representatives of the old republic based on sovereign power and interpersonal association.

The revolutionary impulses of Hurşit Efendi, so spontaneous and immediate, illustrates that the professors and academies had done something more than forge a common moral outlook that enabled communal solidarity. They had been part of an imperial tradition of power and religion. And so hodjas in partnership with aghas had enabled the local population to assert themselves in the imperial system. The old imperial modernity therefore harbored a republican principle. The state was composed as a society, and so it was that society could become part of the state. This old republican principle therefore harbored the potential to serve the new republican principle.

The old republic was founded on a principle of hierarchy, even though it was implemented through participation. The new republic, however, was founded on a principle of participation, even though it was implemented through hierarchy.[25] The Kemalist revolution had become problematic in the district of Of even before the first electoral sounding of public opinion in the Turkish Republic. The devices of authority and association far exceeded nationalist ideology and institutions. The result was splits and di-

24. Umur 1949, 45–46. Although Umur does not explain the hodja's grudge, the central government had favored diminishing the authority of the learned class at this time and was about to undertake further secular reforms of the educational and judicial system (Zürcher 1993, 125–26).

25. For an account of the concepts of sovereignty and citizenship in what I have termed the old republic, see Meeker 1996.

vides in national public culture working through an alchemy of amnesia and prohibition.

In the remainder of this chapter, I shall return to the revolution in public culture in the town of Of during the first decade of the Turkish Republic. In doing so, I explain the extent to which principles were contradicted by practices.

THE DEPOSITION OF FERHAT AGHA

Ferhat Agha Selimoğlu, the ascendant of every public office holder in the early 1960s (see fig. 2), first became the mayor of the town of Of sometime around 1910. Although he is said to have been an active participant in the Battle for Of, he chose to remain in the district during the Russian occupation from 1916 to 1918, continuing to serve as mayor. Many leading individuals from large family groupings elected to stay in their districts, and some of them worked with the military authorities as representatives of the local population.[26] This put them in a delicate position with respect to the nationalist movement once the Russian troops withdrew.

After the beginning of the Independence War, but before the declaration of the Turkish Republic, the local elites in Rize, Of, and Sürmene are said to have been contacted by emissaries of Mustafa Kemal Pasha. Each was asked how many men in arms they might be able to assemble and dispatch in support of the nationalist struggle. According to my interlocutors, the actual purpose of these inquiries was to assess the strength of local elites in anticipation that they might choose to support the imperial government. Those who were considered too powerful because they had too many men or too much money were called before the independence courts (*istiklâl mahkemeleri*).[27] Some leading individuals from large family groupings were there accused of collaborating with the Russians. This was not because they were guilty of any crime, so it was said, but rather it was a move to weaken them by detaining and dishonoring them.

Ferhat Agha managed not only to survive the turmoil of the interregnum but also to remain the mayor of the town, by default since there were

26. Ferhat Agha explained his decision in a letter dated June 6, 1916, which was sent to the müftü of Of, then in hiding (Yiğit 1950, 124–25). It would have been difficult for the Russian army to govern the eastern coastal districts without them. It is therefore quite likely that their absence would have only compounded the suffering and hardship of the general population. Their "collaboration" can therefore be plausibly justified, even by the criteria of nationalist patriotism.

27. Early on, the nationalists had set up the independence courts to deal with their opponents (Shaw and Kural 1977, 352–53; Zürcher 1993, 159).

no local elections. However, his luck finally ran out in 1926 when a new district officer (*kaymakam*) took steps to force him out of office. The timing of his deposition is significant since it occurs at the moment of confrontation between the nationalist movement and the old state societies in the provinces of the Turkish Republic. From 1925, the Kemalist leadership of the National Assembly had begun to take steps to suppress their opponents and consolidate their hold on the central government. The ongoing Kurdish rebellion of Shaikh Sait had served as an initial pretext for their doing so.[28] But subsequent incidents provided further justification. The adoption of the Dress Law (*Kıyafet Kanunu*) in the fall had led to a number of armed rebellions in different parts of Anatolia, some of them occurring in the eastern coastal districts.[29] Then, in the following summer, the discovery of a plot to assassinate Mustafa Kemal in Izmir provided the occasion to crush the opposition. Soon afterward, the Republican People's Party (RPP) became the only legal political party, initiating more than twenty years of a one-party regime (1925–45).[30]

The deposition of Ferhat Agha occurred in this context. One of my interlocutors recalled the occasion as follows:

> During the year 1925, a new district officer (*kaymakam*) was appointed to the district of Of. [The next year] this man went to Ferhat Agha and told him that he would no longer serve as the mayor of the town. In reply, Ferhat Agha gave the district officer two slaps (*tokat*) across his face. The district officer then proceeded to telegraph Trabzon for reinforcements. Taking a number of gendarmes (*jandarma*) with him, he surrounded the office of the mayor, which was next to the Town Square Coffeehouse. He ordered Ferhat Agha out of the office and announced that a new mayor would be chosen.

The district officer and his subordinates (*memur*) are remembered to have become the dominant authorities in the district of Of after the deposition of Ferhat Agha. Probably as never before, district state officials were able to take a range of actions without first reaching agreement or receiving assistance from local elites. The enhancement of the state system at the expense of the old state society was recalled by one of my interlocutors as the onset of moral laxity and decline:

28. Zürcher 1993, 376–80.

29. Shankland (1999) notes that an armed uprising against the Dress Law that occurred in Rize on November 25, 1925, first began in the district of Of. If this is true, my interlocutors discreetly avoided mentioning it to me.

30. Lewis 1961, 269; Zürcher 1993, 181–83.

> With the news [of the declaration of the Turkish Republic in 1923], there were celebrations in the town of Of. Crowds assembled and bonfires were built. There was a sense that the future would be different, but the first change to be noticed was the misbehavior of young men. This was especially the case during the "time of the waiter girls" (*karson kızlar devresi*), sometime around 1926–27. A building was turned into a kind of theater (*tiyatro*) in the town of Of. Films were shown using an electric generator that was run by a little water wheel. [There was no cinema in the 1960s.] Sometimes singers and musicians would come to the town, appear on the stage, and perform for audiences. [There was no nightclub in the 1960s.] Besides the theater, there was also at least one new kind of coffeehouse. One of the new nationalist regulations permitted women to work as waitresses in the coffeehouses. [There was no such coffeehouse in the 1960s.] To encourage this reform, local officials declared that the prices in coffeehouses with men rather than women waiters would have to be set higher. Someone, either a state official or a private party, set up a coffeehouse with women waiters and a group of musicians and permitted the patrons to dance. [There was no public dancing in the 1960s.] Some of the local youths began to attend this establishment, going there to smoke cigarettes, have the girls wait on them, and dance among themselves. They considered themselves very modern and very revolutionary. [There was no place where young men could drink or smoke in the 1960s.] Soon there were disturbances in the coffeehouses, as the young men quarreled with one another and fights broke out. Unwilling to tolerate this, local state officials revoked the experiment, called in a minivan [sic], and packed off the women and the musicians to Trabzon. Still, these kinds of excesses had changed the relationship of fathers and sons. Sons became less respectful of their fathers. The young men no longer went to the mosque or the Friday prayers. They failed to keep the fast during Ramadan. [In the 1960s, by contrast, it was uncommon for young men in the town to avoid the weekly prayers or to break the fast.]

It is not surprising that the revolution, by which the state system had moved to overturn the state society, was remembered as a moment of filial rebellion. The Kemalists had reinforced the ligaments of official authority even as they had also relaxed the ligaments of social authority. Every citizen now had to wear a hat instead of a fez, so why should one attend to fathers and uncles who had worn the fez instead of a hat? But then, as we have already seen, memory can play tricks. The recollection of the unraveling of social and familial hierarchy has to be put in the context of a revolution that promised more than it eventually delivered.

Let us return to the last half of my interlocutor's account of the deposition of Ferhat Agha:

> The district officer ordered Ferhat Agha out of the office and announced that a new mayor would be chosen. The district officer and Ferhat Agha then entered into negotiations. They agreed that a new mayor would be appointed, but by their mutual approval. It was then that Hasan [surname omitted] was appointed to the mayoralty, which he held for six or seven years. He was a physician, and he spoke some French. We knew this because one day a boat stopped here and a French general and his wife disembarked at the pier. Hasan [surname omitted] received them and spoke French to them. The Frenchman wore a little brimmed pillbox hat [*kepi*] and was named De Limerjine, which everyone understood as "Crazy Merjin" (*Deli Mercin*).

To a point, this memory fits the previous recollection of moral laxity and decline. Speaking to me in 1967, my interlocutor was recalling how the Oflus had become aware of a part of the physician's consciousness that was otherwise hidden from them. This had come about when he had come into contact with foreigners whose dress and manners were incongruous, if not absurd. The new mayor had welcomed a Frenchman who was said to be a general in that nation's army, but he stepped off the boat in the company of his wife, wore a funny little brimmed hat, and had the same title as an irregular soldier under the old imperial regime. Some general! Some nation!

The two "asides" that appear in the account of the deposition of Ferhat Agha are equally revealing. After a show of force, we are told, the district officer and Ferhat Agha had "entered into negotiations," and eventually they agreed that a new mayor would be appointed "by their mutual approval." These are signs that the practices of the old regime would continue to be the practice of the new regime. Kemalist ideology and institutions might have been designed to replace the old state society with a new nation of citizens in the long run, but the state system would continue to work through the old state society in the short run.

By this assessment of the deposition of Ferhat Agha, the reforms of the early Republic bear a resemblance to the reforms of the late Empire. Whenever the state system was strong and the state society was weak, the provincial governor had confronted local elites in the eastern coastal districts, sometimes deposing them from state offices and replacing them. When the provincial governor did so, he chose successors in order to insure the cooperation and assistance of those he had dismissed. Similarly, the district officer who deposed Ferhat Agha understood that it was best to make gestures of deference to this man rather than ignore him. The district officer in question, who is remembered as exceptionally intelligent and competent, was also more pragmatic and less ideological than some of his successors.

The aforementioned Hasan, the physician, continued as mayor of the town for about five years (not six or seven as my interlocutor stated). He was then briefly succeeded by yet another member of the Selimoğlu family line, by circumstances about which I have no information. The more interesting period of the mayoralty begins sometime later during the early 1930s, not long after the death of Ferhat Agha.

THE SELIMOĞLU FAMILY LINE DURING THE EARLY REPUBLIC

Mehmet Selimoğlu was born in 1901 in the interior "home" village of the Selimoğlu family line, about twenty kilometers up the western valley-system.[31] At some point, he attended a middle school (*rüşdiye*), probably in the town of Of. Later, he dabbled in "trade and farming," probably in the town of Of. In 1927, the year after the deposition of Ferhat Agha, he joined the Republican People's Party. He was elected chairman of the RPP in the district of Of in 1932, and he was elected mayor of the town in 1934. He continued to hold both of these offices until he was elected to represent the province of Trabzon in the National Assembly in 1946.

Mehmet was remembered as educated (*tahsilli*), bright (*zeki*), and energetic (*çalışkan*). He had come of age during the first years of the nationalist movement. He had entered politics at the beginning of the one-party period. He had become mayor at the high point of the program of reforms. His assumption of the mayoralty therefore marks the definitive replacement of the old order by the new order. How was it, then, that the local transition from Empire to Republic resulted in a local public official, later a national public official, that eventually emerged as a leading individual from a large family grouping?

As it happened, Mehmet Selimoğlu was not at all well placed in his family line at the beginning of his mayoralty. He was not descended from Ferhat Agha or any other prominent member of the Selimoğlu during the late imperial period. He was from the interior "home" village of the family line, and so not a member of any of the "sets" (*takımlar*) of the family line that were most numerous and visible in the town of Of.[32] He did not have a large number of brothers, uncles, or cousins, since he was also not part of any large set of the family line in the home village. He married an older woman only

31. A short biography appeared in the *Halk Gazetesi* (Apr. 28, 1949).

32. Each of these sets were built around a core agnatic lineage of the family line, as in the instance of the sons and grandsons of Ferhat Agha (see fig. 2). I use "set" in the place of "lineage," there being a local term for the former but not the latter.

after he had become mayor, did not have any children afterward, and so was not in a position to consolidate a wide circle of agnates, relatives, and friends. He was maternally (not paternally) related to a set of the family line in the town, but the relationship was strained by an earlier event of bride abduction followed by a vengeance murder in the 1910s. There were rumors that the sons of Ferhat Agha had abused and humiliated him when he was a boy. So he would not have had especially warm feelings for the set of Ferhat Agha, which was the largest circle of agnates, relatives, and friends in the town of Of. My interlocutors who were old enough to recall Mehmet Selimoğlu as a youth referred to him as "Little Mehmet" (*Küçük Mehmet*). The nickname is significant. He was "Little Mehmet," that is, not "Big Mehmet," a son of Ferhat Agha, who was senior to him. So "Little Mehmet" was not initially a leading individual of his family line.

At the time, any young man of the Selimoğlu who had become a Kemalist would not have been well positioned in the patronymic group. The senior prominent members of the family line were too closely wedded to the old regime to be able to adapt themselves to the new regime. Accordingly, Mehmet became mayor of the town without resorting to the old state society. And after becoming mayor of the town, he continued to remain apart from the vertical and horizontal solidarities of the old state society. That is to say, he made no move to use the office of mayor to consolidate a broad circle of agnates, relatives, and friends. On the contrary, during most of the decade he served as mayor, his associates were drawn from a narrow circle of district officials, civil servants, professionals, and merchants. He had become the mayor of bureaucrats, businessmen, and professionals in a small town where there were not very many of these representatives of the new modernity. By my estimation, his core constituency would have roughly consisted of five bureaucrats, one military officer, two judges, three lawyers, one doctor, five teachers, seven merchants, and three businessmen, some of who were not Oflus. All of these individuals would have been members of the RPP, and hence more or less radical secularists. Accordingly, Mehmet Selimoğlu felt no need to display himself in public as a believer, and he is not remembered as a man who was religiously observant. On the contrary, he is said to have had a number of unfortunate petty vices, including drinking and partying.

Mehmet Selimoğlu had personal qualities that had never before had a bearing on the rise to prominence of an individual in the district of Of, qualities that had no relationship to aghas and agha-families or hodjas and medreses. But even though his education, intelligence, and energy must be acknowledged, it was also the case that he would have been only one of a number of exceptional individuals in the town of Of, and therefore only one of several potential candidates for the mayoralty. That the Kemalist leadership nonetheless selected Mehmet Selimoğlu points to a policy of relying on local elites of the old regime. That is to say, they accepted one of the Selimoğlu. And in doing so, they may even have thought he was a leading individual of this large family grouping.

The response to another radical measure of the program of reform, enacted during the same year that Mehmet became mayor, provides further evidence of this peculiar situation. The Name Law of 1934 required every citizen to adopt an official surname. It was at this time that the man who had been Mustafa Kemal became Kemal Atatürk. Similarly, all the citizens in the district of Of also chose new surnames. At this point the correction of a common misunderstanding is required.

It has been observed that "the Turks, like most other Muslim peoples, were not in the habit of using family names."[33] Surnames were indeed exceptional, although not unknown, in many parts of the country. However, there were appellations that resembled surnames in the rural areas of much of Anatolia. It was commonly the case that a collection of agnatically related households in a village might designate themselves by a collective name. So household or family groupings sometimes chose surnames that were derived from these lineage or tribal names. But they more typically chose a new surname from lists of officially approved surnames, since the lineage or tribal appellations were not always understood to refer to a family line.

Otherwise, it is not at all accurate to say that the Turks were not in the habit of using what could be regarded as surnames. Everywhere in the districts of Anatolia, from the seventeenth century forward, if not earlier, there were individuals who were designated by reference to the name of their family line. This was especially the case in the eastern coastal districts, where names of family lines were a matter of paramount significance. As I have already pointed out in chapter 1, the names of family lines, whether in the "*oğlu*" or the "*zade*" form, were used, both officially and nonofficially, to refer to the principal figures of the old state society.

Unlike the lineage or tribal names elsewhere in rural Anatolia, these patronymics did not mark a person as a country bumpkin. Instead, they

33. Lewis 1961, 283.

confirmed standing and position in the imperial system; hence, many individuals were loath to surrender them.[34] Consequently, the old patronymics commonly, although not invariably, became the basis for the new surnames, simply by eliding the suffix. In the district of Of, for example, Selimoğlu became Selim, Muradoğlu became Murad, while Tellioğlu became Öztel, Bektaşoğlu became Bektaş, Şisikoğlu became Şişik, and Abdikoğlu became Abdik.[35] The application of the Name Law of 1934 is therefore of utmost interest as an indicator of the transition from the old republic to the new republic.

As the deadline for selecting surnames approached (January 1, 1935), there were disagreements, even heated quarrels, among the members of some large family groupings. As we have already seen, these conglomerations of hundreds of households were comprised of a variety of sets (*takımlar*), and each set was the potential basis for a faction. The members of different sets were sometimes tempted to formalize these latent cleavages, designating themselves by distinctive surnames. Concerned that such disputes might actually lead to civil disorders, the district officer is said to have taken steps to insure that the members of large family groupings all agreed to adopt the same surname. In one instance, it is recalled, he went to the length of summoning all the elders (*büyükler*) of the Tellioğlu, a large family grouping in the vicinity of the sub-district center. They had been quarreling about the adoption of a surname, and the sets were on the brink of splitting into different groupings. The district officer told the elders they were the most numerous family in the area and should stay together. He then informed them that he would himself choose their new surname by preserving in some way their old family name. Thereupon he dubbed them with the new surname "Öztel." So in this instance, a district officer, who is recalled as an ardent Kemalist, arranged for the continuation of the legacy of aghas and agha-families. He had done so as a practical measure of preserving the working relationship of the new state system with the old state society. He was a revolutionary in principle, but a conservative in practice.

34. Each patronymic has a learned, written form in Ottoman, where the Persian suffix "*zade*" replaces the Turkic "*oğlu*." So one also encounters the older Ottoman variants, Selimzade and Muradzade. This would be a pretentious usage during the Turkish Republic, but I have encountered it a few times.

35. It is possible that elision of the suffix was common in informal usage even before the Name Law. Today one often hears the usage "the Murads" (Muradlar), "the Selim" (Selimler), "the Şişiks" (Şişikler), "the Abdiks" (Abdikler), and others.

However, in still another instance, a leading individual from a large family grouping specifically chose to disassociate himself from his agnatic relatives. After January 1, 1935, Mehmet Selimoğlu became Mehmet Sayın, designating himself by a surname that does not seem to have been adopted by any other member of his patronymic group. The name he chose was a neologism, a "New Turkish" creation of the language reform that meant "esteemed" or "respected." At the same time, most of the other members of the family line had adopted the official surname of "Selim," thereby retaining a semantic hold on their old name, hence also a hold on its eminence.

Mehmet Sayın had chosen a surname that at the same time asserted his attachment to the program of reforms and his detachment from the other members of his family line. And whatever his intention, his new surname could not help but suggest that the old name he had explicitly refused was disrespected in that his new name was respected. So by the choice of his surname, Mehmet Sayın appears to have been a radical Kemalist; however, he was pushed by circumstance to become conservative in practice, even if he was a revolutionary in principle.

After Mehmet Sayın assumed the mayoralty, he began to accumulate other public offices as well. He became the chairman of the Turkish Air Association (*Türk Hava Kurumu*), chairman of the Red Crescent Society (*Kızılay Cemiyeti*), chairman of the Children's Protection Society (*Çocuk Esirgeme*), chairman of the Of People's House (*Of Halkevi*), and chairman of the RPP. He was also director of the Ferry Boat Agency (*Deniz Yolları Acenteliği*) and caretaker (*mütevelli*) for the endowment (*vakıf*) of the town mosque.[36] As my interlocutors remarked, "Little Mehmet was the government." In this regard, he had succeeded in fully "replacing" Ferhat Agha, who might also have been described in such terms. But if he was similar to his imperial predecessor, he was also different. He had begun as an outsider to his family line. He had disassociated himself from his agnates by choosing a unique surname, and he risen to prominence under the auspices of the one-party regime.

Although I have relatively good information about his accumulation of public offices, I have very little information about his motives. It is possible that Mehmet Sayın was in a certain sense forced to accumulate offices. Any local office that he allowed to escape his personal control would have been

36. The office of headman (*muhtar*) for the municipality had been abolished at this time.

commanded by a circle of agnates, relatives, and friends, most probably one that would be led by a member of his own family line. He may therefore have concluded that a local public official like himself would have to serve as the dike against the interpersonal associations of the old state society.

There is some evidence for this. In the course of acquiring public offices, Mehmet Sayın was sometimes obliged to anger members of his family line. For example, he became the director of the Ferry Agency, a public office more lucrative than most, only by removing one of the descendants of Ferhat Agha. More tellingly, perhaps, the one public office that he never succeeded in fully controlling appears to have remained in the hands of leading individuals from large family groupings. This was the directorship of the Agricultural Credit Cooperative, another that was more lucrative than most.

The organization of agricultural cooperatives had first begun during last years of the Empire. They were originally intended to curtail the dependence of producers on usurious loans, but they also served a number of other functions.[37] The cooperatives collected contributions from villagers in order to establish a capital fund. The same villagers could then apply for financial assistance as agricultural producers. The cooperatives bought tools and supplies in bulk at wholesale prices, passing along the benefit to the villagers. The cooperatives rented warehouses so that the villagers could store their crops until such time as they might be sold at the best price. And finally, the members of cooperatives were able to take advantage of government programs intended to stabilize prices and encourage production.[38]

The first Agricultural Credit Cooperative (*Tarım Kredi Kooperatifi*) was organized in the district of Of in 1931, before Mehmet Sayın had served as mayor.[39] Its first director earned himself the nickname "heathen imam"

37. The records of the cooperative show that a total of about 4,000 Turkish lira was made available in loans during the fiscal year 1933. The amount of loans outstanding and the number of members at the close of the fiscal year were not given. In 1937, the records show that a total of about 5,000 Turkish lira had been loaned to forty members by the end of the fiscal year.

38. I shall have some rather bleak things to say about the way in which cooperatives were run, but I do not mean to judge them as complete failures. They were organized to serve villagers, and eventually they did. Still, they could not escape the circumstances of the political transformation of which they were a part. I shall use them as examples to indicate the character and problems of that transformation, not to cast doubt on government assistance programs.

39. The cooperative movement had its beginnings in the late Ottoman period, primarily after the revolution of 1908 (Lewis 1961, 453).

(*gâvur imamı*). As for the cooperative, it became known as the "imam's bank" (*imam bankası*). This man appears to have achieved a minimal literacy by studying in one of the religious academies, although he was said to never perform his prayers or attend the mosque. According to the story told to me, the "heathen imam," "uneducated but clever" (*tahsilsiz fakat kurnaz*), would go to the villages where there were members of the cooperative, set up a table, lay out stacks of papers, and place two bags at his side, one on the left and the other on the right. The members would then come to him and sign papers that he presented to them. This done, he would take money from the bag on the left, give the signers a small percentage, and then drop most of the money in the bag on the right. He would then use this money to give loans to various relatives (*akraba*), friends (*arkadaş*), and youths (*delikanlı*) so that they became indebted to him and supported him.

The director of the Agricultural Credit Cooperative, together with some kind of executive council, was elected by its membership. This being the case, it would have been difficult for Mehmet Sayın to control the cooperative since he lacked a circle of agnates, relatives, friends, and partners among the villagers. On the other hand, the "heathen imam" had been a municipal employee of Ferhat Agha, and he was from a family line that had been associated with the Five Party during the previous century. So it is likely that the cooperative had remained in the possession of a circle of agnates, relatives, friends, and partners once centered on Ferhat Agha.

The Agricultural Credit Cooperative was probably the last bastion of the old state society in the town of Of. If it was, this would explain in part how it was that the descendants of Ferhat Agha came to monopolize the public life of the town during the 1940s.

OFFICIAL PRINCIPLE AND OFFICIAL PRACTICE

In the spring of 1939, a few months after the death of Kemal Atatürk, a resident of the provincial capital traveled to Of and reported on his short visit in one of its newspapers. During his stay in the town of Of, he had attended a public address made by Bay Mahmut [sic], a district officer who had recently been assigned to Of.[40] The visitor described how Bay Mahmut had

40. The titles "*bay*" and "*bayan*" can be compared to the French "*citoyen*" and "*citoyenne.*" The former, like the latter, were introduced when titles of the old regime, such as "*bey*" and "*hanım,*" were suppressed. Eventually, they lost currency and were replaced by more generalized usages of "*bey*" and "*hanım.*"

at one point praised the local gendarmes who had resisted the aghas. Turning to speak to a number of the gendarmes who were standing at his side, he had "opened fire" on the aghas:[41]

> "We will thrash the aghas. We will save the simple and pure folk from their influence, their execrable acts, and their deceits and tricks. We will not give them precedence in any manner, with respect to any thing or task." Then turning to the audience, he said, "I am saying this to you. If a villager comes to you, stand up, but if an agha comes before you, do not budge from your place." There were both aghas and villagers in this meeting; there were people from every class. Wherever there are aghas and those who depend on them, they [all of them] are covered in shame, while the people and the villagers are rearing up with thankfulness and gratitude over their downfallen pride.[42]

According to the memory of my interlocutors, government campaigns against aghas during the 1930s were not always limited to denunciation and invective. Sometimes villagers dared to lodge complaints with district officials against a leading individual from a large family grouping. When villagers did so, the gendarmes sometimes arrested and jailed the accused, or even beat him on the spot. Villagers of the "common class" (*ehali takımı, ehali millet*) also began to refuse to assist the descendants of aghas, seeing that the state no longer favored them. Some said the descendants of the aghas, if not the aghas themselves, fell on hard times. The grandsons of Ferhat Agha, later to become prominent public officials, were obliged to work as janitors or waiters. Tellingly, the old gestures of homage, such as stooping to kiss a patron's hand, vanished from public life. Even when a villager of the common class attempted such a gesture of homage, the descendants of aghas began to refuse such gestures.

At the same time, as we have seen, the transition from the old to the new forms of dress and manners was imperfect. As the example of the Name Law indicates, provincial state officials had continued governmental practices that were not consistent with revolutionary ideology and institutions. They might move against an agha or a descendant of an agha in this or that instance. In other ways, they would have chosen to work through leading individuals from large family groupings, or even to support the social think-

41. In all likelihood, the speech against aghas as given by the district officer of Of in April 1939 was also a commemoration of Atatürk.

42. The article was titled "Impressions of a Trip from Trabzon to Of" (*Trabzondan Ofa Gidiş Gelişin Intibaları*) and appeared in *Yeni Yol*, Apr. 22, 1939.

ing and practice on which their position and influence depended. The predicament of Mehmet Sayın was a result of this compromise of principle by practice. He had been officially favored because he was a member of the most prominent family line of the imperial period, but he was obliged to prevent leading individuals from large family groupings from once again dominating the public life of the town and district.

10 Democracy

The Old Republic Inhabits the New Republic

THE TRANSITION FROM THE ONE-PARTY TO THE MULTIPARTY REGIME

In this chapter, I shall explain how the move from a one-party to a multiparty regime vivified both district networks and coastal coalitions. Leading individuals from the Selimoğlu and the Muradoğlu once again came to dominate public life as each aligned himself with one of two national political parties. This development illustrates how the behavioral foundations of the old state society remained in place during the first two decades of the Turkish Republic despite the revolution in public culture.

In April 1945, the National Assembly in Ankara ratified the Charter of the United Nations, confirming membership of the Turkish Republic in that international organization. At the time, some members of the Republican People's Party were already recommending reforms that would bring Turkey into closer alignment with the democratic principles of the new international organization.[1] Then, on November 1, 1945, President İsmet İnönü gave a speech to the National Assembly in which he announced a change in the political system. Opposition parties would soon be allowed to form, after which free and direct elections would occur.[2]

Although the first "free and direct" elections would be held only a few months after İnönü's speech, it would be some years before the RPP allowed

1. Zürcher (1993, 219) concludes that the shift from a one-party to a multiparty system had domestic as well as international causes.

2. İnönü had succeeded to the presidency upon the death of Atatürk in 1938. According to Zürcher (1993, 221), he had first indicated his support for a multiparty system during his parliamentary speech on November 1, 1944.

itself to be challenged by the opposition. At the national level, some party leaders remained vigorously opposed to any weakening of the one-party system, seeing it as the instrument by which the state could both guide and mold the population. And at the local level, many party members of the RPP were loath to contemplate any changes that would upset the framework of patronage and clientage associated with the RPP. The district of Of provides a case in point.

In the summer of 1945, the president of the Republic was traveling by motorcade along the eastern Black Sea coast. Arriving in the town of Of, his entourage stopped in order to offer encouragement to local party activists. During the brief visit, I was told, Mehmet Sayın was presented to İsmet Pasha [sic], who greeted him warmly. As my interlocutor recollected this occasion, he remarked, "It was then that we knew for sure that he had been 'chosen' (*seçilmiş*) [to represent the province of Trabzon in the National Assembly]."

As for Mehmet, one can guess that he had been calculating his chances for some years. And in doing so, he would have understood that his rise to national prominence was contingent on firm control of his local political base, whether there was a one-party or a multiparty system. And so he had already begun thinking of himself as a leading individual from a large family grouping. Before examining how he did so, I must first explain the obstacles to his transformation.

RIVALRIES AMONG THE FAMILY LINE

Mehmet could only become the key figure in a circle of interpersonal association with the support of the Selimoğlu. But his family line carried a heavy burden of history. The sets (*takımlar*) of the Selimoğlu had vied with one another for prominence. On rare occasions, they had come into serious conflict with one another. So Mehmet could not just assume that all the members of his family line would support him. He would have to take steps to address an undertow of resentments and jealousies.

One of the most serious incidents had taken place during the interregnum between the Empire and Republic in the home village of the Selimoğlu. Sometime in 1922, a young man of the family line had abducted (*kaçırdı*) a young woman of the family line with the intention of marrying her. In response, another young man of the family line organized a party of men and succeeded in taking back the young woman. Afterward, it was discovered that the abductor had sexual relations with her (*onu bozdu*), thereby ruining her chances for a suitable match in the future. Thus began a series of events that concluded with the shooting and death of a friend of the abductor, yet another young man of the family line, but a resident of the town of Of, not the home village.

One of my acquaintances told me the story in the 1960s in order to explain the cleavages in the family line. In the citations of my field notes that follow, I have substituted the terms "the abductor," "the rescuer," and "the friend" in brackets whenever my interlocutor mentioned the personal names of those involved:

> At the time of the kidnapping, the government was weak and self-help was common. All the men in the district of Of used to go about armed with pistols and rifles. One could not depend on the police or the courts for justice, and the resort to weapons was not all that uncommon. So when the woman was at last taken back to her family [by the rescuer], and it became known that she had been raped, there was plenty of anger all around and a good chance of further trouble. For his part, [the abductor] of the woman set about to take revenge on [the rescuer] for having taken her back.
>
> Some years before, [the rescuer] had been appointed as a minor official in charge of a government warehouse. Taking advantage of his position, he had sold all the goods that were stored there, pocketed the money, and then burned the warehouse to cover his tracks. Knowing this, [the abductor] began to urge Rasih Efendi [the father of his friend] to go to the government with this story of theft and arson. After he did so, [the rescuer] was soon arrested and brought to trial. However, on the very day he was taken by the gendarmes to appear in court, he evaded his guards, escaped through a back door, and went into hiding in the mountains.

As we have seen in earlier chapters, gender relations played an important role in social standing in the district of Of. Setting aside the issue of emotional attachments, of fathers and daughters as well as of young men and women, the arrangement of marriages was the very stuff of interpersonal association, and hence of district social networks. Ultimately, there could be no leading individuals, and thus no large family groupings, without the regulation of the giving and receiving of women in marriage. An abduction of a young woman would have normally ended in a settlement between the two families involved. The rescue of the young woman made such an outcome less likely on this occasion, but it still would have been possible for a settlement to be reached. When the rape became public knowledge, it became a genuine challenge, if not impossible, to bring the aggrieved parties into agreement. The informing of the police, however, represented a serious deterioration of the situation. Once the quarrel fell into the hands of state officials, it was almost impossible for the members of the family line to resolve it. Then, a chance incident caused a bitter division between the sets of the family line, both those in the village and those in the town. My interlocutor gave me the following account:

> During the following summer, [the rescuer] began to roam about the highland pastures (*yayla*) with a gang of armed men looking for trouble. One day, by chance, as they were loitering about a mosque in one of the summer settlements, by a bad turn of luck, their worst enemies happened to come along, [the abductor] and his friend [the son of Rasih Efendi, the informer]. The two men came by singly, one about a hundred meters behind the other, [first the friend and then the abductor]. After [the friend] had passed the mosque, the party of [the rescuer] began firing on him, striking him once in the shoulder. Both [the abductor] and [the friend] fell to the ground and returned the fire so that [the rescuer] and his group took cover near the mosque. But now another member of their party, who had been napping in a nearby house, was awakened by the shots. Taking his rifle, he came out to discover [the friend of the abductor] lying on the ground before his house, firing at his comrades near the mosque. There and then he shot [the friend of the abductor] dead from behind. Hearing the gunfire, a number of women had by now come out of the houses in an effort to stop the fighting. Seeing that [the friend of the abductor] was already dead, they brought rugs (*kilim*), wrapped both [the abductor] and [the friend] in them, and carried their bodies away as though both were dead. [The rescuer] and his group wanted to assure themselves that the two of them had been killed, but the women would not allow them to do so. [The abductor] had not even been hit once, and so the women were able to save him. As for the party of [the rescuer], they went out in the highland pastures to dance and sing in celebration of having killed their enemies.

After the murder, supporters of the two sides traded charges and countercharges, each blaming the other for the outbreak of violence. Although the principals were reputed troublemakers, the dispute focused on the question of who had or had not conformed with social norms:

> Some said that [the friend] had said "*selamün aleyküm*" to the party of [the rescuer] as he passed them, but had received no "*aleyküm selam*" in return; even so, he continued on his way minding his own business. Others said [the friend of the abductor] did not say "*selamün aleyküm,*" but passed by without speaking and then started to fire at them from a distance. Still others said that [the friend of the abductor] had said, "I will fuck the mothers and daughters of the lot of you!" (*Topunuzun anasını avradını sikeceğim!*) The party of [the rescuer] themselves offered excuses. "Why should we have attacked him? They were only two and we were many. We had nothing to fear."

By the preceding account, the abduction and recovery of the young woman had moved into the background as a justification. In their place, the principals traded accusations of impropriety. This shift of attention probably began to occur even as the news of the shooting reached the village and the town. The abduction and rescue had spiraled out of control, threatening the solidarity of the family line, and even the hierarchy of social relations in the district of Of. My interlocutor concluded his account by describing the falling out of the members of the family line, as well as the criticism of Ferhat Agha:

> When the news reached the Selimoğlu in the district center, they were furious with the Selimoğlu of the village [because a senseless quarrel in the village had resulted in the death of the son of a prominent individual of the family line in the town]. Young men of the Selimoğlu in the district center broke the windows in a house that was owned by the father of [the rescuer], and they tried to catch his brother, who was able to escape to Sürmene by boat. To demonstrate their friendship [with the Selimoğlu of the district center], their friends and allies came from their villages and offered to help track down [the rescuer]. Rasih Efendi was of course especially upset about the murder of his son, and his three surviving sons were no less upset. They openly blamed Ferhat Agha for allowing such a thing to happen, not only in his area, but also in his family line, for which he was held responsible.

My interlocutor then concluded his story by describing how its legacy of bitter memories scarred the relationships of members of the family line for years to come:

> [The rescuer], who was held responsible for the death of [the friend of the abductor], was eventually caught and sentenced to a long jail term, but freed a few years later by amnesty. His close relatives [among the Selimoğlu of the village] did not come to the town for several years, and [the rescuer] himself did not dare show his face there until after the death of Ferhat Agha in 1931.

At the time, Mehmet was situated exactly in the middle of all those members of his family line in the village who had been involved. He was a close paternal cousin of the rescuer, and so also of the father of the young woman who had been abducted. At the same time, he was also the maternal half-brother of the friend who had been murdered, and so also close to those who had abducted the young woman and then informed on the rescuer.

During the 1930s, after Mehmet had become mayor, the memory of the abduction, rescue, and murder complicated his relationships with the sets of the family line in the town. As I have explained, the sons of Rasih Efendi and descendants of Ferhat Agha had been angered by the members of the family line in the village, just as their relationships with one another had been embittered when the former blamed the latter for not insuring the peace. So Mehmet did not have the best relations with the sons of Rasih Efendi (his half-brothers) because of his connections with the rescuer and his associates, and he did not have the best relations with the descendants of Ferhat Agha since he was connected with the sons of Rasih. All these hard feelings were compounded by the fact that he, an obscure member of the family line from the village, had become mayor, rather than a prominent member of the family line from the town.

So Mehmet was more or less distrusted by all the sets of the family line in both the town and the village. But he was also in a position to ally himself with any set of the family line, since he was equally close to all, even as he was equally distant. During the 1930s, his relations with his agnates appear to have been more in the register of distrust than alliance. He had chosen a surname different from all his agnatic relatives. He had managed to garner for himself almost every public office open to a local resident, in effect preventing his agnates from doing so. In acquiring these public offices, moreover, he had brought about the dismissal of a Selimoğlu on more than one occasion, giving rise to resentment among both the descendants of Ferhat Agha and the sons of Rasih Efendi. By the early 1940s, he had begun to work with individuals of these two sets of the family line, but he could not yet be described as a leading individual from a large family grouping.

MEHMET BEY AND THE DESCENDANTS OF FERHAT AGHA IN THE ELECTIONS OF 1946

By the winter of 1945, Mehmet was still contemplating his elevation to the National Assembly sometime during the general national elections, then formally scheduled for 1947. At the same time, he had just become aware that he might have to face an opponent in what might well be a free and direct election. It was in this context that he made a decisive move to become the leading individual of his large family grouping. During a meeting of the executive council of the local branch of the RPP, Mehmet surrendered his membership and chairmanship in that governing body. On this same occasion, a son of Rasih Efendi and a son of Ferhat Agha were elected to the executive council, the former as its chairman and the second as a member.[3]

3. See the *Halk Gazetesi,* winter of 1945. The two individuals were among seven men elected as members of the executive council by all in attendance. The son of Ferhat Agha, in a tie with one other man, received the most votes of all those

So Mehmet had ceded his positions to senior members of two sets of the family line in the town, preparing for a new era when popular support would perhaps play a larger role in the political process.

On January 7, 1946, former members of the RPP registered the Democrat Party (*Demokrat Partisi*) as an opposition party in anticipation of a general national election the following year. Alarmed by the party's enthusiastic reception among the public, the leadership of the RPP decided to hold the elections immediately. On the occasion of the national RPP congress in May, before any branches of the new party had yet been opened in the province of Trabzon, it was declared that municipal elections would take place immediately, and national elections would quickly follow in the summer.[4] The leadership of the DP decided to boycott the snap municipal elections but entered the national elections nonetheless. Although direct and free in principle, both the municipal and national elections fell far short of such an achievement, especially in the eastern coastal districts (by then divided among the provinces of Rize, Trabzon, Giresun, and Ordu). The first branch of the DP had not been opened in the town of Trabzon until June 1946, the same month as the municipal elections and only shortly before the national elections. In addition to having a late start, the opposition party was also faced with a corrupt electoral process, the casting and counting of votes being obviously rigged in many places.

The news of imminent elections would have caught Mehmet off guard as much as his potential opponents in the town of Of. He was obliged to accelerate his plans to devolve his local offices to members of his family line. He decided to allow (or perhaps he could not prevent) the descendants of Ferhat Agha to seize the public offices open to local residents in the town of Of. Yakup, a son of Ferhat Agha, ran successfully for the office of mayor, a position he was to retain for twenty-seven years. Yusuf, a grandson of Ferhat Agha, ran successfully for the newly revived office of town headman (*muhtar*), serving until 1952, when he was succeeded by another member of the family line (see fig. 2).

As it happened, Mehmet had recently done a favor for the man who would succeed him as mayor. When Yakup's house had burned down not long before, he had directed a public campaign to raise contributions for rebuilding his residence. So he may have been cultivating Yakup as his own

elected to the executive council (twenty-five votes each). The son of Rasih Efendi was afterward elected by the seven members of the executive council as their chairman, replacing the former chairman, Mehmet Sayın.

4. Lewis 1961, 298–300.

personal representative in the town of Of. On the other hand, it is more likely that he was forced to favor the descendants of Ferhat Agha over the sons of Rasih Efendi. When the "heathen imam" was removed from the Agricultural Credit Cooperative a few years earlier, Salih, the younger brother of Yusuf, had become its director, even though he was virtually an adolescent at the time. And when the Hazelnut Marketing Cooperative was organized in the same year as the national and municipal elections, Eşref (a son of Ferhat Agha) was appointed as accountant, then as director three years later (see fig. 2). These developments are further evidence that cooperatives, having leaders elected by a large membership, inevitably became the special preserve of leading individuals from large family groupings.

So by the time of the municipal elections of 1946, the configuration of local offices, more or less as I discovered it twenty years later, was coming into place in the town of Of. The very set of the Selimoğlu that would have been the primary target of campaigns against aghas and agha-families in the 1930s was dominating the public offices in the town of Of. Two months after the municipal elections, Mehmet was himself elected as a member of the National Assembly for the province of Trabzon. And from this time forward he is locally remembered as "Mehmet Bey," an appellation that designated someone who held a position in the state system.[5] He had therefore doubly transformed himself by the results of the municipal and national elections. He was no longer the mayor of a town with a narrow constituency of officials, civil servants, professionals, and merchants. He had newly become a member of parliament in Ankara, even as he had also newly become the patron of the descendants of Ferhat Agha. But he was not yet, as we shall see, a leading individual from a large family grouping.

The RPP had emerged relatively unscathed from the municipal and national elections in most parts of the country; nonetheless, the one-party system had been seriously destabilized. The DP had received substantial numbers of votes in some places, even if it had not done especially well in the eastern coastal districts, suggesting that the arrival of a multiparty system would also mean the defeat of the RPP. In the aftermath of the elections in Trabzon, the provincial newspapers that sided with the opposition began to

5. Although the title *bey* had been abolished along with the Sultanate and the Caliphate, informally it had never fully lost currency in the district of Of. It was used to refer to anyone who had served as a state official. So far as I know, Hasan Bey Selimzade was the only other member of the family line accorded the title. He had been appointed as a sub-district officer (*nahiye müdürü*) sometime during the late nineteenth century.

report mass resignations from the RPP and a surge of support for the DP. The victories of Mehmet, Yakup, and Yusuf were also accompanied by a certain amount of local unrest. The DP had received no more than ten votes in the town of Of; nonetheless, Mehmet Bey did not enjoy broad popular support. Even some members of the Selimoğlu family line were ready to join any kind of credible opposition.

Mehmet Bey, member of the National Assembly and resident of Ankara, received news of the unrest among his constituency during the winter of 1946 and hastily organized a trip back to the district of Of to put things back in order. After he arrived, he immediately began to make the rounds of his supporters, especially those who were said to be displeased and contemplating resignation. He promised them this perk or that office, if only they would give up the idea of joining the opposition party. By these moves, so I was told, he managed to halt, and even reverse, the resignations. Those who had recently joined the DP began to rejoin the RPP. Mehmet Bey was almost completely successful in suppressing support for the new opposition party. The members of the DP had been reduced, some of my interlocutors claimed, to a mere handful. Even so, the handful in question included prominent members of the family line.

On the occasion of his visit, Mehmet Bey had been unable to appease his three half-brothers, the sons of Rasih Efendi. They resented the favors that he had granted the descendants of Ferhat Agha, whom they saw as their rivals. Why had he preferred these other Selimoğlu when they were more closely related and just as active in public affairs? Mehmet Bey had all along attempted to curry their support and grant them favors. During the winter of 1945, as already mentioned, the eldest had been elected chairman of the executive committee of the RPP. But this had not been nearly enough for his three half-brothers. They felt they had assisted in insuring the election victory in 1946. They believed they deserved to enjoy its full fruits but had instead been pushed aside by the descendants of Ferhat Agha. Now, in the winter of 1946, they were on the verge of resigning from the RPP and going over to the DP, thereby openly splitting the family line. During his visit Mehmet Bey therefore resumed his efforts to pressure his half-brothers to remain within the RPP fold. One day, two of them were summoned to the government building. There they were received by both the district officer of Of and a member of the National Assembly, who lectured them about the virtues of loyalty and the vices of conflict. They were informed that there was no need for an opposition party in the district. Reportedly, the sons of Rasih Efendi could not be mollified and remained determined to become activists in the new opposition party, the DP.

Unable to dissuade them in the usual ways, Mehmet Bey had at least isolated his half-brothers so that they had little support from the family line. He returned to Ankara reasonably confident that the DP was weakening in the district of Of. In the town itself, he had nothing to worry about other than a few jealous relatives who had never been entirely happy with him. Some months later, an incident took place in the town that was designed to confirm the collapse of the DP as an alternative to the RPP. One night, a raid was carried out on the DP's newly opened town headquarters. Someone had broken into the office, destroyed all the records of membership, and carried away the chairs, tables, and typewriter, leaving nothing but a bare room. A few days later, most of these items were discovered to have been dumped into the nearby river. According to rumor, word had come down to the police some days before that they should look the other way on that night. Regardless of whoever was responsible for it, the sacking of the DP headquarters had a clear meaning. In the town of Of, anyone who chose to join the DP would have to face the descendants of Ferhat Agha at the local level, and the one-party regime at the national level.

THE RESURGENCE OF THE OLD REPUBLIC IN THE ELECTIONS OF 1950

If indeed they had given the go-ahead for the raid, the local leadership of the RPP had not sufficiently analyzed the situation. The possibility of a shift from a one-party to a multiparty system had brought into view a new kind of political equation. Since the members of the National Assembly were henceforth to be chosen in direct and free elections, anyone at the local level who could turn out thousands of votes would have a claim on the leadership of a political party. And if a particular political party succeeded in winning a national election, then the person who could produce thousands of votes would also be able to make things happen at the level of the state system.

By the later 1940s, this new political equation was on the horizon. The leadership of both the RPP and the DP had made contact with local elites of the regional social oligarchy in the provinces of Rize, Trabzon, Giresun, and Ordu. According to an announcement in a provincial newspaper that appeared on July 1, 1949, Reşat Agha Muradoğlu, together with his two sons, had resigned from the RPP in order to join the DP. Reşat Agha was a direct descendant of the first several generations of aghas of the Muradoğlu family line, one of the last of the local elites in the old imperial style. The news of his support for the DP caused a sensation in the district of Of and near panic among the local RPP activists in the town, given the prospect of national elections in the spring of the following year. There were many more members of the Muradoğlu than members of the Selimoğlu. Furthermore, the former had a reputation for sticking together, while the latter had a reputation for quarreling among themselves. More significantly, the countrified Muradoğlu were themselves farmers who resided in their villages, and so they were potentially able to communicate with the average Oflu much more effectively than the citified Selimoğlu, who sat in offices behind desks in the district center. In other words, the Muradoğlu had a more extensive and a more operational district network of agnates, relatives, friends, and partners. Some of the descendants of Ferhat Agha, who had a clear understanding of what their rivals might be able to accomplish, feared that Reşat Agha might personally be able to sway the votes of a major segment of the rural population. Mehmet Bey himself, too long accustomed to the elitist and statist practices of the RPP, still had an imperfect understanding of the electoral importance of numbers, solidarity, and populism. Asked about Muradoğlu support for the DP during a Giresun congress of the RPP, he appeared unconcerned. "These shepherds (*çoban*) might attract five thousands votes," he is said to have replied, "but what is that going to get them?" As it happened, Mehmet Bey had counted correctly but reached the wrong conclusion.

Receiving word of Mehmet Bey's insult, "The Muradoğlu are nothing but shepherds," Reşat Agha became all the more determined to bring out a massive vote for the DP by mobilizing his relatives, friends, partners, and allies. He is reported to have toured the villages, specifically telling his audiences that they should not be afraid to vote for the DP. He would see to it personally that they would not be subject to reprisals. The first sacking of the DP offices had been the last. With the assistance of his two sons, both men of strong character and determination, Reşat Agha could energize a circle of interpersonal association for the purpose of bringing out a large vote for the DP in the national election. At the local level, electoral politics and party organizations were reawakening the legacy of the leading individuals, family lines, and district social networks. The mechanisms of social relations that had been able to pour seven or eight hundred men in arms into the district center as late as 1908 were now being used as a means to bring out the vote.

So Mehmet Bey, whose only solid constituency had once been a narrow circle of officials, civil servants, professionals, and merchants in the town, was in deep trouble. He was openly opposed by the sons of Rasih Efendi, his half-brothers, who had joined the DP in the belief that he had slighted them in the distribution of favors. Leading individuals among the Muradoğlu were touring the villages to bring out their friends, relatives, and partners to the polls. His control of the town of Of was slipping away to his clients, the descendants of Ferhat Agha, the latter having always believed that he had usurped their rightful position. And resentful of the descendants of Ferhat Agha, the sons of Rasih Efendi were also touring the villages to urge their agnates, relatives, friends, and partners to support the DP. But worst of all, the political party through whose ranks he had risen was facing the possibility of a resounding electoral defeat.

It is at this point that Mehmet Bey made a belated move to become a leading individual from a large family grouping. He assumed a new name. Formerly known as Mehmet Bey Sayın, he now became known as Mehmet Bey Selimoğlu.[6] He was far from being the first or the only person of his family line to make an adjustment in his surname. On the contrary, he was among the last. For some years, the members of large family groupings in the coastal region had been reverting back to the original form of their old patronymics, even with the addition of the suffix "*oğlu*" (occasionally even using "*zade*"). In a few instances, large family groupings that had actually split their surnames, despite the counsel of state officials, reunited as they reverted to the old patronymic.[7] The prospect of free and direct elections of the representatives of the National Assembly had given a new meaning to the old vertical and horizontal solidarities. The old republic was acquiring a new purpose and becoming a political force in the new republic.

The DP roundly defeated the RPP in the national elections held in May 1950.[8] The fortunes of the two parties were, however, mixed in the provinces of Rize, Trabzon, Giresun, and Ordu, the part of the coastal region that formerly comprised the old province of Trabzon. The DP did very

6. In a notice about the RPP congress in Of that appeared in *Yeni Yol*, dated December 1, 1939, he is referred to as "Mehmet Sayın." In references to him that appear on July 11, 1944, in *Yeni Yol*, he is called "Mehmet Sayın, the mayor of Of." In a biography that appeared in 1949 in the *Halk Gazetesi*, he is called "Mehmet Selimoğlu."

7. The same kind of reversion was less common elsewhere in the country, where the old lineage, clan, and tribal names were not a claim to eminence in the state system, but rather a negative sign of rusticity and marginality.

8. Nationally, the RPP won 69 seats and the DP won 408 seats of a total of 486 in the National Assembly. In the province of Trabzon, the RPP won 9 and the DP won 3 seats. In the province of Rize, the RPP won 0 and the DP won 6 seats. See D.I.E. 1966.

well in Rize and Giresun, but the RPP was able to hold its own in Trabzon and Ordu. Still, Mehmet Bey was not reelected to the National Assembly.[9] The Muradoğlu were only able to turn out five thousand votes for the DP in the district of Of, as opposed to seven thousand votes for the RPP. But the "shepherds" could nonetheless take satisfaction in having determined that Mehmet Bey would lose his seat in the National Assembly.[10]

Mehmet Bey is said to have come to the town of Of from Trabzon on the night when the election returns were announced. He was seen walking through the streets with the district officer (*kaymakam*) on one arm and the district judge (*hakim*) on the other. He had been drinking and his face was drawn. The interlocutor who told me of this memory seemed to recall the scene as the end of an era. Mehmet Bey had been selected by national party leaders because of his presumed position as a dominant figure in the district of Of. We can guess that he must have occasionally hinted to them that he was the heir of the old aghas of the Selimoğlu. In fact, his place in the family line, and hence in the social networks of the district of Of, was tenuous. He would run again in the national elections of 1954, but the DP would take all twelve seats for the province of Trabzon. On this occasion, the votes he personally garnered fell below the totals he had received in 1950.[11]

ELITES OF THE OLD REPUBLIC AND ELITES OF THE NEW REPUBLIC

Before describing how family lines and national parties came into perfect alignment during the 1950s, I must first explain why new social groups that became dominant in other towns and cities were pushed aside in the district of Of. For example, why was it that circles of civil servants, profes-

9. The votes for the RPP and DP, respectively, were as follows: Ordu, 50 percent vs. 50 percent; Giresun, 38 percent vs. 62 percent; Trabzon, 49 percent vs. 46 percent; Rize 30 percent vs. 70 percent; total for the four provinces, 44 percent vs. 55 percent (ibid.).

10. The votes for Mehmet Sayın, followed by the average of votes received for the RPP and DP in each district of Trabzon, are as follows: Trabzon (town): Mehmet Sayın 12,651, RPP 14,000, and DP 10,500; Of: 7,091, 7,000, and 5,400; Çaykara: 4,679, 4,750, and 5,500; Sürmene: 10,868, 11,500, and 10,500; Maçka 6,717, 7,000, and 4,100; Vakfıkebir 7,341, 7,850, and 14,500; Akçaabat 10,263, 10,700, and 9,500. See *Yeni Yol*, results of national elections of May 17, 1950.

11. See the results for the national elections as announced in *Yeni Yol*. The RPP received 33 percent and the DP 57 percent of the total vote in 1954. Mehmet Bey received about half the number needed to win a seat.

sionals, property-owners, and merchants were unable to dominate the RPP and the DP, and then to mobilize the turn-out of voters in the villages through their own networks of patronage and clientage? Some of them had been the backers of Mehmet Bey and the RPP for years. Others had founded the DP when it first arose as a threat to Mehmet Bey and the RPP. Elsewhere in the Turkish Republic, including some other districts in the province of Trabzon, these kinds of individuals had constituted the political leadership of the RPP and DP at this time. As for the district of Of, the old order of leading individuals and social formations had remained more or less dormant during the one-party period. It was not already in existence at the moment when the prospect of open elections first appeared on the horizon. Why, then, did the political parties, along with local networks of patronage and clientage, slip once again into the hands of leading individuals from large family groupings?

Two anecdotes will serve to illustrate why representatives of the Muradoğlu family line were essential for the success of the opposition in the district of Of. Given the circumstances of 1950, the descendants of Ferhat Agha could not have been displaced by a "civil" opposition. What the situation required, as the sacking of the DP demonstrated, was at least the specter of an "uncivil" opposition.

The first anecdote illustrates how leading individuals from large family groupings saw to it that their relatives were accorded respect and deference. In effect, it illustrates the dark side of the imperial tactic of gaze, discipline, and rule. During the spring and summer harvest, the villagers carried large baskets of tea leaves to government stations, where they were weighed and graded by officials. There were sometimes disputes when the villagers felt that their leaves have been improperly graded. One of my interlocutors recounted the following events:

> Two years ago, [a member of a large family grouping, but himself of no special prominence] was working as an agent in a tea-collecting station. An angry villager, unhappy with the grade assigned his leaves, gave the agent two slaps (*tokat*) in the face. The agent drew his gun in response, but his assailant was also armed. Firing his pistol first, the villager killed the man then and there with several shots. He was soon arrested by gendarmes and held in prison in Trabzon. One month later an unknown assailant shot and killed this man's son, firing at him through the window of his house as he was eating his dinner. The man himself [who shot and killed the agent] is still in jail, but he will not live out his life. Even if he does not return to the district of Of, he will be tracked down and killed in retaliation. I know who is responsible for this. It is

> [a leading individual from a large family grouping but not someone who was closely related to the agent].[12]

The important point is the belief of the narrator that a leading individual of a large family grouping, but not the close kinsmen of the man who was killed, would carry out retribution. Neither the anticipated murder of the accused nor the actual murder of his son can be described as a vengeance murder. By the logic of vendetta, which was not unknown in the district of Of, a family member of the agent, probably an adolescent son or a younger brother, would have been obliged to take vengeance. The murder of the son who was eating his dinner was something else. Leading individuals, who had an interest in the social standing of their family line, would not tolerate attacks or insults directed against their relatives or, for that matter, even friends of their relatives.[13]

The man who told me this story also assumed that the individual who had shot the son in retribution was not himself a member of the family line. Some of the leading individuals from various agha-families were known to have clients among the "mountaineers" (*dağlılar*), the poor folk from the valley highlands. These clients were said to do whatever dirty work their patrons might require of them. A woman might be assaulted. A man might be beaten up. A fire might destroy a granary or a house. Livestock might be pilfered or butchered. A few shots might be fired through the window or floor of a house.[14] Some say this was more the style of those leading individuals from large families who were until recently farmers and herders, like the Muradoğlu. The prominent members of the Selimoğlu, the sacking of the DP headquarters in 1946 notwithstanding, positioned themselves as officials, bureaucrats, and professionals, and as such were able to assert themselves in a more subtle fashion. Ordinary villagers and towns-

12. I heard a similar story about an incident in Çayeli, but no leading individuals from large family groupings were involved in it. An official in a tea factory was assaulted by an ordinary villager. The latter was shot dead by an unknown assailant sometime later. The brother of the official was suspected as the murderer. This man, a resident of one of the district villages, was obliged to avoid the precincts of the town of Çayeli permanently. When he wished to go to market or to sit in a coffeehouse, he was obliged to go to Pazar instead. If he had been a leading individual from a large family grouping, he might have been less vulnerable to retaliation.

13. I have never determined if the prediction of my interlocutor actually came about.

14. Many of the older houses have stables on the ground floor. I heard stories of individuals who gave their rivals a warning by stealing into the stable, shooting through the floor planks to terrorize the inhabitants, and then quickly vanishing into the night.

men might have hesitated to oppose Mehmet Bey and the descendants of Ferhat Agha. But once prominent members of the Muradoğlu chose to support the DP, they too could afford to do so.

The second anecdote concerned an attempted abduction of a woman, similar to the incident that had occurred in the home village in 1922. As we have seen, the control of women by their fathers before their marriage and by their husbands after their marriage was one of the principles of the old vertical and horizontal solidarities. The story that follows illustrates how leading individuals of different family lines were eager to avoid civil disorders that might arise from quarrels over women:

> A maternal granddaughter of the "X-oğlu" [a large family grouping], a married woman, had come to the bus station in Of in order to take a bus to Giresun. In Of, women from Giresun are considered to be loose. Overhearing her destination, several men loitering about the station [they are named and some are associated with large family groupings] hatched a plot to abduct her. They misled her, saying her bus had already departed, and told her a car would be coming for her, which she could take instead. They arranged to have a car come to the bus station, and they persuaded her to get in. Meanwhile, one of the Selimoğlu overheard their conversation with the woman and became suspicious. He asked about the bus for Giresun at the ticket counter, learned that it had not yet departed, and realized that the woman had been deceived. He immediately informed the gendarmes (*jandarma*), who apprehended the car and its occupants just outside town. The affair was hushed up because of the family lines that were involved, and no formal complaints were ever lodged against the abductors.

My interlocutor then explained how the elders of the family lines involved went about insuring that the incident would not lead to further trouble:

> Within a week, one of the key perpetrators of the abduction, a "Y-oğlu," was married to a woman of the Muradoğlu, who were friends of the "X-oğlu." This was interpreted as a move to neutralize those individuals most likely to take vengeance, that is, the Muradoğlu. Although the woman was only a maternal descendant of their family line, they were judged to be the party most likely to reassert the untouchability of anyone who might be conceived to be under their protection. Another of the key perpetrators, who was a "Z-oğlu," arranged to move to Eskipazar, where one of the Muradoğlu had been persuaded to give him protection. Again, this was a way of neutralizing the group most likely to resort to vengeance in the affair. All the men who had attempted to abduct the woman stayed in hiding for several months. A year after the incident, they were just beginning to show themselves regularly in public.

In other words, when a dispute threatens to divide a family line or its injure its relationship with other family lines, one should send those responsible into hiding and tie them into knots of social relations with those who are eager to punish them. In effect, the anecdote illustrates the kind of steps that Ferhat Agha might have taken, but apparently did not take, in order to settle the hard feelings provoked by abduction in 1922.

THE OLD REPUBLIC INHABITS THE NEW REPUBLIC

During the national elections in 1954 and 1957, the two dominant large family groupings in the district of Of gradually came into alignment with the two dominant national parties in the Turkish Republic. By the end of the decade, the Selimoğlu were the local representatives of the RPP and the Muradoğlu were the representatives of the DP. The relative efficiency with which local social formations aligned themselves with the major national parties was impressive. I shall briefly review the steps by which this came about.

From 1949 to 1957, there was no perfect alignment of the two families and the two parties. The descendants of Ferhat Agha (Selimoğlu) held a firm grip on the public offices in the town and were RPP leaders and activists in the district (see fig. 2). Nonetheless, they were weakened by the fact that the RPP did not receive enough electoral support to form a national government from 1950. Meanwhile, the sons of Rasih Efendi (Selimoğlu) had been joined by the sons of Reşat Agha (Muradoğlu) as party leaders and activists in the DP, ever since the run-up to the elections of 1950. These two sets of the two large family groupings continued to work together during the period in question, when the DP, led by Adnan Menderes, was able to form the national government.[15]

During the run-up to the national elections in the summer of 1957, however, a crisis in the DP at the national level reverberated at the local level in Of. Adnan Menderes, who had been moving to restrict the political process, was being challenged from within his own party as well as from

15. In June of 1949, Kazım Üstündağ was first chairman, and a son of Reşat Agha (Muradoğlu) was second chairman, of the Of congress of the DP, while a second son of Reşat Agha and a son of Rasih Efendi (Selimoğlu) were members of the executive council. See *Yeni Yol*, June 15, 1949. In 1953, a son of Reşat Agha was first chairman, and a son of Rasih Efendi was second chairman, of the Of congress of the DP, while a second son of Reşat Agha was one of the members of the executive council. See *Yeni Yol*, undetermined edition. In May 1957, a son of Rasih Efendi was named chairman of the Of congress of the DP, and the members of the executive council ominously listed no Muradoğlu whatsoever. See *Yeni Yol*, May 14, 1957.

the opposition parties. Instead of changing course, however, the leadership of the DP moved to suppress dissent, first by purging their party membership. Similarly, in the countryside, the local leaders of the DP also began to purge local party membership.[16]

One of my interlocutors recounted the incidents that followed in the district of Of:

> In preparation for the coming elections, [the sons of Rasih Efendi] had been touring the villages signing up people as members of the DP party. They had been organizing the membership to elect delegates to attend a DP party convention to be held in the town of Of. They engaged in a number of maneuvers. They would sign up people, mix up the papers, and so attempt to let their own people in and keep other people out of the meeting. When someone came to the meeting they would tell him that his papers were not in order so he would not be admitted to the meeting.
>
> [The sons of Rasih Efendi] were intent on packing the meeting with their own supporters. What they were trying to do was to gain control over the DP so they could run it as they liked. The Muradoğlu heard about their intentions and came in a crowd to the meeting. They were ready to make their way into the room whatever anyone said to them or did to them. They eventually forced their way inside and chased two of the three brothers out of the meeting. This was the end of the Selimoğlu influence in the DP.[17]

The sons of Rasih Efendi had run the local branch of the DP in an authoritarian manner, emulating party leaders at the national level. When they were driven out of the DP, they founded a local branch of a new national political party, the Freedom Party (*Hürriyet Partisi*). The FP had been organized in late 1955 by DP dissidents at the national level who had been dismissed for refusing to accept party discipline.[18] So now the sons of

16. See Zürcher 1993, 240–43.

17. My interlocutor thought that this had taken place in 1954, but I think that 1957 was the more likely date. As noted above, in May 1957, a son of Rasih Efendi was chairman of the Of congress of the DP, which for the first time included no Muradoğlu whatsoever on its executive council. Only four months later, a second son of Rasih Efendi, along with one of the former members of the DP executive council, announced his resignation from the DP to join the Freedom Party (*Hürriyet Partisi*); see *Yeni Yol*, September 12, 1957. Then, a few weeks later, the first son of Rasih Efendi himself was named as chairman of the Of congress of the FP, while yet another former member of the DP executive council was named as a member of the executive council of the FP; see *Yeni Yol*, October 1, 1957.

18. Zürcher 1993, 242.

Rasih Efendi were emulating DP dissidents at the national level who had been objecting to the authoritarian manner of party leaders. The FP failed miserably in the national elections of 1957 and soon vanished from the scene both locally and nationally. Until the 1970s, all the political activists and most of the voters from the Selimoğlu family line were affiliated with the RPP.

A similar sorting out of family lines and political parties took place among the Muradoğlu. Harun Agha was the elderly bearded man for whom youths had stood at attention in the restaurant in Eskipazar during my brief stopover in 1965 (see chap. 1). Impressed that his kinsman, Reşat Agha, had been able to defeat Mehmet Bey in the national elections, he also became a party activist. Sometime during the early 1950s, Harun Agha had announced that he had joined the Nation Party (*Millet Partisi*). Founded by dissident members of the RPP and DP, this party called for a program of moral uplift based on family and religion.[19] Eventually, Harun Agha became the chairman of the NP in the district of Of. During the run-up to the national elections of 1953, he toured the villages of the district soliciting or, more exactly, demanding support for the NP. Like Reşat Agha, he was one of only a very few individuals who were still accorded the title "agha."[20] Unlike Reşat Agha, however, he had a much harder time adapting himself to the demands of electoral politics. According to the memory of an acquaintance who had also joined the party and toured the villages with him, Harun Agha was better at intimidating the villagers he encountered than at winning their sympathies for his party. For example, he used to travel by minibus from village to village, carrying a staff (*bastinado*) in the manner of some of the old aghas of the imperial period. This gesture succeeded very well in reinforcing his stern appearance, not to mention bringing to mind his fearsome reputation. If a driver of the minibus asked him for a fare, he would simply refuse to pay. If the driver persisted, he would threaten to punish him with his staff. This kind of behavior apparently decreased whatever support there might have been for the Nation Party to the vanishing point.

The failure of Harun Agha and the Nation Party deserves special comment. The platform of the Nation Party appealed to popular resentment of the secular reforms; nonetheless, the NP succeeded in garnering only 5 percent of the vote in the province of Trabzon in 1950. So a national party

19. Ibid., 244.

20. A photograph of Harun Agha, together with a photograph of Ferhat Agha, appears in Yiğit's account of the Battle for Of (1950).

that attempted to make the most of the religious issue actually did very poorly in a region where one would have expected success. The failure of the NP underlines the fact that leading individuals, large family groupings, and district social networks did not constitute an Islamist reaction to the Turkish Republic. They were social formations from the old state society that were assuming a place in the new state system. These social formations were founded on an imperial version of Islamic belief and practice, but they were otherwise oriented toward the official state system of the Turkish Republic. The most successful members of the Selimoğlu and Muradoğlu family lines were no more interested in an extreme Islamist agenda than in a "leftist" or "rightist" agenda. They were not intending to challenge secularism. They wanted to be recognized by and participate in the state system, as did their ascendants during the late period of decentralization.

The rapidity and efficiency with which the two major groups of local elites aligned themselves with two major national parties was then a direct legacy of the old state society. With the shift from one-party to multiparty politics, the local elites were poised to serve as the intermediaries between the government and the population. They were still positioned within a framework of competing social formations. They still believed they had a right to participate in sovereign power. So from the time of the national elections of 1950, leading individuals from the two dominant family lines polished their skills as electoral politicians. They learned how to turn out the vote. They learned how to lobby party leaders.

Their education in electoral politics was accelerated by international circumstances. During the 1950s, the United States was providing the Turkish Republic with agricultural loans and military assistance. This money appeared in the eastern coastal region in the form of subsidies for the development of agriculture, especially the expansion of tea cultivation, as well as funds for road and bridge projects. But there were always questions about how agricultural subsidies were distributed in the coastal region, and where roads and bridges would be built first and last. It was now possible for the Oflus to see a connection between vertical and horizontal solidarities in the district and the configuration of sovereign power in the state system. Consequently there was an extraordinary interest in elections and parties during the 1950s and into the 1960s. Some of the Oflus were described as afflicted by "political fanaticism" (*siyaset hastası*). They felt obliged not only to read every newspaper and listen to every broadcast, but also to travel from place to place to attend political rallies and speeches. Some were said to have ruined their families and business through their preoccupation with politics.

Once the sons of Reşat Agha dominated the DP, they quickly became formidable political competitors. Adnan Menderes was prime minister, and the DP dominated the National Assembly. The man and his party were to become notorious for their skillful use of patronage and clientage as political weapons. As a consequence, the sons of Reşat Agha were able to break down the single channel between the central government and the district population that had been established by Mehmet Bey Selimoğlu and inherited by the descendants of Ferhat Agha. By 1960, the town of Of was no longer the single conduit between state officials and the district population that it had once been.

The first blow to the town of Of and the Selimoğlu came in the later 1950s. At the time, there was a cooperative for tea producers in the town that was managed by Hüseyin Selimoğlu, a brother of Yusuf and Salih. But now a group of the Muradoğlu proposed to organize a second cooperative to be based at Eskipazar that would become a competitor of the already existing cooperative. The supporters of Hüseyin Selimoğlu argued against this measure, saying that one cooperative was sufficient for the district. They had a great deal at stake since cooperatives were also concentrations of capital and, as such, slush funds for clients. In the end, however, the government permitted the new cooperative to come into existence. The decision made perfect sense, since some of the most productive tea gardens were owned by the Muradoğlu and in the vicinity of Eskipazar. Still, this challenge to Mehmet Bey would not have occurred a few years previously.

A second blow soon followed. During the later 1950s, the officials of the government tea monopoly determined that a tea factory was to be built in the district of Of. But where would the factory be located? The answer to this question was an important one for the two dominant family lines. The tea factory would have administrators and workers, that is to say, a payroll.[21] The construction and maintenance of the tea factory would also provide a stimulus for local tradesmen. The key difference between the various proposals for the tea factory was that the Selimoğlu wanted to situate the factory in the town of Of, the Muradoğlu near the market of Eskipazar. I was told a barely credible story by one of my interlocutors, which seems nonetheless to have been true. State officials had finally made a decision. The new factory would be built near the town of Of. All the building materials, the cement and iron, were brought to that site in preparation for the

21. In 1961, the tea factory at Eskipazar had 68 permanent and 520 temporary workers (Tekeli 1961, 14–15).

beginning of the construction. At this point, the Muradoğlu came to the proposed site and carried all the building materials "on their backs" to a site near Eskipazar, where the Muradoğlu had taken the initiative to set aside land for the factory. In response, the officials of the state tea monopoly changed their minds and decided to locate the factory just outside Eskipazar. The market of Eskipazar, which had consisted of only a few shops, thereafter became a small town.

The military coup of 1960 was eventually followed by the execution of Menderes and the banning of the DP. But the descendants of Ferhat Agha, now leading individuals in a district network and a coastal coalition, enjoyed only a brief advantage. After the return to electoral politics in 1961, the sons of Reşat Agha were once again associated with a national party, now the Justice Party (*Adalet Partisi*), which had replaced the banned Democrat Party. The two family lines were therefore once again aligned with the two major political parties at the national level.[22]

Sometime around 1964, the government proposed to build a lumber mill somewhere along the coast. Although the stakes were smaller than in the instance of the construction of the tea factory, this installation would also have important commercial benefits for the immediate area in which it was located. It was said that the Selimoğlu began to quarrel among themselves about who might benefit from selling their land to the government as a site for the lumber mill. Then, in the midst of the confusion, the Muradoğlu offered a site nearer Eskipazar at a reduced price. The thriving marketplace was pushed further along the path toward becoming a town.

By the time of my arrival in the district of Of, leading individuals among the Muradoğlu could claim political clout of mythic proportions. A son of Reşat Agha was reputed to have the power to shift seven thousand voters in an election. Whether he was in fact able to do so was perhaps beside the point. The belief that he controlled so many votes was just as firmly held in Trabzon and Ankara as it was in Of. So when this son of Reşat Agha made a trip to the provincial or national capital, as was his regular practice, he was certain to have an attentive audience among both party leaders and state officials.

During the 1950s and 1960s, the RPP never enjoyed a period of majority government as did their rivals, first the DP and then the JP. So the local

22. The RPP and the JP initially formed a coalition government until 1962. The RPP thereafter formed coalition governments without the JP until 1965, when the JP won the national elections with a landslide and formed a majority government. See Zürcher (1993, 258–65).

clients of the RPP, such as the Selimoğlu, were in a less enviable position than the local clients of the DP or JP, such as the Muradoğlu. Still, the descendants of Ferhat Agha remained formidable political competitors. They continued to hold all the public offices open to local residents in the town, and hence most of those in the district. The town was also still the district center, and therefore the location of most government offices and the residences of most state administrative, judicial, military, and police officials. Furthermore, many of the staff, secretaries, and janitors were agnates, relatives, friends, and partners of the Selimoğlu. So the descendants of Ferhat Agha were in a good position to learn about and respond to government programs and policies.

They were also able to develop their skills in electoral politics in ways reminiscent of machine politics in the ethnic wards of Chicago. During the 1960s, a majority of the voters in the district favored the JP, successor to the DP. So as the population of the municipality increased, the electoral strength of the RPP, and thus the power of the descendants of Ferhat Agha, steadily weakened. Already in 1965, it was said that the town was JP during the day, when the villagers came to the market, and then RPP at night, when they returned to their mountain hamlets. To counter the trend, local elections had to be engineered by bringing truckloads of supporters into the municipality from those villages whose inhabitants could be expected to support the descendants of Ferhat Agha. For good reason, the town of Of came to be known as the citadel (*hisar*) of the RPP and the descendants of Ferhat Agha.

In 1967, I met the son of Reşat Agha who was said to be able to deliver seven thousand votes in a local election. At the time, he counseled me to move to Eskipazar, where an American like myself would find a warmer welcome: "We are capitalists (*kapitalist*)," he told me, "but they [the descendants of Ferhat Agha] are socialists (*sosyalist*)." The comment was inspired by the new "left of center" (*ortanın solu*) orientation of the RPP that had been formulated by Bülent Ecevit.[23] Sometime later, Hüseyin Selimoğlu, the rival of the son of Reşat Agha in the town of Of, wholeheartedly agreed with his assessment. Referring to his personal commitment to Bülent Ecevit, he said to me, "Yes, we are left of the center. We are even left of the left of center!" He did not mean he was more leftist in his ideology than the

23. RPP supporters said, "Left of center is the way of Atatürk" (*Ortanın solu, Atatürk yolu*), to which the reply from the JP was "Left of center is the way to Moscow" (*Ortanın solu, Moskova yolu*). Cf. Zürcher 1993, 265–66.

party leader. His formulation was intended to express his personal loyalty to the party leader. That is, he was thinking in terms of a discipline of interpersonal association, not in terms of leftist, liberal, or rightist ideology. As for the son of Reşat Agha, he was of course no more a capitalist than Hüseyin was a socialist. They were both representatives of the old republic, which now inhabited the new republic.

11 Civil Society
Coffeehouses and Cooperatives

COFFEEHOUSES: FORUMS OF PUBLIC LIFE

During the 1960s, there were about ten coffeehouses (*kahve*) in the town of Of, some of which were also called reading rooms (*kıraathane*) or teahouses (*çayhane*). Despite the name commonly applied to them, the coffeehouses were not places where one went to drink a good or bad cup of coffee. They were the forums of public life, for the town, but also for the entire district. During the course of a week, thousands of villagers came down from their mountain hamlets to spend some time sitting and talking in a coffeehouse, exchanging pleasantries, making business deals, debating politics, learning the latest gossip, playing card games, or hearing newspapers read aloud. The coffeehouses in the town of Of therefore confirm the existence of a level of interpersonal association beyond the family and household, and even beyond the village or a group of villages. I shall first describe the usual pattern of encounters in coffeehouses and then examine the different kinds of coffeehouses in the town of Of.

I cannot recall ever hearing anyone make a speech to an audience in a coffeehouse. Such an event could conceivably take place, but it would have been unusual.[1] The coffeehouse was not like an assembly room, a parliament, or a town square, where a single individual might address an audience. And yet those who sat and talked in the coffeehouses could be said to represent a general public. For example, I was strolling in the town one winter evening with an acquaintance. As we passed several coffeehouses, we looked

1. For an exception, see my account in chap. 2 of the school secretary, who transformed our coffeehouse conversation into a kind of sermon, but on an occasion when the audience was composed mostly of youths. For another exception, see my account of the rehearsal speech for Liberation Day, given in the Town Square Coffeehouse.

through the fogged windows and saw unusually large crowds of men sitting at the tables. Moved to comment on the spectacle, my acquaintance observed, "The public is sitting" (*millet oturur*). My translation is a free one.[2] The Turkish word in question, *millet,* can also translated as "community," "folk," "people," or "nation." In this instance, I think the translation "public" is appropriate. The interactions that occurred in coffeehouses were based both on the assumption of common public norms and the existence of a general public body. I shall give examples to illustrate these points.

One commonly sat with agnates, relatives, friends, and clients in coffeehouses. During these sittings, one exchanged salutations, offered and accepted hospitality, and made conventional inquiries. In this regard, many of the gestures and utterances on such occasions were part of what could be described as a normative performance. Such a performance usually involved only two to four individuals sitting at a single table, but sometimes extended to several tables. For example, a host might bring a guest of some prominence into the coffeehouse, and the guest might himself come with an entourage. On such an occasion, the guest might attract the attention of men sitting at several tables, seven, eleven, or fifteen people. The guest might even find that everyone in the room had turned to hear what he had to say. But he would address the room not as a speechmaker, but only as a conversationalist. His comments would be followed by the replies of others in the room, in accordance with an etiquette of conversation.

As the example implies, individuals who associated in a coffeehouse did not always know one another. Anyone sitting in a coffeehouse was ready for new encounters with persons he had not yet met. Some individuals went to coffeehouses hoping for just such a novelty to break the tedium of an ordinary afternoon or evening. These new encounters involved meetings among Oflus who could easily locate a thread of relationships or a set of experiences that linked them. Encounters between strangers followed a similar pattern as encounters between acquaintances, except they required a little additional work. Where are you from? Is your house the building just beyond the bridge on the hill to the left? Who is your father? Is he the

2. In translating the Turkish word *millet* as "public," I have in mind similar usages in Of. On the occasion of the departure for the pilgrimage, when hundreds of Oflus were boarding buses in the town square, I heard the remark, "the public is going on the pilgrimage" (*millet haca gider*). On an occasion when large crowds of men were strolling along the coastal highway, I heard the remark, "the public is taking its pleasures" (*millet keyfeder*). To emphasize how Oflus associated with one another when they left the district to work in cities, an interlocutor observed, "We stick together" (*milletçileriz*).

Ahmet who married the daughter of İsmail, the greengrocer whose shop is just before the mosque? These exchanges did not have to be invented on the spot. They were based on the norms of a public body. The stranger was not assumed to be a stranger, but rather someone who was intimate and familiar by a connection yet to be discovered.

The coffeehouses as forums of public life were not recent inventions. They were once the instruments of the regional social oligarchy of the post-classical period. To better understand their function in the 1960s, therefore, it is useful to situate them in the transition from Empire to Republic. In this respect, the relationship of the coffeehouse (*kahve*) to the salon (*oda*) is significant. In most of the villages and towns of rural Anatolia, not so very many decades ago, one or more individuals maintained salons in their houses where male friends and followers met. In these household settings, they conversed, drank tea or coffee, and sometimes shared a meal, pausing at appropriate times to perform their ablutions and prayers. The more prominent the individuals involved, the more spacious and elaborate the salon. Some featured carved ceilings, conical fireplaces, elevated daises, and cushioned benches (*sedir*). These gatherings can be considered the equivalent of the gatherings in the petition room of the palace complex (see chap. 4). The salon, like the petition room, featured normative performances of interpersonal association, the gaze of the agha being the equivalent of the gaze of the sultan.

The greater and lesser aghas of the eastern coastal districts maintained such salons in their governmental mansions during the period of decentralization (see chap. 1). And later, when they were no longer allowed to have governmental mansions, they continued to maintain salons in district centers (see chap. 8). However, there were relatively few salons in the villages of the eastern coastal districts by comparison with rural Anatolia. The paucity of salons in places such as the district of Of did not indicate a lack of social structure or organization, but rather the opposite, a more developed regional social oligarchy. The greater and lesser aghas did not allow ordinary villagers of prominence to build and maintain salons, even if they had the means to do so. The salons were places of interpersonal association, and hence the instruments of building a following, and therefore a move toward the assertion of sovereign power.

At the same time, the circles of interpersonal association in the district of Of involved many individuals, such that a single salon could not accommodate all of them. Accordingly, coffeehouses supplemented the salons in the eastern coastal districts. The aghas owned or sponsored coffeehouses, during and after the period of decentralization. Their followers were obliged to patronize them by sitting and talking there, if not also sleeping and eating there, since they sometimes included dormitories and kitchens. The immediate associates of the aghas, if not the aghas themselves, also appeared in the coffeehouses. The result was a greater separation of family and household from the forums of public life than in the rural areas of Anatolia. The men of the eastern coastal districts, if they wished to be considered anybody at all, were obliged to leave their hamlets more or less every day to see and be seen in coffeehouses. In this respect, the coffeehouses stand to the salons much as the palace middle court stands to the petition room. They were devices for the staging and performance of an interpersonal association that was otherwise centered on a single individual.

During the 1960s, the coffeehouses in the district of Of still featured a legacy of the imperial period. The old aghas and mansions were gone, but leading individuals and circles of interpersonal association remained. So the coffeehouses, some more than others, remained the key sites of a regional social oligarchy. The absence of occasions when a speaker addressed a general audience in a coffeehouse is an example of this. Leaders were not related to followers by an impersonal and abstract framework of rules, the kind of setting usually associated with citizens and their assemblies. Rather, the interactions of individuals in the coffeehouses worked through an idiom of intimacy and familiarity, conventionally expressed if not emotionally felt. Although the most prominent individuals were sometimes referred to with an honorific, such as "Mehmet Bey," they were usually referred to by their first names alone, and sometimes even by nicknames, such as "Little Mehmet." They were never referred to by the title of their offices, such as "the mayor" (*belediye reisi*) or the "national assemblyman" (*milli mebus*).

HIERARCHY AND COFFEEHOUSES

The idiom of intimacy and familiarity in social relations was associated with hierarchy as much as equality. For example, women were fully qualified citizens of the Turkish Republic, but they were never to be found sitting and talking in coffeehouses. Their exclusion was consistent with other features of the imperial period. Women were not household heads (*hane reisi*). They were not members of family lines, and so did not have family names. They could not represent households or family lines in public life. They could not be leading individuals, nor were they counted among the leading individuals' followers. They therefore did not go to coffeehouses, just as they did not go to the Friday prayers. Men represented their families and households in public life, and women were restricted to these represented families and households.

These were unshakable rules in the 1960s, as suggested by my interlocutors' bizarre recollection of the "time of the waiter girls" (see chap. 9). One could ask the Oflus all kinds of questions about their lives, but one was expected to avoid the subject of the family and household, and certainly the subject of the women who were part of it. It is even possible that women were not considered to constitute the public body (*millet*) in the district of Of. The proper names of wives and daughters were not recorded in the census office.[3] Men did not count their daughters when asked the number of their children.[4] A number of circumlocutions were possible. One might inquire about the "family" of a friend or associate (*çoluk çocuğunuz iyi mi?*), but an inquiry about the welfare of a spouse (*eşiniz iyi mi?*) was going too far. This explains why the reader can safely assume that every one of my directly quoted interlocutors was male (see figs. 10 and 11).[5]

The hierarchy of gender relations was related to a hierarchy of age. When an older man entered a coffeehouse, it was not uncommon to see one, two, or three younger men leave the room. The latter would have been the junior kinsmen—brothers, sons, or nephews—of the old man. They left the coffeehouse out of recognition that he represented them in public life. If they had remained, thus presenting themselves as individuals in public life, this would have been a gesture of challenge or defiance. They would be saying, "I am also a competent public actor like you. I, too, can have friends and associates in public life. I am therefore free of the obligation to defer to you. I am not of your immediate family or household." For this reason, the obligation to leave was especially incumbent upon a younger man who was a member of the same household as the older man, then eased as the relationship became more distant.

The two examples, hierarchies of gender and age, illustrate how the family and household were shaped by their connection with a certain kind

3. When I attempted to use census records in the government building as the basis of family genealogies, I discovered that most daughters and wives were registered under one name, "Eve" (*Hawa*).

4. Some now claim that anthropologists overstated the significance of this practice because they did not understand that the word for "child" (*çocuk*) was gendered, referring only to boys. So they had unwittingly asked, "How many boys do you have?" While the point is well taken, it remains the case that a common word used to inquire about children was gendered as male rather female.

5. Otherwise, my wife was able to pass on to me valuable observations about the social relations of townswomen.

Figure 10. A descendant of Ferhat Agha (in fedora), an elder (in turban), and women.

of public life. It was not the other way around. A study of the family in the eastern coastal districts would uncover all kinds of differences among households, the traces of Turkic, Kurdish, Lazi, Armenian, Greek, Georgian, Circassian, Bosnian, and Albanian influences. At the same time, all these differences had been more or less submerged by the norms of a certain kind of public life. The circles of agnates, relatives, friends, and clients associated with coffeehouses were public rather than private formations. Older men did not have the privilege of sitting and talking in coffeehouses as a consequence of family and household structure. Distinctions of gender and age were rooted in public life, and these distinctions in turn had an impact on family and household structure.

If villagers no longer stooped and kissed the hands of leading individuals, the conduct of social relations in coffeehouses was precisely adjusted to express social precedence and standing. For example, the villagers in the town and district of Of almost never drank coffee in the coffeehouses. They bought themselves and their associates small glasses of tea for a few pennies, consuming numerous servings during an afternoon or evening. Coffee, served *alaturka* in small demitasses, was reserved for guests of some

Figure 11. A townsman at home.

special distinction. So the choice of refreshment offered was just one way in which the conduct of social relation expressed hierarchy. Others included the arrangement of chairs, who was served first and last, who spoke most often and who listened most often, and whether a speaker received the attention of only one table or several tables. The idiom of intimacy and familiarity in coffeehouses was then an expression of a certain kind of civility, an ottomanism that had been adjusted to, even if was also partially dislocated by, republicanism.

A curious arrangement typical of most of the coffeehouses in the district of Of provides a striking illustration of this civility. A smaller room was set apart from the main room of the establishment by some kind of partition, so that it comprised an interior within the interior. These little rooms could be more effectively heated on a damp and cold winter day, but this was not really the reason for their existence. The small rooms were places for a more intimate and familiar kind of association, where sensitive matters could be discussed more freely. The arrangement of an interior within an interior was not restricted to coffeehouses. Shops and offices also featured a small room set apart from a larger room. The shopkeeper could receive a customer, and the official could receive a citizen, in a setting of intimacy and familiarity.

They could therefore sit and talk in accordance with a discipline of sociability, even though business or government had brought them together. Some of the small shops were especially interesting because they had little partitions that could accommodate no more than two or three persons crammed inside, knee-to-knee, with a Primus stove and a pot of tea precariously poised on a shelf to one side. So one could enter a place of business or government and be treated as a customer or a citizen. But you could also enter the shop or office as "İsmail of the Muradoğlu from Balek village" or "Ahmet of the Ramoğlu from the town of Of" and be treated differently, after the exchange of greetings, drinking tea, and having a conversation. The interiors within interiors were then a feature of a discipline of interpersonal association. They were places devoted specifically to face-to-face interactions that differentiated those "further in" from those "further out."

One or more of the little rooms within the large rooms of coffeehouses may have originally been built by one of the aghas of the later imperial period. As Günday informs us, the aghas from surrounding villages once directly maintained salons in the town of Of (see chap. 8). It seems likely that these aghas would have set themselves up in little meeting rooms that adjoined larger assembly rooms. If they did so, tea and coffee most certainly would have been served in the latter. These meeting and assembly rooms probably would have evolved into coffeehouses in some instances, if indeed they had not originally been built as such. And one might guess that the conversion of meeting and assembly rooms into commercial coffeehouses would have been a way to evade government restrictions.

I would not claim that these structures in the town of Of were explicit imitations of palace architecture, which also featured interiors within interiors (see chap. 4). Rather, I would claim they were the result of the dissemination of an imperial tactic, sovereign power through interpersonal association, from center to periphery. Accordingly, it also makes no sense to see the normative performances in the coffeehouses of Of as imitations of palace ceremony and protocol. They were the result of the spread of ethical practices of political authority, rather than the aping of palace formalities.

My interlocutors in the town of Of will have a good laugh when they learn that I have associated their coffeehouses with normative performances. I heard many criticisms from the Oflus regarding the bad manners of their compatriots in coffeehouses. Some sat akimbo and dressed badly. Some fell asleep in their chairs or on the table. Some spoke loudly and used coarse language. I was treated to praises of Oflu masculinity, punctuated by pistol shots, in a coffeehouse. I saw huge rolls of cash exchanged in the course of the purchase of a large Vabis truck. I sat at card games where each card was placed on the table with a sound resembling a fist blow or a pistol shot. I exchanged information on what were purported to be exotic sexual practices in the United States and Turkey. I heard discussions of how one went about bribing municipal officials in Istanbul. But then I also heard debates on the work ethic and its importance for national development. I was counseled about the terrible fate awaiting unbelievers in the afterlife. I heard detailed analyses of Turkish, Greek, and American foreign policies. I was questioned about the details of space travel.

Sometimes my interlocutors complained that the conduct of social relations in the coffeehouses had deteriorated in recent years. I heard the opinion that card playing, laughter, gambling, and drinking were once virtually unknown in the coffeehouses of Of. But other interlocutors affirmed that these practices had always taken place in at least some coffeehouses. The fact of the matter is that the normative standard of behavior among the Oflus, as well as their neighbors to the east and west, is probably more rough-and-tumble than elsewhere in Anatolia. Nonetheless, if the Oflus might sometimes have used coarse language and rough gestures, they also had a keen sense of a discipline of interpersonal association.

COFFEEHOUSES OF THE NEW VERSUS THE OLD REPUBLIC

I have described the conduct of social relations in coffeehouses as a form of public life. But it was a nonofficial rather than an official form of public life. This had been the case during the Ottoman Empire, and it was once again the case in the Turkish Republic. The conduct of social relations in coffeehouses was a kind of work leading to the construction and maintenance of district networks. Neither the work itself nor the district networks as its result had ever been explicitly prescribed and enforced by official statutes or procedures. Its hegemony depended on a social system of gaze, discipline, and rule rather than the laws, courts, and police of the state system. Accordingly, the old republic could colonize the new republic even after the nationalist revolution had led to the suppression and replacement of the imperial state system.

Before examining how coffeehouses played an important role in this colonization, I shall first mention an important distinction in the types of coffeehouses in the town of Of. Some coffeehouses were places for elites of the new republic rather than elites of the old republic. The New City Club (*Yeni şehir Kulübü*) and the Municipal Reading Room (*Belediye Kıraathanesi*) were situated in the new center of the town, built after the declaration of the Turkish Republic (see chap. 1). Both of these coffeehouses attracted a select clientele from which villagers were altogether absent.

The New City Club was located behind the government building, away from the town, not far from the beach. It was usually patronized by officials, professionals, and businessmen who were often, but not always, from somewhere other than the district of Of. These included most of the higher government officials, such as the district officer, the public prosecutor, the district military officer, and the two judges. But it was also patronized by a certain segment of the town professionals, some of whom were Oflu, but most of whom were Rizeli, Bayburtlu, or Trabzonlu. They included two lawyers, a doctor, a banker, a pharmacist, a paint shop owner, and a major appliance dealer. This was a place where one could do some drinking, card playing, and backgammon playing, the latter not being a favorite pastime of villagers.

The Municipal Reading Room was located opposite the entrance to the government building, just across Atatürk Square. It included an adjoining room that was designated as the "Of Teachers' Association" (*Of Öğretmen Derneği*). This coffeehouse was part of a line of offices and apartments that included the residences of clerks and officials. Here one could play cards or backgammon, but no alcoholic drinks were served. It was frequented by a few lower-ranking clerks and functionaries, a number of primary and middle school teachers, and young men who had graduated from the high school or completed a university degree but were as yet unemployed. Most of these individuals were from the district of Of.

The atmosphere in each of these two establishments was distinctive. The patrons of the New City Club were secularist and nationalist. They might sometimes discuss national politics, but they usually avoided discussing individuals or incidents in the district of Of. As far as their dress, speech, and behavior were concerned, they would not have been out of place in one of the middle-class quarters of Trabzon, Ankara, or Istanbul. The patrons of the Municipal Reading Room, besides the teachers and functionaries, were mostly younger, educated youths who went there in order to avoid their elders who would be sitting in other coffeehouses. Their conversations were also oriented toward the world beyond Of, focusing on careers, sports, fashion, novels, and films.

I do not think that the conduct of social relations in these two coffeehouses could be described as the basis of a form of public life, whether nonofficial or official. This is not to say that those who attended them were free of a discipline of social thinking and practice. On the contrary, the clientele of the New City Club and the Municipal Reading Room had received extensive educations. Most had attended primary, middle, and high schools. Some had attended higher institutes, acquiring academic degrees or professional certificates. Because of such backgrounds, they too were members of circles of interpersonal association. But these circles, the nature of which lies beyond the scope of this study, had not been constructed and were not maintained in the conduct of social relations in coffeehouses.

In many towns in Turkey, including some along the eastern Black Sea coast, the sociopolitical groups who patronized coffeehouses like the New City Club and the Municipal Reading Room dominated public life in the 1960s. In the town of Of, however, these kinds of citizens were outnumbered by tens of thousands of other villagers and townsmen who were part of vertical and horizontal solidarities.

The town of Of was different from other towns only in degree rather than in kind; Of simply serves as an especially striking instance of the way in which the old republic inhabited the new. Taking advantage of this, I shall describe the relationship of coffeehouses and cooperatives to illustrate this double character of public life in the Turkish Republic. To do so, I shall focus on the three sons of the oldest son of Ferhat Agha.

THREE GRANDSONS OF FERHAT AGHA IN THE MULTIPARTY PERIOD

During the 1950s and 1960s, Yusuf, Hüseyin, and Salih attempted to build a local political base in the district of Of so that one of them might be elected to the National Assembly (see fig. 2). Yusuf, the oldest brother, had become the first headman (*muhtar*) in the town, then the chairman of the Turkish Air Association. By the 1960s, he was described by my interlocutors as the most powerful man in the town of Of, the *éminence grise* of the descendants of Ferhat Agha. His reputation, which was also a kind of notoriety, was not due to his hold on a public office, but rather to his position in the vertical and horizontal solidarities of the old republic. Salih, the youngest brother, had become the director of the Agricultural Credit Cooperative as a youth in 1941. He was the first of the descendants of Ferhat Agha to hold a public office, and he would eventually serve as a civil servant for some fifty years, longer than any other member of his family line. In contrast to Yusuf, who was at the center of a nonofficial circle of agnates, relatives, friends, and associates, Salih was a leading individual because he managed an official public institution with a sizable budget.

Hüseyin, the middle brother, would become the candidate for national political office. He would have been in his early adulthood in 1946, when Mehmet Sayın was "chosen" to represent the province of Trabzon in the National Assembly. At the time, his agnate's achievement appears to have deeply impressed him. More than any of the other descendants of Ferhat Agha, Hüseyin emulated the militant Kemalist orientation of his eminent kinsman. During the later 1940s, when he would have still been in his late twenties, he was an outspoken supporter of the Kemalist program of reforms. He even gave one of his children a Turkic, rather than an Islamic, name, an extraordinary gesture for a resident of the district of Of. It was probably during this same period that Hüseyin first adopted the dress and manners of RPP partisans. He always wore a suit coat, fedora, dress shirt, and cravat. He donned these items in such a way that they lost all their qualities as fashion to become entirely absorbed by their function as a uniform.

Also in the same manner as Mehmet Sayın, Hüseyin began to accumulate public offices. At first, he was obliged to be content with relatively insignificant chairmanships, since his close agnates already held the really important posts. Just before the national elections of 1950, he became chairman of the Of People's House (*Halkevi*), a kind of culture club that had been designed to foster participation in official public life. Soon afterward, he became the chairman of the Red Crescent Society (*Kızılay Cemiyeti*), then chairman of the Primary School Parent-Teacher Association (*İlk Okul Aile Birliği*), and then chairman of the Middle School Parent-Teacher Association (*Orta Okul Aile Birliği*).

Otherwise, Hüseyin appears to have been more imaginative than Mehmet Bey was, perhaps too imaginative to be entirely successful as a practical politician. The Kemalist program of reforms had relied on control of the printed page, its script and its language, as an instrument for the revolution in public culture. Hüseyin seems to have been paying attention. During the later 1940s he had opened a shop in the town of Of that sold newspapers, magazines, books, and stationery.[6] In doing so, he had political as well as commercial interests at stake. In the run-up to the national elections of 1950, he began to accompany Yakup, mayor of Of and RPP chairman, as he toured the villages in an effort to turn out the vote. Realizing that the elections were a battle for the minds of the voters, he began to bring out a weekly newspaper, *New Of* (*Yeni Of*), the first and perhaps

6. I have not determined when he opened this shop. I am assuming that it preceded his publication of the newspaper, which is mentioned below.

still the only such publication to appear in the district of Of.[7] The newspaper was published irregularly during periods of relative political calm, then regularly in the run-ups to municipal or national elections. Its columns often reported local social events, funerals, weddings, and so on, but it also included political commentaries, that took issue with provincial newspapers that favored the DP rather than the RPP.

For some years, Hüseyin achieved little more than visibility, and perhaps notoriety, as a figure in the public life of the town and the district. Then, in 1955, he managed to become the director of the first tea cooperative in the district of Of.[8] At the time, the very first tea gardens in the district of Of were beginning to reach full production. Most were in eastern Of, where the Muradoğlu resided, rather than western Of, where the Selimoğlu resided. But somehow the three brothers, Yusuf, Hüseyin, and Salih, got the jump on their rivals, the sons of Reşat Agha (Muradoğlu).[9] Moreover, they had done so even though this was the period when Menderes was prime minister, that is, a period when patronage and clientage were in the hands of the DP, not the RPP.

Soon afterwards, Hüseyin began to consider how he might use the cooperative as a means for repeating the feat of Mehmet Bey, election to the National Assembly. Eventually, he would do so by combining his "work" as directorship of the cooperative with his "work" as a leading individual in one of the coffeehouses.

THE TOWN SQUARE COFFEEHOUSE AND TEAS PRODUCERS' COOPERATIVE

The Town Square Coffeehouse (*Meydan Kahvesi*) stood at what had been the center of the town after its initial incorporation as a municipality around 1874. When I first resided in the district in the 1960s, the outlines of the

7. The newspaper continued to appear sporadically until 1957. It consisted of two to six pages, each about half the size of the page of a regular daily newspaper.

8. The province of Rize began to be an important center of tea cultivation sometime around 1938. I was told that the Of Tea Producers' Assistance Cooperative had first been organized by ten individuals, four of whom were Selimoğlu. They had all been members of a large tea cooperative in the town of Rize that had once had fifty thousand members. I was told that this tea cooperative had been left with only twenty thousand members after splits in the 1950s.

9. The sons and grandsons of Ferhat Agha benefited from more extensive experience as public officials, while the sons of Reşat Agha had benefited from more experience as farmers. This probably explains why the former were able to organize the first cooperative, and the latter were able to develop the best tea gardens.

old town square were still visible, despite encroachments by shops and warehouses. A municipal building had also previously been located on one side of the old square, just to one side of the coffeehouse. During the 1910s and 1920s, Ferhat Agha had sat in his offices in this municipal building.[10] As mayor of the town, he would have received residents of the town and district, who had by then become citizens of the Empire, on official business. At the same time, he would also have sat with, hosted, and talked to a circle of agnates, relatives, friends, and clients in the coffeehouse next door.

By the early 1950s, the descendants of Ferhat Agha received residents of the town and district, now citizens of the Republic, in the offices of their various directorships and chairmanships. These offices, none located exactly on the old square, were scattered about the town. But during the afternoon or evening, when their offices were closed for business, they sat with, hosted, and talked to agnates, relatives, friends, and clients in the Town Square Coffeehouse. The latter included shopkeepers and merchants from the town, as well as a certain number of high and low government employees. In fact, it could be said that most of what transpired in the government building (*hükümet*) was exposed to the eyes and ears of the descendants of Ferhat Agha who gathered in the Town Square Coffeehouse. This means that the district officer in Of during the 1960s faced circumstances very similar to those faced by the provincial governors during the 1880s (see chap. 8).

In addition to the descendants of Ferhat Agha, some other leading individuals—especially those from the family lines once associated with the old Five Party—also sat and talked in the Town Square Coffeehouse. However, there were individuals from the town or district that never sat, hosted, and talked in its rooms. For example, members of the Muradoğlu family line, or their relatives and friends associated with the Twenty-five party, were never to be seen there. The latter had their own regular coffeehouses in or near Eskipazar, and during their visits to Of, they would go to a coffeehouse other than the Town Square Coffeehouse. A good number of my acquaintances also scrupulously avoided the Town Square Coffeehouse, but not always because they were close to the Muradoğlu. They did not want to be implicated in any of the circles of interpersonal association in the town or district. These uncommitted individuals would have certainly been

10. I mistakenly wrote in an earlier paper (Meeker 1994a) that Ferhat Agha had himself received petitions in the Town Square Coffeehouse. I have since discovered an entry in my notes that indicates otherwise. However, it is probable that Ferhat Agha did receive visitors nonofficially in the Town Square Coffeehouse.

welcomed by the descendants of Ferhat Agha in the Town Square Coffeehouse, but they did not want to incur the obligations that were part of the framework of vertical and horizontal solidarities.[11] For this and other reasons, the district officer, the public prosecutor, the two judges, and the district military officer also avoided the Town Square Coffeehouse. They were obliged to meet regularly with the descendants of Ferhat Agha, since the latter held public offices, but they chose not to meet them in their coffeehouse. As for most of the schoolteachers and university students, they would have endured a thousand tortures before setting foot in the Town Square Coffeehouse.

The descendants of Ferhat Agha who held public offices commonly entertained distinguished visitors. But when they did so, they treated them to banquets in restaurants and never invited them to the Town Square Coffeehouse. So they dined with state officials and inspectors, provincial party leaders, and other public figures, and they also regularly included district officials and town professionals. Almost certainly, the descendants of Ferhat Agha deducted expenses for these banquets from the treasuries of the municipality, cooperative, or society in question. The banquets were not the same as sitting and talking in coffeehouses. The official and the nonofficial republic were visibly separated by clear and distinct boundaries.

The Town Square Coffeehouse featured the most elaborate example of an interior within an interior of any such establishment. A larger room accommodated fifty to seventy-five persons at tables for four. A smaller room accommodated sixteen to twenty persons, also at tables for four. The smaller room was set apart from the larger room by a windowed partition that appeared to be of recent construction, no earlier than the 1950s. In the smaller room it was not possible to conduct a private discussion between two or three people since it was so easy to overhear what was being said at every table. At the same time, it was impossible to overhear what was being said in the smaller room from the larger room, which was usually crowded and noisy.

The atmosphere of intimacy and familiarity in the smaller room discouraged anonymous individuals from entering it. One felt obliged to be invited to join the company of those who were already sitting there. The smaller room was also brightly illuminated by a single bare electric bulb of comparatively high wattage that hung from the center of the ceiling. So

11. Umur (1949, 18–19) noted that some individuals and families chose not to affiliate themselves with parties (*fırka*) even during the period of decentralization, "the time of the aghas" (see chap. 1).

everyone in the room was fully present to one another by the absence of both shadows and compartments. Moreover, everyone in the larger room could see the occupants of the smaller room, but they could not hear what they were saying when the door was shut. So the occupants of the smaller room were a group that was "further in" on display to a public body that was "further out."

The smaller room could be considered a structure of the old imperial modernity; nonetheless, it was decked out as a structure of the new republican modernity. The portraits of national leaders Kemal Atatürk, İsmet İnönü, and Cemal Gürsel were hung near the ceiling of one wall.[12] To the right of the three portraits there was a plaque inscribed with the words "People's House" (*Halkevi*). A large map of Asia Minor was located in the center of another wall. It represented what was to become the Republic of Turkey at the time of the Independence War, indicating the occupation zones of the European powers, Britain, Greece, Italy, and France. There was also a hat rack on the wall, a symbolic fixture since only Kemalist nationalists would have donned fedoras (*şapka*) in Of.

The smaller room was usually not occupied during the day, and it was not always occupied in the evening. But the three brothers, Yusuf, Hüseyin, and Salih, were by far its most frequent users. One, two, or all of them might sit there together, always in the company of an inner circle of friends and clients. During the fall of 1966, they welcomed me to sit with them as a special favor, and I did so on many occasions, becoming one of the regulars. On the first occasion I entered the smaller room, the three brothers, in the company of others, were calculating the possible votes they could muster in certain villages in the upcoming local elections. On one of the last occasions I entered the smaller room, they were vigorously disputing the fairness of the distribution of the fertilizer annually allotted to the tea cooperative.

These two incidents, which involved the business of elections and cooperatives, were exceptional. The three brothers more normally assembled in the smaller room to socialize with their inner circle of friends and clients. When they were there, they almost always listened to the evening news broadcast, turning the radio on just before the news began and turning it off immediately afterward. The reactions that followed the news tended to conform to the current party line of the RPP. One man from one of the villages, considered to be a specialist in party ideology, provided guidance in

12. General Cemal Gürsel was the leader of the military coup in 1960 and the president of the Republic from 1961 to 1966 (Zürcher 1993, 356–57).

this respect. He would also sometimes read aloud from a newspaper while others listened. For my benefit, perhaps, he sometimes read aloud from party tracts, explaining and justifying them. If I asked a question, he would occasionally be called on to give an "official" response. But the discussion was not always restricted to party politics. The topics of conversations included economics, religion, philosophy, and, perhaps more often than usual because of my presence, international affairs.

Often I found one of the brothers, most commonly Yusuf but often Hüseyin and sometimes Salih, in the larger room. Along with Yakup, the mayor of the town, they were the descendants of Ferhat Agha who were most likely to be found there. Hüseyin hosted his closest friends and clients at his table, but he also hosted ordinary villagers who were passing through town or attending the weekly market. He would even invite men he did not know to his table, offer them tea, ask them about news of their villages, and sound them out about their political opinions. This was the fashion for any leading individual of a family line who aspired to extend his contacts and influence among the villagers. They were obliged to sit in the same place at certain hours each day, afternoon and evening, ready to receive anyone who might wish to consult with them. The sons of Reşat Agha, for example, could also be found sitting and talking in customary places in Eskipazar. Hüseyin's behavior, however, is especially revealing. From time to time, he would leave his table to go to the old town mosque. There, he would remove his hat, coat, and shoes, roll up his sleeves and take off his socks, and then carry out his ablutions. Fully transformed from Kemalist to Muslim, he joined the ordinary villagers to perform the prayers. Afterward, he would return to his table in the Town Square Coffeehouse, where he appeared as a leading individual of the old republic. But he might be obliged to return to his office in the tea cooperative, where he appeared as a public official of the new republic.

Soon after I began to attend the "salon" in the smaller room of the Town Square Coffeehouse, Hüseyin invited me to pay him a visit at his workplace. When I first went to the Of Tea Producers' Assistance Cooperative (*Of Çaycılar Yardımlaşma Kooperatifi*), he received me in his private office, a spacious room furnished in the style of a high government posting. He was seated in a steel chair behind a steel desk, both of which were stationed on a raised platform. A large wooden frame enclosing a crimson quilted textile was attached to the wall behind the desk. Several large matching steel armchairs were just in front of and below his desk, facing the crimson quilted background. These were unusually luxurious furnishings for a town where most tables, chairs, and cabinets were locally made by carpenters and ironworkers.

I was invited to sit in one of the chairs. Doing so, I found myself in a position of lowness regarding Hüseyin in a position of highness. He appeared from behind his desk, framed by the crimson background. As I surveyed the office, other messages of bureaucratic and administrative eminence came into view. There was a portrait of Kemal Atatürk on the wall, as there would have been in virtually any state or public office at the time. More exceptionally, there was also a portrait of Mithat Paşa, the most eminent of the Ottoman bureaucratic modernizers. A telephone, a more or less rare instrument in the town of Of at that time, was on the desk and covered with an embroidered cloth. Soon after I sat down, the telephone rang. Hüseyin removed the cloth, picked up the receiver and spoke for a few moments, then put the receiver back and replaced the cloth. He then asked me what I would like to drink, and then called upon a servant (*odacı*) to bring my request. I relate these details for a reason, not to make fun of my amiable host.

Hüseyin had modeled his office on the style followed by higher government officials at the time. The elevated platform, steel furniture, quilted and framed fabric, and private telephone could not be matched as a combination by any district official, not the bank director, the two judges, or even the district officer himself. One would have to look to the offices of the provincial governors in Rize and Trabzon to find something that matched or exceeded the quality of these furnishings. So Hüseyin was presenting himself to the public in the district of Of, as well as to visiting dignitaries from elsewhere, as a person of importance. And, of course, he was doing this at the expense of the members of the tea cooperative.

More interestingly, Hüseyin's manner of presenting himself tells us how bureaucratic and administrative eminence in the Turkish Republic still bore the traces of the imperial system. The elevated desk, the cloth background, the cloth telephone cover, the large steel chairs, and the offering of refreshments in the republican office were the remainders of the elevated dais, the cushions, and the hospitality of the imperial salon. The hard-edge, high-tech qualities of the furnishings signified modernity, even as the comfortable qualities of the furnishings signified sociability. A state officialdom had once ruled through a tactic of sovereign power based on a discipline of interpersonal association. Hüseyin had gone to lengths to present himself in the guise of a state official of the republic (even though he was only the director of a cooperative), and in doing so he had combined the symbols of the new modernity with the symbols of the old modernity. That he had done so was hardly an accident, since the cooperative in the new part of town was coordinated with the coffeehouse in the old part of town.

THE OF TEA PRODUCERS' ASSISTANCE COOPERATIVE

The membership of the Of Tea Producers' Assistance Cooperative included from 2,500 to 2,900 tea producers in the latter part of 1967, the uncertainty of the total being related to a looming membership crisis.[13] The cooperative had a staff of six employees, including the director, clerks, accountant, and janitor. Their offices were also well arranged and furnished, although not the equal of that of the director. The operating capital of the cooperative was almost one million Turkish lira, and its assets were valued at about two million Turkish lira.[14] The accumulation and disbursement of these large sums was regulated by a special law pertaining to tea cooperatives. There were provisions for the regular auditing of accounts and the verification of conformity with its charter.

A producer joined the cooperative by committing himself to paying 1,000 Turkish lira into the common fund, beginning with a down payment of 250 Turkish lira. This fund was then supplemented with capital provided by special state funds through the Agricultural Bank (*Ziraat Bankası*). Once a member, a producer was entitled to loans drawn on these funds, which were supposed to be used for purchasing fertilizer, agricultural implements, or insecticides. Some of these items, such as fertilizer, were also sold by the cooperative to their members at prices far below the market rate. Once each year, the tea cooperative was required by law to hold a meeting during which its members approved or rejected amendments to the articles of its constitutions and elected new representatives to its governing board. These occasions were witnessed by inspectors, who afterward submitted documents confirming that the meeting had been conducted properly.

13. Since its founding in 1955, four other cooperatives had been organized in the district of Of. Three of these were located in areas that were not under the influence of the Selimoğlu (Eskipazar, Taşhan, and Dumlusu). The fourth, organized in 1965, was located in the town of Of by a group of members who were separating from Hüseyin's cooperative. I shall eventually have more to say about this schism, which was taking place at the time of my residence.

14. The organizing capital of the cooperative was officially listed as 2,247,000 Turkish lira by obligation. Of this, 784,000 Turkish lira had been paid by the members as of the last accounting before January 1967. These were very considerable sums of money at the time. See chap. 1, note 8, for currency equivalents and annual *per capita* income estimates.

The government sponsorship of tea cooperatives was intended to encourage farmers to expand production at their own initiative. The program was subject to abuses, but it succeeded in fulfilling its objectives, perhaps more effectively than intended, since the eastern coastal districts were producing more tea than the government could process in its factories by the early 1980s. Still, I have to say that the laws regulating tea cooperatives were violated, at least in the instance of this particular tea cooperative. I knew this to be the case by direct witness, indirect evidence, open admission, and persuasive hearsay.

The producers were not always required to pay the stipulated membership fees in order to induce them to join the cooperative. The interest-free loans that they were given for fertilizer, implements, or insecticides were not always so used, but misdirected into nonagricultural activities. The fertilizer allotments were not used on their tea gardens but resold on the black market at substantial profits.[15] The funds of the cooperative were not always deposited in the Agricultural Bank as they should have been, and so accumulations and disbursements were not subject to proper accounting procedures. The nomination of officers was not free and open. The ballots for these officers were prepared before the annual meeting took place, and the ballot boxes were stuffed before the very eyes of the local and provincial inspectors.

It is easy to disapprove of Hüseyin's machinations. But I appreciated his openness and generosity, and I admired his inventiveness and determination. He was trying to accomplish something important, and he was working with everything that had come to him. In one way or another, he was willing to use all sorts of strategies: Kemalist secularism, the public interest, family elitism, party politics, and social Islamism. From his twin bases in the coffeehouse and cooperative, he was attempting to do something for himself and his brothers, but also for his family line, and even, somewhere down the road, for the town, if not also the district. Any director of an agricultural cooperative in Of would have been under enormous pressure from agnates, relatives, friends, and clients. So it was to be expected that the regulations applying to cooperatives, based on the principle of equality before the law, would be compromised by favoritism and cronyism.

15. I was told that the market price of a bag of fertilizer was about 80 Turkish lira in Akçaabat, where it could be used for growing tobacco, while the subsidized price in Of was about 20 Turkish lira. The reselling of cooperative fertilizer was another way of raising cash, but not necessarily for investment. Some claimed that the profits from illegal fertilizer sales were used for frivolous purposes, saying "They eat it."

The shortage of capital in the district of Of, as in all of Turkey, only served to intensify the pressures on the directors of cooperatives. Disputes over which members would be given money or fertilizer were fueled by the capital shortage. Should the large growers receive funds to finance their existing gardens? Or should the small growers receive funds to convert more of their cornfields into tea gardens? The regulations favored the former; nonetheless, the latter had an argument that seemed just and won sympathy. Although tea cultivation could provide a handsome profit, trucking offered even greater returns at the time. If one could borrow enough cash, one could buy a truck, hire drivers, and run the truck from city to city anywhere in Turkey, making a profit while paying off interest and wages. Indeed, a number of individuals were engaged in tea cultivation, an activity that could be conducted entirely by the women of a household, in order to acquire capital for financing truck purchases.

The director of a tea cooperative was therefore in a position to adopt policies that favored a constituency, and the constituency so favored did not have to be limited to those members who were serious tea cultivators. As it happened, Hüseyin had been using the cooperative as a device for promoting his political career since the later 1950s, probably with the support of many of its members. Inevitably this involved stretching, if not breaking, the official regulations governing the management of cooperatives. Some members were receiving more money and more fertilizer than they deserved, and consequently others were receiving less. The only way to conceal this problem was to bring in more and more members, which was possible since the number of producers was rapidly expanding during the later 1950s and early 1960s. Hüseyin was therefore obliged to acquire and retain as many members as possible. This entailed waiving the fees that the capital-hungry members owed to the cooperative in order to prevent them from deserting to other cooperatives, while nonetheless drawing funds from the Agricultural Bank for their membership. But if the number of members were to decline, then Hüseyin's expenditures on lavish office furnishings, restaurant banquets for officials, and frequent trips to Ankara for conferences would all appear as shortages in the cooperative accounts.

In my estimation, many of the members of the cooperative had first considered Hüseyin's questionable activities as a kind of investment on future returns that they could expect as his political career advanced. Because of this same expectation, they had also turned a blind eye to his practice of using the cooperative to reward friends and clients in order to garner votes on the occasion of local and national elections. However, Hüseyin did not prevail when he first entered the national elections in 1961.[16] And by 1965, it had become evident that his standing with provincial and national party leaders had slipped. More and more of his former supporters were having second thoughts. The result was a revolt within the Of Tea Producers' Assistance Cooperative.

THE REVOLT OF THE MEMBERSHIP

As early as 1958, some of the members of the Tea Producer's Assistance Cooperative had split to form a new cooperative with its offices in Eskipazar. Hüseyin is said to have done all he could to prevent the flight. But the Muradoğlu, who were among the principals of the new cooperative, were not going to be stopped. Then, some years later, two other tea cooperatives were organized in other parts of the district of Of. But the real crisis in membership came just before my arrival in the town of Of during the summer of 1965. A dissident group from within Hüseyin's own tea cooperative had set up a new tea cooperative in the town of Of itself, and they had succeeded in attracting a large proportion of the membership of Hüseyin's tea cooperative. The director of the new cooperative was a leading individual from the Selimoğlu, but he was not one of the descendants of Ferhat Agha. The executive committee included leading individuals from other family lines once associated with the Five Party, as in the case of the old cooperative.[17]

Backed by a loyal core of supporters, Hüseyin had done his best to manage all these difficulties. He had first attempted to oppose the organization of the new cooperative, just as he had opposed others in the past. Backed by his executive committee, he had then refused to grant the necessary papers or return funds to members who wished to join the new cooperative. Then, as the new cooperative was proving to be successful in attracting members,

16. A young member of the Muradoğlu was able to win election to the National Assembly some years later by a different strategy than that adopted by Hüseyin. He resided in Ankara for several years, worked as a bureaucrat, and had connections in the national party headquarters. The support of his agnates, relatives, friends, and clients could win him electoral support in the district of Of, but this was not enough. He needed a broader political backing and experience in order to attract voters elsewhere in the province of Trabzon and gain a seat in the National Assembly.

17. These family lines were agha-families and merchant-families whose members had been part of the core of the coalitions traditionally composed by leading individuals from the Selimoğlu. When I visited the offices of the new cooperative I found a son of Rasih Efendi (Selimoğlu) lounging about the office, but neither he nor his two brothers appear to have been in the leadership.

he had asked for the support of the descendants of Ferhat Agha. In response, the director of the Hazelnut Agricultural Sales Cooperative, his uncle, proceeded to seize all the warehouses in town so that the new tea cooperative had no place to store its fertilizer.

But these measures only impeded rather than prevented the membership growth of the new tea cooperative. When I returned to Of the next year, Hüseyin and his partners were bitterly denouncing the needless proliferation of tea cooperatives, even though they had themselves at one time deserted the tea cooperative in Rize to form their own association. As a more serious indication of crisis, Hüseyin's management of the tea cooperative had become openly controversial, bordering on the scandalous. In the winter of 1967, a number of townsmen complained to me about the management of agricultural cooperatives in Turkey. Naming no names, they said that cooperatives were run by "gangs" (*şebeke*) who defeated their purpose as free and open associations of agricultural producers. They could have cited examples of problems in cooperatives up and down the coast, but they obviously had a particular cooperative in mind at the time.

One of my interlocutors specifically mentioned problems in the Tea Producers' Assistance Cooperative, going so far as to say that Hüseyin lacked credibility. This interlocutor then launched into a condemnation of the laxness of government inspectors, improper use of agricultural loans, illegal membership in multiple cooperatives, and so on. From still another man, I heard that Hüseyin had been quarreling with the director of the Agricultural Bank. It was said that Hüseyin had withdrawn cooperative funds from the bank, keeping them in the cooperative safe. The gossip was especially impressive, not only as a hint of possible irregularities in cooperative finances, but also because the director of the bank was a regular of the Town Square Coffeehouse. I was surprised to hear these stories since it was common practice not to mention any local problem before an outsider, and certainly not before me, a visiting American. This suggested an absence of fear, in turn suggesting the anticipation of a fall.

The annual meeting of the Tea Producers' Assistance Cooperative, which took place in late March of 1967, did not exactly bring a climax to all these problems, but it did offer an indication of just how serious they were. The following account that appears in my notes has been edited:

> During the general assembly of the cooperative, the members were lively and outspoken. A crowd of men had jammed themselves into the rooms of the cooperative. Other men, who were unable to get inside, were standing in groups in the street. The crowd on the inside of the meeting room seemed to be divided into separate blocs. When a man

> would speak in one part of the room, he was noisily seconded by a group standing around him. In all there seemed to be four or five blocs. [By the insistent offer of a glass of tea as a gesture of hospitality], I was obliged to sit in a separate and adjoining room, the office of the director, indirectly observing and listening through a doorway to what transpired in the main meeting room. A number of the Selimoğlu and their supporters [names deleted] were with me, pretending to be disinterested in the discussion that was taking place. However, when a particularly harsh criticism of the cooperative was made by one of the members, one of them would remark, "Who said that?"
>
> Hüseyin was leading the meeting, haranguing the crowd about this and that, occasionally assisted by Salih, and another relative from the home village of the family line. There was a good deal of shouting from among the members. At one point, Hüseyin stood on the table before the executive committee, waving his arms and shouting back in an effort to make his point over the din. The headman of [a village composed entirely of the members of a single family line, one that had formerly been associated with the Five Party] was carrying a stick that he occasionally used to silence those around him. I had the impression that he sometimes objected to the proposals of the executive committee. All in all, the polite consensus that usually characterizes such meetings was not in effect.
>
> Yusuf stood toward the back of the room in the midst of a claque composed of the clerks and janitor of the cooperative. When Hüseyin, or one of the executive committee, made a proposal, Yusuf would lead the clerks and janitor in shouting out, "Accept! Accept!" (*Kabul! Kabul!*). Yusuf himself never attempted to hold the floor but muttered and glowered at the critics in the meeting room. Sometimes the reactions of the crowd were harsh and angry. But there were also moments when someone shouted out a joke of some kind, causing everyone to laugh together, including Hüseyin and his executive committee.

The three issues that most impassioned the general assembly were 1) the distribution of fertilizer to the membership, 2) the resignation of members who wished to join the new cooperative, and 3) the question of whether the funds of the cooperative would be deposited with the Agricultural Bank.[18] All of the following violations were alleged. The directors did not want those who owed money to resign leaving their debts. The directors refused to return the deposits of those who did not owe money. The directors would not provide the documents indicating that a member had officially resigned.

18. During the meeting, I heard one man shout, "Fertilizer, fertilizer, we don't want anything else but this" (*Gübre, gübre, başka bir şey istemiyoruz*).

At one point, Hüseyin called on several angry villagers who had been shouting out such charges to come forward. There and then he gave them their official documents of resignation, but no one else dared to press him on this issue.

At the close of the meeting, Hüseyin asked for approval of fourteen new articles, and he received it. He then said that the terms of two members on the executive committee were expiring, and so it was necessary to elect two new representatives. Since the old members had done so well, however, he recommended they be renominated for another term. The two members in question were from two large family groupings that had once been associated with the Five Party. There were shouts from the crowd and then countershouts from the claque. Other nominations were offered, for a total of five. All these nominations were eventually accepted. At this point, Yusuf and two of his close associates came into Hüseyin's office, where I was sitting. Yusuf took a large number of envelopes from one of the drawers and began to stamp them, assembly line–style, with the seal of the cooperative. One of his associates, a district cooperative inspector (*müfettiş*), then produced a large number of slips with the names of the five nominated individuals already typed on them. They then began to stuff these slips into the envelopes and seal them. When they were finished, they took the envelopes and passed them out to members, who dutifully turned them over to one of the cooperative employees as they left the offices. This man then brought all the envelopes back into Hüseyin's office, where they were opened before both the district and provincial cooperative inspectors, who then verified the count of all these pretyped ballots. Each of the two men nominated by Hüseyin received some eighty-odd votes. The other three nominees each received forty-odd votes. The reelection of the incumbents was then confirmed by the inspectors, who filled out an official document testifying to this fact.

The directors had triumphed, receiving approval for all the articles and the reelection of the two representatives they had wanted. But they were not reassured by the outcome, which had only been achieved by an unseemly process that carried the risk of a flight of the membership. When I encountered Hüseyin coming out of the meeting and asked him how he was, he replied, "I am covered in sweat. I am not well" (*Terliyim. İyi değilim.*). He then left for one of the town restaurants, where he and the other members of the executive committee feted the district and provincial cooperative inspectors. Later that evening, in the smaller room of the Town Square Coffeehouse, some of his concerns came to light. Yusuf, Hüseyin, and Salih were all there, hosting their guests who had come down from the villages for the annual meeting. When I entered the smaller room, I understood something was wrong. The aforementioned headman (of the village composed of a single family line) was dissatisfied and complaining. The producers in his village had not received their fair share of the fertilizer allotment. To make his case, he cited the amount of fertilizer that had been allotted to the producers of the home village of the Selimoğlu. At this point, most of the men sitting in the smaller room became silent, since they were not from either of the two family lines. The principals began to argue with one another, vigorously but not angrily. Yusuf, who had no official capacity in the tea cooperative whatsoever, reminded the headman that he had himself received a very large amount of fertilizer, concluding, "We have always loved you!" (*Seni severdik!*). The headman admitted that he could not say that he had received less than his full share, but he would not be able to explain to his villagers why they had received so little.

RECONFIGURING THE OLD REPUBLIC IN THE NEW REPUBLIC

Hüseyin had run the cooperative as a resource for a circle of agnates, relatives, friends, and clients. But once his political prospects dimmed, his associates had begun to recalculate. These events were indications that the configuration of the old and new republic was shifting during the 1960s. In conclusion, I will explain this shift.

The office of the new tea cooperative, the one that had been organized in the town itself by dissidents from the old cooperative, was located in a building of no special distinction in the older part of town. The rooms were not particularly large. Their floors consisted of bare wooden planks. The walls lacked any kind of decoration, save for a calendar. The desks and chairs were wooden, secondhand, and rickety. The staff consisted of just three individuals, a director, an accountant, and a janitor. I was not able to see the books of the cooperative, but I was told by a man on the executive committee that they had almost five hundred members, and would have had many more were it not for the restrictive measures taken by the other cooperative. It was as though the new cooperative had been specifically designed to emphasize frugality, that is, how little had been spent on rent, furnishings, and decor, and therefore how little the director wished to aggrandize himself.

The director, Süleyman Selimoğlu, had himself been the accountant of the old cooperative. When I met him, he was unshaven, tieless, and coatless. He explained to me how the new cooperative had resulted from quarrels (*geçimsizlik*) about the distribution of loans and fertilizer. He took care not to criticize specific individuals. But he did say that those producers who had developed excellent tea gardens were not favored by the directors of the old cooperative. Instead, the resources of the cooperative had been needlessly squandered or diverted. His group of founders had therefore resigned from the old cooperative in order to organize a new one that would focus solely on encouraging tea cultivation. The gossip in the town agreed with the director. The administration of the new cooperative was said to conform with government regulations, heretofore a novel procedure.

The old and new tea cooperatives held their annual meetings on the same day at the same time, so I was only able to attend the meeting of the former. According to a report, there was no shouting at all during general assembly of the new cooperative, although there were some points of contention. One of the members of its executive committee laughed with pleasure when I gave him my account of the brouhaha during the general assembly of the old cooperative. Still, the new cooperative was not entirely different from the old. Süleyman, the director of the new cooperative, was still a leading individual from the Selimoğlu, although of a set (*takım*) distinct from both that of Ferhat Agha and Rasih Efendi.[19] The members of the executive committee of the new cooperative also included individuals from the same sets of large families as the members of the executive committee of the old cooperative. So the founders of the new cooperative were not ordinary villagers and townsmen.

Both the old and new cooperatives were founded by individuals who represented the old republic in the new republic. But the two cooperatives were not administered by the same methods or for the same objectives. The old cooperative had been run in a way that recalled the late imperial period. Local elites, with the support of a circle of agnates, relatives, friends, and clients, set about to colonize the state system. They did so with the understandable intention of subverting the ends of the centralized state system so that it served the ends of the local state society. The new cooperative had been set up as it became apparent that the old methods and objectives were no longer working. Leading individuals from large family groupings were now obliged to recognize that their clients possessed more economic alter-

19. Süleyman had replaced Yusuf as headman of the central quarter of the town in 1952, continuing to serve until 1960 (see fig. 2). During my residence, his first cousin, also of the Selimoğlu, but not of the descendants of Ferhat Agha, had become the headman of the central quarter of the town. As for Süleyman, he would remain the director of the new cooperative for many years, after which he would follow in the footsteps of Yakup Selimoğlu, successfully running for mayor in 1984.

natives than ever before.[20] They were still able to monopolize all public offices open to local residents, but they were now forced, if not inclined, to run local institutions in a manner that was more compatible with the economic interests of their membership. This was the situation whose logic came to light during the annual meetings of the two tea cooperatives in late March 1967.

In the analysis of coffeehouses and cooperatives in this chapter, I have repeatedly pointed to the role of the old republic in the new republic, that is, to the imperial legacy of the district of Of. In doing so, I do not mean to suggest that nothing had ever changed in Of, Trabzon, or Turkey. Indeed, change has always been a prominent feature of public life, from earlier, during the Empire, until now, during the Republic. So the echo of the past in the present is not inconsistent with displacement and dislocation. Let us return briefly to the coffeehouses, which were taken to be a measure of the old republic in the new republic at the outset of this chapter.

In the old days, the government had occasionally burned down the mansions, coffeehouses, and markets of aghas, just as the aghas had occasionally burned down the mansions, coffeehouses, and markets of their rivals. The resort to violence was a consequence of the dissemination of sovereign power through interpersonal association. By the logic of such a regime, circles of interpersonal association were under the constraint of military necessity. As a consequence, aghas from agha-families owned and sponsored coffeehouses, and the ordinary villagers and townsmen who constituted their followings were obliged to sit and talk in these coffeehouses. From the later imperial period, however, new kinds of coffeehouses had begun to appear, ones in which a discipline of social thinking and practice had no strong connection to the leading individuals from large family groupings. Perhaps in fits and starts, but nonetheless inexorably, new kinds of circles of interpersonal association had been gaining ground, especially during periods of greater economic activity and opportunity.

The transition from a one-party to a multiparty system had led to a resurgence of leading individuals from large family groupings in public life. Nonetheless, the Town Square Coffeehouse was the only coffeehouse

20. One successful trader in the market spelled out this analysis for me in 1967 (almost thirty years before I realized the significance of what he was telling me). He explained that political power and influence had become diffuse in Of. It was no longer possible for one man or a group of men to gain control of the affairs of the town, and certainly not the district. He said this was an entirely new development that had only recently come about and would have not been true twenty years previously.

in the town of Of that had a strong connection with leading individuals and large family groupings. Otherwise, ordinary villagers and townsmen could elect to sit in one of at least seven other coffeehouses in the older part of town, including the "teahouse" (*çayhane*) managed by my companions in the Crystal Palace (see chap. 2). This was a gathering place for villagers and townsmen who were "not from the aghas" (*ağadan değil*). Leading individuals from large family groupings were never to be seen there.[21] So ordinary villagers and townsmen were able to form their own circles of interpersonal association, more or less independently of leading individuals from large family groupings. They did so in the course of all kinds of economic engagements, labor migration, entrepreneurial adventures, and business dealings, which were not limited to Of, but extended to Trabzon, Erzurum, Adana, Istanbul, Munich, and Berlin. Income from tea cultivation was rapidly rising as gardens first planted some years before became increasingly productive. Transportation and construction firms run by Oflus in various cities had become increasingly profitable with increasing urbanization. Cash remittances sent home from Germany by migrant workers had become substantial.

All these special factors were compounded by the effects of a general economic expansion during the 1960s. Ordinary villagers were making money as never before. As a consequence, the total value of commercial transactions in the town market was soaring, inflating land prices and building rents. The sociopolitical hegemony of leading individuals from large family groupings was then compromised by market differentiation and expansion during the 1960s. Such a phenomenon was not unprecedented. There had been earlier rises and falls in economic activity in the eastern coastal districts, and hence earlier rises and falls in the claims of aghas and agha-families on ordinary townsmen and villagers. Nonetheless, the sheer scale of the increase in economic opportunities in the twentieth century was unprecedented, especially after the beginning of the multiparty period. Whether these opportunities are judged to represent a new kind of liberty or a new kind of subjection, they unquestionably eroded the hegemony of leading individuals from large family groupings.

Already by the time of the general assembly of the tea cooperative, Hüseyin had begun his long and slow descent from a position of prominence. He was still chairman of the Red Crescent Society at the time, but the number of his other public offices was dwindling. He had been replaced as chair-

21. Actually, the owner of the Crystal Palace Hotel was "from the aghas," but he had chosen to lease his property to my companions.

man of the RPP. The new chairman was a lawyer from a merchant family of local origin rather than from one of the large families. And Hüseyin had also been replaced as the chairman of the Middle School Parent-Teacher Association. The new chairman was a lawyer who had moved to Of from Bayburt who had no standing with the large families of the district. At the annual meeting of the Parent-Teacher Association in the spring of 1967, Hüseyin had stood up to deliver a speech, but he was not well received. The audience of about a hundred fathers (no mothers) began to grumble as he continued to declaim, and he was eventually asked to sit down by the new chairman before finishing what he had to say.

One or more circles of professionals and merchants would continue to assert themselves in the public life of the town, for the most part, in the sphere of educational endowments and institutions. But there were other segments of public life that would for a long while remain closed to them. If, for example, the founders of the new tea cooperative had not been who they were, if they had not been leading individuals from large family groupings, their office equipment and records might well have ended up in the river one dark night. So the old republic would continue to inhabit the new republic in the district of Of, as it does even to this day, but only insofar as its representatives adopted new methods and objectives in order to cope with new political and economic realities.

12 The City
Nations and Empires

LIBERATION DAY: THE TURKISH NATION IN THE DISTRICT OF OF

The celebration of Liberation Day in Sürmene occurs three days before the same celebration in Of (February 28), since the Russians had withdrawn from Sürmene earlier. With the idea of making a comparison between the celebrations, I traveled from Of to Sürmene with a friend during the early spring of 1967. Since that town extends for a considerable distance along the coast, we initially had difficulty locating the place where the celebration would occur. A man we met at a minibus stop told us where we should go, but he dismissed the entire affair as "nonsense" (*fasafariya*). A little later, we joined a large crowd watching a parade consisting of a military corps marching in formation, the Trabzon municipal band playing nationalist marches, and children from the primary and middle schools. After the parade, municipal and district officials made speeches, and a few of the children recited poems celebrating Turkish heroism during the Independence War. The proceedings could be described as an official celebration, so well organized that it was formal and tedious.

Back in the district of Of, an entirely different mood was already noticeable that same evening.[1] It was expected that the ceremonies would once again be attended by a significant fraction of the district population. Yusuf, *éminence grise* of the descendants of Ferhat Agha, and his bosom buddy,

1. As it had happened, the Battle for Of in 1916 had begun on virtually the same day of the year that the Russians had evacuated the district two years later in 1918. So Liberation Day simultaneously marks resistance to as well as liberation from the Russian military occupation.

Molla İshak, a Greek-speaking hodja from Çaykara, had been making plans for weeks. Yusuf would lead a group of citizens dressed in period costume as the "militia forces" (*milis kuvvetleri*). Molla İshak would deliver a speech he had been writing in praise of those who had bravely fought the Russian troops.

The evening just before the ceremonies, in the Town Square Coffeehouse, the two of them were excitedly anticipating their performances. The molla was dressed in his newly tailored militia uniform, consisting of black baggy pants, black vest, black headscarf, and white shirt. He was also equipped with several new and old pistols, a powder horn, and binoculars. He demonstrated how one of his pistols had to be fired with a hammer since it lacked a trigger, producing an ear-splitting gunshot and blinding smoke within the confines of the coffeehouse. He then dramatically delivered his speech at the top of his voice, benefiting from his experience as a sermon-giver, to the approval of all those in attendance.

Early the next day trucks overflowing with men and women from the villages began to arrive in Atatürk Square. By nine o'clock in the morning thousands of people had assembled for the celebration, the men milling about the square, the women standing on rooftops and balconies. As the crowds continued to swell toward ten or twenty thousand, the municipal loudspeakers repeated again and again that anyone firing weapons would be subject to arrest and fine. After the parade and speeches were over, these warnings would be flouted as men roamed the street firing weapons all afternoon. One favorite stunt was to sneak up behind the resident ethnographer, then fire a pistol or rifle close to his ear, producing a reflexive leap into the air.

Toward eleven o'clock in the morning, gendarmes arrived to clear a small space in Atatürk Square. Swinging long switches, they slowly drove the crowd back from a pole mounted in the center of the square. This done, a professional folklore team consisting of seven men from the western coastal district of Akçaabat assembled near the pole. Dressed in period costumes and adorned with international medals, they began to dance the *horon* in a quick step, first squatting and then standing, as one of their members played a reed flute (*zurna*) and another beat a drum (*davul*) with sticks. This was the first of many dances that they performed intermittently throughout the day.

Around noon, the gendarmes returned to clear a larger space in Atatürk Square, this time with more difficulty. The square was jammed with men, while the rooftops and balconies of the surrounding buildings were crowded with village women wearing blue, red, black, and white body shawls. Once the gendarmes had done their work, the parade entered the square. It began, as in Sürmene, with the military corps, followed by the Trabzon municipal band. The group of citizens organized by Yusuf and the molla came next, dressed in the costumes of the militia forces of the late imperial period. The schoolchildren concluded the parade, as in Sürmene, but they too had taken pains to present themselves in a special way. The boys of the primary school were dressed as the men of the Imperial College. They had moustaches painted on their faces and wore imitations of the tall fold-over headgear. They marched in the janissary style, turning to the left and right as they proceeded, and they sang janissary songs. The girls of the primary school who followed them were dressed as the women of the imperial harem. They wore "silk" baggy pants, caftans, and gossamer veils.

Each of these groups, after passing through the square, assembled at different stations in the square, facing the bust of Atatürk. The militia forces, however, moved out of sight. The first speech was then given by the school secretary, that is, the Kemalo-Islamist hodja of the town worthies (see chap. 2). He read a brief account of the heroism of the Oflus during the Russian advance in 1916 and the Russian retreat in 1918. As he finished, he called out in a loud voice, "Let the militia forces move into action!" At first nothing happened, so that he was obliged to repeat the command several times. At last, the militia forces appeared, noisily firing their weapons, which were armed with blanks (see fig. 12). Yusuf came first, mounted on a horse, thus representing one of the old aghas, presumably his grandfather, Ferhat Agha. He wore a brimless hat that evoked the old style of military headgear, and he carried a rifle strapped to his back. He was followed by a second man, representing his adjutant, who was mounted on a supply horse. A man next to me said it should have been a mule, since no one but an agha could have ridden a horse.[2] These two were followed by the main body of the militia forces, all on foot, with one exception to be mentioned below. They were led by a hodja (whom I did not know) dressed as an imam with a turban on his head. From time to time, the hodja would draw a sword and call for the militia forces to charge. The hodja was immediately followed to one side by a man riding a Vespa motor scooter, a vehicle that had lately be-

2. I was repeatedly told that no one was allowed to mount a horse in Of except the agha, a point that was intended to illustrate how the old imperial hierarchy had been supplanted by republican equality. Compare the Ottoman sultan on his horse in the middle court (chap. 4).

Figure 12. The parade on Liberation Day.

come popular in the town. Like all the men following him, he too was dressed in period costume and carried a rifle. So far as I could tell, all those who composed the militia forces had a connection with the descendants of Ferhat Agha, some of them being clerks and janitors of the various cooperatives.

The militia forces advanced toward the pole in the center of Atatürk Square, on which was hung a black flag representing the foreign troops. They then began firing their rifles and pistols, still armed with blanks. After some moments, someone took down the black flag, placed it on the muzzle of his rifle, and tore it to shreds by repeated discharges. This impromptu performance much pleased the crowd. Once the flag had been destroyed, the Trabzon municipal band played the national anthem. The crowd listened quietly and respectfully but did not sing. After the band had finished playing, Molla İshak gave his speech in honor of the militia forces, firing off his ancient pistol with a hammer at the conclusion, to the puzzlement of his audience. A girl and boy from the middle school followed, reading speeches they had written and passionately reciting a patriotic poem. The district officer concluded the ceremony by saying a few words and then reciting a poem by Mehmet Akif. The latter was the author of the Turkish national anthem, but also a critic of secularism and therefore a favorite of religious conservatives. The district officer had taken care to select a poem that fit the religious sentiments of the majority of those in attendance.[3]

The Liberation Day celebration, attended and enjoyed by a significant fraction of the district population, was an impressive demonstration of the public spirit of the Oflus. On an occasion that commemorated a local episode in a struggle that led to a national awakening, they were able to imagine themselves as something more than mountaineers living in remote and isolated hamlets. Many in the audience knew of ascendants who had taken part in the Battle for Of, and so had participated in the building of the Turkish Republic. A few also knew that more distant ascendants had taken part in imperial campaigns, and so had participated in the building of the Ottoman Empire. Despite a mishmash of local customs, an unacceptable Turkish dialect, an embarrassing non-Turkic language, and country manners, the Oflus did not consider themselves bystanders in world history.

But what exactly was being celebrated in Atatürk Square, and who exactly were the celebrants? The elements of Liberation Day in Of, as in Sürmene, were much the same as those of nationalist commemorations everywhere in the Turkish Republic. The officials, soldiers, bandsmen, citizens, teachers, and children represented the past, present, and future of the Turkish Republic. But the elements of Liberation Day in Of, in contrast to those in Sürmene, were presented in such a way that they departed from conventions that had until recently been in force. The citizens appeared as militia forces of the late Ottoman Empire. The children appeared as the men and women of the sultan's palace. This was the imperial past, not the national past.

During the early years of the Turkish Republic, it would have been unlikely, if not strictly forbidden, for schoolchildren to dress up as janissaries and concubines. After all, the revolution in public culture had been conducted against the Ottomans, first by force of arms, and later by legal reforms, at least according to official national history. But by 1967, if not sometime earlier, a deviation from radical Kemalist principles had become permissible. Now, the imperial period could be the subject of children's make-believe. In this context, the costumes and pantomimes of the schoolchildren could be seen as a sign of the success of the revolution in public culture in the later 1960s. The classical imperial period could be recuperated as a moment of triumph and glory, since no one believed that classical

3. He appealed to religious conservatives on other occasions as well. During the month of Ramadan, when attendance at the morning prayers was heavy, he stood outside the mosque to greet the crowds of men as they left the building.

imperial institutions had any claim whatsoever on the present. Children could therefore "play" at being janissaries and concubines.[4]

On the other hand, citizens had represented an agha and a hodja as the leaders of the local militia on the occasion of a foreign invasion. Such a scene, or something much like it, had actually occurred repeatedly on the occasion of successive Russian incursions around the years 1787, 1810, 1828, 1877, and 1916. To so represent the Battle for Of was to trace the origins of the Turkish Republic to the regional social oligarchy of the post-classical Empire. Yusuf and the molla had played out this little drama before the bust of the founder of the Turkish Republic. But Yusuf, the "play agha" in the parade, really was the most powerful man in the town of Of, just as the molla, the "play hodja," really was his closest confidant, and the "play militia" really was drawn from a circle of agnates, relatives, friends, and clients. The little drama was both a play and not a play. So this part of the parade in Atatürk Square raised a question about the success of the revolution in public culture.

At the time, none of my interlocutors mentioned to me the significance that I have just attributed to this event. The little drama with antique flintlocks, blanks, and a black banner was dismissed by a good many as just so much "nonsense." But it is unlikely that the district officer who had addressed the public in 1939 would have tolerated any such nonsense if he were as good as his word: "We will thrash the aghas. We will save the simple and pure folk from their influence, their execrable acts, and their deceits and tricks. We will not give them precedence in any manner, with respect to any thing or task" (see chap. 9). By this radical Kemalist dictum of the time, the little drama of Liberation Day would have to be described as counterrevolutionary. It overtly asserted that aghas and hodjas had led the people of Of into the initial phase of their national history. It covertly asserted that the descendants of aghas and hodjas continued to lead the people of Of in the present phase of their national history. In this regard, the little drama during Liberation Day of 1967 was an unprecedented departure, inconsistent with existing accounts of the events in question.

Neither Altay Yiğit nor Hasan Umur had described the Battle for Of in counterrevolutionary terms (see chap. 9). Yiğit hoped to confirm that aghas from agha-families in 1916 were a local leadership that had already become

4. Some years later in Istanbul, groups of an Islamist orientation would begin to commemorate Mehmet II's conquest at the old walls of the city. This presumably would have raised the question of whether the palace could henceforth remain a subject of children's play.

a nationalist leadership even before the declaration of the Turkish Republic. This is why he described how they carried out the orders of the "Turkish" commander of a "Turkish" army, why he showed their faces in photographs, and why he suppressed references to hodjas and mollas. Taking these steps, he hoped to persuade his readers, and no doubt himself, that the revolution was still moving forward in 1949, as the descendants of aghas and agha-families were gaining control of nationalist organizations and institutions. Similarly, Umur also hoped to move the revolution forward by offering helpful criticisms based on his unusual experiences. He praised the role of professors and academies in the founding of the Turkish nation, but with the intent of pointing to an existing gap between the Turkish state and the Turkish people. He hoped to persuade his readers, and no doubt himself, that Islamic teaching and learning, properly supervised by the state system, might be a resource for narrowing this widening gap. He certainly did not intend to turn back the clock to the post-classical imperial period. Directly and succinctly, he described the "time of the aghas" as a time of misgovernment based on violence and terror.

Yusuf and the molla were not of such reflective dispositions. They were celebrating their own social standing, which they simply assumed to be historically sanctioned and legitimate. And in doing so, they exemplify how national public culture was continuing to split and divide from the 1950s to the 1960s. Kemalist representations of the nation-state and nation-people were increasingly challenged by other representations. In the instance of Liberation Day in the district of Of, officials, military forces, schoolteachers, and classrooms were going out of focus. Local elites, the descendants of aghas and hodjas, were coming into focus.

The colonization of the new republic, based on official hierarchy and authoritarianism, by the old republic, based on social hierarchy and authoritarianism, may explain in part the fury of the younger generation that was to follow in the 1970s. Many young people of both leftist and rightist persuasions were saying that the revolution had failed, making more radical steps an imperative. But this very special period, which appears in retrospect to have been a decisive transition, lies beyond the scope of my study. I shall conclude by sketching still other ways in which national public culture was splitting and dividing as a consequence of urbanization.

OFLUS COME TO THE CITY

I first heard about the Of Culture and Assistance Association (*Of Kültür ve Yardımlaşma Derneği*) at the time of its founding in the winter of 1967. By chance, I had encountered one of my early acquaintances who had been away from the town for some weeks. He had been looking after his firm in Samsun, where he was constructing an apartment building. Now he was planning to move the firm to Istanbul, where business was more promising. As he told me this, he mentioned that some Oflus living in Istanbul were launching a new association for the many thousands of their fellow Oflus who lived there.[5] Each member would pay dues of so much a month, not to exceed 125 Turkish lira a year ($10 U.S.). With the accumulated capital, grants would be made first to needy students, but then to entrepreneurs who required start-up money for new businesses in the city. The organizers had anticipated that their association might eventually have as many as ten thousand dues-paying members, and they had calculated that there might be twenty thousand students in need of some assistance.

Some hours later, I heard someone report the same news to Salih Selimoğlu, who was sitting and talking with his friends in the Town Square Coffeehouse. They laughed together heartily, considering the whole thing a great joke; nonetheless, Salih was careful to interrogate the man who gave him the report and to learn exactly what the organizers intended to do. Eventually, I came to understand that the new Oflu association was similar to others that had been organized by urban migrants from other parts of the country from the 1950s through the 1960s. These associations were a direct result of the appearance of urban colonies of provincials in Istanbul, Ankara, Adana, and Izmir.

In the fall of 1986, I was able to visit the Of Culture and Assistance Association for the first time. It was located in the crowded Laleli quarter of Istanbul, just a few steps away from the old covered bazaar.[6] The association still had thousands of members, probably more than ever. Its members had consistently sponsored various charitable projects for Oflus over the years, both in Istanbul and in Of. They continued to disburse monthly grants to students, and they were then raising funds for a student hostel to serve the new high school (*lise*) in the town of Of. When I learned of the composition of the association's executive committee at that time, I recognized the names of some of the most prominent merchants in the town of Of during my earlier residence there.

5. Hasan Ulusoy, father of one of the organizers of the new association, had contributed a substantial sum of money in the late 1960s (some said forty thousand Turkish lira) for the rebuilding of the minaret of the old mosque in Of.

6. The association has since moved into luxuriously furnished quarters on the top floors of a tall building in the Fatih quarter.

On the occasion of my visit, I entered the coffeehouse (*kıraathanesi*) that was part of the association, referred to by my companion as the "Of Locale" (*Of Lokalı*). It was more or less like the coffeehouses in towns and cities all over the country. Small groups of men were sitting, drinking tea or coffee, playing cards or backgammon, and talking at tables. There were no women present. My companion immediately encountered someone who knew him. The conversation that followed was broken by long pauses. It was as though we were sitting in a coffeehouse in the district of Of. The following excerpts are from my field notes:

> We were greeted by two men sitting at a table in the Of Locale [1st pers.: *selamün aleyküm*; 2nd pers: *aleyküm selam, hoş geldin*; 1st pers.: *hoş buldum*; 2nd pers: *merhaba*]. They were invited to sit and drink tea with them [1st pers.: *merhaba*; 2nd pers: *nasılsın?*; 1st pers.: *iyiyim, sen de nasılsın?*, etc.]. One of them was well acquainted with [my companion]. The other man did not know him, but said he had known his father. He told [my companion] that they were related to one another (*hısımlığımız var*); the sister of [so-and-so] was said to have married [so-and-so].
>
> The man then asked [my companion] his birth date, rather than his age [thereby contextualizing him generationally in the past rather than biographically in the present]. They discussed whether this individual and that individual was alive or dead, when the funeral was held and where, and also who had married whom. [My companion] was having some dental work done and apologized for his slurred speech. The man then told us that he had been in Australia for five years. He spoke admiringly of it as rich country with factories that had been financed with English and American capital.

The two men told my companion that in the coffeehouse a register was kept in which Oflus living in Istanbul listed their addresses and telephone numbers, both residential and business. My companion asked for the register and wrote down the name and address of his son, who had just set himself up in Kadıköy (across the Bosphorus) as an architect.

Some weeks later, the editor of a new magazine invited me to be interviewed by a group of students at the Of Locale. His magazine was written and published by Oflus and directed at an Oflu readership, especially those Oflus living outside the district in the larger cities of the country, not only Istanbul, but also Adana, Ankara, Izmir, and Trabzon. On the occasion of my second visit to the Of Locale, I was shown a complex just to the side of the coffeehouse. I met with the students there in a conference room with comfortable armchairs and couches. After the interview, I encountered individuals whom I had known during my residence in the town of Of during the later 1960s. They had since moved to Istanbul, where they now had places of business. I also met men in their later twenties who said they remembered me from when they were children. I naively asked one of my acquaintances the location of the squatter settlements (*gecekondu*) in which migrants from the district of Of had congregated. Offended, he told me that the Oflus lived in apartments and houses in the better parts of the city, not in squatter settlements.[7]

During a third visit to the Of Locale that same year, I attended a lecture that was given by a retired military officer who addressed a group of businessmen in the conference room. He was one of a number of Oflus who had distinguished themselves in the Turkish military (especially the army, but also the navy). Indeed, a resident of the old district of Of (the district of Çaykara) had been a member of the General Staff during the 1960s, after which he had become president of the Republic after election by the National Assembly. The talk by the retired military officer consisted of an insightful commentary on the contemporary political situation. A lively discussion followed, during which members of the audience asked the speaker penetrating questions. There were no women present.

Afterward, I was shown still other rooms behind closed doors. When I was taken behind the first set of doors, I discovered a few tables, waiters passing through, and a kitchen. I had been entirely unaware of the existence of this part of the association during my earlier visits. My hosts arranged for a meal to be served to me there, and I was able to talk with some children who had been born in Istanbul. I asked them whether they were themselves Oflu. One of the little girls insisted that she was not an Oflu, but an İstanbullu, a response that amused my hosts. After my meal, I was briefly allowed to look behind yet another set of doors. To my astonishment, I discovered yet another dining room, crowded with men sitting at tables eating, drinking, smoking, and talking. There were interiors within interiors within interiors in the Of Locale.

Early the next year, I was invited to the annual celebration of the Of Liberation Day in Istanbul, which was held as close as possible to the official day itself, that is, February 28. The events were organized by the Of Culture and Assistance Association and took place in a music hall (*gazino*) in the Aksaray quarter of Istanbul, between the Laleli and Fatih quarters. I would estimate that about two thousand people attended this occasion. As the celebrants, both men and women, entered the hall, they were received by two

7. I would be surprised if this were universally true.

lines of young men in formal evening dress who greeted them and escorted them to their tables. The seating was generally segregated by table, with the men sitting on one side of the table facing the women sitting on the other side. The women in attendance were dressed in various ways, according to their age, taste, and wealth. Some women kept their heads and arms covered, but there were also women without head coverings wearing fashionable dresses. In the course of the evening, some men left their tables to greet friends sitting elsewhere in the room. Most people remained seated at their tables talking among themselves and occasionally listening to the music. There were no formal speeches, such as I had heard during the meetings of cooperatives in the town of Of.

The entertainment consisted of performances according to the conventional format of a music hall in Istanbul, although some restraints were apparent. Men and women singers accompanied by different instrumental groups performed folk, pop, and classical songs. Alcohol was served at some tables but not at others. There was no belly dancing, otherwise common in most music halls. At one point, one of the members of the executive committee of the association called on those present to give generously to the building fund for the student hostel. He and others then passed through the tables with sacks for cash contributions. Toward the end of the occasion, after the professional singers had concluded their performances, a group of young Oflus mounted the stage and began to dance an Oflu *horon* to the frenetic music of the eastern Black Sea fiddle (*kemençe*), rather than the shrill music of the western Black Sea flute (*zurna*).

The celebration of Liberation Day did not make any reference whatsoever to the old republic of local elites, the aghas and the hodjas. This was a gathering of civil servants, professionals, shopkeepers, businessmen, and their families. They were men and women who had different political opinions and who followed different social conventions. They composed a Turkish nation not so much as a citizenry, but as a society, one that tolerated difference in the urban context, at least up to a certain point. It was possible for women to cover themselves or remain uncovered. It was possible to drink or not drink. It was even possible for the young men, some of who must have been born in Istanbul, to celebrate being Oflu by a folklore performance. In the district of Of, singing, dancing, and fiddling were frowned upon by the hodjas. Other than on Liberation Day, I never saw any such performances in the town of Of during the 1960s. But in Istanbul, young people from the district could represent themselves as a folk, perhaps for the first time in five hundred years. But this was but one of a number of new ways the Oflus of Istanbul were reimagining themselves as a society of a nation that had once been a society of an empire.

Before the end of my two-year residence in Istanbul (1986–88), I was invited to attend the opening of a second branch of the Of Culture and Assistance Association in the city of Kadıköy, across the Bosphorus. The earliest colonies of Oflus in Istanbul had been concentrated on the European side, but there were now also many Oflus who lived or worked on the Asian side. The second branch had been organized to provide the latter with a more convenient meeting place. When I attended the opening celebration, I was able to enter one of the association's inner rooms, which was crowded with men dressed in suits and ties who were standing and talking. Everyone was shaking hands, exchanging information regarding family backgrounds, village origins, and business activities. Those in attendance expected to meet Oflus whom they did not know. Some approached me to introduce themselves and to shake my hand, only to discover with some surprise that I was an American. The two branches of the Of Culture and Assistance Association were social clubs, not political clubs. The membership of both branches seemed to be distributed among a variety of political parties, as well as nationalist and religious parties. I cannot say in what proportion.

Of course, the Of Culture and Assistance Associations in Laleli and Kadıköy did not represent all the ways in which the Oflus had mutual interests and contacts. The Oflus also shared some new intellectual projects. For example, I have already mentioned the editor of the new magazine for Oflus. His name was Haşim Albayrak, author of *Of and Çaykara (1986),* which describes the social history of the old district of Of.[8] A picture of "Gazi Mustafa Kemal Atatürk" appears on the frontispiece. A chapter bears the title, "Were Turks the first settlers of Of?" and then reaches a positive answer to the question. On the other hand, the book cover represents the tombs of three hodjas credited with converting Christian Oflus to Islam during the seventeenth century. By these features, the work composes a history of the district of Of that fuses the official nationalism of the Turkish Republic with the official religion of the Ottoman Empire. Just a few years later, Ömer Asan would publish another kind of book, *Pontic Culture.* The title of the book uses a word that has negative connotations for Turkish nationalists since it is a word that Greek nationalists use to refer to the eastern Black Sea region. One of the initial sections bears the heading:

8. Altay Yiğit (1981) had also published a second volume thirty years after his account of the Battle for Of. It was a study of the history and folklore of Çaykara.

"Who were the first natives of Of?" The author asks the question only to illustrate that it cannot be definitively answered. To make his point, he illustrates how any kind of official history or official identity is insufficient to recognize fully the richness of a people's past. He then argues that "Pontic culture," that is, eastern Black Sea culture, combines all kinds of heritages, but especially Hellenic and Turkic. The last section of his book consists of a Turkish-Greek dictionary of terms current in the villages of the districts of Of and Çaykara. These two examples of different intellectual projects mirror different circles of interpersonal association among the Oflus of Istanbul. Albayrak's readers are probably not Asan's readers. But there were still other kinds of projects and circles among the Oflus in Istanbul as well.[9]

To survive in the great city, the Oflus had deployed a discipline of sociability in all kinds of ways for all kinds of ends. Several of the Oflus had become prominent Mafia bosses in the city, while a large number of Oflus appeared among their followers. I had heard about "Oflu Hasan" during the 1960s, when he was one of the most infamous of the "fathers" (*babalar*) in Istanbul. By the late 1980s, others had taken his place. One of the Oflu "*baba*" was said to receive daily visitors who came to pay him homage in the old style, stooping down and kissing his hand. One of my interlocutors told me that the Oflus had only learned the "mafia business" (*mafia işleri*) after coming to Istanbul, but they were very good at it because they "stuck together" (*tutkunluğumuz var*).

Some of the Oflus were also followers of religious leaders (*şeyh*) who were connected with religious brotherhoods (*tarikat*). The latter were principally Nakşibendi, but some were perhaps Kaderi. I have the impression that these kinds of religious associations were not circumscribed by place of origin, and so not necessarily headed by, or limited to, circles of Oflus. But I have very little information about such religious leaders and brotherhoods.[10] Most of my friends were pious, regularly performing their daily prayers, but they were not interested in religious leaders or brotherhoods. Perhaps this was a characteristic of the educated generation that came of age during the first decades of the Republic.

Although I am not at all well informed about *baba* or *şeyh*, I will venture a generalization. In regard to the Oflus, I would say that these two new

9. For examples of other intellectual projects in an urban context, see Meeker 1991, 1994b.

10. See Shankland 1999 for a good overview of the place of religious leaders and brotherhoods in the politics of Turkey.

types of leaders represented the reformulation of the tradition of old local elites in the urban context. The *baba* can be seen as a "fallen" version of the old agha. He is surrounded by armed followers. He receives visitors who pay him homage. He even serves as an intermediary between the state and citizens, fixing traffic citations and so on, for example. But unlike the old aghas, he is a shadow figure of urban life who lacks the legitimacy of state appointments or a community following. In contrast, the religious *şeyh* can be seen as a "risen" version of the old hodja. He would appear to be a religious exemplar rather than a person of learning who offers instruction in ethical thinking and practice. So in effect he is "above" the context of a state society based on ethical thinking and practice. He is the focus of religious identification and association among urbanites whose daily lives are structured by economic rather than communal interactions.

I have been told that one of the *baba* from Of was a descendant of one of the old aghas. I have also been told that one of the *şeyh* from Of was one of the last graduates of the old hodjas. If these facts are true, and my information is rather poor, I would nonetheless insist that both are new figures of the urban context (both in Of and in Istanbul), but at the same time adapted from the old imperial coordination of power and religion.

It was the prior existence of a public life in the district of Of that enabled the Oflus to immigrate and prosper in the greater cities of the country. However, in the absence of aghas and hodjas, who were still dominant figures in the district of Of, the Oflus in the greater cities formed associations that were less conventional, hence more inventive, and as a consequence, more differentiated and variegated.[11] By the 1980s, however, the town of Of was becoming more and more like a city.

THE CITY COMES TO OF

During my initial residence in the town of Of, my interlocutors had been preoccupied with aghas or, more exactly, with the quality of "agha-ness" (*ağalık*), as they had come to call it.[12] The ghosts of the old regime had somehow recently surfaced in the district of Of, probably beginning in the later 1950s. Agha-ness was said to be everywhere once again, in the streets of the town, in its coffeehouses, in the management of tea cooperatives, in the administration of the municipality, and in the organization of political

11. For a recent study of money and association in the city, see White 1994.
12. The use of this term would appear to be a neologism, since "agha-ness" would have once referred to a state appointment of an individual to serve as an agha in accordance with certain defined duties. See chaps. 7 and 8.

parties. Some said that the "agha mentality" (*ağa zihniyeti*)—meaning both to behave as an agha and to respect those who behaved as an agha—had never been eradicated in the district of Of. But others claimed that a pattern of leadership and followership, similar to what had existed in the old regime, had spread and intensified by a process of "aghafication" (*ağalanıyor, ağalanacak*).

As we saw in the last chapter, this intimation of an unwelcome return of aghas and agha-families was a consequence of a shift in the position of leading individuals from large family groupings. The new awareness of aghas and agha-families was actually a harbinger of a new degree of institutional rationalization that was accompanying economic differentiation and expansion. Aghas and agha-families had actually come into view because it was more possible than ever to imagine that they were unnecessary and unworkable. Eventually, institutional rationalization would lead to a diminution of the awareness of "agha-ness," but it would not lead to the disappearance of leading individuals from large family groupings. Leading individuals from large family groupings continued to adapt and adjust to public life. It therefore became harder and harder to understand where they had come from or what they represented.

In 1988, I was able to pay a visit to the district of Of, the first in about ten years. The population had doubled, redoubled, and then doubled again since the 1960s, so that it probably exceeded twenty thousand. Now there were three tea-processing plants, seven banks, eight pharmacies, six doctors, and five dentists. Previously, there had been only one of each. Now there was a high school (*lise*), a school for imams (*İmam-Hatip Okulu*), and a girls' vocational school (*Özel Meslek Kız Lisesi*) in the town, as well as several middle schools (*orta okulu*) in different parts of the district. Before a single middle school in the town had served the entire district, and the only high schools had been in other parts of the province of Trabzon. The grid of streets had been expanded to include a large esplanade, and many more shops and warehouses had been constructed. There were also thousands of new apartments and many more planned. A significant number of people had made a lot of money, some by selling their gardens at hugely inflated prices, others by building or renting apartments to the crowds of new residents who had moved from the villages to the town.

Measured against my earlier experiences, encounters on the street were comparatively anonymous. In the 1960s, a stranger like myself would have been noticed upon stepping off the bus. He would have immediately been asked who he was and what he wanted. When I mentioned this change to my friends, they agreed, saying they commonly encountered individuals whom they did not know, and so they no longer thought to ask their names, business, or place of origin. I was also impressed with the new urban atmosphere of the town. Before, many of the residences were actually small farms surrounded by tea gardens and with livestock in their basements. When I sent a friend a postcard, it was not even necessary to have his street address. Just a name and surname were sufficient: "Mehmet Öztürk, Of, Trabzon." Now the postman could not possibly know the thousands of residents who lived in blocks and blocks of six-story apartment buildings.

Along with the new anonymity and urbanism, the old public sanctions had lost their force through differentiation of consumption patterns. Before, the wife of the only pharmacist in the town had been cursed and spat upon for leaving her hair uncovered during the weekly market. Now young women employees strolled through the market with bare forearms, something that would have been shocking two decades earlier. Before, a leading individual from a large family grouping had entered the studio of the town photographer and destroyed the photograph of one of his nieces that had been placed in the street window. Now, a son of the same photographer had opened a new boutique, a franchise of a national chain, with the latest women's fashions from Istanbul. Before, Hüseyin had run a stationery shop and bookstore as a way of involving himself in Kemalist politics and reform. Now his son, who was managing the store, had added a substantial video library. There was even a hint of cosmopolitanism. A large and comfortable hotel, The Tea City Hotel, had been opened. It featured an outdoor cafe where one might enjoy a splendid vista of the Black Sea coast. It also featured a restaurant with tablecloths and uniformed waiters, and dishes that matched the quality of those in the best Istanbul restaurants. The hotel, cafe, and restaurant had become a site for government and business conferences, and it had also become a regular stop for German tour buses passing between Trabzon and Rize.

I could hardly recognize the coffeehouses because of all the construction. The Crystal Palace Teahouse, where I had been so warmly welcomed, was no longer to be found. The Town Square Coffeehouse was also gone, but it was eventually replaced by a smaller version across the square. Otherwise, there were many new coffeehouses, some of them incorporated as private clubs, just as there were new kinds of social groups who attended them. But even though there were more coffeehouses than before, the proportion of the population who frequented them must have diminished.[13] The arrival

13. After the collapse of the Soviet Union, another bizarre interlude, the "time of Natashas," repeated the "time of the waiter girls" of the 1920s.

of television, already with several channels and with many more soon to come, had brought with it the living room as a meeting place for family and friends, including both men and women. Because of this change, the coffeehouses, still unattended by women, could not have been quite so important as forums of public life as they had been in the 1960s.

And yet many, if not most, of the public offices open to local residents in the town were still reserved for members of the Selimoğlu. How was it possible for circles of agnates, relatives, friends, and clients to continue to dominate public life? The discipline of interpersonal association had depended on all kinds of constraints that were now eroding. These included men's control of women, men's presence in coffeehouses, restricted intellectual engagements and resources, a political economy of patrons and clients, the imposition of authority by occasional threats of retaliation, the relative immobility of the rural population, and limited economic opportunities. Given that each of these conditions had been more or less compromised, how could circles of interpersonal association, based as they were on normative performances, survive in this town that was becoming a city?

The example of the Oflus in the greater Istanbul region provides the answer. A discipline of social thinking and practice was a resource by which the Oflus adapted to the city. The city was an anonymous urban environment, but it enabled interpersonal associations by concentrating the population, facilitating communication, and expanding economic opportunities. In Istanbul the Oflus were able to devise new kinds of interpersonal associations, some of them mercantile, some of them benevolent, some of them intellectual, some of them religious, and some of them criminal. In just the same way, circles of interpersonal association persisted in the town of Of even as they were becoming more differentiated and variegated in character.

THE PORTRAIT OF MAYORS IN THE MUNICIPAL BUILDING

One afternoon during my brief visit in 1988 I entered the new municipal building, where an employee invited me into the office of the mayor. Süleyman Selimoğlu, who had been the director of the "dissident" tea cooperative during the 1960s, was not in his office at the time. He had first been elected to the mayorship in 1984, his parsimonious style of management having apparently won the day with the voters. The municipal employee kindly offered me tea. Soon other employees joined us, as well as a number of town worthies. Together we recalled the days when I had been a resident. In the course of our conversation, I was shown a large framed picture hung on one wall. It was a montage of identity card photographs, purporting to represent all the mayors of the town since 1874. There were nine photographs in all, each accompanied by a name and dates of service. As we were examining the photomontage, one of the employees said that the mayorship of the town of Of had remained in the same family line for almost a 120 years. One of the town worthies present, an ex-mayor himself, said that this record of service for a single family line was without parallel anywhere else in the Republic of Turkey.

The portrait of mayors was indeed remarkable, even if not exactly for the reasons given. There were years in which the mayor had not been from the Selimoğlu family line, both before and after the declaration of the Turkish Republic.[14] The period of service of two of the other mayors had been inaccurately expanded to cover these gaps. There were also years when Mehmet Selimoğlu had served as mayor under a different surname. This detail was overlooked, although with justification, since he eventually reassumed the name of the family line. So the photomontage, by its inaccuracies and omissions, established what had not really been the case.

The portrait of mayors did, however, confirm that the hegemony of the family line still prevailed in the town of Of, since it was possible to assert a claim that was not strictly true. This having been said, one would have to add that the photomontage actually understated rather than overstated the historical prominence of the family line. Members of the Selimoğlu had figured in the government of the district of Of even before the town existed, for perhaps as long as 250 years, more than twice as long as the claimed 120 years. This is indeed a remarkable record that would surely have few parallels anywhere else in the Turkish Republic. The Selimoğlu had outlasted the "Hazinedaroğlu," the line of Süleyman Pasha and Osman Pasha. They had even outlasted the "Osmanoğlu," the line of Mehmet II and Süleyman I. So what we have to consider is not how members of the family line could claim so much, but rather why they were content to claim so little.

The photomontage commemorated the mayorship as the responsibility of the entire family line. It accurately recorded the fact that the mayorship had not been monopolized by the descendants of Ferhat Agha, but had passed from set to set (*takım*). In doing so, as I have noted above, it did not recognize that the aghas and ayans of the district had come from the family line since the eighteenth century. So, in effect, it ignored the opportunity to claim a strong connection with the imperial period. But at the same

14. Some of my acquaintances had cited the names of several individuals who had been the mayor of the town before and after the Great War but were not members of the Selimoğlu family line.

time, it did not recognize the role of leading individuals of the family line in the Battle for Of. So it also ignored the opportunity to claim a strong connection with the transition from Empire to Republic. Instead, the photomontage correlated leading individuals of the family line with the municipality. They had served as its mayors from the moment of its initial founding in 1874, fifty years before the national revolution, right down to the present. In so doing, the photomontage identified leading individuals of the Selimoğlu with the history of bureaucratic modernization in the eastern coastal region. This history had begun in 1874 with the incorporation of all district centers of the province of Trabzon as municipalities, even though many of them did not even have towns. The representation of the mayors of the town by photographs was itself a way of emphasizing this identification. The mayors appeared more convincingly as bureaucratic modernizers precisely because they also appeared in the form of an identity card photograph, a token of bureaucratic modernization.

One would have to credit Hüseyin Selimoğlu with the idea of so legitimizing the role of the family line in the district of Of, perhaps as early as the 1950s. He had chosen to hang a portrait of Mithat Paşa (a photograph being unavailable) above the quilted and framed fabric behind his desk in his office in the tea cooperative. But Hüseyin had only had the idea of legitimizing the family line in this way. In contrast, Süleyman Selimoğlu had come to prominence by insisting on the practice of bureaucratic modernization. As I recounted in the last chapter, he and his allies had successfully organized a second tea cooperative in the town in the face of opposition by the descendants of Ferhat Agha. He had done so by stressing his commitment to fairness and efficiency. Some years later, he had entered the race for mayor and won the office, presumably on the basis of his reputation as the director of the tea cooperative. And now, altogether appropriately, his mayoral office featured a portrait of mayors that identified the family with the period of bureaucratic modernization.[15]

So the "argument" of the photomontage was not the same as the "argument" of Liberation Day in 1967. The Selimoğlu had traveled a certain distance since the time of my residence in the town. The old tactic of sovereign power through interpersonal association, which had been revived

15. I do not know which mayor was responsible for the photomontage, or when it was first hung in the office of the mayor. My point is that the career of Süleyman brought the importance of fairness and efficiency to the foreground. Other members of the family line would have learned this lesson even before Süleyman became mayor.

during the early years of multiparty politics, was now in the background. It had been replaced by a claim to public service that stretched back to the imperial period of bureaucratic modernization. This indicated that "class" distinctions characteristic of a modern nation-state now supplemented the circles of interpersonal association of a regional social oligarchy. That is, leading individuals of the Selimoğlu claimed the mayorship by their professional training, experience, and contacts, even as they continued to rely on agnates, relatives, friends, and clients. This was a striking change from the 1950s, when some said that the mayor did not know how to read and write very well.

The capturing of public offices by a combination of bureaucratic professionalism and interpersonal associations was, however, subject to challenge. There were sectors of the population who saw bureaucratic procedures as mechanisms of domination and exclusion, and these same sectors of the population also featured circles of interpersonal association. Before my visit to the town of Of in 1988, I had been told by an acquaintance that the residents of the town of Of now included a large number of supporters of the Welfare Party (*Refah Partisi*), whose national leader was Necmettin Erbakan. This party appealed to those who resented the secularist policies of the Turkish Republic, since they experienced them as instruments of repression rather than participation. For example, many of those who voted for this party supported a return to the sacred law of Islam. Such a move, they could imagine, would at the same time legitimize their place in the Turkish Republic and reinforce their social solidarity, thus enhancing their political position.

Given the tradition of official Islam in the district of Of, it is not at all surprising that many, if not a majority, of the villagers who had moved to the town would vote for this Islamist political party. My acquaintance had also told me that the Selimoğlu were no longer able to muster enough votes to win the mayorship without the support of the Welfare Party. The leading individuals from the family line were therefore required, he maintained, to work closely with representatives of the Welfare Party, the latter having not yet fielded its own candidate for the mayorship. The fact of such a partnership would soon be plain to see in the evolving urban character of the town of Of.

THE IMPERIAL GREAT MOSQUE IN THE TOWN OF OF

I have already described how the town featured an extended grid of streets with blocks and blocks of new apartment buildings at the time of my 1988 visit. But I did not mention an impressive architectural project that had been initiated but not completed. A gigantic mosque in the style of the classical Ottoman mosques was being constructed in the old market center. An Oflu firm was going to use reinforced concrete to build a likeness of the domes and minarets that mark the skyline of Istanbul. The new mosque was to be situated at the western side of town in such a way that its grounds overlooked the Solaklı River at the point where it entered the Black Sea. By this arrangement, the new mosque would bring to mind the imperial great mosques that overlook the Golden Horn and Bosphorus Straits.

The construction of the new mosque was part of a trend throughout the country that was not in any way peculiar to the district of Of. During the years immediately following the military coup of 1980, the generals who had taken charge decided to place a new emphasis on religious education in the public schools. The Turkish military, a Kemalist bulwark in the Turkish Republic, thereby compromised the founding principle of a secular public culture. This departure was inspired by the hope that an updated version of official Islam might counter radical leftist and rightist political orientations among Turkish youths. In effect, the Turkish military had adopted the idea of Hasan Umur in his little book *Of and the Battles for Of,* but not with the end that he had in mind. They were not interested in bringing the state into closer alignment with the Islamic beliefs and practices of the people. They were interested in rectifying and improving the people so that they would occupy their proper places in a state society.

In other words, the generals had opted for a version of what I have elsewhere termed "Kemalo-Islamism." Partly as a result of this policy, but also partly as a consequence of the demoralization of the radical left and right, religion acquired a degree of respectability in national public culture. All kinds of groupings and movements were inclined, if not obliged, to align themselves with the updated version of official Islam. During the early 1980s, for example, new public monuments and memorials oriented toward imperial rather than national history began to be built in towns and cities all over the country. The building of the great mosque in the old market center of the town of Of was just one of many such undertakings.

The building project was widely supported by public donations, including gifts from Oflus who lived both inside and outside the district. But leading individuals from the Selimoğlu had also made an important contribution. The part of the old town center where the great mosque was to be located was also the site of the graves of leading individuals from the Selimoğlu family line. Some portion of the grounds for the new mosque was reported to have been donated by members of the family line, in emulation of an ascendant who donated the grounds for the old mosque in the old town center. And eventually, one side of the court of the great mosque would become the site for the reconstructed graves of leading individuals of the Selimoğlu family line. The old graves, some going back to the period of decentralization in the early nineteenth century, would be enclosed in white marble borders. They would be set with new white marble headstones and re-inscribed in the Latin letters of new Turkish. The refurbishing of the old graves thereby accomplished what had been missing from the portrait of mayors. The leading individuals of the Selimoğlu family line had not only been bureaucratic modernizers. They had also been among the founders of an ottomanist provincial society that went back to the post-classical period of the Ottoman Empire.

The leading individuals of the Selimoğlu still headed circles of interpersonal association, but now in a town that had assumed the character of a city. They were therefore inclined to supplement these circles of interpersonal association with a politics that would wrest an electoral majority from a diverse urban population. On the one hand, they represented themselves as fair and efficient bureaucrats, thereby appealing to a citizenry that had good reason to fear corruption. This was some part of the meaning of the portrait of mayors. On the other hand they were also supporters of Islamic monuments and institutions, thereby appealing to a citizenry resentful of bureaucratic domination and proud of its Islamist traditions. This was some part of the meaning of the old graves at the side of the great mosque.

The Muradoğlu, rivals of the Selimoğlu, faced another, more straightforward, version of the problem of changing political circumstances. The Muradoğlu family line was traditionally based in the villages rather than the town. They had never represented themselves as bureaucrats, like their rivals, but claimed instead to be close to ordinary Oflus in the countryside. They were less inclined to rely on the control of public institutions and organizations, and accordingly they had more readily aligned themselves with the Islamist sentiments of the majority of the population at an earlier date.

During a visit to Of in 1978, I had been shown the refurbished graveyard of the founders of the Muradoğlu family line, principally İsmail Agha and Memiş Agha (see chap. 6), and of some of their children and wives. Members of the family line had collected funds to enclose the graveyard with white marble borders and arches. They had also arranged for the setting of new white marble headstones, inscribed in the old Arabic letters, rather than in the Latin letters of new Turkish (see fig. 13). During the same period, funds had also been collected to build a new mosque at the eastern

Figure 13. Graves of the founders of the Muradoğlu family line.

edge of the district of Of, not far from the town of Eskipazar. This mosque was intended to commemorate one of the tombs of one of the hodjas credited with the mass conversion of the Christians in the district of Of (the Maraşlılar) during the post-classical period. The mosque was not large, but its construction materials and facilities were especially fine and luxurious.

So by the later 1970s, the Muradoğlu were commemorating ascendants who had been prominent in the government of the district during the period of decentralization, before the beginning of bureaucratic modernization. By their claim to be a family line that extended back to the post-classical period, the Muradoğlu had also been able to align themselves with the Maraşlılar, who converted the district of Of to Islam and initiated its tradition of professors and academies. Following the coup of 1980, the members of the Muradoğlu were therefore far better positioned than their rivals in the town of Of to respond to the new policy of encouraging religious identification and expression. They had soon taken part in the building of a great mosque at Eskipazar, one that also used reinforced concrete in imitation of the classical imperial style. The construction of this mosque was already more advanced than the great mosque in the town of Of in 1988.

By these developments, the Selimoğlu and the Muradoğlu continued to represent local elites closer to the state system and local elites closer to district networks. The difference between them is therefore analogous to the difference between Osman Agha Şatıroğlu and Memiş Agha Tuzcuoğlu (see chap. 6).

EPILOGUE

The ruling institution of the Ottoman Empire is often understood as a household state, based on the model of a family.[16] In my opinion, this obscures important features of the imperial system. The Ottoman palace was founded on a discipline of face-to-face, person-to-person relationships, one that was unhinged from any local setting of primordial customs and habits. In this respect, it was against family, just as it was also against tribe, community, and ethnicity.[17] One did not have to be born into it, and perhaps all the better that one was born out of it. The discipline in question was derived from an ethico-religious system of scholarly construction, but it came to be used as an imperial instrument. Being valid for all times and places because not limited to any time and place, a tactic of sovereign power through interpersonal association could produce a state society out of all kinds of families, tribes, communities, and peoples. But precisely because the imperial system was both transmissible and assimilable, it was also off balance and out of kilter. Its strategies of centralization always featured problems of decentralization.

The project of the nation features similar qualities insofar as it is a repetition of the project of the Empire. The fractures in the state society of the Empire—officials with and against aghas but also aghas with and against hodjas—reappear as fractures of the Republican period—Kemalists with and against local elites but also local elites with and against Islamists. The splits and divides in national public culture, such as I have described them in the district of Of, can therefore be seen as indications of the transformative and inventive potential of the old imperial devices in the environment of modernity. In the city today, the structural relationship of state and society is still apparent in the differentiation of Oflu associations,

16. This may be a result of the influence of Max Weber's views of patrimonial domination, but Findley (1980, 7) notes that the Ottomans themselves sometimes ascribed to such a viewpoint.

17. Cf. Delaney 1991, who has explored the prevalence of patriarchal symbolism in Turkey.

which range from high religiosity to low criminality. On the other hand, this structural relationship is neither closed nor inescapable. As we have seen, it was possible for a little girl to challenge her interrogator: "I am not an Oflu; I am an Istanbullu." This child's play might seem to be but a recent instance of more than three hundred years of Oflu identification with the great imperial city. But this would be a misunderstanding of my argument, and perhaps as well a misinterpretation of the child's meaning. The Oflus never identified with Istanbul as a city, but rather with the universal imperialism that the city claimed to represent. As for the child, she may have been asserting her identity as an Istanbullu, not an Oflu. But more likely, since she spoke with defiance, she was saying that she was not going to let others tell her who she was. If this is correct, her statement was a sign of a transformative and inventive potential of another kind, one unanticipated by either Mehmet II or Kemal Atatürk. Just where it might lead is anyone's guess.

References

MANUSCRIPTS

Brant, James. 1835. PRO FO 195/112. First part: Report of a Journey through a Part of Armenia and Asia Minor. Also published in Brant (1836).

Fettahoğlu. Circa 1950. Fettahoğullarının Tarihi (The History of the Fettahoğulları), approximately 17 single-spaced, typed pages, transliterated from a handwritten document and available in photocopy.

Muradoğlu documents. Official Ottoman documents in the possession of family members, and available in photocopy. No. 1 dated March 25, 1834/1249, No. 2 August 14, 1834/1250, No. 3 October 25, 1834/1250, No. 4 September 24, 1846/1262, No. 5 March 16, 1847/1263, No. 6 April 15, 1847/1263, No. 7 April 21, 1847/1263.

Palgrave, William Gifford. 1873. PRO FO 526/8. Report, on the Lazistan Coast, and the Corresponding Inland Districts between Shefkatell, or Port St. Nicholas, on the Russo-Caucasian Frontier and Trebizond, in the Summer of the Year 1872. Jan. 29.

ARCHIVAL SOURCES

Başbakanlık Arşiv Dairesi: Cevdet Asker 40224, dated 1789/1204. Istanbul. Available in photocopy.

MAE CCCS: Republic of France. Ministère des Affaires Étrangères. Correspondance Consulaire et Commerciale. Turquie, Sinope. SANS: 1801–11.

MAE CCCT L.: Republic of France. Ministère des Affaires Étrangères. Correspondance Consulaire et Commerciale. Turquie, Trébizonde. Livres 1–13: 1800–1901. BPMT: Bulletin Politique et Militaire de Trébizonde. An official characterization of some of these consular reports.

MAE CPCE L.: Republic of France. Ministère des Affaires Étrangères. Correspondance Politique des Consuls. Turquie, Erzeroum. Livres 1–2: 1841–47.

MAE CPCT L.: Republic of France. Ministère des Affaires Étrangères. Correspondance Politique des Consuls. Turquie, Trébizonde. Livres 1–6. 1848–95.

PRO FO: United Kingdom. Public Record Office. Foreign Office. Consultation of consular reports classed under 195/4, 101, 173, 225, 812, 1238, 1329, 1381, 1420, 1521, 2135; 524/1, 2; and 526/8.

Umur, Hasan. 1951. *Of Tarihi: Vesikalar ve Fermanlar.* Istanbul: Güven Basımevi. Transliterated or summarized documents, Nos. 1 through 129, dated from 1575/983 to 1875/1292.

Umur, Hasan. 1956. *Of Tarihine Ek.* Istanbul. Transliterated or summarized documents, Nos. 1 through 100, dated from 1557/965 to 1880/1297.

PUBLICATIONS

Ahmet Cevdet Paşa. 1892/1309. *Tarih-i Cevdet.* 12 vols. Istanbul: Matbaa-yi Osmaniye.

Akarlı, Engin. 1988. Provincial Power Magnates in Ottoman Bilad Al-Sham and Egypt, 1740–1840. In *La vie sociale dans les provinces arabes à l'époque ottomane.* Vol. 3. Zaghwan, Tunisia: Centre d'Études et de Recherches Ottomanes, Morisques, de Documentation et d'Information.

Aksamaz, Ali İhsan. 1997. *Kafkasya'dan Karadeniz'e Lazların Tarihsel Yolculuğu.* Istanbul: Ceylan Matbacılık.

Aksan, Virginia. 1999a. Locating the Ottomans among Early Modern Empires. *Journal of Early Modern History* 3: 103–34.

———. 1999b. Ottoman Military Recruitment Strategies in the Late Eighteenth Century. In *Arming the State: Military Conscription in the Middle East and Central Asia 1775–1925,* edited by Erik J. Zürcher, 21–39. London: I. B. Tauris.

Akşit, Bahattin. 1991. Islamic Education in Turkey: Medrese Reform in Late Ottoman Times and Imam-Hatip Schools in the Republic. In *Islam in Modern Turkey: Religion, Politics, and Literature in a Secular State,* edited by Richard Tapper. London: I. B. Tauris.

Aktepe, Münir. 1951–52. Tuzcuoğulları İsyanı. *Tarih Dergisi, İstanbul Üniversitesi Edibiyat Fakültesi,* 5–6: 21–52.

Albayrak, Haşim. 1986. *Of ve Çaykara.* Ankara: Cantekin Matbaası.

Albayrak, Sadık. 1980–81. *Son Devir Osmanlı Uleması.* 4 vols. Istanbul: Medrese Yayınlık.

Anderson, Benedict R. O'G. 1991 [1983]. *Imagined Communities: Reflections on the Origins and Spread of Nationalism.* London: Verso Press.

Andrews, Peter Alford, and Rüdiger Benninghaus. 1989. *Ethnic Groups in the Republic of Turkey.* Wiesbaden: Reichert.

Arberry, A. J. 1955. *The Koran Interpreted.* New York: Macmillan.

Asad, Talal. 1993. *Genealogies of Religion: Discipline and Reasons of Power in Christianity and Islam.* Baltimore: Johns Hopkins University Press.

Asan, Ömer. 1996. *Pontos Kültürü.* Istanbul: Belge Uluslararası Yayıncılık.

Ayverdi, Ekrem Hakkı. 1973. *Osmanlı Mi'mârîsinde Fâtih Devri 855–886 (1451–1481).* Vol. 3. Istanbul: Baha Matbaası.

Barkan, Ömer L. 1942a. Les fondations pieuses comme methode de peuplement et du colonisation. In *Vakıflar Dergisi.* Vol 2. Ankara: Vakıflar Umum Müdürlüğü.

———. 1942b. Osmanlı İmparatorluğunda Bir İskân ve Kolonizasyon Metod Olarak Vakıflar ve Temlikler. In *Vakıflar Dergisi.* Vol 2. Ankara: Vakıflar Umum Müdürlüğü.

Barkey, Karen. 1994. *Bandits and Bureaucrats: The Ottoman Route to State Centralization.* Ithaca, N.Y.: Cornell University Press.

Beauchamp, Alphonse de. 1813. Mémoire géographique et historique du voyage de Constantinople à Trébizonde. In *Voyage en Perse, en Arménie, en Asie Mineure, et à Constantinople,* by Jacques Morier. 3 vols. (Vol. 2: 261–320). Paris: n.p.

Benninghaus, Rüdiger. 1989a. Zur Herkunft und Identität der Hemşinli. In *Ethnic Groups in the Republic of Turkey,* edited by Peter Alford Andrews and Rüdiger Benninghaus, 475–79. Wiesbaden: Reichert.

———. 1989b. The Laz: An Example of Multiple Identification. In *Ethnic Groups in the Republic of Turkey,* edited by Peter Alford Andrews and Rüdiger Benninghaus, 497–502. Wiesbaden: Reichert.

Bentham, Jeremy. 1791. *Panopticon; or, The inspection-house: containing the idea of a new principle of construction applicable to any sort of establishment, in which persons of any description are to be kept under inspection: and in particular to penitentiary-houses, prisons, houses of industry . . . and schools: with a plan of management adapted to the principle.* London: T. Payne.

Bijişkyan, P. Minas. 1969 [1817–19]. *Karadeniz Kıyıları Tarih ve Coğrafyası.* Translated by Hrand D. Andreasyan. Istanbul: Edebiyat Fakültesi Basımevi.

Bilgin, Mehmet. N.d. (a). Fetihten Sonra Trabzon Sancağında Erken Dönem Osmanlı Toplumunun Oluşturulması Üzerine Bazı Gözlemler. Forthcoming.

———. N.d. (b). Sürmene Şehrinin Kurulduğu Yerler. Forthcoming.

———. 1990. *Sürmene.* Istanbul: Sürmene Belediyesi Kültür Yayınları.

Birinci, Ali. 1989. Trabzon'da Matbuat ve Neşriyat Hayatı (1865–1928). In *Trabzon '88-'89: Kültür — Sanat Yıllığı,* edited by İ. Gündağ Kayaoğlu et al. *Istanbul: Trabzonlular Kültür ve Yardımlaşma Derneği.*

Birken, Andreas. 1976. *Die Provinzen des Osmanischen Reiches.* Wiesbaden: Reichert.

Brant, James. 1836. Journey through a Part of Armenia and Asia Minor in the Year 1835. *Journal of the Royal Geographical Society of London* 6: 187–223.

Brendemoen, Bernt. 1987. Trabzon Çepni Ağzı ve Tepegöz Hikayesinin Bir Çepni Varyantı. In *Trabzon '87: Kültür — Sanat Yıllığı,* edited by İ. Gündağ Kayaoğlu et al. *Istanbul: Trabzonlular Kültür ve Yardımlaşma Derneği.*

———. 1990. Laz Influence on Black Sea Dialects? In *Proceedings from the 32nd Meeting of the Permanent International Altaistic Conference, Oslo, June 12–16, 1989,* edited by Bernt Brendemoen, 49–64. Oslo: Altaica Osloensia, Universitetsforlaget.

Bryer, Anthony. 1966. Some Notes on the Laz and Tzan, Pt. 1. *Bedi Kartlisa* 21–22: 174–95.

———. 1967. Some Notes on the Laz and Tzan, Pt. 2. *Bedi Kartlisa* 23–24: 161–68.

———. 1969. The Last Laz Risings and the Downfall of the Pontic Derebeys, 1812–40. *Bedi Kartlisa* 26: 191–210.

———. 1970. The Tourkokratia in the Pontos: Some problems and preliminary conclusions. *Neo-Hellenika* 1: 30–54.

———. 1975. Greeks and Türkmens: The Pontic exception. *Dumbarton Oaks Papers* 29: 115–50.

———. 1988. The Crypto-Christians of the Pontos and Consul William Gifford Palgrave of Trebizond. In *Peoples and Settlement in Anatolia and the Caucasus, 800–1900*, edited by Anthony Bryer. London: Variorum Reprints.
Bryer, Anthony, and David Winfield. 1985. *The Byzantine Monuments and Topography of the Pontos.* Washington, D.C.: Dumbarton Oaks Research Library and Collection.
Cahen, Claude. 1968. *Pre-Ottoman Turkey: A General Survey of the Material and Spiritual Culture and History, circa 1071–1330.* London: Sidgwick & Jackson.
Cansız, Mustafa. 1948. Of Kazasının Umumî Tarihçesi. *İnan Dergisi* 38 (March): 11–14.
Certeau, Michel de. 1984. *The Practice of Everyday Life.* Berkeley: University of California Press.
Cuinet, Vital. 1890–95. *La Turquie d'Asie: géographique, administrative, statistique, decsriptive et raisonnée de chaque province de l'Asie Mineure.* 4 vols. Paris: E. Leroux.
Decourdemanche, J. [Osman Bey]. 1874. Lazistan. *Izvestija Imperatorskogo Russkogo Geograficeskogo Obscestua* 10: 356–64.
Defner, Michael. 1877. Five Weeks Among the Renegades (Abjurers) in Of. Translated from Greek to English by Alan Taylor. *Hestia* 2: 547–50.
Delaney, Carol. 1991. *Seed and Soil: Gender and Cosmology in Turkish Village Society.* Berkeley: University of California Press.
Deringil, Selim. 1998. *The Well-Protected Domains: Ideology and the Legitimation of Power in the Ottoman Empire, 1876–1909.* London: I. B. Tauris.
D.I.E. 1966. *1950–1965 Milletvekili ve 1961, 1964 Cumhuriyet Senatosu Üye Seçimleri Sonuçları.* Publication No. 513. Ankara: Devlet İstatistik Kurumu.
Emiroğlu, Kudret. 1993–95. *Trabzon Vilayeti Salnamesi 1869, 1870, 1871, 1872, 1873, 1874, 1875.* Vols. 1–8. Ankara: İmge Ajansı.
Ergin, Osman. 1939. *Türk Şehirlerinde İmaret Sistemi.* Istanbul: Cumhuriyet Matbaası.
Esposito, John. 1991. *Islam: The Straight Path.* Oxford: Oxford University Press.
Evans-Pritchard, Edward E. 1940. *The Nuer, a Description of the Modes of Livelihood and Political Institutions of a Nilotic People.* Oxford: Clarendon Press.
———. 1949. *The Sanusi of Cyrenaica.* Oxford: Clarendon Press.
Evans-Pritchard, Edward E., and Meyer Fortes. 1940. *African Political Systems.* London: Oxford University Press.
Ferrières-Sauveboeuf, Comte de. 1790. *Mémoires historiques, politiques et géographiques des voyages du Comte de Ferrières-Sauveboeuf, fait en Turquie, en Perse et en Arabie, depuis 1782, jusq'en 1789.* 2 vols. Paris: Chez Buisson.
Findley, Carter V. 1980. *Bureaucratic Reform in the Ottoman Empire.* Princeton, N.J.: Princeton University Press.
Fontanier, V. 1829. *Voyage en Orient, entrepris par ordre du gouvernement français* de 1821 à 1829. Paris: Librairie Universelle.
———. 1834. *Voyage en Orient, entrepris par ordre du gouvernement français de 1830 à 1833.* Paris: Librairie de Dumont.
Fortes, Meyer. 1953. The Structure of Unilineal Descent Groups. *American Anthropologist* 55: 17–41.
Foucault, Michel. 1975. *Discipline and Punish: The Birth of the Prison.* New York: Vintage Books.

Fresne-Canaye, Philippe du. 1980 [1897]. *Le voyage du Levant de Philippe du Fresne-Canaye*, edited by M. H. Hauser. Genève: Slatkine Reprints [Paris: E. Leroux].

Freud, Sigmund. 1958 [1919]. The Uncanny. In *On Creativity and the Unconscious: Papers in the Psychology of Art, Literature, Love, and Religion*, edited by Benjamin Nelson. New York: Harper & Row.

Gellner, Ernest. 1983. *Nations and Nationalism.* Ithaca, N.Y.: Cornell University Press.

Gökbilgin, M. Tayyib. 1962. XVI. Yüzyıl Başlarında Trabzon Livası ve Doğu Karadeniz Bölgesi. *Belleten* 26: 293–337.

Gologlu, Mahmut. 1975. *Trabzon Tarihi: Fetihten Kurtuluşa Kadar. Ankara*: Kalite Matbaası.

Gould, Andrew. 1976. Lords or Bandits? The Derebeys of Cilicia. *International Journal of Middle East Studies* 7: 485–506.

Guarracino, Frederick. 1845. Notes on an Excursion from Batum to Artvin. *Journal of the Royal Geographic Society of London* 15: 296–305.

Günay, Turgut. 1978. *Rize İli Ağızları: İnceleme-Metinler-Sözlük.* Ankara: Ankara Üniversitesi Basımevi.

Günday, A. Faik Hurşit. 1960. *Hayat ve Hatıralarım.* N.p.: Çelikcilt Matbaası.

Güngör, Bülent. 1987. Trabzon Evleri. In *Trabzon '87: Kültür — Sanat Yıllığı*, edited by İ. Gündağ Kayaoğlu *et al.* Istanbul: Trabzonlular Kültür ve Yardımlaşma Derneği.

Hamilton, William J. 1842. *Researches in Asia Minor, Pontus, and Armenia.* 2 vols. London: John Murray.

Hann, Christopher M. 1990. *Tea and the Domestication of the Turkish State.* Modern Turkish Studies Programme. Occasional Papers No. 1. Huntingdon, Eng.: Eothen Press.

Hann, Christopher M., and Ildiko Beller-Hann. 2001. *Turkish Region: Culture & Civilization on the east Black Sea Coast. Oxford: James Currey.*

Hobsbawm, Eric. 1990. *Nations and Nationalism Since 1780: Programme, Myth, Reality.* Cambridge: Cambridge University Press.

Hoefer. 1965 [1856]. *Nouvelle bibliographie générale.* Copenhagen: Rosenkilde et Bagger.

Hourani, Albert. 1974. The Ottoman Background of the Modern Middle East. In *The Ottoman State and its Place in World History*, edited by Kemal H. Karpat. Leiden: E. J. Brill.

Humlum, Johs. 1942. *Zur Geographie des Maisbaus.* Copenhagen: Einar Harcks Forlag.

İnalcık, Halil. 1973. *The Ottoman Empire: The Classical Age: 1300–1600.* New York: Praeger.

———. 1977. Centralization and Decentralization in the Ottoman Empire. In *Studies in Eighteenth-Century Islamic History*, edited by Thomas Naff and Roger Owen. Carbondale: Southern Illinois University Press.

Issawi, Charles. 1970. The Tebriz-Trabzon Trade, 1830–1900. *International Journal of Middle Eastern Studies* 1: 18–27.

———. 1980. *The Economic History of Turkey: 1800–1914.* Chicago: University of Chicago Press.

Janin, R. 1912. Musulmans malgré eux; les Stavriotes. *Echos d'Orient* 15: 495–502.

Kafadar, Cemal. 1995. *Between Two Worlds*. Berkeley: University of California Press.

Karadenizli, Kemal. 1954. *Trabzon Tarihi*. Ankara: n.p.

Karpuz, Haşim. 1989. Doğu Karadeniz Bölgesinde Bazı Ahşap Camiler. *Sanat Tarihi Araştırmaları Dergisi* 3: 37–45.

Kayalı, Hasan. 1997. *Arabs and Young Turks: Ottomanism, Arabism, and Islamism in the Ottoman Empire, 1908–1918*. Berkeley: University of California Press.

Keyder, Çağlar. 1987. *State and Class in Turkey: A Study in Capitalist Development*. London: Verso Press.

Koch, Karl. 1846. *Wanderungen im Orient während der Jahre 1843 und 1844, Volume 2: Reise im Pontischen Gebirge und Türkischen Armenien*. Weimar: Druck u. Verlag des Landes-Industrie-Comptoirs.

———. 1855. Reise von Redut-Kaleh nach Trebizond. In *Die Kaukasischen Länder und Armenien*, edited by K. Koch, 65–114. Leipzig: C. B. Lorck.

Kunt, İ. Metin. 1974. Ethnic-Regional (Cins) Solidarity in the Seventeenth-Century Ottoman Establishment. *International Journal of Middle East Studies* 5: 233–39.

———. 1983. *The Sultan's Servants: The Transformation of Ottoman Provincial Government, 1550–1650*. New York: Columbia University Press.

Kuran, Aptullah. 1968. *The Mosque in Early Ottoman Architecture*. Chicago: University of Chicago Press.

Levend, Agâh Sırrı. 1958. *Türk Edebiyatında Şehr-Engizler ve Şehr-Engizlerde İstanbul*. Istanbul: Baha Matbaası.

Lewis, Bernard. 1961. *The Emergence of Modern Turkey*. London: Oxford University Press.

———. 1968. Some English Travellers in the East. *Middle East Studies* 4: 296–315.

———. 1988. *The Political Language of Islam*. Chicago: University of Chicago Press.

Lewis, Geoffrey. 1974. *The Book of Dede Korkut*. Harmondsworth: Penguin Books.

Lowry, Heath. 1977. *The Ottoman Tahrir Defters as a Source for Urban Demographic History: The Case Study of Trabzon* (ca. 1486–1583). Ph.D. diss., University of California, Los Angeles.

Machiavelli, Niccolo. 1992 [1515]. *The Prince*. Translated by W. K. Marriott. New York: Knopf.

Mahmood, Saba. N.d. Feminist Theory, Embodiment, and the Docile Agent: Some Reflections on the Egyptian Islamic Revival. In *Cultural Anthropology*. Forthcoming.

Mardin, Şerif. 1969. Power, Civil Society and Culture in the Ottoman Empire. *Comparative Studies in Society and History* 11: 258–81.

McWilliams, Carey. 1973. *Southern California: An Island on the Land*. Salt Lake City, Utah: Peregrine Books.

Meeker, Michael E. 1969. Note on "The Last Laz Rising and the Downfall of the Pontic Derebeys" by A. Bryer. *Bedi Kartlisa* 26: 150–52.

———. 1970. The Black Sea Turks: A Study of Honor, Descent, and Marriage. Ph.D. diss., University of Chicago.

———. 1971. The Black Sea Turks: Some Aspects of Their Ethnic and Cultural Background. *International Journal of Middle East Studies* 2: 318–45.

———. 1972. The Great Family Aghas of Turkey. In *Rural Politics and Social Change,* edited by Iliya Harik and Richard T. Antoun, 237–66. Bloomington: University of Indiana Press.

———. 1991. The New Muslim Intellectuals in the Republic of Turkey. In *Islam in Modern Turkey: Religion, Politics, and Literature in a Secular State,* edited by Richard L. Tapper, 189–219. London: I. B. Tauris.

———. 1992. The Dede Korkut Ethic. *International Journal of Middle East Studies* 24: 395–417.

———. 1994a. Oral Culture, Media Culture, and the Islamic Resurgence in Turkey. In *Exploring the Written in Anthropology,* edited by Eduardo Archetti, 31–63. Oslo: Scandinavian University Press.

———. 1994b. The Muslim Intellectual and His Audience: A New Configuration of Writer and Reader Among Believers in the Republic of Turkey. In *Cultural Transitions in the Middle East,* edited by Şerif Mardin, 153–88. Leiden: E. J. Brill.

———. 1996. Concepts of Family, State, and Society in the District of Of, Trabzon. In *Turkish Families in Transition,* edited by Dr. Gabriele Rasuly-Paleczek, 46–60. Frankfurt: Peter Lang.

———. 1997. Once There Was, Once There Wasn't: National Monuments and Interpersonal Exchange. In *Rethinking Modernity and National Identity in Turkey,* edited by Sibel Bozdoğan and Reşat Kasaba, 157–91. Seattle: University of Washington Press.

Morier, James Justinian. 1812. *A Journey through Persia, Armenia and Asia Minor, to Constantinople.* London: Longman.

Nagata, Yuzo. 1976. *Muhsin-zade Mehmet Paşa ve Ayanlık Müssesesi.* Study of Languages & Cultures of Asia & Africa Monograph Series, No. 6. Tokyo: Toyo Shuppan.

Necipoğlu, Gülru. 1991. *Architecture, Ceremonial, and Power: The Topkapı Palace in the Fifteenth and Sixteenth Centuries.* Cambridge, Mass.: MIT Press.

Odabaşıoğlu, Cumhur. 1987.*Trabzon Doğu Karadeniz Gazete ve Mecmuaları 1869–1928.* Trabzon: Karadeniz Gazete ve Matbaacılık.

———. 1990. *Trabzon: Belgelerle Milli Mücadele Yılları 1919–1923.* Akçaabat: Top-Kar Matbaacılık.

Özkaya, Yücel. 1977. *Osmanlı İmparatorluğunda Âyânlık.* Ankara Üniversitesi Dil ve Coğrafya Fakültesi Yayınları, No. 273. Ankara: Ankara Üniversitesi Basımevi.

Özkaynak, Kemal. 1954. *Akseki Kazası: Tarhi, Coğrafaya, Turizm, Biyografya.* Ankara: Akgün Matbaası.

Palgrave, William Gifford. 1887. *Ulysses or Scenes and Studies in Many Lands.* London: Macmillan and Co.

Peysonnel [sometimes Peyssonnel], M. de [Charles]. 1765. *Observations historiques et géographiques, sur les peuples barbares qui ont habité les bord du Danube & du Pont-Euxin.* Paris: Chez N. M. Tilliard.

———. 1787. *Traité sur le commerce de la mer Noire.* 2 vols. Paris: Chez Cuchet.

Pierce, Leslie. 1993. *The Imperial Harem: Women and Sovereignty in the Ottoman Empire.* Ithaca, N.Y.: Cornell University Press.

Planhol, Xavier de. 1963a. Geographica Pontica. *Journal Asiatique* 251: 293–309.

———. 1963b. A travers les chaines Pontiques: plantations côtières et vie montagnarde. *Bulletin de l'Association de géographes français* 311–12: 1–12.

———. 1966a. La signification géographique du livre de Dede Korkut. *Journal Asiatique* 254: 225–44.

———. 1966b. Aspects of Mountain Life in Anatolia and Iran. In *Geography as Human Ecology: Methodology by Example,* edited by S. R. Eyre and G. R. J. Jones, 291–308. New York: St. Martin's Press.

———. 1972. Regional Diversification and Social Structure in North Africa and the Islamic Middle East: A Geographic Perspective. In *Rural Politics and Social Change,* edited by Iliya Harik and Richard T. Antoun, 103–17. Bloomington: University of Indiana Press.

Poutouridou, Margarita. 1997–98. The Of Valley and the coming of Islam: The Case of the Greek Speaking Muslims. *Deltio Kentrou Mikrasiatikan Spoudon* 12: 47–90.

Robinson, Richard. 1963. *The First Turkish Republic: A Case Study in National Development.* Cambridge, Mass.: Harvard University Press.

Rottiers, Le Colonel [Bernard E. A.]. 1829. *Itinéraire de Tiflis à Constantinople.* Bruxelles: Chez H. Tarlier.

Sakaoğlu, Necdet. 1984. *Anadolu Derebeyi Ocaklarından Köse Paşa Hanedanı.* Ankara: Yurt Yayınevi.

Şakir Şevket. 1877/1294. *Trabzon Tarihi.* Istanbul: Umran Matbaası.

Selekler, Macit. 1960. *Antalya Çevresi Folkör ve Genel Ahvali ve Bilhassa Antalya'da Kemer Melli — Ibradı Serik.* Istanbul: Orhan Mete Matbaası.

Shankland, David. 1999. *Islam and Society in Turkey.* Huntingdon, Eng.: Eothen Press.

Shaw, Stanford. 1976. *History of the Ottoman Empire and Modern Turkey: The Rise and Decline of the Ottoman Empire, 1280–1808.* Cambridge: Cambridge University Press.

Shaw, Stanford, and Ezel Kural. 1977. *History of the Ottoman Empire and Modern Turkey: Reform, Revolution, and Republic, 1808–1975.* Cambridge: Cambridge University Press.

Şimşir, Bilal. 1982. *British Documents on Ottoman Armenians 1856–1880. Vol. 2.* Ankara: Türk Tarih Kurumu.

Skiotis, Dennis N. 1971. From Bandit to Pasha: First Steps in the Rise to Power of Ali of Tepelen, 1750–1784. *International Journal of Middle East Studies* 2: 219–44.

Slade, Adolphus. 1833. *Records of Travels in Turkey, Greece, etc. and of a Cruise in the Black Sea, with the Capitan Pasha, in the years of 1829, 1830, and 1831.* 2 vols. London: Saunders and Otley. 2nd edition.

Stirling, Paul. 1965. *Turkish Village.* London: Weidenfeld and Nicholson.

Strasser, Sabine. 1995. *Die Unreinheit ist Fruchtbar: Grenz überschereitungen in einem türkischen Dorf am Schwarzen Meer.* Vienna: Wiener Frauenverlag.

Sümer, Faruk. 1992. *Tirebolu Tarihi.* Istanbul: Tirebolu Kültür ve Yardımlaşma Derneği.

Sümerkan, M. Reşat. 1987. Halk Dilinde Mimarlık: Doğu Karadeniz. In *Trab-*

zon '87: Kültür — Sanat Yıllığı, edited by İ. Gündağ Kayaoğlu et al. *Istanbul: Trabzonlular Kültür ve Yardımlaşma Derneği.*

Tapper, Richard, and Nancy Tapper. 1987. Thank God We're Secular: Aspects of Fundamentalism in a Turkish Town. In *Studies in Religious Fundamentalism,* edited by Lionel Caplan, 51–78. Houndmills, Basingstoke, Hampshire: Macmillan.

Tekeli, Sait Tahsin. 1961. *Rize Bölgesinde Çay Yerleştirmenin ve İşletmenin Meseleleri.* Ankara: T. C. Tarım Bakanlığı.

Toumarkine, Alexandre. 1995. *Les Lazes en Turquie (xixe–xxe siècles).* Istanbul: Isis Press.

Tournefort, M. Pitton de. 1717. *Relation d'un voyage du Levant. . . . 2 vols.* Paris: L'Imprimerie Royale.

Tursun, Mehmet. 1998. Of'un Sosyo Kültürel ve Dini Yapısı Üzerine Bir İnceleme. Diss., Cumhuriyet Üniversitesi Sosyal Bilimler Enstitüsü, Sivas.

Uğur, Ali. 1986. *The Ottoman Ulemâ in the Mid-17th Century.* Berlin: Klaus Schwarz Verlag.

Umur, Hasan. 1949. *Of ve Of Muharebeleri.* Istanbul: Güven Basımevi.

———. 1951. *Of Tarihi: Vesikalar ve Fermanlar.* Istanbul: Güven Basımevi.

———. 1956. *Of Tarihine Ek.* Istanbul: n.p.

Uzunçarşılı, İ. H. 1979. s.v. "Âyân." *İslam Ansiklopedesi,* Vol. 2. Istanbul: M. E. B.

———. 1984. *Osmanlı Devletinin Saray Teşkilâtı.* Ankara: Türk Tarih Kurumu.

Van Bruinessen, Maarten Martinus. 1978. *Agha, Shaikh and State: On the Social and Political Organization of Kurdistan.* Risjwijk, Netherlands: Europrint.

Veinstein, Gilles. 1975. Âyân de la région d'Izmir et le commerce du Levant (deuxième moitié du xviiie siècle). *Revue de l'occident musulman et de la Méditerranée* 20: 131–46.

———. 1991. On the Çiftlik Debate. In *Landholding and Commercial Agriculture in the Middle East,* edited by Ç. Keyder and F. Tabak, 35–53. Albany: S.U.N.Y. Press.

Vryonis, Jr., Speros. 1968. Byzantium and Islam: Seventh–Seventeenth Century. *East European Quarterly* 2, No. 3: 205–40.

———. 1971. *The Decline of Medieval Hellenism in Asia Minor and the Process of Islamization from the Eleventh through the Fifteenth Century.* Berkeley: University of California Press.

White, Jenny B. 1994. *Money Makes Us Relatives: Women's Labor in Urban Turkey.* Austin: University of Texas Press.

Winfield, David, M. Q. Smith, Selina Ballance, and Ann Powell. 1960. The Yakupoğlu Konak: An Old Turkish House at Sürmene Kastil. *Anatolian Studies* 10: 197–203.

Yiğit, Altay. 1950. *Birinci Cihan Savaşında Doğu Karadeniz Muharebeleri.* Trabzon: İstikbal Matbaası.

———. 1981. *Çaykara ve Folkloru.* Ankara: Kent Matbaa.

Zilfi, Madeline C. 1988. *The Politics of Piety: The Ottoman Ulema in the Postclassical Age (1600–1800).* Minneapolis, Minn.: Bibliotheca Islamica.

Zürcher, Erik J. 1993. *Turkey: A Modern History.* New York: I. B. Tauris.

Index

Compositor: G&S Typesetters, Inc.
Text: 10/13 Aldus
Display: Aldus
Printer and Binder: Edward Brothers, Inc.